THE POLITICAL THOUGHT OF

WOODROW WILSON

1875–1910

THE POLITICAL THOUGHT OF

WOODROW WILSON

★ 1875–1910 ★

by Niels Aage Thorsen

★

PRINCETON UNIVERSITY PRESS

PRINCETON, NEW JERSEY

Copyright © 1988 by Princeton University Press

Published by Princeton University Press, 41 William Street,
Princeton, New Jersey 08540
In the United Kingdom: Princeton University Press, Guildford, Surrey

This book has been composed in Linotron Baskerville

Clothbound editions of Princeton University Press books
are printed on acid-free paper, and binding materials are
chosen for strength and durability. Paperbacks, although satisfactory
for personal collections, are not usually suitable for library rebinding

Printed in the United States of America by Princeton University Press,
Princeton, New Jersey

Designed by Laury A. Egan

Library of Congress Cataloging-in-Publication Data

Thorsen, Niels.
The political thought of Woodrow Wilson, 1875–1910 / by Niels Aage Thorsen.
p. cm.—(Supplementary volumes to The papers of Woodrow Wilson)
Bibliography: p.   Includes index.
ISBN 0–691–04751–0 (alk. paper)
1. Wilson, Woodrow, 1856–1924—Political and social views.
I. Title. II. Series.
E767.1.T47 1988
973.91′3—dc19   88–2495   CIP

Dedicated to
Lisbeth J. Thorsen

CONTENTS

★ ★

PREFACE

★ ★

The present work is a study of Woodrow Wilson's political and economic thought from the time he entered Princeton College in 1875 until
he entered public office in 1910, when he was elected governor of New
Jersey. Soon he was deeply involved in the internal politics of the Democratic party and, in the course of a dramatic national party convention
in 1912, he was nominated as the party's presidential candidate. The distinction between the academic political thinker and the active politician
was important for Wilson himself. The differences between the two roles
are crucial if one wants to focus upon Wilson's contribution to American
political thought rather than upon his place in the history of American
politics.

As a political figure, Wilson eventually came to be associated with progressivism, a term that is generally used to refer to the popular political
current born after 1900 in the sentiment of outrage over the social costs
of large-scale industrial capitalism. Progressivism began in a program
that aimed to cleanse government of the incompetence and corruption
caused by business interests. This current, to put it broadly, sought to
preserve the liberal values of equal opportunity by reversing the liberal
strategy. Instead of protecting free enterprise and capitalist growth
against government encroachment, liberals now found themselves fighting to protect government authority and regulatory competence against
the actions of the large corporations. Wilson's route to the new liberalism
has long been a matter of controversy. Wilson did not inspire the mood
of social activism and political reform usually associated with progressivism. In fact, most historians agree that he converted to the progressive
temper rather late and largely for opportunistic reasons, but he eventually came to have great influence on the progressive agenda, and he en-
acted many of the reform proposals that were considered part and parcel
of the progressive movement.

The present study is an attempt to show that the genealogy of Wilson's
ideas is more interesting and in some respects more coherent than this.
The argument is not, however, that Wilson was a "progressive" before
progressivism existed as a recognized current in any of the major parties.
Indeed, the transformation of Wilson's ideas into practical politics lies
beyond the chronological scope of this investigation, which is an attempt

ix

to sketch Wilson's development as a political thinker rather than as a politician. There is no attempt to comment upon the debate between the New Freedom and the New Nationalism, nor have I tried to compare Wilson's ideas with the ideas of recognized progressive intellectuals, such as Herbert Croly or Walter E. Weyl. Indeed, I have largely tried to avoid the term *progressivism*, because its general use is chronologically beyond the scope of the topic. But the notion of progress is, of course, a different matter, because it had been an enduring part of the American heritage from the Enlightenment. I have tried to be attentive to Wilson's use of this term, on the assumption that the origins and processes of political thinking need not be less interesting than the finished product. Wilson's academic career exemplifies the transformation of political imagination in America under the impact of industrialism and against the backdrop of the Civil War. It is in this limited sense that the present study may be considered both a study of Wilson's political and economic thought and, in addition, an attempt to watch the genesis of the political plane upon which the notion of progress eventually came to signify, not only a new political party, but also a broad current in the established parties and finally, in historians' retrospect, a whole epoque in American history.

Many historians have found progressive political ideas to be both vague and incoherent. This seems to be the natural result of a persistent effort to extract political ideas from a pool of varied and disparate social interests, such as the Social Gospel movement, urban reform groups, business groups, professional groups, muckraking journalism, farmers' associations, and others. The problem is that none of these groups exhibited a sustained interest in the general features of political life, and few of them had more than a marginal concern for political institutions. Looking for general political ideas in the midst of special interests has not proved to be a rewarding exercise. Progressive ideas may perhaps be construed in different terms, that is, as a set of general presuppositions rather than an ideology of reform. Such presuppositions came to look vague or incoherent only in retrospect, not because they died out, but because they became indistinguishable from the perceived reality of the twentieth century. If this line of reasoning is accepted, Wilson's academic writings deserve consideration as a repository of some of the early perceptions behind the making of a modern political culture.

The most prominent features of Wilson's political scholarship were, first, a mode of thinking in which social and economic diversification was seen as a condition for the growth of national power; second, a sustained attention to political leadership as a remedy for the preceived failings of American democracy, and, third, a maturing conviction that scientific knowledge of economic, political, and administrative practices could be introduced into the conduct of government. Taken together, these principles implied the abandonment of a more traditional form of political theory which had proceeded upon the assumption of the social contract and nourished a political culture based upon constitutionalism, egalitarianism, and common sense. Wilson's political writings allow one to observe the processes of both dissolution and reconstruction in some detail. Wilson played a distinctive role in the attempt to establish a new mode of theory that was closely connected with the rise of the social sciences within the university. Predicated upon a vast and complex social body, the dominant forms of political action were to be conceived in the image of national leadership and administrative politics.

Just as historians in recent years have found it difficult if not impossible to specify the political content of progressivism, the historiography of Wilson's early years seems to reflect a note of impatience with his political ideas, combined with a preference for more advanced methods of inquiry. Important studies of Wilson's psychological, religious, and medical makeup have enlightened different aspects of Wilson's personal life. Thus, Alexander L. George and Juliette L. George have attempted to explain Wilson's important decisions and attitudes with reference to his relationship with his father. A new epoch of Wilson scholarship began with the publication of *The Papers of Woodrow Wilson*, edited by Arthur S. Link, David W. Hirst, John E. Little and others. On this new and comprehensive basis, John M. Mulder and later Robert M. Crunden have articulated some of Wilson's political views with reference to his religious ideas, particularly the Calvinist tradition. Thomas J. Hruska, Jr., has attempted to develop a theory of evolutionary psychology, centering on a notion of "organic man," from Wilson's biographical writings and his educational program. Edwin A. Weinstein, M.D., has studied Wilson's illnesses in relation to political affairs at Princeton and in Washington. Most recently, John Milton Cooper, Jr., has reintroduced a broader perspective by showing that a biographical comparison with Theodore Roosevelt reveals hitherto unnoticed features of Wilson's opinions and actions as political leader.[1] Taken together, these works provide a full and detailed

[1] Alexander L. George and Juliette L. George, *Woodrow Wilson and Colonel House: A Personality Study* (New York, 1956); *The Papers of Woodrow Wilson*, 55 vols. to date (Princeton, N. J., 1966–) (hereafter cited as *PWW*); John M. Mulder, *Woodrow Wilson: The Year of Preparation* (Princeton, N. J., 1978); Robert M. Crunden, *Ministers of Reform: The Progressives' Achievement in American Civilization, 1889–1920* (New York, 1982); Thomas J. Hruska, Jr., "Woodrow Wilson: The Organic State and His Political Theory" (Ph.D. Diss., Claremont Graduate School, 1978); Edwin A. Weinstein, *Woodrow Wilson: A Medical and Psychological Biography* (Princeton, N. J., 1981); John Milton Cooper, Jr., *The Warrior and the Priest: Woodrow Wilson and Theodore Roosevelt* (Cambridge, Mass., 1983).

intellectual biography, which I have relied on extensively in order to limit this inquiry to Wilson's political thought.

The methodological and historiographical issues raised by the investigation of Wilson's early career and academic work are discussed in chapter 11. For the present it may suffice to note that a certain amount of evaluation is inherent in a description of Wilson's academic years with reference to the innermost soul, as illuminated by both older and more modern sciences of the self. A preference for explanations that focus on the self often carries with it the tacit judgment that Wilson's ideas about political matters were to some degree arbitrary or incoherent, hence the search for factors of personality that appear more permanent. William Diamond, in what is perhaps the most direct predecessor of the present work, actually warned that in the case of Wilson's political thought, the historian was in danger of describing a consistent system "where system and consistency never existed."[2]

In contrast, I argue that Wilson's political and economic writings of the period under consideration are distinguished by an internal coherence and continuity that extend from Wilson's first effort to pull his ideas of nationality and leadership together. The Civil War and its aftermath played a decisive role in forming Wilson's whole perception of the political world. Wilson's studies at the Johns Hopkins also had a great influence on his thinking. The impact of the modern social sciences has sometimes been slighted by historians, who have payed attention to Wilson's letters from the University but neglected the development of his scholarship once he no longer felt the pressure of exams and assigned readings. Before Wilson came to the Johns Hopkins, he claimed that constitutional fragmentation could be offset by parliamentary leadership. After he had been introduced to Continental European ideas of state sovereignty, he extended his criticism to the liberal conception of politics and economics. Far from glorifying the rights of property and longing for a return to laissez faire, Wilson called the economy to the defense of the nation. Furthermore, Wilson developed the idea that a science of administration could be transferred to America if it maintained an ideological distance from European absolutism and sought to legitimize itself with reference to the needs of a dynamic society.

In retrospect, Wilson's academic writings appear as a theoretical expression of a general tendency to revalue the notion of political leadership in the light of new forms of national power expressed in mass citizenship and industrial capacity. Historically, American nationalism

---

[2] *The Economic Thought of Woodrow Wilson*, Johns Hopkins University Studies in Historical and Political Science, LXI, No. 4 (Baltimore, 1943), p. 7.

had been the cry of the many against the cosmopolitan elite. Jacksonian democracy, for example, had cherished a majoritarian form of nationalism, and the Civil War was widely seen as the people's war against a slave-owning aristocracy. By way of his notion of the state, Wilson was able to cleanse American nationalism of its anti-elitist origins and construct an idea of national leadership that identified administrative functions as the field for political initiative and change, coupled with popular elections to procure political legitimacy. In chapter 10, I attempt to sketch Wilson's conception of the kind of theorist, and new theoretical practice, that the modern age called for. I also present his conception of politics with reference to such theorists as Edmund Burke, Thomas Jefferson, and the Federalists.

THE DEBTS owed by this study go back to 1970 and 1971, when James Penick, Jr., and Robert W. McCluggage of Loyola University in Chicago first introduced me to American history. The subject of the present work was suggested to me by Arthur S. Link, who has advised and guided the study through all its stages with patience and extraordinary care. The warm concern and hospitality that Professor Link and his family extended to me in all matters made me a guest rather than a foreign visitor in Princeton from 1978 to 1980 and again in 1986. Sheldon S. Wolin introduced me to political theory, and he has contributed generously to the form and substance of this work, as well as to the enjoyment of working on it. The student of the history of a foreign country may develop a special kind of attachment to his or her teachers, partly because of one's obvious dependence when abroad, but in a more important way, as one seeks to prolong the conversation after the return home.

In Denmark, Inga Floto, who introduced American history as a regular subject at the University of Copenhagen, has been an unfailing source of support, criticism, and encouragement in regard to this work, as in numerous other matters. In addition, I am grateful to John Milton Cooper, Jr., of the University of Wisconsin, who urged me both to expand the time frame and to consider the work Wilson did not write, and to Jørgen Sevaldsen of Copenhagen University. Both have given much time to a detailed criticism of several drafts of the present work. Göran Rystad of the University of Lund and Stanley N. Katz and Daniel T. Rodgers of Princeton University have also read the entire manuscript and have made very useful comments. Jeffrey Tulis helped me in matters of secondary literature. Carl Pedersen corrected my writing, and Birgitte Sneum and Annette Rasmussen typed the manuscript. The book as a whole owes very much to the care and exactitude of Alan M. Schroder.

At various stages of research and writing I have received financial support from the Fulbright Commission in Denmark, Statens Humanistiske forskningsråd, Princeton University, the John F. Kennedy Institute in West Berlin, and the American Council of Learned Societies. The Department of English of Copenhagen University granted me a leave of absence. A shorter early version of this work was accepted as a dissertation at Princeton University in 1981. The present version is presented to the faculty of the humanities at Copenhagen University.

THE POLITICAL THOUGHT OF
WOODROW WILSON
1875–1910

I

★ ★ ★ ★ ★ ★ ★ ★ ★ ★ ★ ★ ★ ★ ★ ★ ★ ★ ★ ★

THE DISCOVERY OF
THE NATION: WILSON'S FIRST
POLITICAL WRITINGS

Beginnings have a special attraction for historians, because they believe the outset of something to render in a simpler form the essence or the spirit of historical phenomena that become complex over time. The beginning of Woodrow Wilson's political interest has been a subject of considerable controversy, which has focused on his identification with English liberals and especially on his attachment to his father. It deserves attention, however, that Wilson's boyhood and early years in Princeton were spent in the midst of unusual political circumstances that had a bearing on Wilson's family background, on his religious world view, and on the social environment of the college he attended. Wilson may have instinctively identified himself with the South, but his earliest political writings were concerned with the revitalization of national power.

Wilson grew up in an atmosphere haunted by a fear of political disintegration. The conflict over slavery was not settled with the end of the Civil War, but continued in a different form in the South throughout most of the 1870s. The Fourteenth and Fifteenth amendments, ratified in 1868 and 1870, granted the freedmen full citizenship, including the right to vote. The Negro vote, possibly combined with northern radicalism and supported by federal troops, was seen as a direct threat to the established order of society. Only gradually through the first half of the 1870s did the Democrats regain control of the southern states in which Republicans had made up the majority of the electorate. President Ulysses S. Grant's refusal in 1875 to dispatch more federal soldiers to the South only meant that over the coming years political violence and the suppression of the freedmen would be regarded as a local rather than a federal problem. The election of 1876 and the electoral deadlock between Democrat Samuel J. Tilden and Republican Rutherford B. Hayes seemed to reopen the memories of political violence.

3

In the North, large-scale organizations of capital and labor began to make themselves felt in the political arena, most conspicuously during the panic of 1873 and during the great railroad strike of 1877. The economic depression that left its mark on most of the 1870s heightened the sense of the precariousness of the social order. Potential social strife loomed large in the public consciousness, not necessarily because of direct warnings, but because the constitutional framework that had earlier served to defuse potential conflict seemed to have been seriously weakened by the war, just as common civility seemed to have been undercut. Recurrent scandals in the Grant administration—such as the gold conspiracy, the Crédit Mobilier scandal, and the Whiskey Ring fraud—were widely seen as symptoms of a general debasement of public conduct.

This general political setting was supplemented by more immediate influences on the young Wilson. He was brought up in a culture where religion played a most significant role. This influence is not to be understood as a matter of personal piety but of general perception. As James Bryce noted, "the Bible and Christian theology altogether do more in the way of forming the imaginative background to an average American view of the world of man and nature than they do in modern Protestant Europe."[1] The surrounding social environment reinforced rather than challenged Wilson's religious upbringing in a Presbyterian family headed by Rev. Joseph Ruggles Wilson, D.D., who served as a Presbyterian minister. Wilson's mother came from a family of prominent Scottish divines. From his birth, early on the morning of December 29, 1856, in Staunton, Virginia, Thomas Woodrow Wilson was taught to look at and understand the world through the Calvinist tradition.[2]

Wilson began to formulate his own religious ideas before he began to write about political questions. But the reason for paying attention to his early religious writings is not only a matter of chronology, nor just a matter of tracing Wilson's political ideas to specific religious doctrines.

---

[1] *The American Commonwealth* (3 vols., London, 1888), III, 501.

[2] For an extensive discussion of Wilson's religious background, especially Dr. Wilson's views, see Mulder, *Woodrow Wilson*, pp. 2–58. Other accounts of this period include Ray Stannard Baker, *Woodrow Wilson: Life and Letters* (8 vols., Garden City, N. Y., 1927–39), I, 1–103; Henry Wilkinson Bragdon, *Woodrow Wilson: The Academic Years* (Cambridge, Mass., 1967), pp. 3–64; Josephus Daniels, *The Life of Woodrow Wilson* (Philadelphia, 1924), pp. 27–53; Arthur S. Link, *Wilson: The Road to the White House* (Princeton, N. J., 1947), pp. 1–5; George C. Osborn, *Woodrow Wilson: The Early Years* (Baton Rouge, La., 1968), pp. 3–46; Weinstein, *Woodrow Wilson*, pp. 3–45; and Cooper, *The Warrior and the Priest*, pp. 15–20. General assessments of the ways in which Wilson was influenced by his family and the environment of his youth are Arthur S. Link, "Woodrow Wilson and His Presbyterian Inheritance," and "Woodrow Wilson: The American as Southerner," in Arthur S. Link, *The Higher Realism of Woodrow Wilson, and Other Essays* (Nashville, Tenn., 1971), pp. 3–20, 21–37.

Rather, it is to stress that in Western culture religion has frequently served as a register of notions of power and order, two central terms in Wilson's political imagination. In the Judeo-Christian tradition, belief in God is closely associated with the idea of an ultimate power that moves the world and that takes care of the people. A religion that professes to speak about an omnipotent and omniscient God will necessarily teach the believer how to think about more immediate forms of power in the visible world. Not only will religion sketch the terms on which the individual must prepare himself to sustain or suffer the existence of worldly power, but in addition, the Puritan persuasion will tell the believer when to assume a posture of righteousness, based on authority of the highest order, in defiance of worldly might. It is therefore important to investigate the political understandings diffused throughout Wilson's early religious views.[3]

In his first published essay, "Work-Day Religion," written during a vacation with his family after his junior year at Princeton, Wilson grappled with some of the principles and attitudes that his upbringing had imparted to him. In particular, he was concerned about the connection between religious duty and social activity. At the center of his attention was the Calvinist doctrine of a dual calling to redemption and to social vocation. As Wilson wrote; "Life is a work-day. In this rendering an account of the talents which have been granted to us we will find that true enjoyment which the world knows not. With all this diligence and earnestness we should perform every act as an act of which we shall some day be made to render a strict account, as an act done either in the service of God or in that of the Devil." Daily work, he believed, was instituted as a school in Christian discipline. "The most humble and insignificant services of the household and the business office, should be attended to with the feeling that we are serving God." The social surroundings were pregnant with meaning for the Christian. Christian duty is "a progress of the soul," but not a solitary pilgrimage of the inner self. Instead, the soul is a

---

[3] Sheldon S. Wolin, *Politics and Vision: Continuity and Innovation in Western Political Thought* (Boston, 1960), pp. 95–104, 165–94; and H. Richard Niebuhr, *The Kingdom of God in America* (1939; reprint, New York, 1959). See also, Michael Walzer, *The Revolution of the Saints: A Study in the Origins of Radical Politics* (Cambridge, Mass., 1965). Crunden has suggested the opposite procedure, that is, that religious beliefs be tracked down in Wilson's political statements. Crunden argues that Wilson and other progressive figures were frustrated church men and women who lived in an age in which "the ministry no longer seemed intellectually respectable." The reformers sought an escape to the professions, which "offered possibilities for preaching without pulpits." *Ministers of Reform*, ix, 14–15. See also Clyde Griffen's seminal essay "The Progressive Ethos" in Stanley Coben and Lorman Ratner (eds.), *The Development of an American Culture* (Englewood Cliffs, N. J., 1970), pp. 119–50.

repository of "possibilities and noble resources" that were capable of "almost infinite development in power and virtue."[4]

Thus Wilson saw methodical, worldly pursuits and the moral demands of the church as complementary principles that operate in different but interconnected spheres of life. The Christian duty to fulfill one's talents carried over into secular matters. The principle of love with which God had forged the Christian community extended, not only to the duty of man in his relationship to God, but also to relationships among men. As Wilson put it, "One who forms his every-day life after the perfect model of Christ's life will himself be a model which no man can afford to despise, besides thereby gaining for himself an assurance of everlasting life."[5] Whereas Lutheranism stressed the fundamental incompatibility between the spiritual and the secular realms, Calvinist doctrine sought to reconcile them in the concept of a worldly order established by God as a guide for man in his pursuit of progress and order in a chaotic world. This order pertained to the division of labor, the vocations, and the civil laws as well as to political institutions. Wilson's assumption of a mutually supportive relationship between the secular order and the religious order seems to reflect the historical experience of religion in America.[6] Unlike the European countries, where Puritanism had had to fight to make a place for itself within an existing social and political order, Puritan beliefs existed prior to the establishment of the American nation. Christian principles had been built into the foundations of society.[7]

The extent to which Wilson embraced a world view that presupposed that religious meaning was inherent in the secular order is brought out in his early religious essays, composed during the second half of 1876, during and after his vacation at home in Wilmington, North Carolina. Of these essays, "Christ's Army" contains the most elaborate attempt to place the individual in a religious as well as a temporal realm. Although the essay has been dismissed as the manifestation of a "dualistic and rigidly moralistic view of the world and human activity in it," it merits closer attention as an example of Wilson's attempt to bring religious knowledge

[4] "Work–Day Religion," Aug. 11, 1876, *PWW*, I, 176–78; "Christian Progress," Dec. 20, 1876, *ibid.*, pp. 234–35.

[5] "The Bible," Aug. 25, 1876, *ibid.*, pp. 184–85.

[6] Wolin, *Politics and Vision*, pp. 179–83; H. Richard Niebuhr, "Protestant Movements and Democracy," in James Ward Smith and A. Leeland Jamison, eds., *The Shaping of American Religion: Religious Perspectives in American Culture* (Princeton, N. J., 1961), p. 46; and Cushing Strout, *The New Heavens and the New Earth: Political Religion in America* (New York, 1974), p. 107.

[7] George M. Marsden, *Fundamentalism and American Culture: The Shaping of Twentieth-Century Evangelicalism, 1870–1925* (New York, 1980), p. 49.

to bear on civil behavior.[8] His starting point was a traditional Puritan symbolism, the figures of language that represent "mankind as divided into two great armies," whose "field of battle is the world." The essay is not, however, a simple delineation of one battle but rather of three battles that take place on different levels. The first takes place within the individual himself as a struggle between the good and evil forces of the mind. The second battle goes on in the historical world, where "the army of the Saints" battles the "Prince of Darkness." The third takes place between "the Great Captain of Salvation" and "the darkness of Hell" in a transcendental sphere. Wilson's language is heavily metaphorical; indeed, the message is substantially a metaphorical transporting of meanings from one battle to another. The drama on all three levels, however, proceeds in predetermined fashion. The soldiers in the Christian army, "rallying their broken ranks more vigorously upon every repulse," finally overcome the enemy and win their "sure victory and an everlasting reward."

Far from being the work of a religious fanatic, the scenario of "Christ's Army" is pervaded by order and by restraints upon the actions of the individual. The army is itself arranged in a hierarchy of authority extending from its supreme leader to "the Saints"—"the veteran regiments"—and the "younger troops" arrayed on "the great battlefield of every-day life." Against this background of order, Wilson asks how professed Christians recognize their place on the field and the right tactics for advance. Wilson's answer was that he should take his clues from the social surroundings that, together with the word of the Bible, formed a text of instruction. One fights for Christ the way one "would fight for any other cause." The believer must look to his companions and keep pace with them. He must seek the "congenial and pleasant company of the good and upright." "Companionship" is itself involved in the fight, because it protects the individual and makes him feel that he is "not alone in it." A rightful place in the Christian community is the best assurance of a part in the final victory of salvation.[9]

---

[8] Aug. 17, 1876, *PWW*, I, 180–81; Mulder, *Woodrow Wilson*, p. 49.

[9] For a discussion of Joseph Bellamy's use of the metaphor of the world *battle*, see Alan Heimert, *Religion and the American Mind: From the Great Awakening to the Revolution* (Cambridge, Mass., 1966), pp. 344ff. It seems clear that Wilson relied on the version of the millennium popularized by Jonathan Edwards, with whose writings Wilson undoubtedly was well acquainted; see "Wilson's Commonplace Book: 'Index Rerum,' " Feb. 22, 1876–c. Nov. 15, 1876, *PWW*, I, 110. Whereas traditional Calvinism assumed that the millennium would come about as the result of the actual reappearance of Christ, Edwards taught that the millennium would be established before Christ's return and the end of history. The result was that the millennium seemed more continuous with secular history. Edwards himself prophesied that it would begin in America, in the New World, which had been endowed with the

Most important, however, is the view of power implied in the choice of metaphors that serve to bring the divine and invisible forces into contact with traditional notions of the worldly organization of might. Throughout Western history, the army has been seen as the epitome of the power of the state, a meaning that was hardly lost on the South after the Civil War. Wilson's essay presents power in a light that is strikingly different from the liberal view of power as coercion and from the modern view of power as the capacity to make effective decisions.[10] In Wilson's account, power appears to be connected with the life-sustaining forces of ultimate reality. Power, in this view, is not what divides human beings but the spiritual force that ties human beings to one another and creates a community of shared purpose out of human diversity. Hence, power is to be approached, not with mistrust, but with awe. It is a form of energy that makes each person an instrument in a drama beyond human control and comprehension. At the same time, it is a protective bond thrown around the community that aspires to righteousness—"as God's all-powerful arm is ever around us," in Wilson's words.[11]

Although power is importantly dependent upon human action, it is not a human contrivance, because it is not a matter of choice for the Christian. Power is obligatory for the Christian, since it sustains the community and connects individuals with the general purpose. It provides "the stern necessity of fighting for our own safety, as well as the general advance."[12] The army is kept together by the mystical spirit that infuses each member with a common identity, the devotion to the course of victory. As Wilson exclaims, "How . . . glorious to fight for the divine Prince of Peace, under whose glorious standards, whose shining folds are inscribed with *Love to God*." The unity of the Christian community is inherent in the universality of love to God, which implies the love of one's neighbor. The "principle of love to God" is "the foundation and cause of men's duties to God, to each other, and to their own souls."[13] The principles of love are available to man through the Holy Scriptures.

---

mission for spiritual renewal. Strout, *New Heavens*, p. 151. See also the discussion of millennialism in Ernst Tuveson, *The Redeemer Nation: The Idea of America's Millennial Role* (Chicago, 1968), pp. 34–35, 52, 90; and Marsden, *Fundamentalism*, p. 51. Another source of inspiration for Wilson was Thomas Carlyle, *On Heroes, Hero–Worship and the Heroic in History* (London, 1872), iii: "Are not all true men that live or have ever lived, soldiers of the same army, enlisted, under Heaven's captaincy, to do battle against the same enemy, the empire of Darkness and Wrong?" For Wilson's reading of Carlyle, see the "Index Rerum," *PWW*, i, 125–26.

[10] See, for instance, Anthony M. Orum, *Introduction to Political Sociology: The Social Anatomy of the Body Politic* (Englewood Cliffs, N. J., 1978), pp. 124–33, where contemporary usage is discussed.

[11] "Christian Progress," *PWW*, i, 234.

[12] *Ibid.*, p. 235.

[13] "Christ's Army," *ibid.*, p. 181; "The Bible," Aug. 25, 1876, *ibid.*, p. 185.

In addition to the themes of necessity and unity behind Wilson's idea of power, there was a third theme with profound implications for political theory. The religious community, "the followers of this mighty Prince of Light," maintained its contact with the vital truth of God through a distinct body of literature, which required continuous interpretation. The vital spirit of community was supplied by God through the sacraments. Action, however, required knowledge as well as a common education if Christian principles were to penetrate daily behavior. The authority to teach was, of course, entrusted to the minister of the gospel, whose life and preaching must be "a model of Christian consistency," as Wilson put it. The minister must "in all things set his people a godly example."[14] The individual cannot be his own interpreter, any more than knowledge of moral right and wrong is a private matter. The Bible itself, the example of Christ, and the accumulated knowledge of hundreds of years of the practice of Christianity form a complex body of knowledge that require exegesis and explanation.[15] These functions belong to the minister, who is elected to office by elaborate procedures that insure his selfless integrity as well as his solid learning. But since his function is one of interpretation, he cannot be considered infallible. He is a leader of the religious community, not its ruler. His service is a reflection of the trust of the community, not a symbol of divine appointment. Thus the democracy of commitment and dedication at the basis of the community is balanced, not by an aristocracy of religious officers, but by a meritocracy of those who were "pure in all . . . dealings" and whose "conversation must be free from all vanity."[16] The importance of interpretation is readily apparent in the doctrine of "the principle of love to God"—as opposed to the experience of love. As a principle, the foundation of community is available only through intellectual formulation. To identify power and community, it is necessary to have access to the authentic body of knowledge that constitutes its "foundation and cause" as well as the appropriate method for its interpretation. The third theme behind Wilson's early idea of power may be called the notion of authentic knowledge.

Since these ideas behind Wilson's first writings seem closely tied to his religious upbringing, especially to his father's beliefs, it is necessary to touch briefly upon the nature of their relationship. There is no doubt that Dr. Wilson played a most important role in his son's development.[17]

[14] "Christian Progress," *ibid.*, p. 235; "A Christian Statesman," Sept. 1, 1876, *ibid.*, p. 188.

[15] "The Positive in Religion," Oct. 15, 1876, *ibid.*, pp. 211–12.

[16] "A Christian Statesman," *ibid.*, p. 188; see also Wolin, *Politics and Vision*, pp. 178–79.

[17] Woodrow Wilson later expressed his feeling of dependence on his home: "A boy never gets over his boyhood and never can change those subtle influences which have become part of him, that were bred in him when he was a child." "Robert E. Lee: An Interpretation," Jan.

The bonds of affection between them are witnessed by the loving correspondence that tied son and father together when Wilson left home in 1873 to attend Davidson College, and again when Wilson left for the College of New Jersey in 1875. Wilson admired his father's facility with words. Throughout the 1870s he regularly submitted his various writings for publication to the critical review of his father.[18] Wilson was thoroughly impressed with his father's oratorical capacity and sought to develop his own skills in the image of his father. Finally, it is clear that Wilson wholeheartedly adopted the faith of his father.[19]

The close relationship between father and son has led some biographers to believe that Wilson's political convictions and personality were locked into a projection of his father, which placed his religious upbringing in a dual bond of love and rejection.[20] Unfortunately, only a couple of letters from the young Wilson to his father have been preserved. But one letter (or a draft of a letter) from his second year at Princeton seems to indicate that Wilson grew toward independence while retaining a profound affection and admiration for his father.[21] The nature of Wilson's feeling is revealed in the relaxed and humorous tone of the letter as well as in the subtle way Wilson compared his own individuality with his father's.

Although sent to his father, the letter was addressed to the General Assembly of the Southern Presbyterian Church, meeting in Knoxville, whose proceedings Dr. Wilson directed as stated clerk. Wilson continued, jestingly, to write about himself in the third person, as "the son of the said Stated Clerk," and compared the abilities of his father with his own

---

19, 1909, *PWW*, xviii, 631. The key word is *subtle*, which refers to complex patterns of emulation and succession rather than to a one–to–one transmission of values and behavior.

[18] See, for instance, Joseph Ruggles Wilson to WW, July 26 and Aug. 10, 1877, and Jan. 10, 1878, *ibid.*, i, 287, 288, 338.

[19] Mulder, *Woodrow Wilson*, pp. 29–41.

[20] Alexander L. George and Juliette L. George, in *Woodrow Wilson and Colonel House*, pp. 3–13, stress the importance of "a subterranean hostility" in Wilson's relation to his father. They use this to explain Wilson's search for power and security in his personal relations as well as his rigid adherence to legalistic doctrines, rooted in the Presbyterian environment, in his intellectual life. Robert C. Tucker, "The Georges' Wilson Reexamined: An Essay on Psychobiography," *American Political Science Review*, lxxi (June 1977), 606–18, modifies this view. Edwin A. Weinstein *et al.*, in "Woodrow Wilson's Political Personality: A Reappraisal," *Political Science Quarterly*, xciii (Winter 1978–79), 585–98, challenged the Georges' view, which they restated in "*Woodrow Wilson and Colonel House*: A Reply to Weinstein, Anderson, and Link," *Political Science Quarterly*, xcvi (Winter 1981–82), 641–65. The controversy is judiciously reviewed in Dorothy Ross, "Woodrow Wilson and the Case for Psychohistory," *Journal of American History*, lxix (Dec. 1982), 659–68.

[21] WW to Joseph Ruggles Wilson, May 23, 1877, *PWW*, i, 265–66. It is uncertain whether the letter was sent.

misfortunes. In contrast to the father's "clear-sightedness," Wilson reported that his own mind was "remarkably bright and empty." Wilson further described his own appearance by pointing to his "long nose, open mouth, and consequential manner." He then brought characterization to bear on his ideas, his style of writing, his opinions, and his prospects in the upcoming examinations. Thus the distance in the use of the third person for both sender and receiver indicates respect. But behind the veil of formality and behind the contrast between the father's mature competence and his own immature openness to "everything that is afloat" one detects an extraordinary confidence and trust. Wilson presented a critical self-portrait without fear of downgrading himself in the face of overwhelming paternal qualifications. As the letter concludes; "After all, he [Woodrow Wilson] is a good enough sort of fellow and what he lacks in solidity he makes up in good intentions and spasmodic endeavors." Admiration for his father was balanced against his own youthful enthusiasm and confidence in his own potential for development.

SINCE HIS STAY at Davidson College, Wilson had been drawn to politics. But if any single event can be said to have fixed his permanent interest upon political matters, it was the contested election of 1876 between Hayes and Tilden. From the time of Tilden's nomination, Wilson followed the events with "the most harrowing suspense."[22] He rejoiced in the prospect of a Democratic victory and took part in a Democratic student demonstration on November 8 in order to celebrate the news of Tilden's popular majority. Perhaps the final deal, the Compromise of 1877, which traded the office of the presidency for a promise to remove federal troops from South Carolina and Louisiana, seemed to Wilson a supreme triumph for the shabby deals of congressional politics and a gross humiliation of the presidency itself.[23]

More important for Wilson's political development, the extended electoral crisis confronted him with sectional tensions that brought about his discovery of American nationalism. The contest for the certification of electoral votes took place in an atmosphere that was reminiscent of the crisis that had resulted in the Civil War sixteen years earlier.[24] The pas-

[22] Shorthand diary, Nov. 9, 10 (quote), 11, 13, 1876, ibid., pp. 223–25.

[23] Ibid., Nov. 8, 1876, p. 222. Douglas McKay to WW, Nov. 23, 1876, ibid., p. 231: "When I see so plainly that there is an endeavor to make the will of the people subservient to the wishes of a few unblushing scoundrels, such as some of those in power at Washington, I am the more persuaded that while the government of the Republic is beautiful in theory, its practical application fails entirely."

[24] Morton Keller, Affairs of State: Public Life in Late Nineteenth Century America (Cambridge, Mass., 1977), pp. 262–66, contains a summary of the recent interpretations of the crisis.

11

sions of the Civil War ran strong in Wilson's immediate family. His father had served as a chaplain in the Confederate army and maintained strong views on suffrage for blacks and the poor. Assuming that Wilson had inherited these opinions as well as his father's rash temper, Wilson's mother repeatedly warned him not to get into brawls about the election.[25] On November 15, in the midst of rising political anxiety among the students, Wilson wrote his first political speech, "The Union," which was addressed to both northern and southern students.[26]

The significance of the speech must be seen in the context of the strong expressions of pro-British and antirepublican attitudes Wilson had displayed up to this date. As a little boy, he had witnessed his father's church being turned into an emergency hospital for Confederate soldiers during the final stages of the war.[27] Reports about looting and war crimes committed by federal troops were common in the years that followed the defeat.[28] As a boy, Wilson avoided identification with either the victors or the vanquished. In his early fantasies about soldiers and war, he appointed himself the commander of a British squadron.[29] He was less than enthusiastic about the centennial of the Declaration of Independence. In his diary he complained about patriotic writers who compared the United States with other countries and predicted its "future advance and greatness." It was "the old old story." "The American *Republic* will in my opinion never celebrate another Centennial. At least under its present Constitution and laws. Universal suffrage is at the foundation of every evil in this country."[30] Again, a fortnight later on the Fourth of July, 1876:

[25] Janet Woodrow Wilson to WW, Nov. 8, 15, Dec. 1, 1876, *PWW*, I, 223, 228, 233, reveal her strong anxiety. She seems to refer to Wilson's account of the demonstration on November 8. Douglas McKay to WW, Nov. 13, 1876, *ibid.*, p. 232, contains a reference to Wilson's report to his close friend from the Sunday school in Columbia, South Carolina; it is the best summary of the social and political tensions Wilson experienced. McKay wrote; "You speak of your College mates being divided into two parties, Republican and Democrat, and of your nearly getting into scrapes 'with some of the fanatics.' I can readily understand the heated discussions which are likely to ensue between some of the Southern and Northern boys, as there are many among the northern people who are bitterly prejudiced and intolerant, when the question of the Southerner and negro are involved." Joseph Ruggles Wilson's views on slavery and his involvement in the war, which split his family into two camps, are well covered in Mulder, *Woodrow Wilson*, pp. 9–13.

[26] Draft of a speech, "The Union," Nov. 15, 1876, *PWW*, I, 226–28.

[27] Mulder, *Woodrow Wilson*, p. 11.

[28] See, for instance, Wilson's marginal notes to a description of a military occupation: "Much of this account corresponds exactly with the facts concerning the burning and sacking of Columbia[,] South Carolina. All such scenes are more or less alike." Aug. 7, 1876, *PWW*, I, 168.

[29] Notebook, April 5, 1874, *ibid.*, pp. 43–46.

[30] Shorthand diary, June 19, 1876, *ibid.*, p. 143.

The one hundredth anniversary of American independence. One hundred years ago America conquered England [*sic*] in an unequal struggle and this year she glories over it. How much happier [?] she would be now if she had England's form of government instead of the miserable delusion of a republic. A republic too founded upon the notion of abstract liberty! I venture to say that this country will never celebrate another centennial as a republic. The English form of government is the only true one.

Wilson "passed a very quiet day" at home in Wilmington. Noting that there were "splendid illuminations throughout the North," he spent the evening with Macaulay's history of England.[31]

Little more than four months later Wilson found it "very easy" to write his speech on "The Union." He noted in his diary that he was "pleased" with the result and hoped to "make some impression" with the speech. He chose a string of quotations from Daniel Webster, Henry Clay, Andrew Jackson, and John C. Calhoun to emphasize that praise of the Constitution cut across sectional lines. The Constitution was "the mainspring of the Union, . . . the love and theme of our greatest statesmen in their youth, their guide and word in their old age." In striking contrast to his passivity at the centennial, Wilson now claimed that "no American can think of the Union and the principles upon which it is founded without a flush of pride and thrill of patriotism."[32]

This apparent reversal of opinion may suggest that Wilson was involved in a process of intellectual emancipation from his home. At the same time, however, the address reflected less a change of mentality than a political exploration of a religious viewpoint. Wilson argued that the Union was not based upon abstract principles—presumably the principles of equality and individual liberty—but upon a community of "common love of the country," a phrase that suggests a parallel with the foundations of the religious community. Wilson evoked the image of a suffering, consecrated body "endangered by traitors" that had traded its integrity for petty interests, tortured by "the lesions" of the late war, "so near to being fatal" and now being imprecated by the "frantic wavings of the bloody shirt." The present crisis called for extraordinary sacrifice by a leader who would " 'serve no other master' " and who would make his " 'public vows' " on the " 'broad altar' " of the Union. The primary duty was to renew the power of unity and redeem the resources of patriotic love: "He alone manifests true patriotism who labors to smooth over all dissensions, to inspire sympathy and confidence between all parts of the

---

[31] Shorthand diary, July 4, 1876, *ibid.*, pp. 148–49.
[32] Shorthand diary, Nov. 15, 1876, *ibid.*, pp. 225–26; "The Union," *ibid.*, p. 226.

country, and to instill into the minds of the people those principles which will lead them to act in their already grand capacity of a united brotherhood."[33]

The analogy to Christ's Agony was hardly accidental. Christological themes were not unusual in American political rhetoric before and after the Civil War.[34] The most convincing popular attempt to forge an alliance between American nationalism and Protestant eschatology was "The Battle Hymn of the Republic," written in 1862. Indeed, Wilson introduced his speech by remarking that he was aware that he was "treading upon oft-trodden ground" but that he wished to "impress some important conclusions . . . which we are at present very prone to overlook." The general political meaning of these themes was—as in Wilson's address—to exorcise the memory of the national fratricide with a myth of brotherhood—or the "union of the hearts," as Wilson put it.[35]

But the speech had important implications for Wilson's personal development. Psychologically, the discovery that religious terminology could be used to express fundamental political values allowed Wilson to close the gap between his upbringing and his loyalty to the South, on the one hand, and his national sentiment and the continental atmosphere at Princeton on the other. For the first time, he was able to formulate in words what he called in the speech "an enthusiasm which has ever struggled for utterance."[36] The exultant tone in the address and in his private diary suggests that the speech spoke convincingly to a breach in his political attachments that began with the rise of tensions after the election of 1876.

From a different point of view, the importance of the speech lies in its suggestion of a dimension of passion behind Wilson's theoretical undertakings that is apt to be overlooked if the origins of his interest in politics are described as an identification with British liberals, a reverence for British conservatism, or an attempt to provide a moral justification for American capitalism. These explanations leave no room for the strong undercurrent of fear of a political dissolution that is present in "The Union" and elsewhere in the early writings. It has been easy to overlook this undercurrent, because the progressive outlook excelled in the cele-

[33] "The Union," *ibid.*, pp. 226–28 . The final quotation is from p. 227.

[34] Perry Miller, "From the Covenant to the Revival," in Smith and Jamison (eds.), *Shaping of American Religion*, 359–68, and Strout, *New Heavens*, pp. 200–204.

[35] Tuveson, *Redeemer Nation*, pp. 197–99, is a careful interpretation based upon the idea that the strong images of the hymn were chosen, not primarily for their poetic effect, but in order to picture the war as a stage in a historical sequence leading to the coming Kingdom of Christ. "The Union," *PWW*, I, 226, 228.

[36] *Ibid.*, p. 226.

bration of optimism after the turn of the century. It is clear, however, that Wilson regarded the conscious cultivation of a cheerful attitude as a religious duty.[37]

IF THE EARLY religious essays, including "The Union" are regarded as the beginning of Wilson's political writings, it is possible to suggest an interpretation that allows for a more complex view of his political world. Wilsonian progressivism originated in a political context strongly influenced by the dread of a return to sectional conflict. The Civil War represented a stark return to a political state of nature. The four years of armed hostilities involved a loss of American lives comparable to the total loss of European lives during the Napoleonic Wars, which extended over a decade and a half. But this carnage could hardly be explained with reference to dynastic rivalries or bloodthirsty emperors. It was set in a political society that prided itself for having the most liberal constitution in the world, a maximum of popular participation in politics, and a belief in the Jeffersonian doctrines of the advance of the human mind and the natural harmony of social interests.

But once the historical backdrop shifted from pride in the achievements of the American Revolution to horror at the carnage of the Civil War, the notion of progress tended to lose its character of freedom and spontaneity and to become associated with power and stark necessity. In an essay of December 1876, Wilson discussed the idea of "Christian Progress" and concluded with this statement: "He who pretends to fight under the great banner of Love, should rejoice that there is no armor for his back, that to retreat is death, and should thus go forward with an eagerness and will which no slight cause can turn from their object."[38] In a discussion of the idea that governments can only be protected against outside attack, Wilson chose the answer from Daniel Webster that "nothing can save it when it chooses to lay violent hands on itself." "We may be allowed the hope," Wilson added, "that this suicidal course has not so impaired our system that loving hands may not heal its wounds."[39] Behind the apparent optimism of the belief in the inevitability of progress there was the perception of a demand that society be driven forward lest it should again split apart into warring camps.

At first sight, Wilson's early impressions of power and progress, both associated with the idea of the nation, may seem youthful and inconsequential. After all, they were formulated before his twentieth birthday.

[37] "The Positive in Religion," *PWW*, I, 212; "Christian Progress," *ibid.*, p. 234.

[38] "Christian Progress," *ibid.*, p. 235.

[39] "Some Thoughts on the Present State of Affairs," Jan. 30, 1877, *ibid.*, p. 349.

It should be kept in mind, however, that the very term *national* was highly charged politically. It had been carefully suppressed by the Founding Fathers, who had struck it out of the first draft of the Constitution twenty-six times. As the constitutional scholar Francis Newton Thorpe pointed out in 1901, it was only when the southern states took the name Confederacy that "nation" began to be used in its modern sense in the North. Not until the campaign of 1876 did any political party proclaim that "the United States is a nation, not a league." At the same time there was, according to Thorpe, "a common saying that we had become a nation with a big N."[40] Wilson's use of the term *nation* toward the very end of his draft of "The Union" is therefore interesting. In effect the speech, which began with an emphasis upon a compact of emotional fulfillment, moved toward an emphasis on the power of unity. His celebration of the "warmth of patriotism" was augmented by Wilson's hope for a restoration of the "former prestige as a nation of mental and political giants."[41] Thus, in his first political address Wilson began to invest the term *nation* with a set of meanings, which were retained and elaborated in his later and more mature writings. In *Constitutional Government*, written more than thirty years later, Wilson declared that he regarded "synthesis, not antagonism" as "the whole art of government." As he put it emphatically, "I cannot imagine power as a thing negative and not positive."[42]

[40] *The Constitutional History of the United States, 1765–1895* (3 vols., 1901; reprint, New York, 1970), III, 518–19, 529.

[41] *PWW*, I, 228.

[42] *Constitutional Government, ibid.*, XVIII, 139.

II

★ ★

WILSON'S INTRODUCTION
TO THE STUDY OF POLITICS
AND POLITICAL ECONOMY

If Wilson's discovery of American nationalism is reduced to a mere logical argument, it simply asserted that fratricide presupposed a certain
familial unity. But, of course, such a reduction hides the rich resources
of language and energy that became available to Wilson when the violent
conflict that had dominated his boyhood began to assume a new meaning. He used the family metaphor itself as an image of the founding of a
new nation. The Union consisted of constitutional doctrines "founded by
our fathers," but it rested upon "sound principles of government," that
is, the bountiful knowledge that had "developed from the long experiences of the mother country."[1]

While at Princeton, the alma mater of his undergraduate education,
Wilson was introduced to two forms of political knowledge: political
economy and political science. He was nurtured on a fairly traditional
diet. Although by no means a rebel, he worked his way steadily and consciously toward an independent point of view. Wilson began to argue and
write about an extensive range of political subjects.

IN EARLY 1877, Wilson began systematically practicing the skills that
seemed necessary for a political career. He stopped writing religious essays and began a series about political leaders. Where he had earlier written on the topic of "A Christian Statesman," he now composed an address on "The Ideal Statesman" for which he received the second prize
in a sophomore speech contest in the American Whig Society, one of the
two major debating clubs at Princeton. He told his audience: "No doubt
many of us hope in the future to have some hand in the government of
our country:—we hope some day to become statesmen: and I may say

---

[1] "The Union," *PWW*, I, 226.

that no worthier ambition could influence us."[2] Wilson was elected by his class to the board of editors of *The Princetonian*, the campus journal.[3] From its editorial pages he advocated better instruction in oratory and attacked examinations that forced the student to cram his memory with facts for the purpose of simply reproducing the information instead of developing his interests and enthusiasms. "The secret of success," Wilson declared, "is the power of mental vision, of deep, thorough, condensed thought." Warning against the "wandering mind," he praised intellectual discipline as the "training for the great athletic struggles of our future life."[4]

At Davidson College, Wilson had enrolled in the Eumenian Society, one of the two debating clubs on campus. At Princeton he joined the American Whig Society at its first regular meeting after his arrival.[5] He organized and was the driving force behind the Liberal Debating Club, a small debating society that sought to practice parliamentary procedure and promote verbal talents among its members. He was, in fact, so central to the club that it dissolved shortly before his graduation.[6] Wilson saw the literary and political activities of these clubs as an invaluable addition to the regular curriculum and urged the university to support the practice of oratory in the halls of debate. He also supported demands for better instruction in elocution.[7] In an editorial written during his last semester, Wilson defended students who, in an institution that pursued the "classical" curriculum, stood "below the honor list" but were nonetheless "among the brightest men of their class." Students of this sort devoted their time to reading in fields outside assignments and to "the work of literary societies; or the acquirement of skill in writing, speaking and debate." They were preparing themselves for "the special work which awaits them after graduation."[8]

In the debating societies Wilson discussed a broad range of social, economic, and political questions. At Davidson the students debated the two-

[2] Jan. 30, 1877, *ibid.*, p. 242.

[3] This honor meant a great deal to Wilson. It gave him "somewhat of a reputation in college—whether this reputation is deserved or not is inconsequential," as he put it in private. He promised himself to live up to his reputation. Shorthand diary, March 20, 1877, *ibid.*, p. 253.

[4] "True Scholarship," editorials in *The Princetonian*, May 24, 1877, *ibid.*, pp. 268–69.

[5] Minutes of the Eumenian Society, Oct. 4, 1873, *ibid.*, pp. 31–32; minutes of the American Whig Society, Sept. 24, 1875, *ibid.*, p. 75.

[6] "Editorial Note: The Liberal Debating Club," *ibid.*, p. 245; minutes of the Liberal Debating Club, March 22, 1879, *ibid.*, p. 467.

[7] Editorials in *The Princetonian*, Jan. 25 and Oct. 4, 1877, and Jan. 24, 1878, *ibid.*, pp. 239, 294–96, 344.

[8] Editorial in *The Princetonian*, Feb. 28, 1879, *ibid.*, p. 462.

party system, republicanism and monarchy, coeducation, and slavery.[9] The American Whig Society was preoccupied with questions of a more traditional type, such as whether "a man should be judged by his efforts rather than by his success."[10] Wilson supported the proposition that "a liberal education is to be preferred to an exclusively practical one" and voted in the negative on a resolution that advocated a protective tariff.[11] Wilson wanted to debate contemporary political issues. He urged the Lecture Association to take on "some of the many live questions of the day, both of science and politics," and he proposed speeches on the silver question and on free trade.[12]

The Liberal Debating Club argued about matters that clearly reflected Wilson's own current interests, and many of the issues found their way in one form or another into his essays. The topics for discussion indicate his early interest in European political issues—for example, Bismarck's policy, the Treaty of Paris, and the Third Republic in France. A couple of discussions dealt with British imperial politics.[13] This small group of friends also dealt with specific current problems on the American political scene, such as an expansion of the term for members of the House of Representatives, an expansion of the American standing army, the resumption of specie payments, free trade, the introduction of cabinet members into the House of Representatives, and the reform of the party system.[14] Other arguments dealt with broad social issues, such as poverty, the limitation of suffrage through educational qualifications, the establishment of a national university, and Chinese immigration.[15]

His practice of engaging in debate and promoting current issues for discussion reveal Wilson's early ideas about the purpose of a college education. Bored with much of the formal teaching and contemptuous of the cramming of facts that did not stimulate his curiosity, he advocated a more open and politically informed education that would reflect the needs of society. Debating pressing issues would better prepare students

[9] Minutes of the Eumenian Society, Nov. 7 and Dec. 5, 1873, May 8 and Jan. 16, 1874, *ibid.*, pp. 35, 37, 49, 39.

[10] Minutes of the American Whig Society, March 2, 1877, *ibid.*, p. 251.

[11] Minutes of the American Whig Society, Oct. 19, 1877, May 24 and Nov. 12, 1878, *ibid.*, pp. 302, 377, 434.

[12] Editorial in *The Princetonian*, Jan. 10, 1878, *ibid.*, p. 334.

[13] Minutes of the Liberal Debating Club, May 19, Sept. 22, 29, and Oct. 6, 20, 1877, Feb. 2, Sept. 21, and Nov. 6, 1878, Jan. 18, Feb. 8, 15, and March 1, 1879, *ibid.*, pp. 264, 292, 294, 297, 303, 356, 400, 429, 448, 456, 458, 463.

[14] Minutes of the Liberal Debating Club, June 2, Sept. 22, and Nov. 17, 1877, Jan 12, Feb. 9, and March 16, 1878, *ibid.*, pp. 271–72, 292, 320, 339, 359, 363–64.

[15] Minutes of the Liberal Debating Club, Jan. 26, Feb. 16, March 23, 1878, and March 22, 1879, *ibid.*, pp. 347, 359, 366, 467.

for their future responsibilities. The goal of serious debate was not primarily to promote debating skills as a form of playacting but to develop the arts of reasoning and persuasion. As Wilson wrote in the college paper, "the style of oratory developed in such societies [that are devoted to debate] is just that which will help us the most out of College. . . . Few men can develop much earnestness when their sole object is to make a good appearance. But in these societies there is little inducement to make a display, for each knows that his calibre is already measured. The object of the discussion is to arrive at the truth, or to influence the opinions of his comrades."[16]

Wilson's idea that college education should prepare the students for moral citizenship reflected a novel opinion but one that was widely accepted at Princeton. The college he joined was in the middle of an intellectual and administrative reorganization undertaken by Dr. James McCosh, a professor at Queen's College, Belfast, who was elected president of the College of New Jersey in 1868. Despite his own religious background, McCosh set about to ease the orthodox climate at the college. He did place much emphasis on discipline and required that students regularly attend chapel service, but at the same time he modified religious instruction in the classroom and told the trustees: "I speak of *Biblical instruction* for I believe that what the students require are not courses on theological lectures, or general religious teaching, but instruction that brings them into immediate contact with the living world."[17]

Equally important, McCosh brought to Princeton a distinguished scholarly career, a reputation for having stood up to John Stuart Mill in philosophical polemic, great administrative energy, and a distinct solution to the troubling problem of the relationship between science and religion. McCosh argued persuasively that religion and science share a common foundation, that both were dependent upon notions of order and law that were ultimately rooted in the divine creation of the human mind and its intuitive powers. The apparent contradiction between the theory of evolution and evangelical beliefs was resolved by the assumption that God had created Darwinism as well as faith itself. Science and faith, he said, are distinct forms of the transmission of experience to the human consciousness and are therefore both dependent upon divine appointment. McCosh was the last great exponent of the Scottish school of Common Sense Realism, which was best known for its rejection of epistemological complications and for its belief that man has a moral faculty

[16] Editorial in *The Princetonian*, Feb. 6, 1879, *ibid.*, p. 455. See also Wilson's criticism of the Lynde Debates; editorial in *The Princetonian*, Feb. 27, 1879, *ibid.*, p. 461.

[17] Cited in J. David Hoeveler, Jr., *James McCosh and the Scottish Intellectual Tradition: From Glasgow to Princeton* (Princeton, N. J., 1981), p. 253.

that roughly corresponds to the capacity for perception and judgment imputed to the sense organs. His achievement was to reargue the case for the conviction among American theologians that scientific method, as a way of investigating external realities through the observance of natural facts, should proceed undisturbed by the experience of truths based upon revelation.[18] Wilson liked McCosh and followed his courses on psychology and the history of philosophy.

There is little doubt that Wilson looked forward to the study of political science and political economy, which were required courses in the second and third years at Princeton. At Davidson, Wilson had been enrolled for only the freshman year and had not followed the political courses assigned for juniors.[19] At Princeton, political economy and political science were taught by Lyman Hotchkiss Atwater. It is difficult, however, to specify Atwater's influence on Wilson. Much as Wilson was looking forward to study in the areas of his main interest, he found Atwater quite boring as a teacher and as a preacher. But from the pages of *The Princetonian* he praised Atwater for his able instruction in "pressing public questions," such as the silver controversy. Atwater recognized the responsibility of the college's professors "to do all in their power to enlighten the youth under their care, as to all the principles of those branches upon a thorough knowledge of which, on the part of public men, the welfare or, perhaps, the very existence of the government depends."[20] Atwater introduced Wilson to the orthodox view of the social sciences as inquiries into the moral constitution of common life and therefore concerned primarily with the normative foundation of the social order.

Like so many American economists in the nineteenth century, Atwater

[18] James Ward Smith, in "Religion and Science in American Philosophy," in Smith and Jamison (eds.), *Shaping of American Religion*, p. 409, argues that McCosh hardly succeeded in assimilating the claims of religion and science, if science is understood as a method for the investigation of the nature of things. In effect, McCosh proposed a religious acceptance of science, much as "the housewife may accept and accommodate her dishwasher and her television set without the slightest understanding of the spirit of invention which produced them." See also Marsden, *Fundamentalism*, pp. 18–20, and Hoeveler, *James McCosh*, pp. 160–65, for discussions of McCosh's views. The influence of Scottish realism on nineteenth-century academia is assessed briefly in Perry Miller (ed.), *American Thought: Civil War to World War I* (New York, 1954), ix–xi, and discussed in detail by way of an investigation of metaphysical and ethical textbooks by D. H. Meyer in *The Instructed Conscience: The Shaping of the American National Ethic* (Philadelphia, 1972).

[19] *Catalogue of the College of New Jersey for the Academic Year 1878–79* (Princeton, N. J., 1878); "Courses at Davidson College," in Wilson's notebook, Sept. 1, 1873, *PWW*, I, 27.

[20] Shorthand diary, June 4 and Sept. 24, 1876, *ibid.*, pp. 132, 198; editorial in *The Princetonian*, Feb. 7, 1878, *ibid.*, pp. 357–58.

had come to social science from the ministry.[21] From 1854 onward he taught psychology, the history of philosophy, metaphysics, and logic. When McCosh came to Princeton, Atwater was asked to leave psychology and philosophy to McCosh and to begin to teach political science and political economy.[22] Like McCosh, he adhered to the school of Common Sense Realism, which played a significant role in the development of American social science. In this view, society is both an embodiment of traditional and accepted moral practices and an expression of moral sentiment grounded in the nature of man and therefore ultimately related to a divine plan beyond rational comprehension.[23] Atwater's primary intention seems to have been to show that facts from the economic sphere correspond to traditional ethical principles.

Atwater's 1875 essay on current industrial problems may be taken as an example.[24] In this essay he began by noting the paradox of starvation among the unemployed living in a Christian society of material abundance. He then proceeded to explain this anomaly as being in "accordance with the immutable law of God, that 'he that worketh not, neither shall he eat.' " He warned against a redistribution of property on the grounds that capital was an embodiment of "past labor saved and stored" for the purpose of creating future labor. Any kind of poor relief, he contended, contradicts the principles of eternal justice and will "speedily destroy all property, all capital, by removing every motive to abstinence, frugality, saving, and accumulation." On the other hand, Atwater was aware that many starving people were unable to find employment even if they did want to work. His explanation was that men endeavored to evade the "divine ordinance" by strikes, speculation, and waste. He presented, in short, a secularized version of the rituals of moral purification through economic depression.

Though not an original thinker, Atwater enjoyed considerable prestige in the Middle Atlantic states.[25] Devoted to the preaching of universal industrial harmony, he was deeply troubled by contemporary signs of conflict. He explained that conflict between labor and capital is impossible

---

[21] Joseph Dorfman, *The Economic Mind in American Civilization* (3 vols., New York, 1946–59), III, 69–72.

[22] *Addresses Delivered at the Funeral of L. H. Atwater* (New York, 1883).

[23] The relationship between common sense and social science in Scottish realism is discussed by Gladys Bryson in "The Emergence of the Social Sciences from Moral Philosophy," *International Journal of Science*, XLII (Oct. 1931), 304–23; and *Man and Society: The Scottish Inquiry of the Eighteenth Century* (Princeton, N. J., 1945); and by Nicholas Xenos in "Classical Political Economy: The Apolitical Discourse of Civil Society," *Humanities in Society*, III (Summer 1980), 233–39.

[24] "Our Industrial and Financial Situation," *Presbyterian Quarterly and Princeton Review*, New Ser., IV (July 1875), 518–28.

[25] Dorfman, *Economic Mind*, III, 69.

from a theoretical point of view, since both originate in labor. Workers represent present labor, and capital represents past labor. But he stressed that great concentrations of capital, as in the railroads, create social problems, first because workers resent the concentration of capital, and second because the concentration creates a class of "superintendents or officials, who, while they would guard jealously of their own capital, are unscrupulous in the handling of the money of others."[26] Atwater explained strikes as conflicts among workers themselves, between strikers and scabs. He considered speculation to be the result of a conflict between groups of superintendents who want to enrich themselves at the expense of capital. Atwater called for a wide range of reforms to "weed out from these corporations all extravagance, nepotism, indirect sponging of their profits." The natural equilibrium of the market, he said, is in perpetual danger of being upset by human failings, and the primary role of government is to protect property.[27]

Atwater was also worried about the political consequences of industrial development. On the one hand, he viewed the division of labor as a blessing by virtue of which the body politic ascends to "the greatest multiplicity and variety of function."[28] On the other hand, Atwater saw labor as being under "a condition of minuteness" that is destructive of moral capacity. "A man who works only on a needle may be said to be like the needle, having one point and one eye." Farmers were more likely to be better poised and balanced in their judgment than the average person whose work consisted of repetitive motions. "Hence in courts, farmers are preferred as jurymen to any other class."[29] Atwater was concerned about the rise of "the vast proletarian element among us," which, since it carried "an immense vote," would be "cherished and propagated by those who seek offices, but not the welfare, of the people." "It is our impression," he concluded, "that here we have a giant among us, which accidental circumstances have hereto kept slumbering." Its force was foreshadowed by its arousal "in the outbursts and howlings of labor against capital."[30]

Atwater used Aaron Chapin's modernization of Francis Wayland's

---

[26] *Ethics and Political Economy from Notes Taken in the Lecture Room* (Trenton, N. J., 1878), p. 131. These notes were prepared by students in Wilson's class. Their appearance may explain the absence of notes in political economy among Wilson's own classroom notes. Harold Godwin, *A History of the Class of '79* (Trenton, N. J., n.d.), p. 53, describes the publication of Atwater's lectures as "the noteworthy event of the year."

[27] "The Great Railroad Strike," *Presbyterian Quarterly and Princeton Review*, New Ser., VI (Oct. 1877), 740–42.

[28] *Ethics and Political Economy*, p. 97.

[29] *Ibid.*, p. 99.

[30] "The Currency Question," *Presbyterian Quarterly and Princeton Review*, New Ser., IV (Oct. 1875), 741.

work for his textbook in the course Wilson took. Chapin relied on Wayland's laissez-faire doctrines for the laws of the market, but he added a discussion of current problems to his summary. He gave special attention to "the selfish policy and ruinous administration of railroad managers."[31] The laws of the market, he wrote, presupposed a harmony of interests between the railroads and the public interest, but the managers had been able to usurp power over the corporations they were serving. Chapin posed the issue to the public: "How shall the rights of innocent stockholders be guarded against the machinations of unscrupulous managers? How shall these corporations be protected in their just private rights and yet be held under restrictions . . . as agents . . . for great public interests?"[32]

There is no direct evidence to suggest how Wilson was influenced by Atwater and Chapin, but perhaps it is sufficient to note that the doctrines expounded by Atwater do not conform to the standard view of a celebration of free trade and self-interest as the solution to every economic problem. Wilson was presented with a view of the economy concerned with the prospect of scarcity and conflict. Capital had to be protected, not only from the workers, but even from its own managers. To the extent that self-interest was seen as the energizing principle of the economy, it had to be nourished carefully by discipline and moral exhortation. Writers like Atwater who stressed the ethical foundations of the economy and even proposed to see it as a key to the divine order of the universe were necessarily troubled by their Puritan belief that the great majority of mankind was marked by its proclivity for sin and vice. Since Atwater adhered to the doctrines of laissez-faire, he could not even call directly upon government to discipline the masses. He was left with the force of moral suasion of his own discipline. "The ethical element," he declared, "is paramount because the best means of recognizing the true meaning of Political Economy is to attend to the moral element. Faithfulness in keeping engagements is necessary to political economy." These engagements were often less than promising, especially for workers, who had to fight among themselves for the wage fund that could only be derived from the savings of the capitalist.[33]

[31] Francis Wayland, *The Elements of Political Economy*, recast by Aaron L. Chapin (New York, 1879), p. 387.

[32] *Ibid.*, p. 490.

[33] "Notes on Atwater's Lectures on Political Economy in 1877–78, compiled by Wm. R. Barrichlo by means of the Edison Electric Pen," MS. in the Princetoniana Collection, Princeton University Library. Diamond, in his *Economic Thought of Woodrow Wilson*, p. 21, concludes that Atwater imparted to Wilson a view of political economy as "an *à priori* science, deducible from a few obvious maxims." Mulder, in *Woodrow Wilson*, p. 83, relies on Diamond's account. The point is, however, that Atwater had no conception of the economy as being independent

One of Atwater's central assumptions, however, was of enduring importance for Wilson. Atwater's teaching encouraged the conception of a national scope for the economy. The emphasis upon common moral precepts cast the idea of the economy in the form of national unification. The division of labor, the presumption of social interdependence, and the complex exchange relations that were necessary for the procurement of necessities strengthened the sensitivity to material well-being as a symbol of national power and unity. The notion of "Christian progress" could be turned to a secular vision. In his essay on "the Present State of Public Affairs," Wilson referred to "the truth that progress and its attendant prosperity are the severest tests of national character and national institutions," and he argued that the principles of the economy could be seen as a means of strengthening political order on a national scale.[34] But to do so he needed a dynamic view of society, a view that replaced the prospect of scarcity with an idea of national growth sustained by political direction of the economy.

In his course in political science with Atwater, Wilson read Theodore D. Woolsey's textbook on the theory of the state, which is an extensive account of constitutional theory from the earliest times. Woolsey's treatment of the American system is meager in comparison to his detailed discussion of European governments. He warned against the weakening of political stability that resulted from "the changes of society as it respects wealth, diversity of employment, and the growth of the cities; the infusion of new elements, especially from the lower classes of Europe; and the gradual reception of doctrines of political rights, which belong to extreme democracy."[35] Economic and social development, he said, is reflected in the corruption of political parties caused by the institution of universal suffrage. Woolsey deplored that the lower classes, which could have been excluded from the polls by "a very small property qualification," had been demoralized by party demagogues, while "the best part of society will not attempt to instruct them."[36]

---

of ethical principles. His principles were obviously derived from noneconomic sources. For the argument of the autonomous nature of the economy in Britain, see Karl Polanyi, *The Great Transformation: The Political and Economic Origins of Our Time* (Boston, 1957), pp. 111–25. See also Meyer, *Instructed Conscience*, pp. 99–107, and Anna Haddow, *Political Science in American Colleges, 1636–1900* (1939; reprint, New York, 1969), pp. 160–64.

[34] Jan. 30, 1878, *PWW*, I, 351, 354.

[35] *Political Science; or, The State Theoretically and Practically Considered* (2 vols., New York, 1878), II, 141. The work was reviewed in the *North American Review*, CXXVI (1878), 171–74, where it was criticized as being unscientific because of its lack of concern for "predictability" as the standard for modern political science.

[36] Woolsey, *Political Science*, II, 122.

This conservative warning was repeated in parts of the reading that Wilson completed on his own. During the summer of 1876 he discussed with his father the famous exchange between Jeremy Bentham, James Mill, and Thomas Babington Macaulay on the proper basis of government. Back in school, Wilson continued his reading of Macaulay and discussed his style and opinions in letters home and in the Liberal Debating Club.[37] In the exchange between the Utilitarians and Macaulay, Wilson sided with Macaulay in his criticism of universal suffrage. Rejecting the claim to a natural equality among citizens as a proper basis for influence in government, Macaulay emphasized the responsibilities of "the higher and middling orders [as] the natural representatives of the human race." The American Constitution played a special role in this debate, because all the participants saw the United States as a country of high wages and extensive opportunity for the lower classes. Since in America even laborers had a chance to better their worldly lot by their own efforts, it would not be necessary "even for the immediate advantage of the poor to plunder the rich." But conditions in England were different, Macaulay stressed. In England "the great majority" had no other prospects than a "life from hand to mouth." He predicted that the United States would have to face this conflict when economic opportunities had been exhausted.[38] Thus the issue of the fateful consequences of common franchise reverberated in Wilson's surroundings. But after his identification with the Union, Wilson rejected the issue in its customary conservative form. He did not ask whether the unworthy deserved to lose their vote but turned to the question of positive leadership. He conceived of the idea of political knowledge largely as an issue of perfect leadership. His biographical sketches and essays on general topics reflect a gradual development of his ideas on leadership. He turned from the notion of the great statesman to the idea of a political elite and, finally, to the idea of political education by oratory and debate.

WILSON saw the true statesman as the embodiment of commanding authority, an idea that owed something to Carlyle's celebration of heroes and hero worship. Wilson saw the great leader as able to rise above both particular selfish interests and historical factuality as someone ahead of his age. "Across the mind of the statesman," he wrote, "flash ever and anon brilliant, though partial, intimations of future events. . . . That

[37] Shorthand diary, July 18–20, 1876, *PWW*, I, 155, 156; Robert Harris McCarter to WW, July 18, 1877, *ibid.*, p. 283; minutes of the Liberal Debating Club, Jan. 12, 1878, *ibid.*, p. 339.

[38] Thomas Babington Macaulay, *The Miscellaneous Writings of Lord Macaulay* (2 vols., London, 1860), I, 320, 315, 313; Joseph Hamburger, *Macaulay and the Whig Tradition* (Chicago, 1976), pp. 55–62, 124–36.

something which is more than fore-sight and less than prophetic knowledge marks the statesman a peculiar among his contemporaries."[39] He is the selfless instrument for the advancement of the common good, and patriots will win "many a victory prouder than party victory—victories of principle and of right." Yet Wilson's great men are placed only above the common people, not soaring toward the heights of divinity, as are Carlyle's heroes. True leaders are ordinary men with special gifts who will "elevate the people to the heights of principle and justice in spite of themselves." The dynamics of leadership consist neither in divine appointment nor in an overpowering personal will. Wilson's idea of leadership was associated with guidance rather than rule. He believed that oratory is the strong bond that both arouses the followers and holds the leader under a tight rein.[40]

Wilson's interest in oratory obviously derived from his father's high standing as a preacher and a teacher of elocution. But over the years at Princeton, Wilson changed his idea of oratory so that it became a political rather than a religious mode of communication. He accommodated the Calvinist tradition of preaching to political oratory. It seems likely that Wilson's reading of Oliver Goldsmith's essay on eloquence played a role in this process. Goldsmith described oratory as a form of the social control of popular sentiment that in recent years had moved from religion to politics: "Enthusiasm in religion, which prevails only among the vulgar, should be the chief object of politics. . . . It [is] the duty of those whom the law has appointed teachers of this religion, to enforce its obligations and to raise those enthusiasms among people, by which alone political society can exist."[41] This idea of politics rested on an understanding of the primacy of emotion and interest with which David Hume and Edmund Burke had undermined the Enlightenment belief in reason as the basis of moral judgment. The orator was a man who was able to transfer "the passion or sentiment with which he is moved himself, into the breast of another." The rehabilitation of political sentiment involved a new emphasis on a standard of truth that was dependent upon the sensitivity of the speaker and the receptivity of the audience rather than on

[39] "The Ideal Statesman," Jan. 30, 1877, *PWW*, I, 244.

[40] *Ibid.*, p. 243; "Some Thoughts on the Present State of Public Affairs," *ibid.*, p. 354. Wilson's preoccupation with Thomas Carlyle's idea of the hero is illustrated in the "Index Rerum," in which Wilson made notes from his reading and concluded that "to enthrone the Ablest Man, [is] the true business of all Social procedure: the Ideal of Constitutions." Feb. 22–Nov. 15, 1876, *ibid.*, pp. 125–26.

[41] On Wilson's preoccupation with Goldsmith, see "Index Rerum," *ibid.*, p. 103, and Shorthand diary, Oct. 16–20, 1876, *ibid.*, pp. 212–15. "Of Eloquence (and Sermons)," in Oliver Goldsmith, *The Works of Oliver Goldsmith*, edited by J.W.M. Gibbs (5 vols., London, 1884), II, 426.

the demands of logical rigor. Goldsmith stressed the collective dimension of oratorical action: It is impossible for the orator to "affect the hearers in any great degree without being affected" himself. One could not "convince without being convinced." "It is much easier to deceive our reason than ourselves: a trifling defect in reasoning may be overseen . . . for it requires reason and time to detect the falsehood; but our passions are not easily imposed upon,—our eyes, our ears, and every sense, are watchful to detect the imposture." These views allowed for Goldsmith's exultation about oratory as the means by which power was generated: "This is the eloquence the ancients represented as lightning, bearing down every opposer; this is the power which has turned whole assemblies into astonishment, admiration, and awe—that is described by the torrent, the flame, and every other instance of irresistible impetuosity."[42]

Wilson's great leaders—Daniel Webster, William Pitt, Gladstone, John Bright, Alexander Hamilton, even Bismarck—were formed to fit this frame. He pictured them as leaders of parties in a constitutional setting. He saw oratory as the crown of leadership that integrates the different talents of the personality and turns into political genius: "To set off his business talents, to defend his independence, to support his positions, and to paint in startling colors the future which dwells in his mind the statesman must possess an orator's soul, an orator's words, an orator's action. To nobleness of thought he must add nobleness of word and conduct."[43] When the orator impresses his opinions upon his listeners, he is himself transformed. Wilson considered William Pitt a perfect example of a public speaker who was able to command the attention of the public. Pitt, as a person, "stood, in fact, almost alone," Wilson wrote, "above the masses who, from sheer admiration, supported him, and in their enthusiasm idolized him." He commanded "a vivid imagination" and "warm enthusiasm."[44] In the search for historical illustrations, Wilson even praised Bismarck's verbal powers. Though Bismarck was not a great debater, Wilson admitted, he embodied "a sort of rugged strength and beauty in his speeches. . . . Habitual terseness and frankness engrave his words upon his hearers' memories, imprint his sentiment upon their hearts."[45] Behind the ability to be heard, to carry the audience into the statesman's quadrant of thought, Wilson saw the special kind of political genius fit for a democratic age. The statesman is dependent upon his "divine insight into human nature," he has to develop "deep sympathy with all the efforts and strivings of the common mind." The relationship

[42] *Ibid.*, pp. 421–22, 427.
[43] "The Ideal Statesman," *PWW*, i, 244.
[44] "William Earl Chatham," Oct. 1878, *ibid.*, pp. 408–409.
[45] "Bismarck," Dec. 6, *ibid.*, p. 326.

between the leader and his audience is fundamentally of a psychological nature.[46]

The call for leadership is likely to become a fairly trivial exercise if it is not followed by an identification of groups or institutional arrangements that seem likely to produce the human dispositions that are called for. The importance of Wilson's answer lies in its distance from the two dominant tendencies of nineteenth-century politics in America. While American conservatism largely relied on some variation of the hope that the men of class and property would dominate public office, American liberalism was traditionally marked by a hostility to any notion of permanent political elites that would be able to establish a monopoly on the art of ruling. Based on his contention that "a representative government depends in great measure upon the existence of a large body of upright and intelligent men who make politics a career," Wilson argued for the prerogatives of "the thirty thousand young men who are pursuing studies at the different colleges of this country." This group of men would supply a continuous source of political talent and competence.[47]

While the statesman should lead the masses, the new college men should educate them. The need for education was sharpened by the common franchise. Without new sources of political instruction, "liberal institutions, political freedom, universal suffrage would be, one and all, the worst mockery of freedom, the sorest curse of humanity."[48] While both American conservatives and liberals had traditionally conceived of political preparation with reference to experience, either as the experience of the administration of property or the experience of political organization, Wilson focused on the need for general instruction supplied in the institutions of higher learning and transmitted by their graduates to the public at large. "While it is indisputably true," Wilson asked rhetorically, "that the people can comprehend great truths, is it not as true that they are not primarily acquainted with these truths and that they must be educated into an acceptance of them?" The truths that form the body of political knowledge are, in short, "political economy in connection with history and development of government."[49] In a forceful statement Wilson projected the features of a new politics in which objective knowledge would bring forth a new national dimension of political education:

[46] "The Ideal Statesman," *ibid.*, p. 243.

[47] "The Present State of Public Affairs," *ibid.*, pp. 350, 353.

[48] Editorial in *The Princetonian*, Jan. 10, 1878, *ibid.*, p. 336.

[49] "The Present State of Affairs," *ibid.*, p. 352; outline of a speech; "Independent Conviction," July 16, 1877, *ibid.*, p. 280; see also an editorial in *The Princetonian*, Jan. 10, 1878, *ibid.*, pp. 357–58.

If men in their youth allow blinding party prejudice to rule them there is less hope that they will throw off its shackles in later life. If, on the other hand, they conscientiously and thoroughly study the interests of the country, they will flood the land with vitality; will go forth prepared to lift the people to the comprehension of the great principles of political economy: raising the masses to the level of each great principle rather than lowering the principle to the level of the masses and thus degrading both.[50]

With this general conception of a new politics in mind, Wilson began to look for an institutional setting that would fit its national scope and its educational purpose.

This search was the primary motive behind Wilson's most ambitious articles from his last year at Princeton. "Cabinet Government in the United States," which he composed in early 1879, was Wilson's first essay to appear in a major national journal.[51] Encouraged by this success, he wrote "Self-Government in France" at about the time that "Cabinet Government" appeared in print. The two articles were closely related. Just as he used the English parliamentary experience to place the dynamics of leadership in perspective, Wilson used the French experience to enlighten the dynamics of mass behavior, understood as "political habits." The energetic reasoning that runs through both essays is related to at least three aspects of Wilson's political personality: his interest in parliamentary procedure, as seen in his organization of the Liberal Debating Club and his participation in its debates;[52] his practice of oratory and his reflections on its political importance; and finally his preoccupation with political theorists such as Walter Bagehot, Alexis de Tocqueville, and Edmund Burke.

THE EXPLICIT ARGUMENT in "Cabinet Government" is fairly simple and is readily apparent in the title. Wilson advocated constitutional changes that would require the president to select the heads of executive departments from among the members of Congress. Executive officers would be afforded the right to initiate legislation as well as to sit on the standing committees. Moreover, the secretaries of the departments would be po-

[50] "The Present State of Public Affairs," *ibid.*, p. 354.

[51] Aug. 1879, *ibid.*, pp. 493–510. The article was published in the *International Review*, VI (Aug. 1879), 146–63.

[52] Wilson's constitution for the Liberal Debating Club gives an early picture of this ideal of parliamentary organization. The secretary of state, appointed by the president and responsible to the majority of the members for his opinions upon matters under debate, was the key officer in terms of decisions and proceedings. "Constitution of the Liberal Debating Club," Feb. 1, 1877, *PWW*, I, 245–49.

litically responsible to the majority in Congress. This reform, Wilson claimed, would destroy the secrecy of the standing committees, which had caused political debate to deteriorate to the level of bargaining and trade-offs. If political issues were forced into the open by the need to gain the confidence of the majority in Congress, the result would be the selection of politicians with a capacity for principled reasoning and leadership. Read as a proposal for congressional reorganization, the essay was clearly inspired by Bagehot. Although Wilson seems to have conceived of his reform proposal independently of American sources, Bagehot's work on the English constitution had already stimulated an American discussion about congressional responsibility in the light of English cabinet government.[53]

Innumerable textbooks on American government later adopted Wilson's argument as a proposal for reorganizing Congress in the name of efficiency. But with regard to Wilson's own intellectual development, the essay is probably best understood as an attempt to reconcile the idea of the nation with the practice of universal suffrage. He achieved this reconciliation by turning some of the dominant assumptions of the age upside down. As John Tomsich and John G. Sprout have shown, political pundits of Victorian America worried endlessly about how ignorant voters would be able to choose "the best men" for leadership.[54] Wilson's reasoning implied that this was the wrong question to ask. At the outset of the essay he attacked the prejudice that congressional corruption and incompetence should be blamed on the popular vote: "A marked and alarming decline in statesmanship, a rule of levity and folly instead of wisdom and sober forethought in legislation, threaten to shake our trust not only in the men by whom our national policy is controlled, but also in the very principles upon which our Government rests." Wilson identified Theodore Woolsey as representative of those who delighted in blaming the voters and who therefore wanted to solve the question of corruption in government by purging the constituencies "of their ignorant elements." This, Wilson suggested, was to look for a "scapegoat for all our national grievances" by making "too superficial an analysis." The real question, Wilson pointed out, should not be "What representatives shall we choose to represent our chances in this haphazard game of legislation?" but "What plans of national administration shall we sanction?" While the "haphazard game" of politics was a matter of "the conflicting interests of innumerable localities represented," the notion of administra-

[53] "Editorial Note: 'Cabinet Government in the United States,' " *ibid.*, pp. 492–93.
[54] John Tomsich, *A Genteel Endeavor: American Culture and Politics in the Gilded Age* (Stanford, Calif., 1971); and John G. Sprout, *"The Best Men": Liberal Reformers in the Gilded Age* (New York, 1968).

tion presupposed a "directing power."[55] In effect, Wilson proposed to reconstitute the politics of competing local interests according to the new national scale. The suffrage, he said, is not an evil to be deplored but a boon to be exploited. The suffrage need not weaken governmental efficacy; instead it can actually legitimize the power and authority of the nation.

Wilson's argument turned upon a distinction between two kinds of political behavior. With reference to his religious essays, the standard types may be termed the politics of darkness and the politics of light. The most important features of the politics of darkness derived from an institutional setting characterized by deep institutional niches, by political cubbyholes, by the system of a separation of powers, and by the isolation and secrecy of decision making in congressional committees. It was a natural breeding ground for "party trickery" and "legislative jobbery," and it furnished the ideal conditions for organized economic and political groups who worked "in the interest of corporations," "under lobby pressure from interested parties," or "by the all-powerful aid of party machinery." The politics of light, in contrast, was conditioned on "full and free debates" characterized by "severe, distinct, and sharp enunciations of underlying principles, the unsparing examination and telling criticism of opposite positions, the careful, painstaking unravelling of all the issues involved."[56] Wilson envisioned an open system of competition rather than a closed system of interests. Under a system of cabinet responsibility, the public would be able

> to exercise a direct scrutiny over the workings of the Executive departments, to keep all their operations under a constant stream of daylight. Ministers could do nothing under the shadow of darkness; committees do all in the dark. . . . Corruption in office would court concealment in vain; vicious trifling with the administration of public business by irresponsible persons would meet with a steady and effective check. The ground would be clear for manly and candid defence of ministerial methods.[57]

While actual decision making, understood as "ministerial methods," would be removed from the legislative body, Congress would assume a primary responsibility for the creation of national opinion. Congressional debate would become the primary symbol of a successful combination of nationalism and general suffrage, because it would absorb the principle

[55] "Cabinet Government," *PWW*, 1, 493–94, 502.
[56] *Ibid.*, pp. 499–500.
[57] *Ibid.*, p. 503.

of political equality and rearrange it in the image of national policy. Wilson reproached those who were willing "to cast discredit upon that principle the establishment of which has been regarded as America's greatest claim to political honor,—the right of every man to a voice in the Government under which he lives." The transforming power of true debate is so great that it would allay conservative suspicions of the general assembly as the instrument for the tyranny of the majority. True debate would make Congress the vehicle of national unity. Congressional debate would take place "in the presence of the whole country." While the cabinet would govern, Congress would provide "an atmosphere of publicity." Its activities would be the equivalent "of the country speaking in open and free debate." The vital function of Congress would be to organize itself so that "the different sections" could "learn each other's feelings and interests."[58] The idea of a nationalized debate was the necessary condition and the guiding value behind Wilson's proposal of a change from committee to cabinet government:

> Committee government must fail to give effect to public opinion. In the first place, the exclusion of debate prevents the intelligent formation of opinion on the part of the nation at large; in the second place, public opinion, when once formed, finds it impossible to exercise any immediate control over the action of its representatives. There is no one in Congress to speak for the nation. Congress is a conglomeration of inharmonious elements; a collection of men representing each his neighborhood, each his local interest; an alarmingly large proportion of its legislation is "special;" all of it is at best only a limping compromise between the conflicting interests of the innumerable localities represented. There is no guiding or harmonizing power.[59]

This conception of politics as the overcoming of localism and as the stage for the formation of national political opinion was at the center of Wilson's argument, because it connected the political elite with the voting masses again after the link between the representatives and their local constituencies had been weakened. The crucial difference was that opinion would no longer flow primarily from the bottom up but from the top down. Congressional debate might be "the best, the only effective, means of educating public opinion." Although the educational value would flow in two directions, both "upon the members of the legislature themselves, and upon the people whom they represent," voting, of course, is essen-

---

[58] *Ibid.*, p. 494.
[59] *Ibid.*, pp. 501–2.

tially mute.[60] In this respect, Wilson's views on the nature of representative government followed Bagehot's dictum that "it is for our principal statesmen to lead the public, and not to let the public lead them."[61] This relationship would be essentially duplicated in the relationship between the officers of executive action and the deliberative assembly, which would criticize the government rather than meddle in its affairs. The strong emphasis upon political education as a primary function of Congress distinguished Wilson's conception of politics from Walter Bagehot's approach.

Bagehot's work *The English Constitution* was important for Wilson because of its frank proclamation of the "secret" that the efficacy of British power depended, not on the separation of functions, but on "the close union, the nearly complete fusion, of the executive and legislative powers" in the cabinet. In addition, however, Bagehot claimed to have discovered a political mechanism, hitherto unnoticed, that explained the apparent stability of English politics despite the expansion of the suffrage in 1832 and 1867. This mechanism revealed why the traditional political elite had been able to retain control of Parliament and government despite its position as the minority. The enfranchisement of the workers had not carried the antagonisms of economic life over into the political arena.[62] As Bagehot laid out his theory of political deference; "A country of respectful poor, though far less happy than where there are no poor to be respectful, is nevertheless far more fitted for the best government. You can use the best classes of the respectful country; you can only use the worst where every man thinks he is as good as every other."[63] Popular respect in England, rooted in affectional custom, was most clearly expressed in reverence for the Crown and the House of Lords. Bagehot claimed that these institutions fulfilled a "theatrical" function in contrast to the "efficient" function of government, which was placed in the House of Commons and in the cabinet. The "theatrical show" of wealth and power, the "spectacles" of the aristocratic classes and the queen, had a quality of visibility that coerced the imagination of the lower classes and made them respect "the real rulers," who were "obeyed implicitly and unconsciously."[64]

[60] *Ibid.*, pp. 500–501.

[61] *The English Constitution* (Garden City, N. Y., n.d.), p. 19.

[62] *Ibid.*, pp. 69, 19–21. Analyses of Bagehot's theory of deference include David Spring, "Walter Bagehot and Deference," *American Historical Review*, LXXXI (June 1976), 524–31; and Samuel Beer, "Tradition and Nationality: A Classic Revisited," *American Political Science Review*, LXVIII (Sept. 1974), 1293–95.

[63] Bagehot, *The English Constitution*, p. 290.

[64] *Ibid.*, pp. 63, 287–89.

Though he inquired into an issue similar to Bagehot's, Wilson gave a different answer. Where Bagehot had argued that the cabinet was an effective political body to the degree that broad public attention to political substance would be deflected to the nonpolitical parts of government, Wilson argued that the congressional committees—the most effective bodies of decision making—should be opened to public inspection. In England, according to Bagehot, political stability required that the authority of the state be separated from the power to decide. In the United States, Wilson argued, the power to decide should be surrounded with the means of national persuasion. Wilson seemed to suggest that national policy required that the legislature be surrounded with theatrical effects that would focus popular attention on the center of national debate. National power would be made more efficient in the process of its self-legitimation: "A responsible Cabinet constitutes a link between the executive and legislative departments of the Government which experience declares in the clearest tones to be absolutely necessary in a well-regulated, well-proportioned body politic. None can so well judge the perfections or the imperfections of a law as those who have to administer it."[65] For examples of this argument, Wilson referred to taxation and to the need for increased effectiveness in the "civil, military, and naval services." These functions were central to his conception of state power.[66]

The revaluation that follows from Wilson's use of the metaphors of light and darkness and from his emphasis upon the redeeming function of national debate may be contrasted with the American belief in the necessity of constitutional checks and balances. The separation of powers had been institutionalized on the assumption that political power is a dirty business, a reflection of man's fallen nature and an enduring testimony to his lust for power, and that while it is impossible to suppress individual and group interests, it is possible to check power by setting ambition against ambition, as the Federalists had argued. The Jeffersonian solution was to keep government to a minimum to avoid contamination of the social sources of freedom.[67] In contrast to this bleak view of

[65] "Cabinet Government," *PWW*, i, 502.

[66] *Ibid.*, pp. 502–3. Wilson's insistence that effective power be protected by institutional means is seen in an exchange in *The Princetonian* at about the time when Wilson wrote "Cabinet Government." Wilson proposed that the board of the journal should select its members rather than having each class elect its representative by general vote. In replying to criticism, Wilson maintained that editorial competence and continuity could be combined with an indirect form of voting. The students would regulate the tone of the paper by refusing to subscribe to it "unless the editors continue to be in sympathy with college sentiment." *The Princetonian*, April 4, 18, and May 2, 1879, Princetoniana Collection, Firestone Library.

[67] *The Federalist*, ed. by Jacob E. Cooke (Middletown, Conn., 1961), No. 10, pp. 56–60; Gerald Stourzh, *Alexander Hamilton and the Idea of Republican Government* (Stanford, Calif.,

politics, Wilson sketched a positive vision in which power is purified in the process of its legitimation. The metaphor of light was important because it allowed Wilson to join the images of openness, searching discussion, and rationality with a national range of power. The argument of the essay is that the prerequisite for a national policy is an institutional context that allows for the transformation of leadership from a local to a national scope.

EVEN WHILE his friends were congratulating him on the publication of "Cabinet Government," Wilson was about to finish its sequel, "Self-Government in France."[68] The new essay, which is usually seen as primarily a journalistic exercise, has not received much attention, perhaps because Wilson did not succeed in having it published despite several attempts during the following year.[69] Actually, it had its origins in the same reform proposal as the previous essay, and Wilson could very well have titled it "Cabinet Government in France." Wilson concluded his exposition of recent French history with the observation that it is "an instructive fact that [the] great changes were made possible by just such a system of ministerial responsibility as we consider unsafe and unsteady, and impracticable. . . . And yet this delicate system of official responsibility works without serious strain in passionate, inexperienced France."[70] The course of French history proved that English institutional arrangements and political experience were able to overcome the problems of popular self-government that revolution and abstract political doctrines had only deepened.

The important change from "Cabinet Government in the United States" was that Wilson now wanted to examine mass politics rather than the opportunities for parliamentary leadership. As stressed in his introductory remarks, he wished "ever and again to lay fresh emphasis upon the peculiar, distinctive character of the French *people* as it has issued, by the evolution of revolution, from the darkness and trials of political servitude into unaccustomed paths of self-government."[71] While constitutional procedure had been at the center of "Cabinet Government," Wil-

---

1970), pp. 95–106; and Joyce Appleby, "What is Still American in the Political Philosophy of Thomas Jefferson?" *William and Mary Quarterly*, xxxix (April 1982), 287–309.

[68] WW to Robert Bridges, Aug. 8, 1879, *PWW*, i, 511–13; "Self-Government in France," Sept. 4, 1876, *ibid.*, pp. 515–39.

[69] Bragdon, *Woodrow Wilson*, pp. 63–64, and Mulder, *Woodrow Wilson*, p. 60, characterize the article as primarily a journalistic exercise, strong on recent events in France but weak in its Anglophile bias.

[70] "Self-Government in France," *PWW*, i, 537.

[71] *Ibid.*, p. 516.

son used a concept of collective habit as his analytical point of departure in "Self-Government in France." This choice came to color his view of popular politics very deeply. The term "political habits" appears several times in the essay. It is even supplemented by several other terms that are meant as synonyms, such as "the character of the people," or "the humor" or "the inner life" of the nation. The emphasis Wilson gave this concept is perhaps most conspicuous in his use of more unusual constructions, such as "the habit of acquiescence," "the habit of obedience," and "the habit of revolution."[72]

Where did the notion of political habit come from? Most of Wilson's description of social life in France was taken from a contemporary literary account, *Round My House: Notes of Rural Life in France in Peace and War*, by Philip G. Hamerton.[73] The idea itself owed much to Tocqueville's *Ancien Régime*. When he read *Democracy in America* a few years later, Wilson noted that it was "quite the best philosophy since Aristotle. Political institutions presuppose a particular moral and sentimental state of the community, one of his [Tocqueville's] valuable reflections."[74]

But the most important inspiration was Edmund Burke's reevaluation of habit as the root of social unity. Burke's rhetorical style had early captured Wilson's political imagination.[75] But in addition, Burke was a historical witness to the enduring power of traditionalism in politics. His idea of constitutionalism conveyed a sense of the relationship between rulers and ruled that was infused with responsibility, honor, reverence, and sentiment rather than with cold reason and interest. In particular, Burke provided a staunch defense of the popular prejudices that the Enlightenment had vilified as superstition perpetuated by despotism. Prejudices and their manifestation in moral norms, according to Burke, contained the wisdom of the ages and provided their own kind of reason based upon experience which was vastly superior to "naked reason" as the basis for civil society. "Prejudice renders a man's virtue his habit; and not a series of unconnected acts. Through just prejudice, his duty becomes part of his nature."[76] As Bruce James Smith put it, Burke saw custom as the embodiment of "the collective habits or prejudices of a people.

[72] "Self-Government in France," *passim*.

[73] Boston, 1877. Hamerton acknowledges his dependence on Tocqueville (pp. 191ff).

[74] "Self-Government in France," *PWW*, I, 519; marginal notes, Jan. 19, 1883, *ibid.*, II, 293–96. A decade later, Wilson related the "habit of obedience" to the English discussion of sovereignty, but it has been impossible to determine his knowledge of this debate in 1879. He was probably introduced to the concept by McCosh or Atwater. The emphasis on habit in Scottish Realism is discussed in Bryson, *Man and Society*, pp. 155–72.

[75] "Index Rerum," Feb. 22–*c*. Nov. 15, 1876, *PWW*, I, 87–88, 94–98.

[76] *Reflections on the Revolution in France* (New York, 1961), p. 101.

Such collective habits were so thoroughly ingrained in a nation as to be indistinguishable from natural propensities—a kind of 'a second moral nature.' "[77]

Wilson used the notion of "political habit" to show that social and political behavior take on a fixed character through frequent repetition and that acquired dispositions and tendencies had become instinctive impulses reaching through the whole structure of French society. Throughout the essay, the term *habit* refers to the process of internalized behavior. It conveys a set of generalized constraints within French society, which had previously been seen as the primary example of revolutionary upheaval. The idea of habit was the antidote to the view that identified the majority in France with unpredictable political passions. The effect was to place social conservatism at the base of society, among the most numerous classes of the population, such as the peasants and the middle class, whose political passivity had offered the opportunity for monarchical and revolutionary despotism to flourish. In Wilson's account, the peasants had until recently been "over-weeded with the habit of acquiescence in whatever *is*." The French bourgeois had nothing left over for self-government. "His whole soul is wrapt up in saving . . . he can scarcely be called part of the community."[78] Thus in Wilson's view, the emphasis upon the resilience of habit did not offer the comfort of conservatism but the prelude to reform. The human propensity to form habits implies that the citizen can be improved by political institutions, such as cabinet government.

Unlike the modern view, which tends to associate constitutional arrangements with little beyond the rules of the political game, Wilson saw cabinet government as the counterpoint to universal suffrage. The ideal and practice of self-government, he believed, involves more than simply the establishment of the right to vote. Cabinet government and constitutional procedures are the best means of offsetting the impression created by the franchise that each individual, regardless of merit, has the same claim to share in government itself. Cabinet government furnishes the best rules for leadership competition, and at the same time it makes the population fit for government. It promotes the habituation of power as a public enactment of obligations, trust, and responsibility that gradually identify the individual with government. The French misfortune had

[77] *Politics and Remembrance: Republican Themes in Machiavelli, Burke, and Toqueville* (Princeton, N. J., 1985), p. 120.

[78] "Self-Government in France," *PWW*, I, 529, 527. As he put it in a private letter, Wilson was arguing that the French people had "grown up in the habits of political servitude" and were only slowly developing the habits of self-government. WW to Robert Bridges, Aug. 8, 1879, *ibid.*, p. 513.

been to have a population "whose traditions and habits blind them to servitude." "Until now they have learned how to do nothing but over-throw," Wilson exclaimed. Cabinet government was, "above all things else, necessary as the condition of such popular education" as France needed now.[79]

To make the population receptive to political instruction, it is necessary to improve the general level of knowledge. "The French people," Wilson explained, "can be ripened for self-government only by the sunlight of education." Further, education should be freed from the dominance of the church. Popular schooling was a pressing political issue, because education was the only way to break the prejudices of social self-sufficiency and the geographical localism that kept the countryside and the towns hostage to the mood in Paris.[80]

Less than a year later, Wilson brought these ideas closer to home in a series of short articles written for newspaper publication. He argued that state-supported education was imperative for the South. First, education maintained social control and prevented idleness, poverty, and crime.[81] Second, popular education was a prerequisite for the development of southern prosperity. He welcomed the beginning of industrial development in the "New South" and explained that the growth of transportation and communications was a force that would destroy localism in the South and place the region on equal terms with the rest of the national economy.[82] Third, education produces "good citizens for the state." "There is no more solemn problem for the South to solve," Wilson wrote, "than that of how to make universal suffrage a safe, rather than a damning and revolutionary method of rule. . . . One of the chief arguments for education is that upon it the safety and health of popular institutions depend." It is too important to be left to local whim. Education, Wilson asserted, "can be uniformly good only when uniformly organized: it can be uniformly organized only by some power which has authority in all parts of the state: the only such power is government."[83]

[79] *Ibid.*, pp. 535–36.

[80] *Ibid.*, pp. 530–32.

[81] "The Education of the People," article for the Wilmington *Morning Star*, Aug. 20, 1880, *ibid.*, pp. 666–71.

[82] "Stray Thoughts from the South," Feb. 22, 1881, *PWW*, ii, 26–31; "The Politics and the Industries of the New South," April 30, 1881, *ibid.*, pp. 49–55; "New Southern Industries," April 20, 1882, *ibid.*, pp. 119–25; and "Convict Labor in Georgia," Feb. 24, 1883, *ibid.*, pp. 306–11. In these articles Wilson generally placed himself as close to a liberal position as he could while still ensuring that his articles would receive a fair hearing in the South; see a letter from Harold Godwin to WW, April 10, 1881, *ibid.*, p. 42.

[83] "The Education of the People," *ibid.*, i, 668–69, 667. Compare Wilson's views on educa-

POLITICAL HABITS—their reflection of social circumstances, their imprint upon the individual consciousness over time, and their emendation by general education—were the values of routine, discipline, restraint, and ordered conduct in the network of social interdependence. Such values had a private as well as a public meaning, and this interconnection suggests that there was more at stake in the idea of self-government than rules to keep individuals from infringing upon each other's rights. This question preoccupied Wilson throughout his academic career, but already in 1879 he had demonstrated his distance from the liberal view that liberty is primarily to be understood as a matter of individual rights. He argued that liberty in France—if it was not a "mere abstraction, an unsubstantial phantom born of a disordered fancy"—was to be understood as a matter of dependence upon a general conscience, which adapted the citizen's motives to the requirements of the collective order.[84] What appeared as freedom for the individual was better understood in its political aspect as "self-imposed obedience."[85] Freedom was to be seen, not in opposition to, but as a consequence of the steady inducement of regulated behavior.

---

tion with the prevalent mood in the South as described by C. Vann Woodward in *Origins of the New South, 1877–1913* (Baton Rouge, 1951), pp. 63–66, 93–94.

[84] "Self-Government in France," *PWW*, I, 538.

[85] *Ibid.*

III

★ ★

PREPARING FOR LEADERSHIP:

CONGRESSIONAL GOVERNMENT

At Princeton, Wilson had already decided that law was the natural vocation for an aspiring politician. Yet the study and practice of law left him emotionally dissatisfied. Time after time he turned, not to his law books or his prospective clients, but to the vision of national leadership he had entertained as an undergraduate. Wilson continued his studies of politics as a law student at the University of Virginia from October 1879 to December 1880 at home in Wilmington with his parents, and as a young lawyer in Atlanta from August 1882 to the spring of 1883, when he finally decided to return to the study of political science at the Johns Hopkins University.

WHEN HE ENTERED the University of Virginia, Wilson seemed determined to repeat his Princeton experience. He joined one of the two debating clubs on campus, the Jefferson Society. Soon he was appointed to attack the proposition that the government of Great Britain was better adapted to promoting the welfare of society than was the government of the United States. Later he spoke in the affirmative for a restriction of the franchise. At the end of the school year he participated in the annual debate for medals arranged by the Jefferson Society and defended, unsuccessfully, the view that Catholicism was not a menace to American institutions. He also rewrote the constitution of the Jefferson Society, as well as the rules governing the *Virginia University Magazine*.[1]

Wilson was taught common law by the accomplished professor John

---

[1] Minutes of the Jefferson Society, Oct. 18, 25, 1879, and Feb. 28, 1880, *PWW*, I, 576, 578, 608. The debate on Catholicism was summarized in the *Virginia University Magazine*, April 1880, *ibid.*, pp. 643–46. Wilson's attitude toward the Catholic church is spelled out in his "Anti-Sham" letters to the editor, *North Carolina Presbyterian*, Jan. 25 and Feb. 15, 1882, *ibid.*, II, 97–98, 99–103. "Editorial Note: The Constitution of the Jefferson Society, 1881," *ibid.*, I, 688; art. VII, p. 695, relates to the magazine, while the bylaws, art. IV, p. 698, provide rules for debates. "The Constitution of the Jefferson Society, 1881," *ibid.*, pp. 689–99.

Barbee Minor, and constitutional and international law by professor Stephen O. Southall. In the country as a whole, the study and teaching of law was at a low point, and judging from the notes that Wilson took, it seems that both professors adhered closely to the dogmatic school of jurisprudence.[2] On the basis of a comprehensive survey of the methods and doctrines of this school, Lawrence Friedman concluded that the approach was magisterial and uncritical at best, with little regard for its own internal assumptions. There was "no connection between law and life or even of common-law evolution. Beneath sometimes brilliant lectures, there was fundamental hollowness."[3] Although reform had entered Harvard University with the introduction of the case method a decade earlier, and although Oliver Wendell Holmes was working on his new concept of the life of the common law, which was published in 1881, the University of Virginia held on to the older ways.[4] Minor taught from his four-volume *Institutes of Common and Statute Law*; recitation periods and lectures took up most of the students' day, and memorization loomed large over the rest.[5]

To Wilson, this kind of work had very little meaning. He soon confessed in letters to friends that he was "most terribly bored," that the teaching was monotonous and dry, that the students were regarded as "mere studying machines," and law had become a treadmill for him. Even after he had been admitted to the Georgia bar in October 1882, he recalled his "impatience of the dreadful drudgery which attends the initiation into our profession."[6] Even the legal fields that were closest to his own interests apparently had little impact on his thinking and writing, at least for the time being. Wilson's essays on constitutional reform dissociated themselves from the technicalities of jurisprudence and brushed aside constitutional doctrine and interpretation in favor of political life and constitutional practice.[7] The only essay directly related to Wilson's experience with the law at the University of Virginia is a short piece on

[2] Notes on Professor Southall's lecture on international law, Jan. 17, 1880, and notes on Professor Southall's lecture on constitutional law, March 9, 1880, *ibid.*, pp. 594–96, 621–23.

[3] Lawrence M. Friedman, *A History of American Law* (New York, 1973), pp. 529–30; see also Robert Stevens, "Two Cheers for 1870: The American Law School," *Perspectives in American History*, v (1971), 405–550.

[4] Morton Keller, *Affairs of State*, pp. 343–53; and Paul F. Boller, Jr., *American Thought in Transition: The Impact of Evolutionary Naturalism, 1865–1900* (Chicago, 1969), pp. 152–62.

[5] "John Barbee Minor," *Dictionary of American Biography* (24 vols., New York, 1928–79), xii, 26–27; WW to Talcott, Dec. 31, 1879, *PWW*, i, 591–93.

[6] WW to Talcott, Dec. 31, 1879, and to Robert Bridges, Feb. 25, 1880, and Oct. 28, 1882, *ibid.*, pp. 591, 604; ii, 148.

[7] "Congressional Government," *ibid.*, i, 548. Significantly, "Government by Debate" begins with a description of the House of Representatives and its atmosphere, not with a constitutional analysis; *ibid.*, ii, 159.

"Some Legal Needs" written in May 1881. In this essay Wilson deplored the legal confusion that resulted because state legislatures were either inexperienced or too weak to offer much resistance to organized economic pressure groups. He found that state legislatures were ill-equipped to deal with emerging industrial problems on a national scale, such as the regulation of corporations and railroads and the depletion of forests.[8] The basic approach of the essay, with its emphasis on the economic and social functions of the law, seems in retrospect to have been one of defiance toward the doctrinal approach that his professors were following at the time.

Wilson had left Princeton encouraged by the prospect of the publication of "Cabinet Government in the United States" in a national magazine, and he brought to Virginia a good measure of "political dreams," which he shared with his friend Charles Talcott. Against his father's wishes, Wilson entertained hopes of establishing himself as a political writer, speaker, and adviser rather than as a lawyer.[9] He hoped to combine his literary skills with his political interests rather than to commit himself to becoming a party politician. When on their way to law school, the two graduates promised to encourage each other to switch from law to politics, and their correspondence during the following year served to stimulate the political ambitions that each of them entertained.[10] Wilson practiced his voice in his father's church and worked on composition. In his letters, Wilson stressed the need to preserve a character free from the "*pettinesses* of our profession."[11] Behind their exchanges lies an ideal of self-edification that carries the imprint of college life.

Neither Talcott nor Wilson initially gave much thought to participation in the affairs of the local community or to work in party organizations. Any serious renewal of American politics, they believed, had to come from sources untainted by special or partisan interests. Their plan was to strike from the outside on a regional or national level. Reflecting on remarks from Wilson, Talcott distinguished between two political arenas—the masses, which constituted public opinion, and the political establishment. "Both classes can be reached by the press," Talcott wrote, "and, as you have suggested, we should do all in our power during the first years of our professional lives to purify politics by using this instrument and gradually work ourselves into a broader field."[12]

[8] "Some Legal Needs," May 1, 1881, *ibid.*, ɪɪ, 60–63.

[9] For his father's warning that Wilson was becoming too absorbed in "mere literature," see Joseph Ruggles Wilson to WW, Dec. 22, 1879, and Oct. 5, 1880, *ibid.*, ɪ, 589–90, 682.

[10] Talcott to WW, June 1, 1879, *ibid.*, p. 485; WW to Talcott, May 20, 1880, *ibid.*, p. 655.

[11] WW to Talcott, July 7, 1879, *ibid.*, p. 488 (Wilson's emphasis).

[12] Talcott to WW, June 1, 1879, *ibid.*, p. 486; see also WW to Talcott, May 20, 1880, *ibid.*, pp. 603–605.

In two unpublished letters to the editor in early 1881, Wilson spelled out what he had in mind in some detail. To clamor for honesty in government and to attack the spoils system was, of course, a widespread avocation in the 1880s, but Wilson went one significant step further. His suggestions aimed, not only at reform, but also at a system of reform that would be able to direct and control government from the outside, from an independent social base between public opinion and the political establishment.[13] He envisaged a new class of "college-bred men" who would not close their ranks to newcomers and who would retain, in relation to the public and the politicians, "only such an advantage as professional athletes have over amateurs." The two basic characteristics of this social instrument of reform included, first, special knowledge. "The reform of governments is not an every-day business," Wilson stressed, in contrast to the nineteenth-century American belief that reform is basically a question of common sense and honesty. "We must be taught the out-of-the-way trade" to be able to manage the "power of special knowledge." Second, Wilson stressed the stern self-discipline and selfless idealism that would distinguish the class. "To study, then, to study is the imperious necessity which rests upon all young men of ambition." Wilson used the image of a steam engine to show how the new political power source would both strengthen and direct a public opinion that seemed "to have been disappointed of its omnipotence."

> Boil water in an open pot and its vapors impotently dissolve in the air; confine those vapors in an engine's boiler and they are ready to drive power through the pipes. What needs to be done, therefore, is to condense the vapors of public opinion and find or invent some engine that they can successfully propel. There are models which we may copy. There must be a great organized agitation.[14]

In these letters to the editor, as well as in the correspondence between Wilson and Talcott, the emphasis is on the need to dispel the contemporary myth that "society and government can run themselves" stimulated by nothing more elevated than "selfish and unpatriotic" motives and the desire for "personal aggrandisement."[15] The goal that Talcott and Wilson set for themselves was to keep "fresh from the prejudices and free from the foolish inaccuracies of those with whom we will constantly be thrown by the necessity of our law practice." They shared the basic assumption that they, by virtue of their college experiences, represented something new in a body politic that was undergoing radical transformation. Their

[13] "What Can Be Done for Constitutional Liberty?" and "Letters from a Southern Young Man to Southern Young Men," March 21, 1881, *ibid.*, II, 33–40.
[14] *Ibid.*, pp. 35–38.
[15] Talcott to WW, June 1, 1879, *ibid.*, I, 486.

correspondence was carried on in an undercurrent of excited feeling that they had their grip on a political position independent of traditional interests, which could be developed by careful training. They aimed, in short, to realize a new "style and knowledge" that promised to raise political thought and action to a higher level of national concern.[16]

A few years later, in a letter to his fiancée, Ellen Louise Axson, Wilson described his friendship with Talcott as "a solemn covenant that we would school all our powers and passions for the work of establishing the principles we held in common." Wilson explained that his practice of law had been a failure because of an earlier commitment to the study of politics, which he had now just begun at the Johns Hopkins University. "The profession I chose was politics," he wrote, "the profession I entered was the law."[17] As so often in the case of Wilson, it is tempting to see his hopes as strange forecasts that demand some sort of deeper explanation, whether religious or psychological, because his wishes almost ask to be read backward from their eventual fulfillment.[18] The letter was indeed indicative of a rendezvous, not with destiny, but with his future wife. Wilson wrote to enchant Ellen Axson with the seriousness of his high public ambitions and to ask for her support on the basis of allusions to the love between them. Ellen Axson did not miss the message of the story about the covenant. She wrote Wilson back: "When I think of your various gifts and the high, pure and noble purposes to which they are dedicated, I feel a quiet little glow and thrill of admiration, tingling out to my very finger-tips."[19]

[16] WW to Talcott, July 7, 1879, *ibid.*, p. 488.

[17] WW to Ellen Axson, Oct. 30, 1883, *ibid.*, II, 500.

[18] See Bragdon, *Woodrow Wilson*, p. 51; Osborn, *Woodrow Wilson*, p. 45. Mulder, *Woodrow Wilson*, pp. 56–58, 269–77 viewed the letter as a key to Wilson's personality. The accord between Talcott and Wilson expressed "essentially Wilson's covenant for his entire life, pledging himself to a career in politics in which his principles would be realized (p. 56)." Wilson's political interests were understood as a reflection of God's relationship with his chosen people as a "contractual, covenanted order, ruled by a moral law contained in the Bible." As Mulder concluded, "in his agreement with Talcott, Wilson once again used this covenanted theological view of the world and individualized it for himself (p. 58)." The idea that Wilson unconsciously or consciously identified with Abraham or Moses—the primary Biblical examples of "individualized" covenants with God on behalf of a whole people—seems to be a variation of the earlier Freud and Bullitt thesis that Wilson unconsciously identified with Christ. But the idea that an individual could contract with God can hardly be reconciled with Calvinist theology and psychology. No less important is the failure to notice that Wilson's letter was intended to explain, not that Wilson felt committed for life to any solemn covenant, but why he felt free to break his youthful pledge. As the letter continues after the passage on the covenant, "But a man has to know the world before he can work in it to any purpose . . . and this I did *not* know when I left college and chose my profession" (Wilson's emphasis).

[19] Ellen Axson to WW, Nov. 5, 1883, *ibid.*, II, 517.

In January 1881, Wilson withdrew from the University of Virginia. The official reason was ill health. The real reason seems to have been an intolerable boredom with the study of law. He continued his studies independently for a year and a half while living with his parents in Wilmington. In August 1882 he moved to Atlanta, was admitted to the bar, and established a law practice with Edward I. Renick, who had graduated from the University of Virginia in 1881. After a few unsuccessful months in the law office, Wilson began to plan a return to school. In September 1883 he enrolled as a graduate student of political science, history, and political economy at the Johns Hopkins University.

WILSON'S POLITICAL WRITINGS from 1879 to 1883 may be said to fall into two categories. The first deals with the structures of popular politics and with the issue of social and political stability and development. "Self-Government in France" and various essays on the South belong in this category. The second group includes Wilson's best-known work on the organization of government and the problem of leadership, *Congressional Government*, which was published in 1885 but which had been conceived before Wilson came to the John Hopkins. In both cases Wilson hit upon ideas and formulations that were to remain central to his political thought throughout his academic career. During the 1890s, when much of his main work was in the fields of administration and history, he refined his first formulations and gave them a form that fitted the requirements of the public lecture.

The insistence that habit be regarded as a primary value distinguishing the nature of modern popular political behavior did not turn Wilson into a sociologist, nor did it make him a political conservative who insisted that habits be preserved in an unchanging form. Far from diminishing his appreciation of the innovative aspects of politics, the discovery of political habits focused Wilson's attention on leadership as the dynamic and creative force that gave form and purpose to the inert materials of accumulated dispositions. In "Cabinet Government" he had already argued that persuasion was "the one force which can sway freemen to deeds"; in his study of France, Wilson hinted that the popular addiction to abstract words was part of the revolutionary malaise. "How often have words caused a revolution in restless France," Wilson exclaimed. Words that appealed to the imagination and the passions had been the goads that had driven the population to action.[20] How would it be possible to stimulate popular energies for national purposes without weakening the habitual props of political society? The answer, Wilson said, is to cultivate a center

---

[20] "Cabinet Government," *PWW*, I, 495; "Self-Government in France," *ibid.*, p. 535.

of political innovation, where communicative and deliberative action would be organized at some distance from the polity and projected upon the nation as a whole.

Wilson continued his political studies of constitutional organization after the publication of "Cabinet Government." In October 1879 he finished a longer essay, "Congressional Government." From early 1882 to January 1883 he worked on a book-length manuscript, "Government by Debate," in which he again argued for constitutional reform.[21] Both these works were submitted for publication but were rejected by publishers. In January 1884, however, the *Overland Monthly* printed an article Wilson had extracted from the manuscript of "Government by Debate."[22] In late 1883, as a graduate student at the Johns Hopkins University, he began to write *Congressional Government*. It appeared in print in January 1885 and established him as a promising name in the field of political scholarship.[23]

Congressional Government remains Wilson's best-known work. Considering its place in the development of academic political science in America, it may be appropriate to review briefly its current status within the profession before approaching the book itself. This procedure should lead to a clearer perspective on the intentions that Wilson himself entertained in preparing and writing the book, intentions that had an important bearing on the substance of the work. In order to account for Wilson's mode of thinking about political questions and government structures during the early part of his academic career, the book should be compared to an older tradition of political theory, because at this time Wilson was seeking to come to grips with a dramatic mode of deliberative politics.[24] This theme became a permanent element of his thought and

---

[21] Oct. 1, 1879, *ibid.*, pp. 548–74; Dec. 4, 1882, *ibid.*, ii, 159–275.

[22] "Committee or Cabinet Government?" *ibid.*, ii, 614–40.

[23] Jan. 24, 1885, *ibid.*, iv, 13–179.

[24] In their editorial note on *Congressional Government* (*ibid.*, p. 12) the editors present a comparative analysis of the incremental growth of Wilson's knowledge of the constitutional issue that they developed from a consideration of the differences between various manuscripts leading up to *Congressional Government*. The best discussion of the book is John A. Rohr, "The Constitutional World of Woodrow Wilson," in Jack Rabin and James S. Bowman (eds.), *Politics and Administration: Woodrow Wilson and American Public Administration* (New York, 1984), pp. 31–49. In a criticism of Christopher Wolfe's article, "Woodrow Wilson: Interpreting the Constitution," *Review of Politics*, xli (Jan. 1979), 121–42, Rohr argues that Wilson's approach to constitutionalism was "more philosophical and historical than legal" (p. 36). Rohr stresses Wilson's failure to propose specific constitutional amendments to follow through on his proposals. This argument seems to be a variation of Abbott Lawrence Lowell, *Essays on Government* (1892; reprint, New York, 1968), pp. 46–59, where Lowell shows that the realization of the cabinet system in the United States was not a matter of constitutional amendment but of constitutional overthrow.

can be traced in his speeches and writings throughout the 1890s as the problem of leadership in modern government.

A PREVALENT CRITICISM of *Congressional Government* is that the book was written without Wilson ever taking the trouble to sit "for an afternoon in the gallery of the Senate," as Albert Somit and Joseph Tanenhaus put it in their influential book about the history of political science in the United States.[25] The observation is founded in fact, yet its implications are not entirely clear.[26] When it is recalled that "Government by Debate" and several of Wilson's published articles contain rather elaborate descriptions of what the congressional setting looked, sounded, and smelled like, the comment would seem to carry a certain unstated censure.[27] Since few scholars would expand the demand for empirical research to include a requirement that direct sensual experience is a necessary precondition for scholarly reliability, the intimation is that Wilson simply did not do his homework properly. Or, as it is sometimes phrased, the "book suffers from the substitution of rhetoric for facts."[28] A second criticism is that the book succumbed to its model (Walter Bagehot's analysis of the English constitution) and became an extended treatise on Wilson's own prejudices in favor of the British arrangement of parliamentary government rather than an analysis of American practices.[29]

These faults also bear on a third point, as argued by Roland Young, who compared Wilson's work with modern scholarship on the same sub-

[25] *The Development of American Political Science: From Burgess to Behaviorism* (Boston, 1967), pp. 32–33. See also Bernard Crick, *The American Science of Politics: Its Origins and Conditions* (Berkeley, 1959), p. 104.

[26] WW to Ellen Louise Axson, Jan. 22, 1885, *PWW*, III, 630–31: "If I wrote 'Congr. Govt.' without visiting Washington, much more can I write upon the science of administration without doing so!"

[27] See chapter I, "Inside the House of Representatives," *ibid.*, II, 159–68; most of this description reappeared in "Committee or Cabinet Government?"

[28] Mulder, *Woodrow Wilson*, p. 79. Crunden, in *Ministers of Reform*, p. 11, charges that "the book illustrates all too well the abstract, antiempirical nature of Wilson's mind and the superficiality of his research. . . . He preferred to use his books and develop abstract principles to foreordained conclusions."

[29] David Easton, *The Political System: An Inquiry into the State of Political Science* (New York, 1963), pp. 165–66. In his 1947 discussion, Arthur S. Link rendered a verdict that has been much quoted by later historians. Link did not find the book to be "profound." He also pointed out "an amazing neglect or ignorance of economic factors in political life." *Wilson: The Road to the White House*, p. 15. Bert James Loewenberg tried to take a positive view. He pointed out that Wilson was young when the book was written. Also, he said, institutions "came alive" in the book. "Government functioned in dynamic human relationships with palpable consequences in the lives and actions of men. If for no other reason *Congressional Government* is a great book." *American History in American Thought: Christopher Columbus to Henry Adams* (New York, 1972), pp. 410–12.

ject. According to Young, Wilson was incapable of perceiving governmental processes in a "system of action," that is, as a "special type of process with which the legislature resolves conflict in society." In this view, persuasion, debate, and voting are only a few of the means by which the legislature adapts and reflects "maladjustments occurring in society, where there are conflicts of purpose and competitive wants, and its function is that of establishing patterns of order in which various purposes can be achieved."[30] David Easton, in his important study of the state of political science, argued that Wilson only asked what kind of institutional arrangement he wanted and forgot to ask how it was possible to analyze the already-functioning system. Thus Wilson placed the cart before the horse. He wanted "to discover how to achieve a given goal without first having discovered the way in which the institutions he wished to manipulate do in fact operate. This failure to put first things first has a confusing effect upon his whole analysis." Easton also claimed that Wilson's main hypothesis was that the more power is divided, the more irresponsible it becomes. Instead of proving his hypothesis, however, Wilson turned it into an assumption and made it the basis from which he advocated ministerial responsibility. "The major theoretical assumptions," Easton concluded, were "not elevated for careful statement and subsequent proof before the value-oriented task of suggesting changes" was undertaken.[31]

To grasp the significance of these objections, it is necessary to ask what kind of understanding of politics they reflect. The most important element in the compound of presuppositions that seems to govern this reading of *Congressional Government* prescribes how reality must be approached by the scientific mind. The claim is that reality exists independently of the inquiry and the inquirer. Truth, on this assumption, is understood as a correspondence between reality and a proposition about reality that lends itself to verification. Values, sympathies, and political passions have to be kept separate from the propositions in order not to upset the proposition itself and the process of verification. Theory is seen as a means of distinguishing between meaningless facts and important facts and serves as a guide through extended, cumulative inquiry carried on within the scientific community. It follows from these "realistic" ideas that reality itself is left unchanged by the inquiry. A true proposition, while rendering political phenomena visible to the scientist, does not in itself affect its object but leaves it in its place, so to speak.[32]

[30] "Woodrow Wilson's *Congressional Government* Reconsidered," in Earl Latham (ed.), *The Philosophy and Policies of Woodrow Wilson* (Chicago, 1958), pp. 201–13.

[31] Easton, *Political System*, pp. 82–84.

[32] Somit and Tanenhaus, *Development of Political Science*, pp. 177–79.

CHAPTER 3

For the present consideration, the extent to which these assumed gaps can be argued systematically on epistemological grounds is of little concern. But it is necessary to take stock of them, because they tell us something about why *Congressional Government* has become a difficult book to read. Their existence means that modern readers find themselves stumbling about, often without knowing where they are going, fearful of the pitfalls that modern scholarship has discovered in the territory. The book cannot be enjoyed in the manner that one enjoys following the argument of a contemporary monograph through its master plan, its construction of hypotheses, its account of evidence, and its conclusions—all of which alert the reader to views and hazards along the way. Much of the criticism is of a sweeping sort, describing the book as "confusing," "verbose," "repetitive," and "not profound." This is the kind of criticism that conveys a certain distance and incomprehension. It conveys the kind of impatience that comes from looking in vain for a vantage point within the book from which to assess Wilson's own starting point and the direction of his journey.

A good measure of the difficulty derives from the role that Wilson ascribes to the presidency. The president appears to be an almost pitiful figure, selected at a nominating convention by procedures and for reasons that almost guarantee the nominee's inability to exercise leadership in case of election. According to Wilson, this may be just as well: "The business of the President, occasionally great, is usually not much above routine. Most of the time it is *mere* administration, mere obedience of directions from the masters of policy, the Standing Committees."[33] Except for the veto power, Wilson thought that the president might be treated as "a permanent officer." The president was "part of the official rather than of the political machinery of the government, and his duties call rather for training than for constructive genius."[34] In retrospect, it seems almost as if history itself conspired against the book to make it obsolete at the date of its publication, if not at the date of its writing. It was conceived at the lowest point of presidential influence and came out just as Grover Cleveland began to lay the groundwork for a reconstruction of presidential prestige. One might well conclude that if Wilson set out to account for the course of the presidency, or at least tried to clear the ground for a scientific understanding of political change, the book was a failure, interesting for its author's career rather than for its content. The problem, however, is whether this was what Wilson attempted

[33] *Congressional Government, PWW*, iv, 140.
[34] *Ibid.*

50

with his work. Or, to put the question differently, what kind of political landscape did Wilson set out to explore?

One way to approach the question is to start with the essay "Congressional Government," which Wilson wrote about half a year after he—with obvious success—had covered much the same ground in "Cabinet Government in the United States."[35] It has escaped notice that the role of the author differs in these essays. In "Cabinet Government," Wilson saw himself in the role of a herald of gloomy tidings, a messenger to "the people, from whom springs all authority." He warned that "our dangers may overwhelm us, our political maladies may prove incurable."[36] In "Congressional Government," Wilson placed himself in a different role, occasioned by the appearance of Albert Stickney's *A True Republic*, which Wilson read soon after its publication in 1879.[37] Stickney's argument was a plea for a businesslike government, with civil service officers as guardians of the public business. Wilson took the book to task for its antipolitical conclusions, particularly its dismissal of political parties and their function in good government. His marginal notes reveal that he read the book with a view to identifying a possible distinction between political and administrative functions in government. Throughout the essay Wilson contrasted his own "method" of cleansing the parties by creating a cabinet government with Stickney's suggestion of abolishing parties altogether.[38]

The terms on which Wilson chose to enter the polemic with Stickney in "Congressional Government" are remarkable. Wilson consistently selected epithets that characterized the moral qualities of the adversary rather than his arguments. Stickney, the reader is told, is "conspicuously candid and manly" as a writer. He had displayed "unhesitating candor and scrupulous consistency," "bold clearness and fearless distinctness." He "never flinches." After this chivalrous praise, Wilson finally threw down the gauntlet: "But I take issue . . . at the very outset of his argument." Six years later Wilson barely recalled Stickney's argument, but he remem-

[35] See Mulder, *Woodrow Wilson*, p. 61, and Bragdon, *Woodrow Wilson*, p. 75, for critical comments about "Cabinet Government in the United States."

[36] "Cabinet Government," *PWW*, i, 510.

[37] New York, 1879.

[38] Stickney, *True Republic*, with transcripts from Woodrow Wilson's copy, Woodrow Wilson Collection, Firestone Library. See, for example, Wilson's comment on Stickney's suggestion on page 45 that written reports to Congress would replace discussion: "Full written reports may give (often do give) no information whatever, but, on the contrary, skillfully conceal all that is important to be known." Hasty questions in debate, Wilson wrote, "are just the ones which surprise the truth into self-discovery." See Oct. 1, 1879, *PWW*, i, 546–48, for further notes on the margin of Wilson's copy. See also "Congressional Government," *ibid.*, pp. 548–74.

bered that Stickney was "utterly without the *practical* instinct of the states-man." Stickney, he said, "regarded government as an affair of passionless business, rather than, as it really is, an affair of rules of action com-pounded of every human passion."[39] The herald was all trumpet when Wilson called out his warning against the dangers of uninstructed major-ities; half a year later, after the publication of "Cabinet Government," he was self-consciously ready to make his mark on the stage of public opin-ion.[40] He entered the stage with a keen sense of drama and with a temper that made no secret of its heroic intent.

Wilson's concept of political activity as a contest for intellectual mastery and oratorical subjugation of the adversary in a public performance re-mained a salient theme throughout his studies of congressional organi-zation. In "Mr. Gladstone," Wilson concluded that "the secrets of a na-ture such as Mr. Gladstone's" were "warrior qualities—the qualities which display themselves in battle."[41] The idea of the essay is animated by a vivid picture of a debate in the House of Commons: "Above the rear benches and over the outer aisles of the House, beyond 'the bar,' hang deep galleries. It seems a place intended for hand to hand combat; and on that chill, damp November morning, it witnessed a combat such as had seldom awakened its echoes before."[42] In "Government by Debate," Wilson pointed out that debate is a means of inspiration and unity, while interests and spoils are the means of faction. Oratory, he wrote, "cannot inspire when inflated with the mere enthusiasm of a holiday. It must be tuned like a call to battle or voiced like a herald of deeds worthy the doing."[43] In *Congressional Government* he asserted that the roots of political excellence are to be found in martial virtues, such as "the force of char-acter," the "readiness of resource," and the "courage of conviction," all of which are seen among the "horses that draw the triumphal chariot of every leader and ruler of free men."[44] Such language obviously prepares

[39] "Congressional Government," *ibid.*, pp. 553–54; WW to Albert Shaw, June 8, 1885, *ibid.*, IV, 693.

[40] "Not many years ago it required no little bravery to question the principles of our Con-stitution; now every scribbler may declare it a failure unchallenged, and many wise heads are nodded in acquiescence." "Congressional Government," *ibid.*, I, 551.

[41] *Ibid.*, p. 635.

[42] *Ibid.*, p. 641. The scene is arranged in what seems to be a conscious emulation of Macau-lay's account of one of the great debates in the House of Commons. Peter Gay, in "Macaulay: Intellectual Voluptuary," in *Style in History* (New York, 1974), pp. 95–134, quotes Macaulay's description at length and offers a useful introduction to his rhetorical method.

[43] *PWW*, II, 240–41.

[44] *Ibid.*, IV, 118. Throughout the 1890s, Wilson often referred to a ballad of a medieval knight who was given the choice between a horn and a sword in order to awaken a whole army that had fallen into a mysterious sleep. When the knight chose the horn, the army

the reader for a campaign or for a battlefield rather than for the testing of hypotheses.

With this background it becomes clear why Wilson had little room for presidential greatness in his understanding of political power. To put it crudely, the president is not much of a political man, nor can he be, according to Wilson, since the president has no adversaries, no stage of action, no place to excel among equals, and no need to cultivate oratorical performance in order to "compel victory."[45] At best, the president can "tire the Senate by dogged persistence," but he can never deal with it "upon a ground of real equality." "He has no real presence in the Senate," Wilson wrote.[46] In one of the sharpest formulations in *Congressional Government*, Wilson transfixed the line of presidents through the late nineteenth century: "A President's usefulness is measured, not by efficiency, but by calendar months. It is reckoned that if he be good at all he will be good for four years. A Prime Minister must keep himself in favor with the majority, a President need only keep alive."[47]

Thus *Congressional Government* is infused with a conception of the political actor as a hero, a conception that had earlier been stated by Thomas Carlyle.[48] This understanding is most carefully worked out in "Mr. Gladstone," but throughout Wilson's career as a writer, it appeared in allusions and images whenever names such as Patrick Henry, Daniel Webster, John C. Calhoun, and John Bright were mentioned. Yet it is obvious that the emphasis on heroic action has been withdrawn from the surface of *Congressional Government*. Rather than being replaced by a different, more empirical orientation—which might have been more in tune with the emphasis of contemporary political science—it was transformed into a special mode of action that may be called interpretive politics.

In Wilson's view, the political hero is connected to ideas of order and predictability. The supreme act is that of founding a system that organizes political activity within a scheme of self-government. As Wilson wrote in "Congressional Government," "The highest type of statesmanship is

---

vanished. Wilson concluded that the story was a lesson that society cannot accept the disturbance of its convictions lightly. "Let every man be responsible for what he thinks and says; *but let him fight,—make* him fight,—for it. If he will not fight, if he have not the courage of his thought, if he hold not his intentions in fighting earnest, he is not the kind of man by whom we wish to be conquered." Wilson told this story, it should be added, in refutation of John Stuart Mill's warnings against the social suppression of heretical opinions in modern society. "Democracy," *ibid.*, vii, 360–61.

[45] "Mr. Gladstone," *ibid.*, i, 639.

[46] *Congressional Government, ibid.*, iv, 133.

[47] *Ibid.*, p. 138.

[48] Benjamin Evans Lippincott, *Victorian Critics of Democracy* (New York, 1964), pp. 6–53; Ernest Barker, *Political Thought in England, 1848–1914* (London, 1915), pp. 184–90, 201.

the *constructive*, that which is exhibited in the conception and execution of policies, in the building up of uniform systems of law and the establishment of great principles of legislation." At Johns Hopkins he became involved in drafting a new constitution for the Hopkins Literary Society. When his proposal was adopted, the name of the society was changed to the Hopkins House of Commons.[49]

The contrast between the heroic and the organizational aspects of political activity played an important role in Wilson's own choice of a career. In a long letter to Ellen Axson a few months after he had begun his graduate study, Wilson took stock of his interests and future prospects. He explained that he had originally chosen law as his profession because it seemed the proper way to politics. Lawyers were "the only men (except the minister and the physician) who stopped amidst the general hurry of life to get learning" and who would skill themselves "in those arts of forensic contest that were calculated to fit men for entering the lists at political tilts, or for holding their own in legislative debate." The failure of his law practice had made Wilson look elsewhere for a profession that afforded "leisure for reading" and "for original work, the only strictly literary berth with an income attached." His solution was a professorship, which would perhaps not permit him to play an active role in politics but which would at least groom his political interests as thoroughly as would the bar. Since "the occupancy of office had never been an essential part of my political programme," Wilson explained, he had decided to content himself with "becoming an *outside* force in politics." He now wanted to satisfy his "unquenchable desire to excel in two distinct and almost opposite kinds of writing: political and *imaginative*." This explained his choice of vocation.

Wilson's elaboration of the difference between these two kinds of writing makes it clear how closely they were related in his mind. The imaginative side of writing he associated with a kind of emotional community, as in "lay sermons full of laughter and a loving God. . . . I could wish to be the favored correspondent of children, as well as a counsellor of the powers of the earth." His purpose, however, would be to reform the state of political knowledge. He hoped "to contribute to our literature what no American has ever contributed, studies in the philosophy of our institutions, not the abstract and occult, but the practical and suggestive, philosophy which is at the core of our governmental methods. . . . I want to divest them of the theory that obscures them and present their weakness and their strength without disguise, and with such skill and such plenti-

[49] "Congressional Government," *PWW*, i, 572; WW to Ellen Axson, Dec. 15, 1884, *ibid.*, iii, 543.

tude of proof that it shall be seen that I have succeeded and that I have added something to the resources of knowledge upon which statecraft must depend."[50]

Associating political power with the instructive duties of the minister within the religious community made it possible for Wilson to stake out a domain of political activity in which theoretical elements are sublimated as the art of effectual and persuasive representation, "the art of putting things so as to appeal irresistibly to an audience." "And," Wilson asked, "how can a teacher stimulate young men to study, how can he fill them with great ideas and . . . make them to become forces in the world without oratory?" Political interpretation, in Wilson's view, involved a claim to surpass previous theories and understandings; implied also was a claim to a place within the system of political power, even if it be a place for theory as "an outside force." Wilson described his reason for attending the university as a way "to get a special training in historical research and an insight into the most modern literary and political thoughts and methods, in order that my ambition to become an invigorating and enlightening power in the world of political thought and a master in some of the less serious branches of literary art may be the more easy of accomplishment."[51] Less than a fortnight before he wrote this letter he had asked Professor Herbert Baxter Adams to free him from work on the assigned projects of the seminar at the Johns Hopkins. Shortly after writing the letter, Wilson began some additional research and the rewriting of *Congressional Government*.

In his letters to Ellen Axson, Wilson several times returned to the imaginative side of his work. In his view, Walter Bagehot's essential contribution to constitutional studies had been to infuse imagination and life into the study of the English constitution, which had earlier been dominated by a narrow legal reasoning and understanding. Wilson wrote that Bagehot had inspired his study of the American government. "He brings to the work," he said, "a fresh and original method which has made the British system much more intelligible to ordinary men than it ever was before." If a similar intelligibility could be achieved with respect to the United States Constitution, it would result "in something like a revelation to those who are still reading the Federalist as an authoritative constitutional manual."[52] In his reports to Ellen Axson about the progress of his work, Wilson talked little about problems relating to literature or research and preferred to discuss his efforts to develop a "faculty in catch-

[50] WW to Ellen Axson, Oct. 30, 1883, *ibid.*, ii, 500–502.
[51] *Ibid.*, pp. 502–503.
[52] WW to Ellen Axson, Jan. 1, 1884, *ibid.*, pp. 641–42.

ing and holding" the attention of the reader and the effort involved in finding "comprehensible figures in a sketch which everybody will find interesting."[53]

The seriousness with which Wilson approached the problem of style makes it clear that more was at stake than a wish to become widely read or to popularize a difficult subject. Wilson spoke about style in a way that resembles the modern idea of meaning. Wilson complained early about his teachers at the Johns Hopkins because he found that they neglected style in favor of science. "Style," he wrote, "is not much studied here; *ideas* are supposed to be everything—their vehicle comparatively nothing. But you and I know that there can be no greater mistake; that, both in its amount and in its length of life, an author's influence depends upon the power and the beauty of his style."[54] Later he described the task of bringing the political system within the realm of his vision: "There's the pinch: to be these three things, entertaining, exact, philosophical. I can't even put the subject on paper as I see it. I've thrown overboard my faith in the old dogma that in order to write clearly one needs nothing more than a clear vision. The seer does not often . . . have the gift of expression; and readers delight most, not in a writer who sees, but in one who enables them to see readily and pleasantly."[55]

In these efforts and in his concern for the imaginative elements of political analysis there is an emphasis upon creativity, exaggeration, even distortion that links Wilson to an older mode of political theory, which saw these inaccuracies as the necessary means with which to reduce the bewildering mass of political phenomena to an ordered whole.[56] Wilson's struggle to find engaging words and images was more than a matter of literary embellishment. It was, rather, one of the constituent elements of theoretical effort, no longer used to create a distance between theory and political reality, but instead to present a complex and changing picture to an informed audience by attempting to adjust the public's imagination to a new context of American politics. The context that Wilson hoped to displace was the usual contrast between monarchical and popular presidential government, a view that tended to make the American government seem "singular, possessing a character altogether its own," as Wilson explained in the preface to *Congressional Government*. "The two principal types" that ought to "present themselves for the instruction of the modern student of the practical in politics," he said, are the two types

[53] WW to Ellen Axson, Oct. 30, 1883, *ibid.*, p. 504; Feb. 12, 1884, *ibid.*, III, 18–19.

[54] WW to Ellen Axson, Oct. 30, 1883, *ibid.*, II, 504.

[55] WW to Ellen Axson, Feb. 12, 1884, *ibid.*, III, 19.

[56] Wolin, *Politics and Vision*, pp. 17–21; *idem*, "Political Theory: Trends and Goals," *International Encyclopedia of the Social Sciences* (18 vols., New York, 1968), XII, 319.

of "legislative and administrative *machinery*" embodied in congressional and parliamentary governments.[57] This fundamental choice of administrative and practical values over familiar constitutional categories filled Wilson with enthusiasm. In a letter to a friend, Wilson stressed that his intentions with the book were based on this fundamental choice rather than on the descriptive value of the book: "If ever any book was written with a fulness and earnestness of conviction, with a purpose of imparting conviction, that book was." His primary hope was "to *stir* thought," Wilson emphasized.[58] His aim was not to create a photographic image, a duplication of reality. The work was to be understood as a scholarly mission and a project of political conviction.

The implicit location of the author and the strategy for presenting his material contain certain clues as to Wilson's intentions. Whereas Wilson intended "Cabinet Government in the United States" to be a contribution to public debate, "Government by Debate" signaled that he was preparing for an entrance into political life.[59] This is apparent in the striking opening sentence, which leads the reader into the political arena: "The House of Representatives is a superlatively noisy assembly."[60] As the reader is guided around, shown the desks of the congressmen, advised about the properties of the room, and so on, it becomes clear that the building itself serves as a metaphor upon which the understanding of political life is to be built. The break with the usual analysis of the Constitution could hardly be more pronounced. A comparative design—which points out the differences among the British, French, and American constitutional systems—is spun out upon visits overseas to the House of Commons and the French Assembly.[61] Upon the return to the United States, the reader is made to identify with the ordeal that a new member of the House has to go through as he experiences the almost tyrannical

---

[57] *Congressional Government*, PWW, IV, 13–14; compare "Government by Debate," *ibid.*, II, 159.

[58] WW to Richard Heath Dabney, Oct. 28, 1885, *ibid.*, V, 37–38.

[59] In a letter to Robert Bridges about *Congressional Government*, Wilson admitted that it was unusual for a book of its character to use so much space for polemics, but, Wilson said, "I don't see that I can change it." Stickney "is the only other writer who has proposed any considerable changes in our forms of govt. Mine is necessarily a *rival scheme*, and I could not leave him unnoticed. To fortify my positions I must destroy his." Feb. 5, 1883, *ibid.*, II, 298–99. See also WW to Robert Bridges, May 13, 1883, *ibid.*, p. 358.

[60] "Government by Debate," *ibid.*, p. 159.

[61] "Government by Debate," *ibid.*, pp. 161–67, 179. The essence of the description is that while the House of Commons is a "place meet for hand to hand combats," and the French Assembly is characterized by "the right to precedence by main force," the House of Representatives is a place for "privacy," for being left alone.

restraints upon debate in the committees and on the floor of the House.[62] The final paragraph of "Government by Debate" calls upon readers to bend their "strength to the accomplishment" of reform.[63]

The entry into the House of Representatives in *Congressional Government*, written after Wilson's decision to embark on a university career, was considerably more complex. "Like a vast picture thronged with figures of equal prominence and crowded with elaborate and obtrusive details, Congress is hard to see satisfactorily and appreciatively at a single view and from a single stand-point. . . . [I]ts doors are practically shut against the comprehension of the public at large." The institution could no longer be grasped just by looking at it. It was mystifying: "Its complicated forms and diversified structure confuse the vision and conceal the system which underlies its composition." The metaphors no longer stay within the Capitol but take off from the introductory chapter, which contains an historical account of the political and economic forces in the life of the nation.[64] The Constitution is to be understood in the setting of the growing organism of the Union, responding to new circumstances and changing its meaning radically in the course of the nineteenth century. While the Union had been a matter of necessity at the time of the Revolution, it gradually turned into a matter of destiny. "The union of form and of law [became] a union of sentiment, and . . . of institutions. That sense of national unity and community of destiny which Hamilton had sought to foster . . . [became] strong enough to rule the continent."[65]

According to Wilson, the decisive event that upset the balanced government described in the *Federalist* papers was the Civil War. It destroyed the original balance of power between the states and the federal government and caused a rapid movement toward national centralization. Wilson specified in detail the erosion of state power that followed the expansion of the doctrine of implied powers, the growth of the federal civil service, the financing of internal improvements, the development of internal transportation and communications, and the regulation of interstate commerce.[66]

The changes in Wilson's political imagination are perhaps best viewed on the basis of a comparison. In "Mr. Gladstone," Wilson pictured political life in terms that resemble "Christ's Army," written four years earlier. In "Christ's Army" Wilson had approached the question of an ultimate reality governing collective life on the grounds of religious truth as disclosed by conscience. But in "Mr. Gladstone" the picture began to be-

---

[62] *Ibid.*, pp. 171–76.
[63] *Ibid.*, p. 275.
[64] *Congressional Government, ibid.*, IV, 42.
[65] *Ibid.*, p. 29.
[66] *Ibid.*, pp. 20–36.

come more complicated. Freedom from the "shackles of prejudice and the blinds of bigotry" now appeared preferable to "fixedness of opinion." Still using the metaphor of the army of truth, Wilson now asserted that he who follows "the leadings of his progressing convictions without thought of turning back, is no less consistent" than the man "who has from the first occupied the advanced posts of inquiry whither the other has just arrived."[67] In *Congressional Government*, political reality at the deepest level disclosed itself in a crisis that created the present conditions for government:

> The war between the States was the supreme and final struggle between those forces of disintegration which still remained in the blood of the body politic and those other forces of health, of union and amalgamation, which had been gradually building up that body in vigor and strength as the system passed from youth to maturity, and as its constitution hardened and ripened with advancing age.[68]

The "altered conditions of government" required "a new order of statesmanship," fit for "national life."

> The period of federal construction is long passed; questions of constitutional interpretation are no longer regarded as of pressing urgency; the war has been fought, even the embers of its issues being now almost extinguished; and we are left to that unexciting but none the less capitally important business of everyday peaceful development and judicious administration to whose execution every nation in its middle age has to address itself with what sagacity, energy, and prudence it can command. It cannot be said that these new duties have as yet raised up any men eminently fit for their fulfillment. We have had no great administrators since the opening of this newest stage. . . . The questions now most prominent in politics are not of such a nature as to compel skilled and trustworthy champions to come into the field, as did the constitutional issues and revolutionary agitations of other days. They are matters of a too quiet, businesslike sort to enlist feeling or arouse enthusiasm.
>
> It is, therefore, very unfortunate that only feeling or enthusiasm can create recognized leadership in our politics. There is no office set apart for the great party leader in our government.[69]

In short, Wilson's problem was how to surround the practice of businesslike administration with a politics of feeling and enthusiasm that would sustain the sentiment of national unity. As has been shown, Wil-

[67] *Ibid.*, i, 633.
[68] *Ibid.*, iv, 29–30.
[69] *Ibid.*, pp. 114–15.

son's writing of the book was deeply infused with two kinds of emotional energy, both of which had a long history in political thought. The first was the spirit of martial virtues, such as courage, manliness, and vigor, all of which were associated with the practice of political debate. The second was expressed in religiously inspired virtues, such as compassion, sympathetic understanding, responsibility, perhaps even love, all of which were associated with the act of interpretation. How could such virtues possibly be applied to the practice of bloodless, cool, and efficient administration? How could the great traditional emotions of political life be hooked up with the objective need for a clean and regular administrative order?

Wilson's answer at the institutional level was to relocate administrative processes from Congress to the executive department. His basic charge was not that Congress was doing its job badly, but that it was doing the wrong job and therefore neglecting its true function of critical inquiry that stimulated heated and searching debate. Wilson did not attack Congress primarily for its corrupt practices but for its complexity and secrecy, which "divorced" legislative politics from the "general mass of national sentiment." The effect, which Wilson significantly compared to the weakness of the British government before the outbreak of the American Revolution, was to throw constituencies "into the hands of local politicians," who were "more visible and tangible" than even the representatives of the people in Congress. The result was doubt and "confusion of thought" in the "minds of the vast majority of voters." The question for Wilson was not how government could be described scientifically but how political creativity could be restored. The problem was to make ample constitutional room for leaders who would display "plain purposes and act upon them with promptness" so that people could "watch and understand."[70] The idea of the book, as Wilson put it later in writing to James Bryce, was to argue for "the marriage of legislation and practical statesmanship."[71] But to bring about such a marriage, it was mandatory that Congress abandon its illegitimate love of administrative practice, including its affairs with log-rolling, its mutual "exchange of favors," and its "innumerable fingers in the budget pie."[72] In Wilson's view, open and enlightening congressional debate would be possible only if the field of administrative decisions were allowed to develop without legislative interference. "It is absolutely necessary to have financial administration in the hands of a few highly-trained and skillful men acting subject to a very

[70] *Ibid.*, pp. 106–107.
[71] Dec. 18, 1891, *ibid.*, VII, 370.
[72] *Congressional Government, ibid.*, IV, pp. 97–98.

strict responsibility, and this is just what our committee system does not allow," Wilson wrote.[73] At the center of Wilson's argument was his contention that legislation consists of two processes and that each required its own institutional setting. Administrative preparation should be separated from critical inquiry into both the intentions and the effects of laws.

At a second and more theoretical level, Wilson grappled with the intricate and confusing nature of modern power, which expressed itself in the mysterious metaphor of the "organic nation." The chief attraction of this term was its allusion to a dual process that absorbed and adjusted the individual and transformed him as he was enveloped in the growth of national strength. In *Congressional Government* Wilson was content to discuss leadership largely as a function of institutional arrangements. But throughout the rest of his academic career he was preoccupied with the idea of leadership in its organic setting, that is, as a function of the interaction between leaders and followers. What are the processes that imprinted the design of the whole upon the mind of the individual? The answer pertained to the very meaning of modern "political society," which required

(1) *A place of definite and reasonably permanent leadership* for tested minds,—and open processes of self-selection.
(2) *Such processes of government* as will most surely and continuously *hold the attention* and *instruct the understandings* of the people.[74]

Wilson's idea of leadership was predicated upon the assumption that the majority of people had no or only very limited access to political experience. It was part of the standard conservative criticism that the suffrage was placed in the hands of people who were without the elementary knowledge and skills required for public decisions. Wilson's achievement was to adopt the conservative premise but to reject its conclusion that the lack of political experience made popular politics a synonym for political incapacity. On the contrary, he argued that modern society provided the individual with a strong sense of belonging to a vast social totality. Looking at "the great maze of Society," the individual was impressed with "its solidarity, its complexity, its restless forces surging amidst its delicate tissues, its hazards and its exalted hopes." Wilson concluded, "How can we but be filled with awe!"[75] Modern society predisposed its members, if not for political experience, then for a certain kind of social cohesion. Popular ignorance was not an obstacle to national development but an oppor-

[73] *Ibid.*, p. 81.
[74] Notes for lectures on the elements of politics, March 5, 1898–April 29, 1900, *ibid.*, x, 466.
[75] An address, "Leaders of Men," June 17, 1890, *ibid.*, vi, 670.

tunity for modern leadership. In accordance with this view, Wilson re-wrote his conception of the political hero to fulfill the requirements demanded by modern conditions.

Wilson believed that the great leader is the medium for popular action, but he added that the true measure of leadership is the creation of the mass in a political form. While he was careful to emphasize that the leader is importantly dependent upon the habits and the traditional loy-alties of the populace, Wilson also insisted on the modern idea that the mass itself is shaped by political means. First, Wilson argued, the mass is substantively different from the sum of the individuals composing it.[76] Second, the mass is a product of the "restless forces" in a society undergoing incessant change. In such a society there is a continuing need for an integrative vision that welds the social units into a functioning whole. Wilson repeatedly pointed out the potency of the imagination that the leader brought to bear upon the formless crowd: "The whole ques-tion with [the competent leader] is a question *of the application of force.* There are men to be moved: how shall he move them? He supplies the power; others supply the materials upon which that power operates. . . . It is the *power* which dictates, dominates: the materials yield. Men are as clay in the hands of the consummate leader."[77]

Wilson's solution to the paradox of large political emotions in the con-text of administrative order and routine is contained in his perception that modern society both requires and makes possible a form of interpre-tation in contrast to the function of the theorist. Interpretation is not intended to upset political reality but to disclose it. Interpretation uncov-ers the social totality, makes the masses conscious of organization, and animates a spirit of participation. In a passage that contrasts with Tocqueville's description of the theorist who observes the whole from the point of view of the traveler who has climbed a hill outside a vast city, Wilson located the leader-interpreter, not at the margin, but at the center of modern society, "as a sort of sensitive dial registering all the forces that move upon the face of society."[78]

And in the midst of all stands the leader, gathering, as best he can, the thoughts that are completed, that are perceived, that have told upon the common mind; judging also of the work that is now at length ready to be completed; reckoning the gathered gain; perceiv-ing the fruits of toil and of war,—and combining all these into words

[76] *Ibid.*, pp. 648–51.
[77] *Ibid.*, p. 650.
[78] *Ibid.*, p. 671; Alexis de Tocqueville, *Democracy in America*, trans. by George Lawrence (Garden City, N. Y., 1969), p. 408; Wolin, "Political Theory," p. 322.

of progress, into acts of recognition and completion. Who shall say that this is not an exalted function?[79]

Wilson's contribution to American political theory may be assessed in light of the virtual absence of any sustained reflection upon the notion of leadership within the liberal tradition.[80] Allusions to political creativity had been confined to the act of constitution making. The Constitution itself, as Wilson made clear, was conceived on the premise that institu-- tional checks and balances would replace the skills and human abilities required for the sustenance of the republic. Wilson's intention in his discussion of cabinet government was to reformulate the idea of fixed and completed foundations and static balances. He hoped to reconceive the Constitution in the light of "plain evidence" of a continued expansion of federal power, which reflected a manifest demand for a centralization and uniformity of governmental function. Wilson considered the most pressing problems to be those involving the economy and specified them as "the regulation of our vast systems of commerce and manufacture, the control of giant corporations, the restraint of monopolies, the perfection of fiscal arrangements, the facilitating of economic exchanges, and many other like national concerns."[81]

From his earliest writings on this question, Wilson had pointed out that the new leader should receive an education that shaped his talents for constitutional machinery. He described cabinet government as a "practice-school of national legislation and politics," the best place to learn "the practicable methods of government, gaining knowledge of the operation of economic principles, and gathering information as to the resources and the industries of the country."[82] These are skills and knowledge that Wilson would later transfer to his idea of a class of administrators. In the course of his writing on cabinet government, a contrasting concept began to take shape which was partly inspired by his interest in a sort of heroic debate. Wilson extracted the political essence from his idea of grand oratory and combined it with his perception of modern society as being in need of a manifest symbol of national coherence and direction. The result was his appropriation of a traditional notion of theory and its relocation on the plane of mass politics. His insistence that the great leader's "imaginative interpretation" would function as a supplement on the na-

[79] "Leaders of Men," *PWW*, vi, 671.

[80] Madison's hope for the sudden but unexpected appearance of "a chosen body of citizens, whose wisdom may best discern the true interest of their country," is voiced in *The Federalist*, No. 10, p. 62; Wolin, *Politics and Vision*, p. 390; Stourzh, *Alexander Hamilton*, pp. 95–106.

[81] *Congressional Government*, PWW, iv, 40–41.

[82] "Government by Debate," *ibid.*, ii, 272.

tional level to common political experience on the state and local levels contains a distinct opening to the practice of leadership in he twentieth century.

Wilson's insistence on the primacy of political leadership was a fitting dynamic counterpart to his idea of the natural formation of political habits. Taken together, the two notions imply a pronounced rejection of the belief in progress as a spontaneous affair that is best achieved with minimal public direction. As Wilson put it sharply in his lecture on democracy, "*Progress is a march, not a scamper*. It is achieved by advance *in hosts and under discipline*, not by the running hither and thither of inquisitive crowds. It is a slow thing, of *movement together* and in united masses, a movement of *states*."[83]

MOST commentators have discussed Wilson's argument in *Congressional Government* on the basis of origins and sources, presumably because his exposition was leading to a dead end, as Walter Lippmann concluded in 1956. Lippmann suggested that Wilson began to reconsider his views as soon as the administration of Grover Cleveland presented him with a picture of a more vigorous practice of executive leadership.[84] Lippmann marshaled Wilson's 1908 work, *Constitutional Government*, in which he exalted the office of the presidency, as further evidence of the later development of a more mature and balanced view of the constitutional system. Wilson's emphasis on leadership as interpretive action, however, was already present in his first book as an author's point of view over and above his advocacy of cabinet government. This form of political action was also at the center of Wilson's idea of sovereignty.

Wilson first delivered his lecture on sovereignty before the Faculty Philosophical Club in 1891, though it was not published until 1893, when it was included in his collection of essays *An Old Master and Other Political Essays*.[85] The lecture was a polemic against John Austin's view that the seat of sovereignty in America is the constituencies of the state legislatures. As Wilson made clear in his introductory remarks, the notion of sovereignty is not a matter to be taken lightly. The notion itself is burdened with strong connotations of a single and indivisible power presiding over political life and legal order. These vestiges of absolute authority make the concept "a capital test of orthodoxy." In fact, these features make the concept seem not a little outlandish in the context of American

[83] "Democracy," *ibid.*, VII, 365.

[84] "The Political Philosopher," in Em Bowles Alsop (ed.), *The Greatness of Woodrow Wilson, 1856–1956* (Port Washington, N. Y., 1956), pp. 67–78.

[85] "Political Sovereignty," Nov. 9, 1891, *PWW*, VII, 325–41.

constitutionalism.[86] Wilson's contribution was to Americanize the concept. Crudely put, Wilson's strategy was to scale down Austin's severe definition of sovereignty so that it appeared to be less a voice of command than a center of political initiative. Furthermore, he removed the concept from the body of "the people" and from the political constituencies and relocated it in a form of power that unifies government by its capacity to change public opinion in the country as a whole. The states and the Supreme Court are again treated as secondary functions. The Constitution is described as "a formal documentary statement," "the formulations of the habits of obedience"; it is part of "the limitations of sovereignty," but it is not the sovereign power itself.[87]

Although Wilson's essay owes something to contemporary English and German literature on sovereignty, his argument owes a lot more to the quest for a sociological realism of power, which goes back to his earliest writings on politics, in particular to the essay on French self-government.[88] The heart of his argument is a distinction between the creative and the consolidating institutions of power. The former, the governing power, is innovative and advanced power. The latter consists of institutions that transform power into habits and rules. "Power is a positive thing; control, a negative thing. Power belongs to government, is lodged in governing organs; control belongs to the community, is lodged with the people. To call these two things by the same name, Sovereignty, is simply to impoverish language by making one word serve for a variety of meanings."[89] Sovereignty, Wilson concluded, is limited only by its capacity to command obedience. As Edward R. Lewis pointed out in 1937 in his review of the history of sovereignty in America, Wilson's argument was "strikingly *sui generis*."[90]

THE DISCUSSION about what kind of constitutional amendments Wilson should have proposed in order to institutionalize cabinet government in

---

[86] *Ibid.*, p. 325; see also Louis Hartz, *The Liberal Tradition in America: An Interpretation of American Political Thought since the Revolution* (New York, 1965), pp. 44–45.

[87] "Political Sovereignty," *PWW*, VII, 338–40.

[88] The connection with "Self-Government in France" is seen in the paper "The Development of Law," which Wilson delivered to the Johns Hopkins Seminary of Historical and Political Science on March 15, 1889. It contained, as the editors of the Wilson papers note, "the embryo of Wilson's later theories about the limited nature of sovereignty." *Ibid.*, VI, 152–54. Wilson's attempt to limit sovereignty may be seen as a withdrawal of the concept from the German notion of the state in order to give it a political rather than a metaphysical expression.

[89] "Political Sovereignty," *ibid.*, VII, 339.

[90] *A History of American Political Thought from the Civil War to the World War* (1937; reprint, New York, 1969), p. 192. See also C. E. Merriam, *History of the Theory of Sovereignty since Rousseau* (New York, 1900), p. 182.

the United States may be interesting on its own terms, but it is somewhat misleading as far as Wilson's intentions and ideas are concerned. Nor did Wilson present a historical argument for cabinet government. Although he emphasized a dimension of time as a precondition for a full picture of constitutional change, he was quite aware that his proposal was without historical precedent in the United States. To present a historical argument would have required a constitutional investigation of the Lincoln administration.[91] But the ideas behind *Congressional Government* were presented, not as a constitutional proposal, but as a theoretical venture.

Turning now from Wilson's proposal for reform to the issue of descriptive value, we should be aware that *Congressional Government* has often been assessed according to the tenets of the later scientific method. Accepting Albert Shaw's early suggestion that Wilson's work be seen as the first "concrete and scientific study of our political system," commentators have pointed out inexplicable descriptive gaps in the book, such as the virtual absence of the Supreme Court and states rights.[92] As an exercise in prediction it proved to be wrong in a matter of a few years. To this may be added the author's stubborn refusal to withdraw his results, or at least to explain why his mistakes had been worth making from a methodological point of view. In a new preface to the fifteenth "edition" of *Congressional Government* in 1900, Wilson showed no embarrassment whatever. He did point out a few "matters of detail" that had changed over the years. The House Committee on Rules, for example, had created "in germ, at least, a recognized and sufficiently concentrated leadership within the House, although in a form that had only "a very remote resemblance" to responsible leadership. The vindication of his study that might put "this whole volume hopelessly out of date" was discussed with reference to "the greatly increased power and opportunity for constructive statesmanship given the President, by the plunge into international politics and into the administration of distant dependencies," which was the most "striking and momentous consequence" of the war with Spain.[93]

The abandonment of the traditional constitutional frame made room for the formation of a new science of politics upon theoretical foundations that corresponded to the national condition. These foundations consisted of the distinction between "the *governing* power," ("the daily operative power of making and giving *efficacy* to laws," the power that was

[91] Preface to the fifteenth "edition" of *Congressional Government*, Aug. 15, 1900, in *PWW*, XI, 570. William A. Dunning, in *Essays on the Civil War and Reconstruction* (1897; reprint, New York, 1931), eventually presented the constitutional argument.
[92] Review of *Congressional Government* in *The Dial*, v (March 1885), reprinted in *ibid.*, IV, 315.
[93] *Ibid.*, XI, 567–71.

"daily in command of affairs") on the one hand, and the order that supplied the conditions of power, "the conditions of acquiescence, cooperation, obedience on the part of the people," on the other.[94] The character
of Wilson's achievement may also be seen in light of the development of
this distinction in the course of American political science. Most present-
day political scientists seem to have adopted the fundamental distinction
between the interactions that produce directing leadership and the processes that produce consensus and general acquiescence. Contemporary
political science has largely accepted Wilson's claim that "there is no hope
for theory if it is to neglect these obvious distinctions."[95] A modern mirror of these distinctions may be found in the division between the study
of decision making and the study of voting behavior.

[94] "Political Sovereignty," *ibid.*, vii, 333–34.
[95] *Ibid.*, p. 334.

IV

WILSON'S STUDY OF

POLITICAL ECONOMY

Wilson's graduate studies at the Johns Hopkins University from 1883 to 1885 formed a decisive period of his intellectual life. As indicated by *Congressional Government*, Wilson's introduction to a historical perspective on politics was immediately registered in his writings. As might be expected in the case of a student as independent as Wilson, his contemporary letters reveal a mixed personal response to the experience. His engagement to Ellen Axson in September 1883 undoubtedly added to his interest in beginning a teaching career as soon as possible, and he left the university without finishing his degree. Wilson and Ellen Axson were married in June 1885 and moved to the vicinity of Philadelphia, where Wilson began teaching at Bryn Mawr College.[1] In 1886 he was granted a doctoral degree diploma by special arrangement, and *Congressional Government* was accepted as his thesis. But if Wilson was relieved to quit the Johns Hopkins and its spirit of scientific positivism, he was also happy to return. Two years after Wilson received his Ph.D. he reestablished his connection with the Johns Hopkins with his appointment to lecture in a five-week course on public administration. This arrangement continued for the following nine years.

There were two important aspects to Wilson's connection with the Johns Hopkins. The first is that Wilson entered and maintained contact with the primary center of academic vitality in the nation in the 1880s and 1890s. The intellectual atmosphere among the teachers and students at the Johns Hopkins in this period may be seen as a clear anticipation by a few years of "the civic consciousness that soon swept over a vastly

---

[1] Wilson decided in early November 1884 to offer himself "to the highest bidder at the end of this collegiate year" rather than systematically to prepare for the general examinations. Fear for his health played a role in this decision, which was made on the advice of his father. Joseph Ruggles Wilson to WW, Oct. 29, 1884, *ibid.*, p. 385. See also WW to Ellen Axson, Oct. 26, Nov. 8, 1884, and Feb. 26 and May 23, 1885, *ibid.*, iii, 385, 415, and iv, 300, 619.

larger public," as Richard Hofstadter has shown.[2] Second, Wilson's professors, particularly Herbert Baxter Adams, Richard T. Ely, and George Sylvester Morris confronted him with German conceptions of history, government, and society that had an enduring influence on him. This strenuous initiation to a scholarly career at the Johns Hopkins meant that Wilson came to feel at home in the academic world, and it gave his own scholarly production a Continental European outlook that remedied the English provincialism of his earliest writings. Historian have often underrated the impact of Wilson's studies at the Johns Hopkins, because they have paid insufficient attention to his special situation. Great attention has been given to Wilson's complaints in private letters about the heavy load of readings his teachers assigned and about the dull and unimaginative lectures he attended.[3] It has generally been overlooked that most of these complaints appear in love letters to Ellen Axson, where the discipline of work is set up as a counterpoint to Wilson's agony about the separation from his fiancée. Actually, seen in the context of his academic career as a whole, the stay at the Johns Hopkins was a crucial experience for Wilson, who was deeply influenced by the many privileges the university afforded him—its serious scholarly atmosphere, its connections with Continental European scholars in history and the social sciences, and its sense of fellowship with a remarkable group of students and instructors.

In some ways the John Hopkins matched Wilson's aggressive scholarly ambitions. Upon its opening in 1876, Daniel Coit Gilman, the president, had declared that the aim of the university was to provide advanced education to a public-spirited elite drawn from the middle class.[4] Within a

---

[2] *The Age of Reform: From Bryan to F.D.R.* (New York, 1955), p. 205.

[3] Wilson's reading habits have been a matter of some debate because they may be interpreted as a neurological symptom. Evidence concerning this issue may also be seen in the light of the debate in university circles at this time between the conservatives, who want to use reading requirements as a way of disciplining the mental faculties of the students, and the liberals, who stress, as Wilson did numerous times, the value of a free development of the student's imaginative faculties. Since Wilson voiced most of his complaints in letters that bemoan his separation from Ellen Axson, it is also tempting to look for an emotional rather than a psychological or a neurological explanation for Wilson's complaints. See, for instance, WW to Ellen Axson, Jan. 20, 23, 1885, *PWW*, III, 623, 633; Weinstein, *Woodrow Wilson*, pp. 14–18, 49, 60, 120; George and George, "*Woodrow Wilson and Colonel House*: A Reply," pp. 645–48.

[4] Burton Bledstein, *The Culture of Professionalism: The Middle Class and the Development of Higher Learning in America* (New York, 1976), pp. 292–94; Laurence R. Veysey, *The Emergence of the American University* (Chicago, 1965), pp. 158–64; Daniel Coit Gilman, *The Launching of a University and Other Papers: A Sheaf of Remembrances* (New York, 1906), pp. 6–24; Hugh Hawkins, *Pioneer: A History of the Johns Hopkins University, 1874–1889* (Ithaca, N. Y., 1960), pp. 38–78.

few years, Gilman had managed to assemble a young but distinguished faculty. The intention was to domesticate the German system of professional, scientific learning in the United States. Herbert Baxter Adams, who had spent several years as a student in German universities, became chairman of the history department. Richard T. Ely, who held a Ph.D. from Heidelberg, became an associate professor. In 1882 the project of scientific history and politics was enhanced by the gift of the personal library of the late Johann Bluntschli, professor of constitutional and international law at Heidelberg.

While Gilman soon emerged as one of the leading spokesmen in the movement to professionalize university training, Adams and Ely were both active in the creation of professional societies with a scientific outlook in history and economics, respectively. At the university itself, they worked to induce values and skills judged to be fitting for a progressive class that was called to scientific inquiry in public service. Among the educational innovations, the most important was undoubtedly the seminar, which served the dual purpose of teaching and research, carried out in a spirit of critical analysis and scholarly community. Adams described the seminary in the disciplines of history and political economy as a modification of the medieval "training school for priests," which was now being engaged in "advancing philosophical inquiry by the defence of original theses." From "a nursery of dogma," the modern seminary was to be developed as "a laboratory of scientific truth."[5]

Herbert Baxter Adams entertained an evolutionary view of history that sought to account for modern institutions by tracing their stages of development back to their obscure Germanic roots. Wilson complained to Ellen Axson that his professors wanted "everybody under their authority" to work on what was called " 'institutional history,' to digging, that is, into the dusty records of old settlements and colonial cities . . . and other rummaging work of a like dry kind, which seemed very tiresome." But when Wilson voiced his interest in a continuation of his work on cabinet government, Adams immediately freed him from " 'institutional' work," and offered him, as Wilson reported, "all the aid and encouragement he could give me," saying "that the work I proposed was just such as he wanted to see done!"[6] Although at this stage Wilson did not have much personal regard for him, Adams presented him with a modern, interdisciplinary approach to history which emphasized that American history should be seen in a national context, and that history

[5] Herbert Baxter Adams, *Methods of Historical Study*, Johns Hopkins University Studies in Historical and Political Science, 2nd Ser., i–ii (Baltimore, 1884), 64, 27–29, 41–43.

[6] WW to Ellen Axson, Oct. 16, 1883, *PWW*, ii, 479–80.

as a discipline is the bearer of political values. The importance of the new sort of history was, as Adams suggested, to contribute to "an expansion of the local consciousness into a fuller sense of its historic worth and dignity, of the cosmopolitan relations of modern local life, and of its own wholesome conservative power in these days of growing centralization."[7]

Both Herbert Baxter Adams and Richard T. Ely, who taught the courses in political economy, had attended the seminary of Dr. Eduard Engel of the statistical bureau of Berlin, where, as Adams noted, the idea was developed "that the government offices of the statistical bureau should become laboratories of political science."[8] For the first time there appeared to be a way that would turn political economy from a set of theoretical speculations into a positive empirical science. The availability of masses of economic data seemed to herald a future in which economists would not be forced to seek refuge in the simplification of economic life but would be able to face the modern social complexities on equal terms. As Ely pointed out, "If the phenomena of social and industrial life are numerous, so are those numerous in proportion whose business it is to arrange and classify these facts for the student." Within the area of national banking alone, the economist had "at his service a whole army of men who spend their entire time in furnishing him with material." The increasing interdependence of the economy made for a new world of facts. "Thousands of men," Ely wrote, "are employed in statistical bureaus, census-offices, clearing houses, chambers of commerce . . . gathering, arranging and classifying the infinite varied facts of modern economic life." At the time that Wilson entered the Johns Hopkins, Ely was preparing an all-out attack on "deductive" thinking, which was associated with classical economists who refused to acknowledge that new means were available for general progress.[9] The new economics, Ely made clear,

---

[7] Adams, *Methods of Historical Study*, pp. 17–18. Among the works that stress the awkward, preprogressive character of Adams's views on history are Jürgen Herbst, *The German Historical School in American Scholarship: A Study in the Transfer of Culture* (Ithaca, N. Y., 1965), pp. 108, 115–20, 125–28; John Higham, with Leonard Krieger and Felix Gilbert, *History* (Englewood Cliffs, N. J., 1965), pp. 159–62; Richard Hofstadter, *The Progressive Historians: Turner, Beard, Parrington* (New York, 1968), pp. 38–39, 65–68; and Ray Allen Billington, *Frederick Jackson Turner: Historian, Scholar, Teacher* (New York, 1973), pp. 58–108. Significant modifications of this view can be found in Dorothy Ross, "Historical Consciousness in Nineteenth-Century America," *American Historical Review*, LXXXIX (Oct. 1984), 909–28; and John Higham, "Herbert Baxter Adams and the Study of Local History," *ibid.* (Dec. 1984), 1225–39.

[8] Adams, *Methods of Historical Study*, p. 80.

[9] Richard T. Ely, *The Past and Present of Political Economy*, Johns Hopkins University Studies in Historical and Political Science, 2nd Ser., III (Baltimore, 1884), pp. 60–61. Ely asserted that "we must observe in order to theorize, and theorize in order to observe. . . . The very determination to accept hypotheses with caution, and to test them continually by comparing

had no hesitation on this count. It was to be "tacitly assumed that the economist who studies and examines economic life will not neglect to advise and prescribe norms for the most satisfactory economic organism."[10]

Even more important was the fact that the vision of a new body of scientific data, comprehensive and detailed at the same time, was supported by a new idea of public ends. These ends cannot be described as "regulation" if the term is taken to mean a set of general restrictions that were intended to slow the pace of economic change. Ely's idea is better described as a suggestion that the state involve itself in a policy of selective development. The young professors who had studied in Germany were under no illusion that "society" could be regarded as an expression of spontaneous economic activity, as the orthodox school seemed to assume. They had been taught in theory, and Bismarck's regime had shown them in practice, that industrialization was vitally dependent upon state action to arrange the social and economic context required for private industrial production. Ely's advertisement for the German authorities included the observation that Bismarck might be considered the foremost member of the group of "socialists of the chair," because Bismarck himself had denounced English liberal political economy and had pursued economic studies of his own.[11]

Ely did his utmost to engage his students in the clash of doctrines between the Old School, that is, classical English political economy, and the New School, the German historical school, which attempted to bring social considerations to bear on the principles of political economy. While the Old School, had relied on a model of man as a creature of rational self-interest, Ely sketched a broader picture, which included, in addition to self-interest, "a continuous, conscious moral economy and moral persuasion which has its foundations laid in the nature of man and its purpose in the welfare of the people." As Ely's definition makes clear, the purpose was not to formulate a new psychology but to provide a defini-

them with facts unceasingly gathered, is a weighty one, and promises good things for our future economic development." *Ibid.*, p. 47. As Joseph Dorfman noted, Ely developed the idea that "government regulation of industry provided the means of effectively applying the inductive method." "The Role of the German Historical School in American Economic Thought," *American Economic Review*, xlv (May 1955), 26–27. See also Richard T. Ely, *An Introduction to Political Economy* (New York, 1889), pp. 281–82.

[10] Ely, *Past and Present of Political Economy*, p. 58. Wilson noted that "we must proceed not upon the ground of natural rights of freedom but from the stand of the ethical community of which the individual is a member and from the standpoint of the common weal." "Classroom Notebook," *c.* Dec. 7, 1883–May 20, 1884, Woodrow Wilson Collection, Firestone Library.

[11] *French and German Socialism in Modern Times* (New York, 1883), pp. 235–36.

tion of "the state."[12] The attraction of the notion of the state was that it served both as a symbol for established norms of social cohesiveness and as a means of inducing new norms in conformity with general progress. Ely by no means abandoned the assumption of self-interested economic agents. He complemented the principle of self-interest with a principle of socialization—society, which "corrects, modifies and rounds out the individual action." He used Adolf Wagner's term *Zwangsgemeinwirt-schaften* (compulsory economic communities) to describe the modifications that mold the individual for economic action. As exchanges multiplied in industrial society, "dependence" was asserted by the state, "not only in intensity, but in extent." The third principle in Ely's understanding was the "caritative principle," which took note of special cases, such as "voluntary action in behalf of others" and almsgiving. This principle "regulates, modifies and elevates" and "removes hardships from individuals as neither the first or second could by any possibility do." The important task of modern economists was "to develop into intelligent . . . activity all three principles." "The preponderance of any one is injurious," Ely explained.[13]

It is well known that Wilson cared little for Ely's style of lecturing and disliked the manners of the associate professor, who was his senior by only two years.[14] Ely's later reputation as an academic rebel, as a friend of labor, and as religious reformist, had not yet been established in 1883. Wilson thought his teaching anything but rabble-rousing, and if Ely voiced radical political opinions in class, it was hardly noticed by Wilson, who regarded it as an "honorable" as well as a "politic" service to work with him.[15] Ely's importance for Wilson derived from his reversing the

[12] Ely, *Past and Present of Political Economy*, p. 48. Wilson's classroom notebook entry for December 17, 1883, contains Ely's discussion of political space, "the life territories of the people." "The peculiar economic life of the people is that it is the first and most necessary territory of their life." "This territory is . . . apart but is not independent in any practical sense of the word. It is the economy *side* of the life of the people. We must concede causal relations existing between them and the other life territories of the people," such as the jurisdictions of law and political and social administration. Ely's problem was to fit "the market" within the nation. Woodrow Wilson Collection, Firestone Library.

[13] Ely, *Past and Present of Political Economy*, pp. 51–53. On December 12, 1883, Ely commented further on Wagner's "principles of economic activity which together make a sum of economics in organic society," i.e., the individualistic, the socialistic, and the caritative principles. On January 16, 1884, he discussed the caritative principle, warning that it militates against "individual exertion and individual self-restraint, since it weakens self-reliance." Classroom notebook, *c.* Dec. 7, 1883–May 20, 1884, Woodrow Wilson Collection, Firestone Library.

[14] WW to Robert Bridges, Dec. 15, 1883, *PWW*, II, 586.

[15] WW to Ellen Axson, Feb. 19, 1884, *ibid.*, III, 36. It is not entirely clear when Ely began to think of himself as a radical. The standard account is Benjamin Rader, *The Academic Mind*

order of elements that had been central for Atwater's conception of the economy. While Atwater had subsumed economic phenomena under the general frame of a moral science, Ely argued that ethical and moral behavior was best understood in economic terms. Ely was one of the first of a generation of economists who did not come to political economy from the pulpit but who instead came to the pulpit from the science itself. Money and capital was the general medium through which not only self-interest but also duty, thankfulness, public spirit, and other human virtues expressed themselves.[16]

The intellectual revolution that separated Atwater from Ely may be described as the rejection of the view that the development of the economy was restrained by the narrow limits of man's moral capacity both for strenuous work and for the sacrifice of saving for future gain. Atwater had feared that middlemen and managers would blunt the moral content of economic transactions. The danger was that fraud and the exploitation of other people's property would create a false sense of prosperity, hence his cheerless advice that unemployed workers should save themselves by becoming capitalists. If the economy was mirrored in human morality, society was doomed to meager fare.

Against this background, "the state" provided a considerable measure of theoretical relief. The key to Ely's doctrines is his move to transfer the practice and idea of morality and ethical behavior from the individual to a generalized expression in the idea of the state. The result was to free the idea of the economy from its dependence on the scarcity of human virtue. The state was able to save on its own for the public benefit. In

---

and Reform: The Influence of Richard T. Ely in American Life (Lexington, 1966), pp. 1–2, which places Ely's political awakening upon his return from Germany to the United States in 1880. The source is a private letter written five years later to the labor leader Joseph A. Labadie. Labadie to Ely, Aug. 8, 1885, and Ely to Labadie, Aug. 14, 1885, in Sidney Fine (ed.), "The Ely-Labadie Letters," *Michigan History*, xxxiv (March 1952), 15–17. It is unclear how far this letter is a true measure of Ely's radicalism. It appears to have been solicited by Labadie, who wanted to be assured that Ely would not betray the cause before he gave Ely access to information relating to Socialist organizations in America. Ely, in *Ground under Our Feet: An Autobiography* (New York, 1938), p. 38, describes the return from Germany in terms that suggest a different emphasis: "The city was dirty and ill-kept, the pavements poor, and there were evidences of graft and incompetence on every hand. Is this my America? I asked myself. . . . I vowed to do whatever was in my power to bring about better conditions."

[16] Classroom notebook, Dec. 7, 1883, Woodrow Wilson Collection, Firestone Library. Ely supplied a list of virtues that was intended to modify the doctrine of individual self-interest as the basic motive force in the economy. "This error has scarcely a plaxur [place] any longer in the science," Wilson noted, "it is a standpoint which has been passed by. [The] true economic motives" also include a "consciousness of moral duty," such as "religious motives." See also Jean B. Quandt, "Religion and Social Thought: The Secularization of Postmillennialism," *American Quarterly*, xxv (Oct. 1973), 402–404.

Atwater's view, the economy dictated a separation between winners and losers, a division of sheep and goats that in a way, hidden from man's understanding, was a revelation of divine justice. The notion of the state promised to relieve the economy of this ultimate judgment and open the door to the prospect of growing prosperity that depended not on a private willingness to sacrifice but on the public inducement of competition, interdependence, and even a measure of charity for the wretched. Implied in Ely's view was the rehabilitation of middlemen, organizers, administrators, and managers, whether privately or publicly hired. The economy of the market was liberated from individual morality, and society was opened for social science and "experiments in social and economic life."[17]

The idea of the state was expounded from yet another angle. George Sylvester Morris, a professor of philosophy, was the third of Wilson's teachers at the Johns Hopkins whose interests were attuned to German scholarship. Morris had spent two years in Berlin after the Civil War. Back in the United States, he launched a philosophical critique of British empiricism from the position of Hegelian idealism.[18] Since Morris's course on "the philosophy of the state" paid special attention to Herbert

[17] Ely, *Past and Present of Political Economy*, pp. 44–45. Dorothy Ross, in "Socialism and American Liberalism: Academic Social Thought in the 1880s," *Perspectives in American History*, XI (1977–78), 5–79, offers a different account of Ely's views and of his influence on Wilson. According to Ross, Ely influenced Wilson toward socialism, but academic emulation rectified the early views of both men. "With the possibility of access to desirable social positions before them, and their social outlook grounded in emulation of the respectable elite, the American intellectuals could not easily choose a political stance that would alienate their social models" (p. 57). The views of the intellectuals in question seem to have been radicalized in order for their betrayal to appear greater. It is unlikely that at this point either Ely or Wilson would considered themselves socialists in the sense of advocating what Ross calls "collectivistic state action to control the economy, and increasingly . . . state ownership of the means of production" (p. 13). For Ely's distinction between socialism in "the popular sense" as economic equality and in the scientific sense as "simply the social system," see his *French and German Socialism*, pp. 29–30. In an unpublished essay, Wilson reviewed Ely's book *The Labor Movement in America* (New York, 1886) and seemed to draw the same distinction; *PWW*, v, 559–62. Much of the argument turns on a distinction between state and government. On this point, see Ely's *Recent American Socialism*, Johns Hopkins University Studies in Historical and Political Science, 3rd Ser., IV (Baltimore, 1885), p. 73. Also, see Sidney Fine, *Laissez Faire and the General-Welfare State: A Study in Conflict in American Thought, 1865–1901* (Ann Arbor, 1964), pp. 198–251, for an incisive analysis of Ely's economic ideas and their political implications.

[18] Since Morris was not a tenured member of the Johns Hopkins faculty but came to Baltimore each semester from the University of Michigan, his influence on Wilson went unnoticed and was first suggested by the editors of the Wilson papers, who recovered unusually careful notes of Morris's lectures from October 1884 through January 1885. See "Editorial Note: Wilson's Study and Use of Shorthand," *PWW*, I, 15–16.

Spencer and the political theory of organicism, it was not without a bearing on political economy. It appears from Wilson's notes, with their numerous references to Aristotle and Hegel, that Morris was using material that later went into his book, *Hegel's Philosophy of the State and of History*, published in 1887. Morris pointed out that Spencer, in *The Man versus the State*, insofar as he wanted to rely on an organic notion of society, could not limit his conception of the political to a purely mechanistic conception of government; Spencer was in effect forced to acknowledge some kind of higher principle beyond individual interest and coercive government. As Morris argued, "If the state is an organism, man is not complete without it, anymore than a part of the body is complete separate from the body." The effect was to split Spencer's notion of government apart with "the necessary distinction between state, as possibly found in the nature of man, and *government*, or the *machinery* of government."[19]

WILSON worked as hard as his health permitted. "Constant reading probably *does* jade me a little too much," he wrote to Ellen Axson, "but I think that the work is telling on me a little just now only because I have never before held myself down to the systematic performance of set tasks, and that my body and mind will both accommodate themselves to the novel discipline within a few weeks." He had loaded his course work with lectures in political economy. In addition to Ely's undergraduate and graduate courses in this discipline, he followed Ely's courses in Finance and Taxation, Principles and Historical Growth of Commerce, and Methods of Administration in England, Germany, and France.[20]

Soon after his arrival at the university, Wilson was asked to lecture on Adam Smith in Ely's class. The preparation involved extensive reading in *The Wealth of Nations*. The lecture, which was delivered to the class at the beginning of 1884, impressed Ely so much that he invited Wilson to participate in a joint project, a textbook on the history of American political economy. Ely would write on Henry C. Carey, who was considered the single most important figure; Davis R. Dewey, a graduate student like Wilson, would write on the economists before Carey; and Wilson, as he explained in a letter to his fiancée, would "prepare a narrative and critical review on the writings *since* Carey."[21] Although Wilson initially considered the topic too dusty for his taste and later became afraid that his work was superficial, he felt honored by the proposal and stayed with the project. After the publication of *Congressional Government* he began the

[19] Notes on Professor Morris's lecture on Herbert Spencer, *ibid.*, III, 426–28, 457–58.
[20] WW to Ellen Axson, Jan. 23, 1885, and Oct. 6, 1884, *ibid.*, pp. 633, 335 n. 1.
[21] Fragmentary draft of a lecture on Adam Smith, *ibid.*, II, 542–44; WW to Ellen Axson, Feb. 19, 1884, *ibid.*, III, 36.

necessary reading, and in May 1885 he wrote his first draft, which he handed over to Ely for comments and suggestions. Neither Ely nor Dewey, it seems, finished their sections, and the project died after Wilson left the university.[22]

Since Wilson's draft consists of seven unconnected intellectual biographies, and therefore does not include an attempt to make a formal argument, it has not been regarded as a source for Wilson's own opinions. William Diamond found it "a colorless . . . description" and concluded with reference to the heavy use of quotations that it contained "little of Wilson himself."[23] Wilson clearly did not regard it as an original piece of work. He wrote to Ellen Axson: "I don't have to have any opinions of my own in doing *this* writing. I have simply to understand the writing of others, and appreciate their relations to each other and to the general body of thought in their science."[24] Wilson's despair over the lack of originality is a commonplace in his letters. But in this case the final product,

---

[22] WW to Ellen Axson, June 5, 1884, *ibid.*, p. 209; "Editorial Note: Wilson's 'History of Political Economy in the United States,' " *ibid.*, IV, 628–31. Ely's failure to compose his section is difficult to explain, because he was a prolific writer. He mentioned in his autobiography that he found the research on Carey more difficult than he had anticipated. In the summer of 1885, Ely was engaged in the organization of the American Economic Association, and it is possible that the politics of the profession made it inexpedient for him to make his views on his predecessors known at this juncture. Richard T. Ely, "Political Economy in America," *North American Review*, CXLIV (Feb. 1887), 113–19; Fine, *Laissez Faire and the General-Welfare State*, pp. 212–21; Rader, *Academic Mind and Reform*, p. 42; Ely, *Ground under Our Feet*, pp. 112–13.

[23] *Economic Thought of Woodrow Wilson*, p. 30; see also Mulder, *Woodrow Wilson*, p. 84; and Bragdon, *Woodrow Wilson*, pp. 115–16. Diamond inferred that Wilson probably changed his opinions in some way but at heart retained his classical liberal values: "His years at Hopkins seem to have weaned him away from a strict Manchesterianism and towards an historical inductive economics. If the premises of his thought remained essentially unchanged, he found it necessary to reconcile them with the facts so vigorously pointed out by Ely." Although "these facts may have displeased Wilson," he accepted them as reasons for government regulation of the economy (p. 37). See also Charles A. Beard, "American Interpretations of Liberty as Economic Laissez Faire," in his *Public Policy and the General Welfare* (New York, 1941), pp. 130–31. If one adds J. Franklin Jameson's remark some forty years later that Wilson's Hopkins career reflected "pretty much of the old Manchester school" (Diamond, p. 26), there begins to emerge the picture of Wilson as someone with strong emotional ties to Old South paternalism on the one hand and an enduring affection for Old Manchesterianism on the other that Hofstadter painted in his elegant vignette in *The American Political Tradition and the Men Who Made It* (New York, 1948). In *The Age of Reform*, Hofstadter further enlarged the picture in order to explain progressive regulatory activism as a reflection of a regressive moral temper. This picture of Wilson as a ministerial, old-time moralizer caught in a world of hard industrial facts is related to the questions raised for Hofstadter by the New Deal experience, and is colored by the view of Wilson's last years as president. See also Crunden, *Ministers of Reform, passim.*

[24] WW to Ellen Axson, March 12, 1885, *PWW*, IV, 356.

although it summed up an extensive literature and apparently was well received by his teacher, was clearly not meant to be a contribution to the advancement of economic science. Yet, the very process of selecting quotations for later reflection is revealing of certain directions of thought.

Wilson's section of "The History of Political Economy in the United States" was a first draft. The arrangement of page numbers and footnotes, the interlineations, and the misspellings support this observation, which in turn may account for the lack of an introduction and a conclusion, which has made any interpretation difficult.[25] Instead, the context of Wilson's section must be inferred from other sources. First, the terms of Wilson's argument were set by the appearance of Ely's own study of the general issues that had appeared at least two months before Wilson began to write his own section.[26] That Wilson was in fact familiar with Ely's work is apparent, despite the absence of direct references, because Wilson used and commented on some of the quotations from European economists that Ely had drawn attention to in his work. Second, Wilson's section on American economists was related to his earlier lecture on Adam Smith and, more important, to a presentation on American economic writers that Wilson made before the historical seminary on March 27, 1885, that is, after he had done most of his research but before he had begun the draft that he eventually handed to Ely. Finally, Wilson's section was related to his review of the general controversy over economics in his essay "Of the Study of Politics," written in November 1886.

The report to the seminar presented, according to the minutes, "a review of recent American political economists," and it may well have been a test of Wilson's views before his peers and teachers. The minutes of the seminar record further that "remarks were made by Dr. Ely, justifying the method adopted by Mr. Wilson."[27] By "method" Ely seems to have been referring to the distinction between a general and a national approach to economics, an issue that was at the heart of the contemporary dispute over the very nature of economics as a scientific discipline. Two years earlier, more English-oriented economists had formed the Political Economy Club, and progressive economists had attempted to respond by forming a Society for the Study of National Economy.[28] If political econ-

[25] "Editorial Note: Wilson's 'History of Political Economy in the United States,'" *ibid.*, p. 629.

[26] *Past and Present of Political Economy.*

[27] Minutes of the Seminary of Historical and Political Science, March 27, 1885, *PWW*, IV, 421. Wilson's report had been scheduled several weeks earlier but was postponed because, as Wilson explained to Ellen Axson, "Dr. Ely was away, and . . . he was very anxious to hear my report." March 9, 1885, *ibid.*, p. 345.

[28] Rader, *Academic Mind and Reform*, p. 34; Fine, *Laissez Faire and the General-Welfare State*, pp. 212–21.

omy was limited to being a science based on man's desire for wealth, it had as little to do with nationality as the natural sciences had. Ely, however, argued that a national approach, outlawed by liberal economists, was a necessary step deriving from the social and historical elements in economics; the "new" science of economics was constituted by the nature of its object, which called for "method" rather than axioms. Just as Adams had stressed the opposition of the new historical method to "tradition," Ely stressed the opposition to older economic doctrines that proceeded from the practice of taking the "ultimate facts" of economics "from common and familiar experience, or from the declarations of consciousness" in order to develop "an economic system without any further recourse to the external world." Ely emphasized that the "alluring simplicity" and the "enticing unity" of English political economy explained its popular attraction, because it "appealed irresistibly to the vanity of the average man" with its "few easily managed formulas." It required "but a few hours' study to make of the village schoolmaster both a statesman and a political economist."[29]

While Wilson obviously had worked on the assumption that political economy could be conceived of on a national basis, in his presentation before the seminar he offered a line of reasoning that set him off from Ely's hopes for the project. His choice of words at the very beginning of his report reveals Wilson's informing notions. He underscored such characteristics among the political economists as were traditionally associated with the peculiar American values of self-dependence and autonomy. He modified the idea that American economists had been echoing the English models. Although American economics descended from English thought, economists had soon worked their way toward secession: "So independent, indeed, and so individual have our text writers been that it is very difficult to make any satisfactory grouping of them. Each has had his special point of view and his special idiosyncrasies of belief."[30] Wilson's results indicated the existence of an American "public discourse" on political economy, a term Wilson used a few years later in a sketch of Adam Smith's economic thought.[31]

In trying to sort out some of the common characteristics that would

---

[29] *Past and Present of Political Economy*, pp. 8, 17. Similar formulations appeared in Ely's prospectus for the American Economic Association, which was being written in the early summer of 1885 with the assistance of Herbert Baxter Adams, among others. It circulated among economists, and in September 1885 it became the central point of discussion for the platform of the association. It was moderated in order not to be too challenging to more English-oriented economists. Ely, *Ground under Our Feet*, pp. 136–40; *American Economic Association Publications*, i (1886), 5–46.

[30] Report to the historical seminary, March 7, 1885, *PWW*, iv, 422.

[31] "An Old Master," Feb. 1, 1887, *ibid.*, v, 447.

justify a "satisfactory grouping" within the national frame, Wilson referred to an article by Cliff Leslie in the *Fortnightly Review*. The choice of Leslie was significant, since he was considered the leading spokesman in England for the historical school. Leslie argued that American writers had generally rejected Malthus; that American economists had had, and still had, a marked religious background; that they rejected the theory of an equalization of wages and profits over the long run between different occupations; and that there was a strong advocacy of protectionism in American textbooks. Deductive economic reasoning had never received much attention in America.[32] Wilson added that political economy in America had had a practical, not a theoretical, purpose. While classical economics was associated with speculations that tended to become "mere library theories, mere fine-spun threads of logic," the independence of American economists had asserted itself in an "actual dissent":

> Writing in a country where vast, almost unprecedented, developments of industry and movements of population were taking place their imaginations have been impressed, of course, and they have realized the scientific importance of the rapid economic progress proceeding under their eyes. . . . The industrial facts furnished ready to the hands of our writers by the history of almost every American community were much better than any supposititious cases which they could frame for themselves. They lived, so to say, amongst object-lessons in their science. They would have had to be without neighbors to have been without illustrations of the topics upon which they were writing. The experiences of actual life thrust themselves into their speculations and by their very presence affected those speculations.[33]

The mixture of language, on the one hand referring to scientific terms like "supposititious cases" and "industrial facts," and on the other, using words of a more traditional sort, like "community" and "neighbors," underscored Wilson's point that the observation and discussion of economic issues were part and parcel of a political tradition, not a scientific tradition.[34] Economic activities were generally understood as shared ventures, inasmuch as they took place within an economy of individual enterprise. Economic development was not the property of any particular class or any particular expertise, any more than it was imprisoned in libraries or

[32] Thomas Edward Cliff Leslie, "Political Economy in the United States," *Fortnightly Review*, New Ser., xxviii (1880), 488–509.

[33] Report to the historical seminary, *c.* March 7, 1885, *PWW*, iv, 422–24.

[34] Compare the sketch of general economic debate in "Cabinet Government in the United States," *ibid.*, i, 500–501.

in esoteric suppositions and complicated logical operations. It was, so to speak, a homely affair that had affected the community as a whole and had therefore been a natural part of public life.

In contrast to Ely's understanding, Wilson's argument was distinguished by its hesitation to treat American economists as rigid exponents of English liberalism. Economic knowledge in America had, until recently, been inclined "to take very optimistic views of the economic life." Wilson denied that American political economists in general had embraced laissez-faire doctrines. While economists had often criticized government economic policy, they had not attacked the fundamental economic institutions of society. Wilson argued that sheer material abundance seemed to have impeded the rise of doctrines and the clash of fundamental principles associated with a critique of the "existing order of society."[35] General prosperity, Wilson claimed, had " 'spread a sort of poetic haze over the whole machinery of society.' " It had been difficult for Americans to conceive of "a world too fruitless to sustain every human being that might come into existence"; "the boundless continent with its still untaxed resources" appeared to be "a palpable refutation of all the Malthusian forecastings." For Americans to speculate about basic economic laws would have been "like the ingratitude of looking a gift horse in the mouth."[36]

In effect, Wilson was saying that material scarcity was a necessary precondition for economic doctrine and economics in a more scientific form. While abundance had created a fertile ground in the United States for widespread economic thinking and for "careful examination of concrete economic facts," economic theory proper, with its stress on "à priori methods" and "fine-spun threads of logic," was a child of scarcity. Unfortunately, the minutes are too brief to give an impression of the subsequent discussion, but the reporter (who was, incidentally, Davis R. Dewey) noted that "Dr. Ely also called attention to a late letter of Mr. Bryce to Dr. Adams, in which he calls attention to the subject of laissez-faire in the U. S. as a fruitful one for investigation."[37] This was, it seems, the study that Ely had had in mind. If Wilson had proven that early American economic thought had been an echo of speculative economics, he would have provided the perfect sequel to Ely's critique of an economic science oriented toward abstract English theorems rather than real national needs. When Wilson suggested that classification in terms of deductive and inductive methods was not helpful for a description of

[35] *Ibid.*, IV, 422.

[36] *Ibid.*, p. 423.

[37] Minutes of the Seminary of Historical and Political Science, March 27, 1885, *ibid.*, p. 421.

American economists and that there had been few laissez-faire theorists in America, he seems to have upset Ely's initial plans for the project.

The idea of a shared, workaday fund of economic knowledge based on common observations was not a casual notion but a recurring theme in Wilson's writings on economics. It was made explicit in his work on Adam Smith. This has received little recognition among the modern readers of Wilson's work, possibly because we are apt to see Adam Smith as Ely did, that is, as the first scientific exponent of economics, whose genius was to separate economics from its substantive basis in man's procurement of the means for his livelihood and to turn it into a system of formal thought amenable to manipulation by logic if not by mathematical reasoning.

Wilson looked upon Adam Smith with rather different eyes. The stable character of Wilson's perception is suggested by the fact that the argument and concerns he displayed in his early lecture in 1883 were retained in the more elaborate essay "An Old Master," of 1887, which would become the title of the collection of essays he published in 1893.[38] Both the lecture and the essay treat Adam Smith as a philosopher of wealth and a political speaker rather than as an expert on economics. Adam Smith had "examined those political regulations which are founded, not upon the principle of justice, but upon that of *expediency*, and which are calculated to increase riches, the power, and the prosperity of the state." What Wilson found particularly important was Adam Smith's "true instinct of an orator and a teacher," manifested in his ability to argue his politics from the outside—from the world of learning—and to "draw men to his way of thinking, nay, to one who would induce the great mass of men to give any heed to what he was saying." Smith's most valued instruments were "the clear processes of proof which gave speed to thought" and his "vigorous imagination which lent illumination to the argument."[39] Adam Smith was a model teacher of politics.[40]

[38] Fragmentary draft of a lecture on Adam Smith, Nov. 20, 1883, *ibid.*, II, 542–44; "An Old Master," *ibid.*, v, 445–55. *An Old Master and Other Political Essays* was published by Charles Scribner's Sons, New York, 1893.

[39] *Ibid.*, II, 544. It might be argued that Wilson's decision to focus his lecture on Adam Smith's oratory rather than his economic doctrines was based on Wilson's perception that in his lectures Ely had covered Adam Smith's economic assumptions. Wilson hinted in his letter to Ellen Axson of November 4, 1883, that he was unsure of his task, since "the professor himself has in his own lectures touched upon all the leading points of Adam Smith's life and opinions" (*ibid.*, p. 515). The gist of Ely's opinions, as revealed in Wilson's notes from the minor course in political economy, is available for Oct. 29, Oct. 31, and Nov. 2, 1883; *ibid.*, pp. 496–98, 506–508, 512–14. In these lectures Ely emphasized a comparison between Adam Smith and the German school. While Wilson's preparation was quite extensive, as is revealed in his bibliography and discussed in detail in the "Editorial Note: Wilson's Lecture

To view Adam Smith from this perspective was to suggest that he be approached as a political thinker whose special contribution was to point out that wealth forms the nation by linking the people to the state. The linkage was expressed in Adam Smith's definition of political economy.[41] It is on these terms that Wilson's section on the history of American political economy can be regarded as an attempt to grapple with some of the political problems involved in the scientific approach to economic theory. Wilson divided his review of eight political economists into three stages of changing economic ideas. He took Henry Vethake and Francis Wayland to represent a doctrinaire phase, in which orthodoxy had "a strong theological flavor." The second phase contained writers "of our own rearing who have grafted upon that [English] psychological stock some strong branches of American commonsense and practical conclusion." To this group belonged George Tucker, "A Southern Planter," Francis Bowen, Amasa Walker, and Arthur Latham Perry. The third stage was represented by only one writer, Francis Amasa Walker, who received an extensive review.[42]

In his treatment of the earlier economists, Wilson reviewed different ways of defining and describing economic issues. He singled out various doctrines for criticism, particularly those that seemed connected to Ricardo's theory of the wage fund or to Malthus's theory of the growth of population. "His induction is not always quite of a scientific sort," Wilson wrote about Bowen's views, "it is often mere generalizations based on wide but rather miscellaneous *personal observations*." He contrasted the "open-eyed methods of Adam Smith," which took account of "actual economic conditions," with a doctrinaire reliance on "principles of human nature."[43] Thus it was difficult to talk about a distinctive American tradition of laissez-faire. Either Americans had restated English models of

---

on Adam Smith," *ibid.*, pp. 537–42, the single most important source was Walter Bagehot, "Adam Smith as a Person," *Fortnightly Review*, New Ser., xx (1876), 18–42, which introduced Wilson to Adam Smith's times.

[40] *PWW*, v, 445. The theme of the essay is summed up in Wilson's opening question: "Are not our college class-rooms, in being robbed of the old-time lecture, and getting instead a science-brief of *data* and bibliography, being deprived also of that literary atmosphere which once pervaded them? We are unquestionably gaining in thoroughness; but are we gaining in thoughtfulness?" The question may be seen as a comment on Ely's lectures as well as of the prevailing idea of science at the Johns Hopkins.

[41] Adam Smith's definition contained two elements. First, to "provide a plentiful revenue or subsistence for the people," and, second, "to supply the state or commonwealth with revenue sufficient for the public services." Adam Smith, *An Inquiry into the Nature and Causes of the Wealth of Nations*, edited by Edwin Cannan (2 vols., Chicago, 1976), i, 449.

[42] "History of Political Economy in the United States," *PWW*, iv, 633, 653.

[43] *Ibid.*, pp. 639, 637.

little relevance for the practical problems of the American environment or American economics had relied too much upon common sense to form a coherent point of view.

Only Francis Amasa Walker's writings contained an internal coherence that Wilson had sought in vain among the earlier writers. Walker was a prominent representative of a type of northern intellectual whose experience had been profoundly colored by the organization and conduct of the Civil War. After the war he served as chief of the Federal Bureau of Statistics and superintendent of the federal census. In 1881 he was made president of the Massachusetts Institute of Technology, and he was soon after elected the first president of the American Economic Association. As Wilson noted, Walker's contribution consisted largely of his discussion of "many practical questions," which were treated as a matter of "the *art* of political economy," rather than of science. As he put it in a letter to Albert Shaw, "I have just finished going through delicious old A. L. Perry. What a treat to go through so complacent a treatise, where never a doubt obscures even the broadest generalization and where absolute finality of doctrine reassures you on every page! For a decided change of diet, I am going next to Walker. A little 'horse sense' from him will do my etherialized spirit good. The earth will seem real again." As Wilson put it in his essay, Walker's writings were "more truly practical" and "more or less governed by considerations of State policy." Walker was "essentially modern—essentially of to-day."[44] Although Wilson quoted extensively from the distinction Walker made between economic policy and economic science and from his theories of rent, profit, and consumption, it seems that Walker's ideas on the social preconditions of industrial advance were of the most immediate interest to him.

Walker's special achievement was to begin the modern discussion of the reproduction of human resources needed by capitalism in order to maintain itself in a state of expansion. He was probably the first American economist to argue that "reduction of the wages of labor" not only produces human hardship but, far from clearing the way for further production, is likely to impair the industrial capacity of the community. In passages that Wilson quoted at length, Walker argued that economic forces are not self-correcting, as the orthodox economists had thought. The industrial "laboring class" is vitally dependent upon the preservation

[44] *Ibid.*, pp. 652–63; WW to Albert Shaw, Nov. 28, 1884, *ibid.*, p. 738; see also George M. Fredrickson, *The Inner Civil War: Northern Intellectuals and the Crisis of the Union* (New York, 1965), pp. 203–205. Walker's significance as an economist is well laid out in Bernard Newton, *The Economics of Francis Amasa Walker: American Economics in Transition* (New York, 1968). Daniel Horowitz, "Genteel Observers: New England Economic Writers," *New England Quarterly*, XLVIII (March 1975), 78–79.

of competition among employers to weed out the less competent industrialists. Without competition, profits would increase and labor would suffer "economic injury" that would reduce wages and tell "prejudicially upon their health, habits, and spirit, making them thereafter industrial agents of a lower, perhaps of a lower and still lower, order." Pure economics could never save the nation. The economy needed help from the outside:

> In opposition to the orthodox doctrine that all such economical injuries are in their nature temporary and tend to disappear, I hold that, so far as purely economical forces are concerned, they tend to perpetuate themselves and to grow from bad to worse . . . ; [that] the rich tend to become richer and the poor poorer; and that only social and moral forces, like charity, education, religion, political ambition, entering from the outside, or physical forces, like the discovery of new principles of chemical or mechanical action . . . can restore the economical equilibrium if once destroyed by the weakness of the laboring class.[45]

The idea of the precarious nature of industrial progress struggling against regressive forces was supplemented by Walker's original view of the modern employer. He singled out this industrial type from the capitalist and raised the employer to the status of a fourth factor of production, in addition to the factors of land, labor, and capital. Walker laid the foundation of the idea of the "entrepreneurial function" as an economic category with important political attributes. Walker's employer was not an owner of capital but a risk taker, an organizer of production, and a commander of men. Labor needed the modern employer to furnish "technical skill, commercial knowledge and powers of administration; to assume responsibilities and provide against contingencies; to shape and direct production and to organize and control the industrial machinery." "The mere possessor of capital" was helpless on his own; "the employer, the entrepreneur" was destined to become "the master of the situation." Wilson commented that "the whole of Professor Walker's discussion of the employing class in industrial communities is indicative of keen practical insight, and consequently, fruitful of much practical suggestion."[46] The idea of a class whose economic ambitions and political qualifications made their self-interest identical with the mediation of the worker's and

[45] "History of Political Economy in the United States," *PWW*, iv, 660–61; compare Francis A. Walker, *Political Economy* (New York, 1889), pp. 30–32, 40, 256.

[46] *Ibid.*, pp. 205–206, quoted by Wilson in his "History of Political Economy in the United States," *PWW*, iv, 659; Newton, *Economics of Francis Amasa Walker*, pp. 29–38, 63–78, 163–75.

the capitalist's interests was later to play an important role in Wilson's idea of the historical development of the American West.

In general, the importance of Walker's views lay in its underscoring of Wilson's own belief that the maintenance of progressive change presupposed a qualified leadership that was able both to master the technical prerequisites of advance and to exact obedience. But in the context of the joint venture with Ely and Dewey, it appears that the project was doomed to failure, because Wilson had shown convincingly that, although it might be possible to write the biographies of American political economists, it was not possible to write the history of American political economy. There was no history of laissez faire in America; indeed, there was no coherent doctrine around which the individual economists might have been grouped. There were no boundaries of the discipline, because economic discussion in America was tightly woven into more general political issues. This has largely been confirmed by Paul K. Conkin's recent work on early American political economists.[47]

WILSON himself provided a kind of conclusion on his study of political economy at the Johns Hopkins. A year and a half after he had left, when he was preparing to go back to lecture at the university, he wrote an essay, "Of the Study of Politics," which reviewed the political significance of what he called the "open secret that there is war amongst the political economists."[48] He viewed his former teachers with a slightly ironical distance. The critics of John Stuart Mill and Adam Smith, he wrote, wanted to know " 'all the facts,' and [were] ready, if necessary, to reduce every generalization of the older writers to the state—the wholly *exceptional* state—of a rule in German grammar." But he also paid a fine tribute to their efforts. "Their protest is significant, their purpose heroic, beyond a doubt," he said, and he wished it known that he bid "these sturdy workers 'God speed!' "[49] To put Wilson's argument briefly, he showed on the basis

[47] *Prophets of Prosperity: America's First Political Economists* (Bloomington, Ind., 1980), p. 312.
[48] *PWW*, v, 395–406.
[49] *Ibid.*, IV, 395. Wilson's belief in the primacy of politics over economic laws was already quite obvious in *Congressional Government, ibid.*, on pp. 161–62, Wilson quoted William Graham Sumner with approval: "The modern industrial organization, including banks, corporations, joint-stock companies, [and] financial devices . . . is largely the creation of legislation (not in its historical origin, but in the mode of its existence and in its authority), and is largely regulated by legislation. Capital is the breath of life to this organization." Sumner, *Andrew Jackson as a Public Man* (Boston, 1883), p. 226. Interestingly, Wilson drew quite a different conclusion from this observation. While Sumner used it as a springboard to assail "the selfishness and cupidity [that] constantly strive to make use of laws and civil institutions to divert one man's money to another man's use," Wilson went on to state that "even more important than legislation is the instruction and guidance in political affairs which the people might

of examples that the claim of the New School that historical economics could replace the study of politics was naive. Political scholarship would remain of great importance as long as political action was a question of general conviction rather than of refined scientific truth.

Economics, whether based on eighteenth-century English concepts, which reduced man to a self-interested animal, or on German attempts to amass "particulars about the occupations, the habits, the earnings, the whole economic life of all classes and conditions of men," was unable to capture the political dimension of man. Inside the library, men might go "with their masters in thought—mayhap go great lengths with Adolph Wagner, or hold stiffly back, 'man *versus* the state,' with Spencer—outside their libraries they 'go with their party.' " What the New School needed was the element of political imagination or vision that would make it possible to secure mass consent. Such an element was not easily extracted from a science of economics that was constituted upon the attention to "detail." To succeed, the New School just needed "the eventual collaboration of some Shakspere who will set before the world all the standard types of economic character," as Wilson put it. Or they might have to collaborate with "theorists like Rousseau," who was capable of inducing citizens "to rear fabrics of government after their aërial patterns out of earth's stuffs, with the result of bringing every affair of weight crashing about their ears." These fine economists could not "build in the air and then escape chagrin because men only gaze at their structures, and will not live in them." The advanced economists were "closet students of politics." Only political leadership, cut to the stature that Wilson had sketched in *Congressional Government*, could make men "recognize" scientific results and incorporate them into common experience.[50]

Wilson's essay was shaped to provide a kind of answer to economists who thought that economics could replace the idea of political order if economics were buttressed with the communal values that history had generated. But in addition, the essay may be read as an answer to later accusations against Wilson that he harbored a secret animosity toward modern science. This charge was first made after he had been inaugu-

---

receive from a body which kept all national concerns suffused in a broad daylight of discussion." Wilson did not share the conviction of the autonomy of economic development that unified people as different as Ely and Sumner.

[50] "Of the Study of Politics," *PWW*, v, 395–96, 404. The disagreement between Ely and Wilson was nourished later. When a few years later Wilson gave a paper on the development of law at the Johns Hopkins, Ely commented "upon the necessity of the close union between Political Economy and History, between Pol. Eco. and Jurisprudence, [and] expressed his doubts whether the public opinion is so all-powerful, whether the law-making power is being absorbed by the legislature . . . as Dr. Wilson states" (Minutes of the Johns Hopkins Seminary of Historical and Political Science, March 15, 1889, *ibid.*, vi, 153–54).

rated as president of Princeton University,[51] but it has been repeated by commentators who have found some of his economic views nostalgic. These criticisms lack any basis in Wilson's early writings, and it may be suggested that they have only gained some credibility because Wilson, devoted to scientific advance on all fronts, tended to take the view that science needed political power if it was to break into the habits of common people and reshape their lives. Although science might reveal significant truths, it suffered from a certain political impotence, because it could argue these truths only with reference to the common sensibility within the political sphere. In political matters, science was deprived of its own turf: logical interference, the scientific method. "Scientific works," he wrote, which constantly superseded each other and which were barely expected "to outlive the prevailing fashion in ladies' wraps," could not by themselves provide stable political foundations. Even science was not without its political preconditions. Only a great political imagination would be able to direct the economist's "innumerable details" in order to pour them "in a concentrated fire upon the centre-citadels of men's understanding." Before it would be possible to arrive "within full sight of the longed-for time when political economy is to dominate legislation," a new understanding of the state was required.[52]

THE INTENSIVE STUDY of political economy was an important element behind Wilson's turn toward the fields of administration and politics, where his academic work was eventually carried out. Although he was never interested in political economy for its own sake, his introduction to the methods of economics, particularly its method of simplifying and formalizing a complex system of seemingly disconnected actions by independent human agents, changed his understanding of society and paved the way for a new approach to the functions and goals of political arrangements. Wilson's view of the preconceptions of the study of American industrial economy absorbed the ideas of the German historical school and at the same time brought them into a political perspective, a viewpoint that distinguished Wilson's approach from that of his teachers.

[51] The charge was voiced by James McKeen Cattell, the editor of *Popular Science Monthly*, who was referring to Wilson's sesquicentennial address, "Princeton in the Nation's Service." As Wilson pointed out in a letter, this charge was built on a misquotation that began in the middle of a paragraph, leaving out "a strong eulogy of science," and was written with the intention of misrepresenting him "just as much as possible." WW to Robert Bridges, July 17, 1902, *ibid.*, xiv, 21–22.

[52] "Of the Study of Politics," *ibid.*, v, 404.

V

★ ★

FROM FAMILY TO

NATIONAL SOCIETY: WILSON'S IDEA

OF THE DEMOCRATIC STATE

The last half of the 1880s was a very happy and productive period for Wilson. He very quickly came to enjoy a growing reputation as a writer, a teacher, and a public lecturer, and his family life seems to have fulfilled his emotional needs in every respect. As testified by a large number of letters to Ellen Axson Wilson in the course of their marriage, he loved his wife passionately and self-consciously.[1] He regarded their relationship as the spring of his intellectual ambition and capacity for work. The young couple seems to have lived harmoniously and happily together with their three daughters, Margaret Woodrow, Jessie Woodrow, and Eleanor Randolph, who were born in 1886, 1887, and 1889, respectively. After three years of mostly undergraduate teaching at Bryn Mawr, Wilson accepted an appointment at Wesleyan University in Middletown, Connecticut, in 1888. That same year he began his lectures on public administration at The Johns Hopkins University. Two years later, in 1890, he was elected professor of jurisprudence and political economy at Princeton, a position he accepted with much pleasure. These elements of his personal life formed the context in which Wilson developed a theory that attempted to rest the state upon the family.

WHEREAS Wilson conceived of *Congressional Government* as a political statement, the purpose of which was to create a stage for public debate and leadership at the center of government, he conceived of his second book, *The State*, as a project of descriptive or historical theory.[2] Its tone was factual rather than persuasive or imaginative. Wilson planned and wrote it as a textbook, not as a critical argument. Yet *The State* invites

---

[1] Mulder, *Woodrow Wilson*, pp. 111–17; Weinstein, *Woodrow Wilson*, pp. 95–107.

[2] *The State: Elements of Historical and Practical Politics, A Sketch of Institutional History and Administration* (Boston, 1889).

comparison with *Congressional Government* on the assumption that both books represent a search for the means of political revitalization. Wilson expanded the scope of his viewpoint from Congress to Western civilization, and his discussion of collective life from political assembly to historical evolution. This change of perspective throws light both on Wilson's own development and on the development of American political ideas in the late nineteenth century.

In the history of American political ideas, the 1880s are generally seen as the Dark Ages, steeped in laissez faire, Social Darwinism, and a persistent glorification of private capital in its corporate form—a decade of dissolution in political thought before the turbulent 1890s, with their threat of class warfare. After the turn of the century, progressive ideas restored federal authority, supported now by a growing international prestige, and set out to curb industrial misconduct, strengthen social cohesion, and change the tyrants of industrial power into guardians of economic development by way of regulatory commissions.

However one might quarrel with this account, it suggests that the origins of progressive politics flowed from an understanding that was different from traditional liberal ideas about individual rights, consent, and local self-government. A new vocabulary was being formed in which values such as stability, order, efficiency, and national growth turned political discourse from the polity to a new notion of society. As Charles Merriam noted in 1923, the years between the Civil War and the turn of the century were characterized by a subtle change in the content of individualism. "The individualism of the Fathers grew out of the fear of political absolutism. The individualism of the last half century grew out of the fear of business depression or repression. The individualism of the Fathers was based upon an ideal of liberty: the later form upon an ideal of industrial production."[3] This sketch of the larger transformation of political values may provide a backdrop against which Wilson's ideas may be seen more clearly.

Wilson argued that, historically, organic development as exemplified in the life of the family had provided the bonds of purpose, affection, and trust that were necessary to sustain political community. On these terms, Wilson's argument was hardly convincing, something that he himself more or less recognized. Perhaps one gets closer to an understanding of the stakes behind his project if it is conceived in somewhat different terms. His hope was to explore the origins of the state by recourse to notions of authority, dependence, and sentiment associated with the fam-

[3] *American Political Ideas: Studies in the Development of American Political Thought, 1865–1917* (New York, 1923), p. 325.

ily as a sociopolitical institution. His undertaking was to develop a language with which to reveal the processes of political energy generated by the rise of the national democratic state, and he constructed this language on analogies and metaphors of family development.

Since Wilson did not consider his theory to be successful and soon discarded it in favor of a theory of sovereignty and a history of national growth centered on the American West, the present attempt to trace an abandoned metaphysics of the state may seem futile. Yet the very failure of Wilson's project holds a certain fascination in retrospect. It reveals both Wilson's determination to develop his ideas from an organic metaphor of political order and the extraordinary problems that such an undertaking involved. The present account is a study of Wilson's way of connecting political impulses rather than as a settled interpretation of a text. Perry Miller once remarked that the task of intellectual history is to make contact with the feelings rather than with the words of past writers. Such feelings are known by way of their history, and it befits the historian to account for the frustrated as well as the felicitous expression of these feelings.

The State is for all practical purposes a forgotten book. Despite its publication at the beginning of professional political science in America, and despite Wilson's later role as a political actor, one looks in vain for any extended discussion of the meaning and significance of the work. The concept of the state itself seems infused with a kind of awkwardness that makes it almost impervious to modern political scientists. This is at least suggested by David Easton, who attempted to probe its scientific usage and found it in such disarray that he recommended that it be scrapped in the interest of "clarity of expression." "There is little hope," Easton explained, "that out of this welter of differences anyone today can hammer out a meaning upon which the majority of men will genuinely, consistently, and constantly agree." With his formulation of an imperial, if not millennial, criterion for political reason—reflecting, as it were, a claim to science in the tradition of the Hegelian state beneath its obvious plebiscitarian trappings—Easton proposed that modern political science abandon the concept of the state altogether. The reason was, not that the concept was barren, but rather that it was historically suffocating, loaded with vast "confusion and variety of meanings," a quagmire of twenty-five hundred years of "forbidding disagreement," and therefore without hope for the achievement of "uniformity."[4] Judging from the actual writings of political scientists since World War II, Easton seems to express a

---

[4] *Political System*, pp. 107–108.

professional consensus regarding the usefulness of the idea of "the state," notwithstanding its most recent revival both in the guise of "the national interest" and in radical political theory.

It is not surprising, therefore, that Wilson's book has mostly been left to historians. Historians have treated *The State* in the course of biographical accounts of Wilson. Their comments approach the book with hesitation, not least because parts of it can be described as "rather thinly veiled plagiarism" due to Wilson's heavy reliance on German sources for his report on continental European administration.[5] This charge is not without foundation. Wilson acknowledged his use of Heinrich Marquardsen's multivolume edition of *Handbuch des Oeffentlichen Rechts der Gegenwart*, and it is clear that major parts of *The State* do not reflect either Wilson's own inspiration or his own formulation.[6] The fact of Wilson's plagiarism itself, however, may not be without some meaning. It is his recognition of the failure of his project, his acknowledgment of the exhaustion of his imagination.

In addition, historians have characterized the writing of *The State* as obscure, the content as unsynthesized, and its ideas as tainted with Social Darwinism. They have called attention to Wilson's compartmentalization of the relationship between religion and politics, and have suggested that this split is a reflection of a need to "preserve the emotional stability and security which his faith provided him."[7] Other authors point out that on the one hand, the book takes a conservative view, emphasized by references to Edmund Burke and Herbert Spencer and underscored by a celebration of the "organic" processes of society. In this it seems to favor limited government. On the other hand, the book advocates government intervention to protect the labor market and regulate the conditions of competition, and thus seems to propose a progressive course of action. "In detail and in particular cases," as William Diamond summed up the matter, Wilson was "frequently unembarrassedly inconsistent."[8]

These strictures reveal that *The State* has been reviewed in somewhat the same way as a present-day textbook. Although the appraisals are not without substance, they fall somewhat short of an interpretation. It has been difficult to determine what kind of questions the book tried to deal with, and its place in Wilson's scholarship is uncertain, although the work clearly established Wilson's academic reputation. *The State* was, by and

---

[5] Mulder, *Woodrow Wilson*, p. 103.

[6] "Editorial Note: Wilson's 'The State,' " *PWW*, vi, 244–52. The four volumes that Wilson relied on were published in Freiburg and Tübingen between 1883 and 1887.

[7] Mulder, *Woodrow Wilson*, pp. 103–107; Bragdon, *Woodrow Wilson*, pp. 174–78.

[8] Diamond, *Economic Thought of Woodrow Wilson*, pp. 56–57; see also Link, *Wilson: The Road to the White House*, pp. 21–22.

large, well received by contemporary critics, who stressed that whatever its shortcomings, it was the first of its kind in presenting an historical and comparative method for understanding the state.[9] It came out in several revised editions and was translated into Japanese, French, and Spanish. With a remarkable sense of timing, the book was translated back into German in 1913.

The difficulties in approaching the book are real enough. It purports to describe an organic coherence in the development of political institutions, yet the writing is cut up into no less than 1,287 bits and pieces of detail. The arrangement of headings, subheadings, sub-subheadings, and so on often seems arbitrary and in any case is left unexplained. The comparative design extends little beyond the stuffing of minute descriptions of administrative organization in different countries into a single volume. Most of the seven hundred pages were composed in the course of only one summer.[10] Although Wilson drew up plans for the work in the spring of 1886, he did not begin its actual composition until June 1888. By November he was able to send chapters to his friends for review.[11] Evidently he used his lecture notes for most of the chapters.[12] A certain loathing of the work seems to have overcome him at the end. Having finished the last revisions in March 1889, he wrote his wife that he hoped soon to be free of "this tedious burden—this text-book!" "What a job it has been! I am thoroughly tired of it and disgusted with it. I hope nothing with reference to it now except that it may some day be off my mind. Catch me undertaking another fact book! Hereafter . . . I mean to be an *author*—never more a book-maker."[13]

THERE are several reasons for reconsidering *The State*, the most important being that the discovery of Wilson's early papers in 1963 uncovered notes, outlines, and drafts of an unpublished paper, "The Modern Democratic State," which indicated that Wilson conceived the scope and general intentions of *The State* almost immediately after he left the Johns Hopkins. While the work has earlier been related to Burke and Spencer, it now seems clear that its Hegelian language, especially the positive con-

---

[9] See, for instance, the reviews by the New York *Nation*, Dec. 26, 1889, reprinted in *PWW*, vi, 458–62; and the review by Edward W. Bemis in the Nashville *Round Table*, i (March 15, 1890), 14–15, reprinted in *ibid.*, pp. 550–52.

[10] "Editorial Note: Wilson's Plan for a Textbook in Civil Government," *ibid.*, v, 147–49; WW to Horace Elisha Scudder, May 12, 1886, *ibid.*, pp. 218–20.

[11] WW to Robert Bridges, Aug. 26, 1888, *ibid.*, pp. 763–64; WW to Munroe Smith, Nov. 12, 1888, *ibid.*, vi, 20–22.

[12] "Editorial Note: Wilson's 'The State,'" *ibid.*, pp. 246–49.

[13] WW to Ellen Axson Wilson, March 9, 1889, *ibid.*, p. 139.

cept of the state, can be related to George Sylvester Morris and his discussion of political society. Wilson's notes from Morris's lectures reveal that Morris organized his course as an explication of mechanistic and organic concepts of political affairs, contrasting the ideas of Hobbes and Spencer with those of Aristotle and Hegel. The state itself, Morris argued, was located in the consciousness of man, and Morris's formulation aimed at a reconciliation of the contradictions that Spencer claimed existed between man and the state, between particularity and universality, and between community and authority. Wilson's reading of Elisha Mulford's *The Nation* added a national dimension to the theme of state unity.[14]

Second, the view of Wilson's study of political economy as a mere gloss on Adam Smith, Bright, and Cobden can no longer be sustained. Although Wilson was introduced neither to the mathematical analysis of economics nor to the marginal revolution in economics, he was conversant with the most advanced proponents of the historical school in America and absorbed its leanings toward national markets, social science, and statistical measurement as the basis of administration. Perhaps even more consequential were the explicit doctrines of the historical school in America concerning the social interdependence of modern society, which Wilson combined with a teleological conception of historical progress. In his own lectures on the history of political economy, Wilson defined the field as a branch of modern sociology.[15]

Third, the kind of innocent belief in scientific reason and industrial progress that is often associated with early progressive attitudes should be modified. Wilson's first lectures at Bryn Mawr, prepared as the introduction to a two-year course in history and political science, were based on a close rereading of Bagehot's *Physics and Politics*. This work contains a dual argument about the meaning of discussion in modern society. On the one hand, Bagehot asserted, discussion frees politics from the yoke of custom and sets in motion the forces of science, progress, and action based upon reason. On the other hand, discussion is a consequence of the crowded conditions of modern life, in which the real problems are "excessive energy," "the overactivity of man," his tendency to multiply beyond what reason might suggest, and the development of "desire far

[14] "Philosophy of the State," filed Oct. 8, 1884–Jan. 28, 1885, Woodrow Wilson Collection, Firestone Library. See also George Sylvester Morris, *Hegel's Philosophy of the State and of History: An Exposition* (Chicago, 1886), and Elisha Mulford, *The Nation* (New York, 1875); WW to Horace Elisha Scudder, May 12, 1886, *PWW*, v, 219.

[15] Classroom lecture notes, "On the History of Political Economy," filed Oct. 3–19, 1887, and "On the History of Political Thought," filed Feb. 1, 1888, Woodrow Wilson Collection, Firestone Library.

in excess" of what was needed—with a "felt want" much greater than the "real want."[16]

Thus, Bagehot wrote, modern society is endangered by its own success and is threatened with a return to earlier stages of civilization, which would bring back the "secret and suppressed side of human nature" hitherto restrained by "fixed custom." Groping for an agency that could be entrusted to sustain civilization, Bagehot concluded that public discussion takes the form of an instrument of social control, a "union of spur and bridle." This, Bagehot concluded, accounts for the commercial and political success of the Englishman, who has "plenty of energy" but still does not go "too far."[17] As Wilson summed up this argument, discussion turns "the old vigour of the race, which once went to produce eager, restless, oftentimes rash action, into channels of clear creative thought." The result is to produce "that 'animated moderation' in action which the uncivilized man knows nothing of, but which is the perfect flower of social growth."[18]

About a month after writing his summary of Bagehot, Wilson seems to have entered a period of high intellectual productivity, as is indicated by a considerable number of outlines and notes from this period. In early December 1885 he was already able to send his father 121 typewritten pages of "The Modern Democratic State" for comment.[19] The essay was never published, and Wilson realized that his project was much too large in scope for an essay. His father wrote back, commenting that he had trouble seeing what the discussion was all about.[20] Wilson included significant parts of this essay, however, in the opening and concluding chapters of *The State*, he revised other parts and incorporated them into the article "Character of Democracy in the United States," published in 1889, and he included still other parts in his 1887 article of "The Study of Administration."[21]

[16] 1st edn. (1867; reprint, New York, 1948), pp. 191–203; see also Barker, *Political Thought in England*, pp. 151–53.

[17] Bagehot, *Physics and Politics*, pp. 159, 207.

[18] Notes for four lectures on the study of history, Sept. 24, 1885, *PWW*, v, 18–23.

[19] "Editorial Note: Wilson's First Treatise on Democratic Government," *ibid.*, p. 56, printed in *ibid.*, pp. 61–92.

[20] Joseph Ruggles Wilson to WW, Dec. 12, 1885, *ibid.*, pp. 92–93; WW to Robert Bridges, Dec. 20, 1885, *ibid.*, pp. 95–96: "The writing I have been doing has not yet taken definite enough shape to be described. I am feeling after the real conditions which make popular institutions workable, and the most practicable means whereby they can be made and kept healthy and vigorous. If I have 'bottom,' I'll come out all right: if not, I'll decline upon something of more modest dimensions. . . . It will take more definite, describable shape after a while."

[21] Published first in the *Atlantic Monthly*, Nov. 1889, and reprinted in *An Old Master and*

In brief, "The Modern Democratic State" argues that modern democracy cannot be understood as a form of government within the classical typology of government by the one, by the few, and by the many. Instead it is government "by the whole," constituted by the appearance of an informed and responsible public opinion that breathes life into the national corpus and unifies the few who govern and the many who participate in public discussion. Thus modern democracy appears to have outgrown the dangers of the instability and lawlessness that beset the classical republics. It represents a stage of development distinguished by the evolution of the individual and the state through historical growth toward national unity. This unity is signified by the development of communication on a national scale, as indicated by the appearance of a national market and a national press.[22] *The State* defines modern democracy as a system of administration constrained by public opinion and executed by a unified government within an historical typology that applies to Western government from the earliest times. Wilson found here a stable set of administrative functions irrespective of constitutional forms. As he notes in the preface: "The wide correspondences of organization and method in government,—a unity in structure and procedure much greater than the uninitiated student of institutions is at all prepared to find—will appear, to the upsetting of many pet theories as to the special excellencies of some one government."[23] Compared to Wilson's earlier studies, the question was no longer what kind of practices would befit a constitutional state but rather what sort of arrangements were required in the interest of stable administration.

But a summary of this kind fails to come to grips with the radical changes in Wilson's vocabulary, which contains an abundance of phrases like "the ultimate residence of sovereignty," "the intimate nature of the state," "politics as a whole," and "the organic conception of state life." These words turn upon meanings and abstractions that are barely comprehensible today, unless the modern ideas of "economic development" and "social welfare" are seen to contain residues of the organic conception of the state. The difficulties are compounded by Wilson's claim to be dealing with the roots of American political life while at the same time introducing a vocabulary that had no place in the traditional language of American politics.

Before attempting to throw light upon the language of the organic

---

Other Political Essays (New York, 1893), a preliminary draft of "Character of Democracy in the United States" is included as an address, "Nature of Democracy in the United States," May 10–16, 1889, in *PWW*, vi, 221–39. "The Study of Administration" was first published in the *Political Science Quarterly*, ii (July 1887), 197–222, and is reprinted in *PWW*, v, 359–80.

[22] *PWW*, v, 61–92.

[23] *The State*, p. xxxv.

state, it may be useful to consider an example that shows why Wilson found it difficult to express himself within the established vocabulary. The notes that preceded "The Modern Democratic State" included the assertion, "It is indicative of the steadiness of our habit (the naturalness with wh. the expedient seems with us to be the constitutional) that we can break constitutions without either destroying or losing respect for them."[24] This seems to boil down to the observation that the American political habit is to break habits, if it is assumed that the term "constitutions" here stands for political procedures and behavior established over time. While it may seem like a paradox, it implies something more serious. It is, in effect, an attempt to categorize a concept in terms of its reverse, a move that, if successful, is apt to weaken the meaning of the original concept. Wilson's reference to the preservation of old constitutions points to his problem. Political society under neither the Articles of Confederation nor the Confederate States of America seems to have been afforded much respect, certainly not by Wilson himself. To "break" something without "destroying" it is an act that made no sense within conventional American liberalism, with its presumption about a fixed constitution based on consent. Wilson's remark presupposed a Hegelian historical dialectic, according to which the past is not broken but absorbed and diffused in the present. Beneath the formulation one senses Wilson's difficulties in adapting his vocabulary to the new mode of political reason.

In the very first paragraph of "The Modern Democratic State," Wilson moved toward the claim that democracy was losing its right to represent a higher form of political morality. It had lost "its early ideality." It had not proved to be "a universal deliverance" as promised by its "fathers." "Instead of political salvation, the world has extracted from Democracy nothing greater than much instructive and helpful political experience. . . . It is now plain to everyone that its inspiration is of man, and not of God."[25] In contrast to ancient democracy, which had been "a sleeping volcano," modern democracy is less dangerous and more dull. Its essence was "the *commonness* of govt.—its entire openness to criticism by all, and its possible conduct by all,—the absence of distance, exclusiveness, or mystery about it. No hallowed sanctity about it." It deserves notice that Wilson's criticism of the constitutional level of democratic government was preceded by the recognition of democratic vigor at the popular level.

Erroneous as it is to represent government as only a sort of commonplace business, little elevated above merchandizing, and to be regulated by counting house rules, the favour easily won for such a

[24] Memoranda for "The Modern Democratic State," *PWW*, v, 59.
[25] Preliminary Draft of "The Modern Democratic State," *ibid.*, p. 61.

view nowadays is very significant. It means self-reliance in govt. It gives voice to the eminently modern democratic feeling that govt. is no hidden cult, but a common everyday concern of life, even if the biggest such common concern.[26]

The gap between democratic "ideality" and democratic practice offered distinct possibilities for a new mode of political thought, and Wilson expressed these possibilities as a warning and an opportunity. Wilson's perception that democracy was trivializing political life was emphasized by his caution about attempting a political revitalization by theoretical means. Indeed, the idea of "the modern democratic state" and its attending science was born with a distinct antitheoretical bias. To achieve the combination of "order with progress," Wilson wrote, it is necessary to cultivate a certain "aversion from treating principles of government as open questions." The new science should be without "any taint of *a priori* weakness." It should not run the "risk of shaking effective political purposes by questioning too curiously the conceptions underlying them, or by exposing too bluntly the whole fact of our experience in putting political principles into practice."[27] The suppression of the traditional theoretical mode of inquiry proceeded along with Wilson's recommendation of a new set of assumptions that were intended to turn political theory into a mode of governance. Criticizing the "false tendency of reaction against authority," Wilson suggested in his notes that an individual conception of "state life" should be contrasted to an organic conception:

(1) Organic conception: Written constitutions &c. have held us away from this conception and kept us to a mere *formal* idea of state existence. Would the nation not still exist if the Const. and the rest were suddenly swept away?

(2) If organic, personal: if personal, must have means of self-expression through personality (thr. persons of trusted leaders) and abolish forever *impersonal* action, aggregate legislation, subdivided responsibility, &c—*atomistic action.*[28]

These passages may exemplify some of the changes in vocabulary that resulted as Wilson replaced more traditional liberal ideas with the language of organic nationalism. "Nation" and "personality" were associated with action, authority, and the kind of self-expression that Wilson saw as the principle of power in the political leader, whose "thought may be

[26] *Ibid.*, pp. 78–79.
[27] *Ibid.*, p. 64.
[28] Memoranda for "The Modern Democratic State," *ibid.*, pp. 60–61.

individual" but whose substance was "of the common counsel." Interesting also is the close connection between "nation" and "personality," which seems to imply that the movement toward nationhood was at the same time a movement toward a social or political psychology. Wilson invested "personality," in contrast to the "individual," with common mental traits. At the bottom of Wilson's idea of the state there seems to have been a metaphysical base, a myth of the powers that shape identity and form political relations "as naturally, as much without deliberate choice, as is the family." These ideas appear to have been the starting point for Wilson's new conception, which eventually resulted in the writing of *The State*. "The ties of kin and the dependence of youth constitute the amalgam and object of the family; the state founds itself upon the instinctive associations of maturity," Wilson wrote as the stipulated definition of "the democratic state."[29]

Some of these ideas had been anticipated in the historical perspective that Wilson added to "Government by Debate" when he rewrote it as *Congressional Government* and added, rather than developed, an imagery of a complex union of states slowly growing toward national unity.[30] When he left the Johns Hopkins, this vision returned, and the project of *The State* may well be dated from his realization of a need to work out in depth the new political universe that the different influences at the university had inspired.[31]

Wilson began his move toward the idea of a historical evolution of political life with the intention of clearing the ground of some of the conventional institutions, particularly the United States Constitution itself, which had earlier claimed his primary attention. In retrospect, it is at least an interesting paradox that the first casualty of the historical interpretation was the Constitution as an historic monument. Yet Wilson's "historical criticism" was quite explicit on this point. He turned against the principle of "constitutional arrangements" as a static and immobilizing notion because it stood for "deadness in the absence of any exercise of an external creative will." He criticized the fiction that had seen the Constitution as a "final" creation, and he went on, "our fundamental laws were, so to say, put in the *mortmain*. Our national life has been made to seem the manufacture of lawyers."[32] The Constitution itself was not enough to sustain the life of a democratic polity; it was "formal," too

---

[29] "The Modern Democratic State," *ibid.*, p. 77. WW to Robert Bridges, Dec. 20, 1885, *ibid.*, p. 96: "For the last few days I've been engaged upon the thesis, that democracy is the highest and most essentially *adult* state."

[30] See, for instance, *Congressional Government, ibid.*, IV, 29–30.

[31] "Editorial Note: Wilson's First Treatise on Democratic Government," *ibid.*, V, 55.

[32] "The Modern Democratic State," *ibid.*, p. 68.

open to conflicting interpretations, had yielded its authority as the final arbiter in the Civil War, and could not be counted on to hold up against the future. As Wilson warned, "if a democratic polity based on individual initiative prove a failure," people might "be tempted to grope on, in the doubtful light of Socialism, towards a democratic polity based on communal initiative."[33]

Wilson pointed to the risks involved in regarding a written document as the ultimate arbiter in political matters. The Constitution, he said, was the "mere ligaments of law," "the artificial structure resting upon contract only," "the frail thong of contract." "Is the Constitution the only actual bond which keeps us from falling apart into atoms?" he asked. Behind his question was the larger problem of how democratic government could be practiced, not by communities, but by nations. This problem was loaded with the old charge against democracy—recently restated by Sir Henry Maine—that it is inherently unstable, inefficient, and subject to the threat of class rule, all of which is summed up in Wilson's brief but recurring references to "Ochlocracy" and to "the colossal crowd composed of 'all-of-us.' "[34] Wilson's intention was not only to combat potential industrial anarchy but also to contain the revolutionary forces that had asserted themselves during the Civil War and Reconstruction. The key to Wilson's concept of nationality is his attempt to redefine the conditions of social cohesion in order to reinstate the primacy of political authority.

Wilson's response to this challenge contained two elements. First, he suggested a substantive concept that would promote a sense of ideality and authority that traditional political theory had been unable to preserve. The idea of nationality had many of the redeeming features that constitutional and liberal theory lacked: "There is a law greater . . . which makes the Constitution possible, without which the Constitution would be but a dead letter; a law which is the supreme rule of the national life. This is that law written on our hearts which makes us conscious of our oneness as a single personality in the great company of nations." The "real foundations of political life in the United States" were to be "found elsewhere than in our constitutions," which were "but the formal symbol of a deep reality of national character." "Justly revered as our great Constitution is, it could be stripped off and thrown aside like a garment, and

[33] *Ibid.*, p. 62; see also *The State*, pp. 659–60.

[34] "The Modern Democratic State," *PWW*, v, 69, 68, 76. Henry Sumner Maine, *Popular Government* (New York, 1886). In a letter to Horace Elisha Scudder of May 12, 1886, Wilson said that his object in *The State* was "to answer Sir Henry Maine" by "aiming to reckon with all the actual forces of thought and machinery in modern popular government . . . and to do for such political facts something better than I did for the existing facts of our constitutional system in 'Congressional Government.' " *PWW*, v, 218.

the nation would still stand forth clothed in the living vestment of flesh and sinew, warm with the heartblood of one people, ready to recreate constitutions and laws."[35]

The terms Wilson chose for the representation of nationality were partly drawn from religious mystique. Despite Wilson's claim to be giving a historical account of the state, the birth of nationality had obvious religious connotations. It was therefore not without a flavor of myth, an "imaginative and sympathetic conception," as Wilson later called it.[36] Expressions such as "the law written on our heart," the "heartblood," the "single personality," and the "living vestment of flesh and sinew" had reference to religious practice, especially to eucharistic doctrine.

Second, Wilson hoped to recreate a method to restore and possibly expand the vigor and political strength that prevailed at the popular level of democracy. Traditional political theory had proven to be too mundane and skeptical in dealing with the ultimate sources of authority. But it was also badly suited to practical achievement. On both counts it was of little value for the purpose of governance. "Theoretical philosophy" had already been developed and had proven itself an object not to be trusted by "practical statesmen." But there remained possibilities for a "businesslike philosophy suitable for plain men which as yet awaits creation." "It should be considered the business of English political investigation to supply elements of thought which will also be elements of reform and so of progress," Wilson wrote. The new political science should be characterized, not by "scientific aloofness, but *practical interiorness* of view." This method should be "historical, comparative,—the method of fact." "Democracy owes it to itself to be scientific,—not, however, for speculative but for practical purposes," Wilson continued. "It is itself the result of history, not of theory, a creation of experience rather than of speculation; and it ought to be careful to reap the full benefits of history, to know thoroughly the experience of which it is the outcome." Indeed, the very nature of modern democracy meant that government had "ceased to be a matter of speculation, had ceased to be a tenet of philosophy and has become a mere qu[estion]. of fact."[37]

Wilson strikingly pictured the translation of the elevated passions of nationality as "mere" questions of fact and the incorporation of these facts into the system of government in an essay from 1887, "The Author Himself":

[35] "The Modern Democratic State," *ibid.*, p. 69.

[36] Address to the Commercial Club of Chicago, "The Relation of University Education to Commerce," Nov. 29, 1902, *ibid.*, xiv, 239.

[37] "The Modern Democratic State," *ibid.*, v, 64–66.

I presume . . . that our universities are erected entirely for the service of the tractable mind, while the heart's only education must be got from association with its neighbour heart, and in the ordinary courses of the world. Life is its only university. Mind is monarch, whose laws claim supremacy in those lands which boast the movements of civilization, and he must command all the instrumentalities of education.

At least such is the theory of the constitution of the modern world. It is to be suspected that, as a matter [of] fact, mind is one of those modern monarchs who reigns but does not govern. That old House of Commons, that popular chamber, in which the passions, the prejudices, the inborn, unthinking affections long ago repudiated by mind have their full representation, controls much the greater part of the actual conduct of affairs.

To come out of my figure, reasoned thought is, though perhaps the presiding, not yet the regnant force of the world. In life and in literature it is subordinate. The future may belong to it; but the present and past do not. Faith and virtue do not wear its livery; friendship, loyalty, patriotism do not derive their motives from it. It does not furnish the material for those masses of habit, of unquestioned tradition, and of treasured belief which are the ballast of every steady ship of state, enabling it to spread its sails safely to the breezes of progress, and even to stand before the storms of revolution.[38]

As this passage makes clear, it was not Wilson's intention to construct a concept of nationality that embraced a theology of state reason.[39] His aim was to explore the vast resources of social sentiment that had been stored in the popular consciousness over the course of the development of political civilization. The new form of theory was to abandon its inherited rationalist bias and concentrate upon the social energies and the psychological needs of the population. The new science was to commit itself to the analysis of the virtues of social order and coherence, the faith, friendship, loyalty, and patriotism that were essential ingredients if society was to be protected from the repercussions of its recent history and its present changes. The study of nationality was to consolidate the advances of the age by acting as the guardian of social cohesion. In a for-

[38] Dec. 7, 1887, *ibid.*, pp. 635–45; the quotation appears on pp. 643–44.

[39] *The State*, p. 13. Furthermore, Memoranda for "The Modern Democratic State," *PWW*, v, 59: "God is not the head of state; but he is the Lord of the individual and the individual cannot be moral who is immoral in *public* conduct." See also the exhaustive discussion in Mulder, *Woodrow Wilson*, pp. 99, 114–16, 269–77; and Weinstein, *Woodrow Wilson*, pp. 21–22.

mulation that could hardly be improved by a century of political sociology, Wilson phrased the axiom that political authority is located in social emotions, not in political reason. "Thought presides," Wilson wrote, "but sentiment has executive powers, and the *motive* functions belong to feeling."[40]

The reconstruction of authority should start in the political unconscious, the "unthinking affection" of the popular mind. Wilson wanted a science, not a theology, to deal with the irrational features of social solidarity. The religious mystique of the state, the allusions to the consummation of the flesh and to the communion of the blood, may be approached as Wilson's acknowledgment that the popular perception of authority had profound religious dimensions. *The State*, however, was distinguished by the choice of an alternative mystique. Wilson attempted primarily to develop the unity of the state from imaginative sources that depended upon the living experience and the rituals of marriage and family. Such language would also seem to accommodate notions of biologically transmitted predispositions, a tenet in some of Bagehot's writings. More important, however, were the connotations of care, trust, and mutual dependence inherent in the notion of the family, which suggested that the national state contained vital bonds of belonging buried in its superior form of power and in its historical laws of development. The family offered itself as a useful analogy with which to describe and explain political institutions. Just as Wilson had earlier walked through the doors of Congress to visualize political practice in its concrete setting, his work on the state used the doors of the self and family to imagine the development of national life.

Wilson's explication of the state as derived from the family took three basic forms. First, he outlined a genetic explanation of the origins of the state. Second, he used the family as an analogy or model with which to point out certain interconnections between members and function. Third, he used the family as a metaphor with which to suggest emotional bonds of loyalty and affection between the citizen and the state, an association greater than the sum of its members.

The question of the origins of government and the state, Wilson emphasized, could now be settled "not by conjecture, but by history."[41] Re-

[40] "The Author Himself," *PWW*, v, 644.

[41] *The State*, p. 1. In a report, probably prepared for one of Herbert Baxter Adams's courses, Wilson had discussed the origins of the family on the basis of recent literature. The best clue as to the origins of family authority, he said, was to be found among southern Slavonian families, who had been able to preserve original "family forms" and whose institutions reminded Wilson "of those hardy habits of local self-government which our Anglo-Saxon forefathers kept alive." These families dwelled together in groups of near kin,

ferring to various works of anthropological, legal, and historical scholarship, he stated that "the original bond of union and the original sanction for magisterial authority were one and the same thing, namely, real or feigned blood relationship." "Families were the primitive states. The original State was a Family. Historically the State of to-day may be regarded as in an important sense only an enlarged Family: 'State' is 'Family' writ large."[42] The earliest government was not dependent upon physical boundaries or upon possession of a particular land, Wilson claimed with critical reference to Johann Bluntschli.

> The original governments were knit together by bonds closer than those of geography, more real than the bonds of mere continguity. They were bound together by real or assumed kinship. They had a corporate existence which they regarded as inhering in their blood and as expressed in all their daily relations with each other. They lived together because of these relations; they were not related because they lived together.[43]

With this sketch of his argument, Wilson was close to giving away his thesis. Kinship was supposed to express bonds of domination that were more "real" than the relations to the land from which the group drew its sustenance. At the same time, Wilson conceded that blood relations were either "real" or "feigned" or "assumed," which is to say that kinship was a way to express a relationship of bonding and domination. But kinship was neither the cause of this relationship nor the relationship itself. Similarly, Wilson's idea that people lived together because they had "daily relations with each other" seems a fallacy, if not of putting the cart before the horse, then of putting the cart before the cart. But the logical problems created by a naturalistic conception of the origins of government and by an appeal to such "revealed facts" as Wilson considered in consonance with empirical inquiry, rather than by appeal to religion or to reason, are less interesting than their consequences. The thrust of his argument was that political order was inherent in the nature of social relationships, and from there it became the foundation of government as well as the constitution of the individual. "Government came, so to say, before the individual. There was, consequently, no place for contract."[44]

With this formulation, Wilson completed rather than rejected the

---

"House-communities," which were ruled by the eldest or wisest male who had been chosen with "an element of election." "Some Words upon An Essay on the Early History of the Family," Nov. 9, 1884, *ibid.*, xii, 480–85.

[42] *The State*, p. 3.

[43] *Ibid.*, p. 9.

[44] *Ibid.*, p. 13.

mode of thinking about the political order first given its theoretical expression by John Locke. Whereas the traditional model of society was understood as an expression of order imparted by the political center, Locke instituted an understanding in which social relationships, placed before the social contract and legitimizing political order, were seen to carry the superior authority.[45] Wilson's explicit rejection of Locke (and also of Hooker, Hobbes, and Rousseau) was largely an attempt to undercut the element of "human choice" that had been appended to Locke's theory by its association with the American Revolution and Thomas Paine, and that was carried through the nineteenth century by revolutionary liberalism.[46] Wilson sought an understanding that portrayed government as an extension of the family and as its organic expression in society. The price that he paid was that the blood infused into the state made government institutions appear to be somewhat anemic, an impression that Wilson admitted by describing administrative arrangements in terms of mechanics and utility, a weak complement to such powerful precedents as "the reign of custom" and "the bonds of religion."[47] It was no longer "order" that required an explanation, it was the occurrence of "disorder," which had pushed Western man into a state of change. Whereas the majority of mankind had preserved itself against change, "with a favored minority of the race it was broken by war, altered by imperative circumstance, modified by imitation, and infringed by individual initiative."[48]

Although the concatenation between the family and the state was not Wilson's invention, he gave it an emphasis with original features. Wilson's concept of family had little affiliation with Hegelian *Sittlichkeit*, with its stress on the obligations, fortunes, and property of the family. While Wilson retained the transcendental mysticism of German theories of the nation and referred to Bluntschli's definition of the state as "der Mann," he replaced the emphasis on paternal authority and power with an idea of "maturity," which had a certain democratic note to it. The stress on common language and the sense of unity and self-sufficiency in German theories of the nation was replaced by an idea of mutual adaptation. Wilson's family was defined by its daily relations and sustained by its "ties of family affection."[49] Since it was pictured without landed property, it escaped the

[45] Wolin, *Politics and Vision*, p. 308.

[46] *The State*, pp. 13–15; Wolin, *Politics and Vision*, pp. 293–94.

[47] *The State*, pp. 19–20.

[48] *Ibid.*, p. 29.

[49] *Ibid.*, p. 666. Bluntschli's definition is mentioned in "The Study of Administration" but not in *The State*. See William A. Dunning, *A History of Political Theories: From Rousseau to Spencer* (New York, 1920), pp. 307–11, for an assessment of Bluntschli's influence in the United

more ferocious side of patriarchy, in which social status and even physical survival were dependent upon the father. The family was founded upon "custom and tradition," which bound the father "no less than his subjects," since "he was governed scarcely less than they were." Wilson found open coercion to be basically of a psychological nature: the "mere domineering strength of will." What remained of paternal despotism was directed against the emotional and intellectual independence of the individual members, as is apparent from Wilson's comparison of the absolutism of the family to the " 'tyranny of one's next door neighbor' against which there are now and again found men bold enough to rebel," or to "that tyranny of social convention which men of independent or erratic impulse nowadays find so irksome."[50] Wilson saw the family as a flexible structure governed by habits and a spirit of mutual accommodation.

The homely description of political power within the family made the transition to a political state less dramatic. Wilson pictured the transition that occurred when "the headship of this vast and complex family ceased to be natural and became political" in a low key, as a matter of a simplification of authority in response to outside pressure. The impulse was the need for more effective warfare, a strengthening of the "primitive organization" that took place when "a distinct element of choice" entered the family and "the oldest male of the hitherto reigning family was no longer chosen as a matter of course" but was superseded by "the wisest and the bravest." "It was even open to . . . go upon occasion altogether outside this succession and choose a leader of force and resource from some other family." Wilson's stress on the continuity of power relationships and on the imperceptibility of historical change is underscored by his account of the American Revolution. As he noted in "The Modern Democratic State," "there was nothing revolutionary" about the transition to independence; democracy in America did not need to "overthrow other

States; Merriam, *History of the Theory of Sovereignty*, pp. 99–103; and Francis W. Coker, *Organismic Theories of the State: Nineteenth Century Interpretations of the State as Organism or as Person*, Studies in History, Economics and Public Law, xxxviii, No. 2 (New York, 1910), pp. 104–114.

[50] *The State*, pp. 595, 20. Although Wilson presented the idea of the family in secular terms, undoubtedly an important source was the Puritan image of the family as a metaphor for the state. See Strout, *New Heavens*, p. 64. The two institutions were unified by the need for methodical discipline, clear authority, and close organization. But at the time of Wilson's appointment as a professor, Francis L. Patton, the president of Princeton College, wrote him privately and criticized *The State* for its tendency "to minimise the supernatural," to give little place to "Divine Providence," and to be "silent with respect to the forming & reforming influences of Christianity." Feb. 18, 1890, *PWW*, vi, 526–27.

polities: it had only to organize itself." "It did not need to spread propaganda: it needed nothing but to methodize its ways of living."[51]

The invocation of a political man, whose "social function" was "as normal with him as his individual function" and who had "not been without politics, without political association" since the formation of the family, led Wilson to see society as the real foundation of government. "The public order is preserved because order inheres in the character of society." From this perspective, the idea of consent and voluntary compliance were largely beside the point. "Our own approval of the government under which we live," Wilson wrote, "though doubtless conscious and in a way voluntary, is largely hereditary—is largely an inbred and inculcated approbation. There is a large amount of mere *drift* in it."[52]

Society expresses its "common will" in "public opinion," according to Wilson. He seems to have perceived a parallel between the way in which the family grooms the child and the way in which public opinion matured through the ages. Public opinion in the classical world was an expression of an infant stage, in which the corporate being wholly absorbed the individual. During the Middle Ages certain classes rose to "maturity." During the modern age, the people as a whole reached its maturity: "By using their minds, the people gradually put away the childish things of their days of ignorance, and began to claim a part in affairs. Finally, systematized popular education has completed the story. Nations are growing up into manhood. Peoples are becoming old enough to govern themselves." Just as the family implanted both restraints and potential rebellion in the individual, the system of public opinion produced both compliance and the opportunity for dissent. "We are like primitive men in the public opinion which preserves, though unlike them in the public opinion which alters our institutions. Their stationary common thought contained the generic forces of government no less than does our own progressive thought."[53]

The progressive character of public opinion, Wilson explained, is a consequence of certain modern processes. Modern forms of information dispelled local rumor and established themselves as a national system. Local education was basically self-enclosed, Wilson argued. It was "a system rather in idea than in compactness of organization. Each little group learns by itself." Unless "more powerful influences" were at work, such education "would take and retain a distinct local colour, and would be narrowed and minimized by a petty, purblind local application." The

[51] *The State*, p. 28; "The Modern Democratic State," *PWW*, v, 67.

[52] *The State*, pp. 597, 598.

[53] See also *The State*, pp. 608, 597. Memoranda for "The Modern Democratic State," *PWW*, v, 59.

more important development was, therefore, the communication by newspaper: "Looked at in the large, the newspaper press will be seen to be a type of democracy, bringing all men without distinction under comment made by any man without distinction; every topic reduced to a common standard of news; everything noted and argued about by everybody." The press therefore has a vital national function: "It makes men conscious of the existence and interests of affairs lying outside of the dull round of their own daily lives. It gives them a nation, instead of a neighbourhood, to look upon and think about."[54] The value that Wilson had previously placed in parliamentary discussion was now relocated in the social sphere of the modern democratic state. Political deliberation was diffused and absorbed in various social institutions. This was a preliminary to securing ample room and a broad scope for administrative government at the center of the nation.

Wilson's idea of the integrative force of a national system of public opinion explained the development of the American government. It was "the blood" of the nation, expressing the drift of local sentiment into "the national idea." While Wilson in "The Modern Democratic State" stressed such influences as the press, travel, commerce, and "innumerable agencies which nowadays send knowledge and thought in quick pulsations through every part of the body," in *The State* he expanded the idea in two chapters, "Railroads, Expansion, and War aid the National Idea" and "Civil War completes the Union." In discussing the Civil War, Wilson concluded,

> The great effect of the war was, that the nation was made homogeneous. There was no longer any permanent reason why the South should not become like the rest of the country in character and sentiment. Both sections were brought to the same modes of life and thought; there was no longer any obstacle to our being in reality one great nation. The effort made in the war, moreover, to preserve the Union, and the result of the war in making the country at last homogeneous throughout, has made the federal government, as representative of the nation, seem greater in our eyes than ever before, and has permanently modified in the profoundest manner the way in which all the old questions concerning constitutionality and state rights are regarded.[55]

What seemed like an historical observation in fact had a deeper meaning for Wilson. It meant that the Constitution as the central political ref-

[54] "The Modern Democratic State," *PWW*, v, 72–73.
[55] *The State*, p. 480.

erent in the United States had to be replaced by another and more profound object of inquiry—the country's "character and sentiment" and "its modes of life and thought." Public opinion was a carrier of some of the vestiges of political participation:

> [It is] not a single audience within sound of the orator's voice; but a thousand audiences. Their actions do not spring from a single thrill of feeling, but from slow conclusions following upon much talk. The talk must slowly percolate through the whole mass. It cannot be sent through them like the pulse which answers the call of a trumpet. A score of platforms in every neighbourhood must ring with the insistent voice of controversies; and, for a few hundreds who hear what is said by public speakers, many thousands must read of the matter in the newspapers, discuss it interjectionally at the breakfast table, desultorily in the streetcars, laconically on the street, dogmatically at dinner. Through so many stages of consideration passion cannot possibly hold out. It gets chilled by overexposure.[56]

The filtering from top to bottom, from podium to dinner table, was not an accidental feature in Wilson's understanding. It signified that the system of public opinion restrained democracy at the same time that it made democracy possible. National public opinion formed a filter that shielded the political organs of the state. Since common opinion was highly unstable and without any determinate or authoritative means of expression, it was to be counterbalanced by "a new machine of government—a machine which may have *thought* for one of its motive powers, by having officers through whose interests in the public thought, and capacity for catching it, is to be controlled."[57] In effect, the "infinite variety of thought and impulse," which makes up "the national whole," had transformed democracy into the most stable kind of society, because "thoughts which in one quarter kindle enthusiasm will in another arouse antagonism. Events which are fuel to the passions of one section will be but as a passing wind to the minds of another section."[58] Its very pervasiveness rendered public opinion harmless. The multiplicity of information tended to create a kind of anxiety, a restlessness of the reading mind, when it was exposed to many sorts of news items and opinions without any immediate relation to the individual reader. The influences of the press, Wilson observed,

[56] "The Modern Democratic State," *PWW*, v, 83–84.

[57] "Notes on Administration," *ibid.*, p. 49.

[58] "The Modern Democratic State," *ibid.*, p. 82; "Nature of Democracy in the United States," *ibid.*, vi, 226.

may only confuse and paralyze [the] mind with their myriad stinging lashes of excitement. ... They overwhelm [the individual] with impressions, but do they give stalwartness to his manhood; do they make his hand steadier on the plow, or his purpose any clearer with reference to the duties of the moment? ... Is he better able to see because they give him countless things to look at? ... Activity of mind is not strength of mind. It may show itself in a mere dumbshow; it may run into jigs as well as into strenuous work at noble tasks.[59]

This understanding of the nature of democratic opinion, with its tendencies toward both excitement and paralysis, directed Wilson's attention to the psychological power of the family and the state. The family molds the individual "in the period of immaturity in the practice of morality and obedience"; the state creates like conditions for "self-directive activity." While family discipline is "variable, selective, formative," the discipline of the state is "invariable, uniform, impersonal." Wilson often said that a person left his minority and reached his majority when he ceased to be a subordinate in the family.[60]

WILSON did not attempt to develop a more systematic psychology of family-man as a political animal of a certain mental economy. A few clues to his understanding of the development of political character may, however, be gleaned from his personal correspondence and from one of his literary essays from the late 1880s. Unfortunately, very few letters from Wilson to his father have been preserved. But one of these, of December 6, 1888, deserves extensive quotation, because it seems to exemplify Wilson's pre-Freudian grasp of the transmittal of authority through family relations:

My precious father,
    My thoughts are full of you and dear "Dode" [Wilson's younger brother] all the time. Tennessee seems *so* far away for a chap as hungry as I am for a sight of the two men whom I love. As the Christmas recess approaches I realize, as I have so often before, the *pain* there is in a season of holiday and rejoicing away from you. As you know, one of the chief things about which I feel most warranted in rejoicing is that I am your son. I realize the benefit of being your son more and more as my talents and experience grow: I recognize the strength growing in me as of the nature of your strength: I become

---

[59] "The Modern Democratic State," *ibid.*, v, 73–74.
[60] *Ibid.*, p. 78; *The State*, p. 666.

more and more conscious of the hereditary wealth I possess, the capital of principle, of literary force and skill, of capacity for first-hand thought; and I feel daily more and more bent toward creating in my own children that combined respect and tender devotion for their father that you gave your children for you. Oh, how happy I should be, if I could make them think of me as I think of you! You have given me a love that grows, that is stronger in me now that I am a man than it was when I was a boy, and which will be stronger in me when I am an old man than it is now—a love, in brief, that is rooted and grounded in *reason*, and not in filial instinct merely—a love resting upon abiding foundations of *service*, recognizing you as in a certain very real sense the author of all I have to be grateful for. I bless God for my noble, strong, and saintly mother and for my incomparable father. . . .

Your devoted son, Woodrow[61]

This letter has long been considered crucial to an understanding of Wilson's psychological development, and two schools of interpretation have emerged. One school, including Alexander and Juliette George, Sigmund Freud, and William Bullitt, and more recently Robert C. Tucker claims that the letter contains a hidden ambivalence that justifies a search for sinister, "subterranean" currents or for "hypertrophied charges of libido" beneath the loving surface.[62] The other school, which also includes both psychoanalysts and historians, denies that the letter indicates any psychological pathology. In this reading the letter simply indicates that Wilson loved his father and wanted to comfort him after the recent death of Jessie Wilson, Woodrow Wilson's mother.[63] Unfortunately, neither of these readings pays any attention to *The State*, which Wilson was putting into its final draft at the time he wrote the letter. Because of the long-standing assumption of a connection between the figure of the father and political authority through the superego, the neglect of *The State* is unfortunate.[64] In addition, these readings so focus

[61] *PWW*, vi, 30–31.

[62] George and George, *Woodrow Wilson and Colonel House*, pp. 10–13; Sigmund Freud and William C. Bullitt, *Thomas Woodrow Wilson: A Psychological Study* (London, 1966), pp. 58–63; Tucker, "The Georges' Wilson Reexamined," pp. 606–18.

[63] Weinstein et al., "Woodrow Wilson and Colonel House: A Reappraisal," pp. 585–98; Weinstein, *Woodrow Wilson*, pp. 104–105.

[64] Alexander George and Juliette George, in *Woodrow Wilson and Colonel House*, present as their main thesis the idea that "underlying Wilson's quest for political power and his manner of exercising it was the compelling need to counter the crushing feeling of inadequacy which had been branded into his spirit as a child." The thesis is argued negatively: "There is not a shred of evidence that [Wilson] ever once openly rebelled against his father's authority" (pp.

on what is presumed to be the function of the letter that the text itself is quoted as a self-explanatory piece of evidence. It is therefore difficult to join the issue in any direct way. For the present purpose, the letter warrants attention for its elucidation of assumptions relating to "character" as a basic element of power expressed in terms of generational relationships. The essence of character as a core of continuous existence transmitted through the family appears to consist of three basic parts: value, time, and self.

Regardless of whether the letter is seen as a show of submission or as a gesture of comfort and compassion, its content reveals emotions that suggest the positive value of the family as an institution in Wilson's consciousness. The letter consists of an inventory of family assets that brings it close to self-love—an earlier generation of Puritans would probably have called it the sins of pride, ambition, and vanity. Wilson presents values as various skills that have developed over time and that have become bearers of family identity. The representation of time as the function of developing skills and talents may be seen more sharply if one notices the virtual absence of any allusions to concrete memories. Longings for the past, if any, are encompassed in the idea that devotion and respect may be planned for and reproduced in the coming generation.

The key to the letter is the recurrence of words that imply distance by the imposition of consciousness. There are no less than fourteen explicit references to thought, realization, and recognition. They occur in every sentence except perhaps for the last, in which God is posed as a mediator. The letter itself does not express emotions as much as it gives an account of a feeling of filial piety. Self-consciousness has replaced such other forms of interpretation that have traditionally claimed a position for an understanding of the family, whether proceeding from values of place, property, or family honor.

In Wilson's letter, the primary function of the family is to transmit the skills that would lead the individual toward self-control and self-development. These forms of "capital," such as capacity for reason, planning, perseverance, and emotional expressivity, figured prominently in the economy of the mid-Victorian soul. They were fitting for the culture of an emerging professional middle class. Compared to the culture of the commercial man, they signify a move from "credit to credentials," in Burton Bledstein's felicitous phrase.[65] In Wilson's writings, the new values

---

114, 9). It seems, however, that the letter of December 16, 1888, contains a fairly clear statement of succession put forward in terms that were Wilson's own. If something less than a smoking gun can qualify for evidence of psychological patricide, it would seem to be Wilson's claim to succeed his father that is elaborated in the letter.

[65] *Culture of Professionalism*, pp. 129–46.

projected a notion of character as self-administration. Wilson saw emotion and reason as conjoined in the measure of efficiency with which the individual is able to manipulate himself in relation to his surroundings.

Wilson included these understandings in a fictionalized account of character development that he wrote in 1887. He obviously chose the name of the main character, John Hart, with care.[66] It is explicitly connected both to "heart" and to the "hearth" of family. In addition, the short story carries many autobiographical references. In brief, John Hart is a lawyer who has inherited his father's practice. He develops literary interests in the course of living with his sister, a stern and humorless spinster. His subsequent marriage to Edith brings him into a state of consciousness that enables the young man to practice his literary skills with great efficiency. Wilson describes John Hart's talent as "his genius for reacting from his surroundings." John Hart "wrote from a heart which found cheer amid the hardness of the way because of strong faith in the balanced rightness of the world." He "made for himself, wherever he happened to be, a sort of private world of manly sentiment." Yet he needs "Edith's management" to discover his "proper mental economy," which had hitherto not been disclosed to him, "simply because he never meditated hitting upon such an economy." As family life develops, it becomes clear that continuous travel is the best way to expose Hart to conditions that stimulate him to write. Visiting destitute places, he produces "light-hearted" novels; out in the mining regions of the West, he is able to write about "sedate burghers, wearing the full harness of law and civilization." Edith, for her part, assumes "the rôle of business partner, watching the thought market, establishing proper conditions for manufacture, and erecting suitable machinery, while John furnished capital of thought and skill of execution." As Wilson concluded the story: "In brief,

[66] *PWW*, v, 567–84. The story of John Hart grew out of a critical essay, "The Eclipse of Individuality: A One-sided Statement," which Wilson wrote in April 1887 under the pseudonym Axson Mayte. In the essay he tried to claim the maintenance of individualism as the purpose of literature. *Ibid.*, pp. 476–83. For a while Wilson seems to have contemplated a literary life; see "Editorial Note: Wilson's Desire for a 'Literary Life,' " *ibid.*, pp. 474–75. Weinstein, in *Woodrow Wilson*, pp. 87–90, offers a fine psychological interpretation of the short story. For self-references in the story, see Wilson's letter to Ellen Axson Wilson, Aug. 2, 1894: "I was not entirely 'making up out of my head' when I wrote of Edith's 'management' of John Hart. You have yourself just as surely produced the conditions of my success: you are *my* 'manager': my sweet and stimulating atmosphere." *Ibid.*, VIII, 639. On the ability of the southerner to produce literature of "the *spirit*, of the *ideal*," "full of heart and imagination," "catholic, expansive," in contrast to the New Englander, see WW to Ellen Axson Wilson, Sept. 8, 1893, *ibid.*, p. 361. For an overview of literary changes as the country abandoned a sectional for a national fiction, see Larzer Ziff, *The American 1890's: Life and Times of a Lost Generation* (New York, 1966).

the management was a signal success." "In love and tenderness she gave him not only a satisfying home wherever they sojourned, but at last a great reputation and the full honors of intellectual maturity and success."[67]

The turn to fiction seems to have freed Wilson's imagination to state his ideas with greater precision and daring, as it were. The idea of a correspondence between the intimate relationships associated with the family and the sentiments and communication that were crucial in holding the nation together is played out in Wilson's story. As John Hart moves his hearth into the midst of the nation, he is made to signify the development of a national mind. It is clear, however, that the notion of home undergoes certain modifications in the process. Its meaning in regard to place becomes precarious. The new home is bought at the price of permanent dislocation and a permanent estrangement from the neighborhoods and communities that provided him with impulses that were processed in the spirit of the harmony of the aggregate. John Hart is made to stand for a writer who establishes himself in the national market, and his political role is to serve the common sentiment and bring it safely from localism into the national body. He represents Wilson's idea of "the balanced rightness," the "mental economy" of the national form of political opinion.

TOWARD THE END of the 1880s, Wilson turned his attention to the idea of the state, which he saw as the symbol of the authority of familial values applied on a national scale. Wilson adopted "the state" as the general name for the authority that directs individual feelings toward order and competence. He expressed this understanding in his political writings as well as in his private letters. The attempt to transform the idea of the national state in the image of familial habits is reflected in the notes for his definition of the functions of the state:

> *The State directly conditions* both the existence and the competence of the individual:
> *Authenticates* his personality and status;
> *Economic guardian* (post, telegraph, coin, weights, etc.).
> *Spiritual god parent* (Education, suppression of vice).
> *Health* (Sanitation, licensing physicians, etc.).
> *Means of knowledge* underlying reform (Statistics).[68]

Wilson obviously searched for words that would evoke an association with family care and immediate personal forms of dependence. The

---

[67] *PWW*, v, 568, 570–72, 582, 583–84.

[68] Notes for lectures at the Brooklyn Institute of Arts and Sciences, Nov. 15, 1893, lecture on "Political Liberty," *ibid.*, VIII, 407.

functions of the state, however, suggest economic convenience and administrative government. The outcome was a curious mixture of an organic state and a human face that kept its tractable mind busy with the conditions for competition. Wilson developed this second feature of the state as a celebration of the restless vigor of the anonymous mass, which he occasionally saw as a distinctive mark of American nationalism:

> *Modern* democracy in which the people who are said to govern are not the people of a commune or a township, but all the people of a great nation, a vast population which never musters into any single assembly, whose members never see each others' faces or hear each others' voices, but live, millions strong, up and down the reaches of continents; building scores of great cities throughout fair provinces that would in other days have been separate kingdoms . . . and yet not *separate*, but standing fast in a vital union of thought and of institutions, conceiving themselves a corporate whole: acting so, and so accepted by the world. There is no simplicity here! The new democracy is manifold, intense, dramatic, thrilled through and through with a new life, facing a new destiny,—with many questionings, but also with high and confident hope. We must needs look long and earnestly both into the past and into the present to understand *it*.[69]

Wilson pictured the democratic state as an energetic body unified by general social membership and economic activity. This understanding became more pronounced after Wilson in 1891 gave the idea of sovereignty its final formulation. The idea of the state came to refer to "the general vitality of the organism," while sovereignty was a term for "the specific originative power of certain organs."[70] This terminology indicates some of the difficulties that the modern reader experiences in coming to grips with Wilson's language. It appears that what is normally understood as a state in modern terms—that is, a centralized structure of power—is roughly the equivalent of Wilson's "sovereignty" or his "government." What Wilson referred to as the state is broadly coextensive with the modern idea of "society" as the general term for the structure of social relationships.

Although these rough translations may account to some extent for the fact that there was little need for Wilson to repudiate a youthful interest in German metaphysics of *der Staat* in order to become a liberal statesman, the simple rewording does not, of course, exhaust the meaning of Wilson's language. Unlike the conservative followers of Herbert Spencer, who were accustomed to defend society against the state, Wilson's view

[69] A lecture on "Democracy," *ibid.*, vii, 347.
[70] "Political Sovereignty," *ibid.*, p. 333.

permitted him to argue that state and government were supplementary rather than opposed forms of order. Just as Wilson argued that "the law of liberty" should be supplemented by "a law of progress," he was able to stipulate that "it should be the end of government *to assist in accomplishing the objects of organized* society. There must be constant adjustments of governmental assistance to the needs of a changing social and industrial organization." He pictured government as the agent of the state, as "society's controlling organ."[71]

[71] "Democracy," *ibid.*, p. 365; *The State*, p. 660.

VI

★ ★ ★ ★ ★ ★ ★ ★ ★ ★ ★ ★ ★ ★ ★ ★ ★ ★ ★ ★

LEGITIMIZING ADMINISTRATION

IN AMERICA

Wilson's identification of national integration as the basic purpose of the American state may be seen as a precondition for his development of a concept of administration. On the one hand, it enabled him, to insist emphatically on values and ends within the scope of the nation; on the other, it permitted him to put liberal sentiments aside and to analyze the organization of power in a new context. The latter problem involved an attempt to clear the ground for a systematic study of administration, a search for appropriate methods, and a reformulation of the relationship between state and citizen in view of administrative conditions. Each of these questions was a part of Wilson's politics of administration, which was based upon an understanding of the generalized character of the relationship between citizens and government in the industrial age.

It is clear from Wilson's notes that the ideas that went into his celebrated article of 1887, "The Study of Administration," were amplified simultaneously with his ideas relating to the modern democratic state.[1] The article impressed Herbert Baxter Adams so much that Wilson was invited to lecture on the subject on a regular basis.[2] In addition to this article, which is widely respected as the first academic attempt to formulate the boundaries and precepts of administration, Wilson further developed his notion of administration in *The State*. The last chapters of *The State* indicate a shift of interest from the origins to the functions of government as the limits of a concept built on familial authority and organic growth became clear. Wilson partially replaced it with the image of dynamic government machinery at the very heart of the state, where policy originates.

Wilson's notes for his lectures at the Johns Hopkins have been preserved. They reveal both that Wilson extended his study of administra-

[1] *PWW*, v, 359–80.
[2] Herbert Baxter Adams to WW, Nov. 25, 1886, *ibid.*, pp. 393–94.

tion by readings in European scholarship and that he kept in touch with current ideas of administrative reform in the United States.[3] They also reveal that he revised his lectures substantially over the years. During the first two years he relied to a large extent upon the last chapters of *The State*. Reflecting his shift from the idea of the state to the idea of sovereignty, his lectures on administration began to focus on what he labeled "public law," or "positive Administrative Law," which covered the legal and jurisdictional aspects of administrative activity.[4]

Although "The Study of Administration" has a special claim to our attention as the single most important text at the beginning of an academic discipline in America, the lectures may have enjoyed a more direct influence. Not only did Wilson reach a large body of students, some of whom became prominent in public life, but he also associated himself with the movement for municipal reform. In 1896, after nine years of giving twenty-five lectures a year at the Johns Hopkins, Wilson received an invitation to address a civic mass meeting in Baltimore for people, irrespective of party, who opposed the spoils system in the city council. The newspaper report of the meeting indicates that he fully measured up to the main speaker, Theodore Roosevelt, in intention and humor, let alone civic militancy in pursuit of a good cause:

> What I want to know is whether you who are here tonight have come to this meeting "to stay"? By that I mean . . . whether this will be a display of the spasmodic strength on your part, or whether you will . . . put your shoulder to the wheel of good government. All I will say is that if you have come to "stay" the City Council has not. [Cheers.] Take up the sword before you take up the horn.[5]

The following interpretation is an attempt to sketch the discovery of new administrative possibilities within Wilson's own political thought. These possibilities suggested themselves through an expansion of the functions that connected the exercise of creative leadership with common political habits. The following discussion begins, however, with the recent debate about the content of "The Study of Administration," since the debate reveals the importance of Wilson's paper in the modern field of public administration.

[3] "Editorial Note: Wilson's Lectures on Administration at the Johns Hopkins," *ibid.*, vi, 482–84. For an overview of the background and institutional setting of administrative reform in the period, see Stephen Skowronek, *Building a New American State: The Expansion of National Administrative Capacities, 1877–1920* (Cambridge, Mass., 1982), pp. 47–84.

[4] Notes for lectures on administration, Feb. 3–March 10, 1890; Jan. 26, 1891–Feb. 27, 1894, *PWW*, vi, 484–86; vii, 114–18.

[5] Baltimore *Sun*, March 4, 1896, *ibid.*, ix, 485.

IN LARGE MEASURE, the modern understanding of Wilson's idea of administration revolves around the question of whether and how Wilson was able to distinguish between administration and politics.[6] In this debate the term *administration* roughly refers to governmental action carried out by a salaried staff organized in an hierarchical order and funded by federal or local authorities. The term *politics*, in contrast, is usually understood as the determination of policy by elected and by appointed officials competing for influence. Until recently, it was often overlooked that Wilson explicitly regarded the separation of administration from politics as a practical matter to be settled when concrete issues arose in the course of changing governmental functions and techniques. While it was obviously a matter of importance for the practical solution of pressing issues, the separation of administration from politics could not be determined, Wilson said, "without entering upon particulars so numerous as to confuse and distinctions so minute as to distract."[7] The issue of administrative autonomy was submerged in his basic claim that the constitutional identity of the republic was being transformed into an administrative identity. Consistent with his evolutionary outlook, he did not imply that the Constitution had been abandoned. Instead he believed that the order associated with public administration was bound to absorb and reform the politics that had been laid down by the Constitution.

What looks to the historian like a case of misplaced emphasis appears to be pregnant with meaning for the professors and practitioners of public administration who have written at length about Wilson's essay. While Wilson hoped to *establish* the legitimacy of administration in America, the

---

[6] See Lynton K. Caldwell, "Public Administration and the Universities: A Half-Century of Development," *Public Administration Review*, xxv (March 1965), 53–54; Frederick C. Mosher, *Democracy and the Public Service* (New York, 1968), p. 68; Fred W. Riggs, "Relearning Old Lessons: The Political Context of Development Administration," *Public Administration Review*, xxv (March 1965), 71; John C. Buechner, *Public Administration* (Belmont, Mass., 1968), p. 6; Richard J. Stillman II, "Woodrow Wilson and the Study of Administration: A New Look at an Old Essay," *American Political Science Review*, LXVII (June 1973), 582–88. A recent controversy began with Vincent Ostrom, *The Intellectual Crisis in American Public Administration* (Birmingham, Ala., 1973), and rejoinders include Robert D. Cuff, "Wilson and Weber: Bourgeois Critics in an Organized Age," *Public Administration Review*, XXXVIII (May/June 1978), 240–44; Robert T. Golembiewski, " 'Maintenance' and 'Task' as Central Challenges in Public Administration," *ibid.*, XXXIV (March/ April, 1974), 168–76; and Kent Kirwan, "The Crisis of Identity in the Study of Public Administration: Woodrow Wilson," *Polity*, IX (Spring, 1977), 321–43. Jack Rabin and James S. Bowman (eds.), *Politics and Administration: Woodrow Wilson and American Public Administration* is a useful collection of papers that comment on most aspects of Wilson's essay.

[7] "The Study of Administration," *PWW*, v, 371. Rabin and Bowman note in the introduction to *Politics and Administration* that "the mechanics of the relation between politics and administration was not of great consequence to Wilson" (pp. 2–3).

problem for the profession of public administration, which has burgeoned in the twentieth century, has been to *protect* its institutional and professional preserve against political incursion. The common way of doing this has been to argue that the science of administration is or should be politically neutral. While Wilson viewed administration as an instrument to state power, the profession came to identify itself with a scientific view of public administration, and it was only natural to search for support for the scientific view in the texts that had contributed to the rise of the profession. For generations of administrators, this was hardly just an intellectual exercise. Public administration was from the beginning fair game for the party out of power. Its functions, soon termed the fourth or fifth branch of government, seemed to live an uncertain institutional existence despite its claim to indispensability. The administrative class had no foundation in the Constitution and, unlike the established political parties, had an uncertain basis in popular loyalty. If it was not possible for public administrators to distinguish their function from that of the elected politicians, the political managers, the advisers, or the lobbyists, no profession remained. The high prestige of the natural sciences at the end of the nineteenth century virtually guaranteed that the new discipline would try to assimilate the terminology and claims associated with science in order to gain respectability.

The so-called dichotomy, or distinction—sometimes labeled the continuum—between administration and politics that most public administrators read into Wilson's essay represent well-chosen terms for the central ideological assumption that serves to guard established administrative prerogatives.[8] Fortunately for the profession, its practice of nourishing the separation was supported by policy makers who, from time to time, could find their own reasons to support a claim of administrative neutrality. It would often prove useful to mask political choices with references to science or expertise in order to shield complicated issues from public uproar, as Wilson well knew. Most of the disagreement concerning Wilson's essay has centered upon the question of whether Wilson stated the distinction in a realistic or useful way, or whether, instead, his attempt led the profession astray. There seems to be general support of the proposition that administration and politics must be kept separate in theory in order for the two phenomena to interact in practice.

Commentary on Wilson's essay reveals the shifting intradisciplinary moods over the last several decades. As underscored in a recent volume of papers devoted to "reexamining politics and administration" in Wilson's essay, the present situation is one of an identity crisis in the profes-

---

[8] Rabin and Bowman (eds.), *Politics and Administration*, p. 3.

sion.[9] While Wilson's essay was earlier approached with high hopes for the future of public administration, it is now read in a dispirited temper. As Rabin and Bowman make clear, some writers now find Wilson's dichotomy to be "both descriptively and prescriptively inadequate" and the science it created to be little more than a "series of trite proverbs" throughout much of the century. The lack of "enough power at any focal point of leadership" within the American system of politics seemingly smothered the science in its cradle. The impression of failure was only partially offset—or perhaps further emphasized, depending on one's point of view—by a gross acceptance of professional guilt. The last fifty years of government service is now denounced as founded upon a "divorce between politics and administration" that has been "scientifically as well as politically disastrous." "The American Dream, of which public administration had been so much a part, turned into a nightmare during the 1960s and 1970s," Rabin and Bowman explain. In the sobering period of the early 1980s, the profession was finally ready to picture itself as a primary architect of "the 'Iron Cage' prophesied by Weber."[10] The magnitude of these feelings of remorse supplements the earlier gloomy views of Vincent Ostrom, who launched a campaign for a new professional identity in the vanguard of "a new American revolution" that would undo Wilson's "counterrevolutionary doctrine." Ostrom hoped for a return of the republic to the doctrine preached by the Founding Fathers, in particular Alexander Hamilton, that "all our political experiments would be predicated upon the capacity of mankind for self-government." Ostrom's model of self-government was itself predicated upon an image of the citizen as a supreme chooser of "maximizing strategy," acting "*as if* he were 'satisficing.' "[11]

In view of this cycle of professional self-esteem from a firm adherence to a scientific ethos to a close identification with government dating roughly from the New Deal and to the present mood of gloom with forebodings of revolutionary fervor, Wilson's analysis may be of special interest. His sketch of administrative behavior implies that the new profession should not be provided with a firm professional identity, which had tended to produce a state within the state in continental Europe.

In contrast to the modern rationalist understanding of administrative behavior as a theory of choices that are constrained only by external factors, such as time, costs, benefits, information, technological possibilities, Wilson's view was marked by psychological realism. His current interest

---

[9] *Ibid., passim.*

[10] *Ibid.*, pp. 5–7.

[11] Ostrom, *Intellectual Crisis*, pp. 133, 130, 50–52.

in German and French administrative studies did not cause Wilson to drop his earlier appreciation of the hard-nosed and irreverent approach to administration he found in Walter Bagehot. Bagehot's importance for Wilson has been overlooked at least in part because of the trivial fact of an incorrectly cited quotation. In the beginning of his essay Wilson cited a long quotation as being from Bagehot's "Essay on Sir William Pitt," but the reference is really from Bagehot's essay "The Character of Sir Robert Peel," in which Bagehot undertook to diagnose the phenomenon of the administrator as a new type of political man.[12]

Bagehot contrasted the modern administrator with the willful type of hereditary landed proprietors who had ruled the House of Commons by various means of influence and social patronage. The new administrative type was of the manufacturing class but was one generation removed from the "strong, ready, bold men of business" who had "devised a factory system, [and] combined a factory population." The administrative type was schooled not as military or industrial commanders, but as "the receivers of profit" in "the banausics of work." The peculiarity of the new administrators was "that they wished to see the government administered according to the notions familiar to them in their business life. They have no belief in mystery or magic; probably they have never appreciated the political influence of the imagination; they wish to see plain sense applied to the most prominent part of practical life." Bagehot took Sir Robert Peel as the embodiment of the quality of selfless instrumentality. He was "the great administrator," whose mind was "always acted upon." He was without "fixed opinions," and his ideas were all bestowed on him from the outside. He was without personal identity. His ideas could have been "any one's ideas." He was a man of "willing ears" and "placid belief." *Vox populi* was his "natural religion."[13]

Bagehot's analysis of a political personality without any firm identity was appealing to Wilson, for whom a central question was the control of administrative behavior. Wilson explained that there are three basic motives that can be used to keep the administrative identity in a state of

---

[12] Wilson's reference to Bagehot's discussion of "the difference between the old and the new in administration" appears on *PWW*, v, 362. Bagehot's "The Character of Sir Robert Peel," can be found in *The Collected Works of Walter Bagehot*, ed. St. John-Stevas, 9 vols. to date (Cambridge, Mass., 1968–), III, 238–71.

[13] *Ibid.*, pp. 248–53, 256–57. Bagehot's analysis preceded and to some degree anticipated the formulation of modern ideas about the relation between bureaucratic structure and personality that modern sociologists have refined as the notion of "trained incapacity" (Thorstein Veblen), "occupational psychosis" (John Dewey), or "professional deformation" (Daniel Warnotte), all of which describe the personality of the administrator. For a discussion of these ideas, see Robert K. Merton, *Social Theory and Social Structure*, enl. ed. (New York, 1968), pp. 251–59.

suspension. The first is the tendency of the administrator to identify with an *esprit de corps*; the second is the administrator's inclination to make "ingratiating obeisance to the authority of a superior"; and the third is the influence of an administrator's "sensitive conscience." Although the last motive was the most attractive, Wilson implied that it should be balanced by the other motives if the usefulness of the administrator is to be preserved. To build on private conscience was obviously to deduct from public accountability. The first priority of administrative behavior was its flexibility according to shifting political needs. If the administrative personality became too stable, it was already on its way to furthering its own class interest. The psychological realism of Wilson's analysis did not lead him to hope that bureaucratic self-interest could be eradicated, but it led him to conclude that it could be manipulated. Administrative service could be inspired and controlled by shifting appeals to the administrative agent's interest, as by promises of "contributing abundantly to his sustenance, . . . [of] furthering his ambition, . . . [and of] advancing his honor and establishing his character." These were, in brief, the primary means by which administrative identity was kept on a short leash.[14]

WILSON'S IDEAS about modern administration originated in the fall of 1885, perhaps the most creative period of his academic life. His preliminary notes seem to indicate that two ideas were of special importance to him. Both were clearly inspired by the teaching at the Johns Hopkins.[15] The first was that administration in America should be related to "practical means" rather than to "abstract principles."[16] The second was that the contracting social space had negated the Federalist belief that geographic and economic expansion would serve to counteract majoritarian tyranny. Thus Wilson originally perceived administration against the backdrop of depleted economic opportunities. In a passage written a few months before the composition of "The Study of Administration," Wilson spelled out the social presuppositions of an administrative order:

> The grave social and economic problems now putting themselves forward, as the result of the tremendous growth and concentration

[14] *PWW*, v, 380. Wilson's draft contains a slightly more detailed discussion of the balance between training designed to make the administrator's minds "athletic and self-commanding" and encouragement of his "native executive aptitudes" by practical instruction. Wilson underlined the idea that general college training would not be enough, and he urged the establishment of "administrative schools." Nov. 1, 1886, Woodrow Wilson Collection, Firestone Library.

[15] "Notes on Administration," *PWW*, v, 49–50.

[16] Notes to "The Study of Administration," Nov. 1, 1886, Woodrow Wilson Collection, Firestone Library.

of our population, and the consequent sharp competition for the means of livelihood indicate that our system is already aging. . . . There are already commercial heats and political distempers in our body politic which warn of an early necessity for carefully prescribed physic.[17]

Wilson's perceptions of impending political congestion clarify the theoretical purpose behind the historical introduction to "The Study of Administration." It was not intended to be a historical description but a theoretical projection. The picture is one of organic growth toward economic complexity, social discord, and intensified political uncertainty. Wilson mentioned such features as "the complex systems of public revenues and public debts," "puzzled" financiers, the "present complexities of trade and perplexities of commercial speculation," the "giant monopolies," and the tensions between capital and labor, which had reached "ominous proportions." The functions of government were bound to become "more complex and difficult," "vastly multiplying in number." The modern state was saddled with the necessity of making itself the "master of the masterful corporation."[18]

The controlling metaphor is "complexity"; the political space was getting crowded. "In former ages," as Wilson put it later, "there were large cool spaces between individuals. Now there was friction between the forces which had come into existence." The dimension of time was not cyclical but progressive. As Wilson concluded his projection, "If difficulties of governmental action are to be seen gathering in other centuries, they are to be seen culminating in our own."[19] The whole conception constituted a break with the language of agrarian virtue and independence that has attracted much attention as the dominant mode of political discourse in America in the nineteenth century.[20] Wilson's image of complexity conveyed an idea of history where changing social and economic conditions absorbed the past in the course of preparation for secular innovation. Within this conception of history, progress toward an admin-

---

[17] "Responsible Government under the Constitution," Feb. 10, 1886, *PWW*, v, 123.

[18] "The Study of Administration," *ibid.*, pp. 361–63.

[19] Lecture at Brown University, reported in the *Providence Journal*, Nov. 12, 1889, *ibid.*, vi, 417; "The Study of Administration," *ibid.*, v, 361.

[20] J.G.A. Pocock, *The Machiavellian Moment: Florentine Political Thought and the Atlantic Republican Tradition* (Princeton, N. J., 1975), pp. 506–50; J. H. Hexter, "Panoramic Vision: Republic, Virtue, Liberty, and the Political Universe of J.G.A. Pocock," in *On Historians: Reappraisals of Some of the Makers of Modern History* (Cambridge, Mass., 1978), pp. 255–303; Dorothy Ross, "The Liberal Tradition Revisited and the Republican Tradition Addressed," in John Higham and Paul K. Conkin, (eds.), *New Directions in American Intellectual History* (Baltimore, 1979), pp. 116–31.

istrative state was not a matter of reinventing past conditions but of preparing for an inexorable future. It was not a vision of a nation
accomplishing common goals but of one bearing the consequences of
general dependence. In his first more coherent attempt to describe the
subject of administration, Wilson suggested that administration was to be
approached as the most advanced stage of constitutional development:
"The period of constitution-making is passed now. We have reached new
territory in which we need new guides, the vast territory of *administration*.
All the enlightened world has come along with us in these new fields, and
much of the enlightened world has realized the fact and is preparing
itself to understand administration."[21]

Wilson had anticipated this formulation of a new political stage in
Congressional Government, where he called attention to a fourth stage of
administrative tasks, which had replaced the stage of constitutional struggles.[22] The juxtaposition of the constitutional and the administrative state
of development indicates the character of the interpretive movement
Wilson found himself engaged in. Whereas he merged the historical attachment to the Constitution with the idea of the nation, the "fact," or
the constitutional practice, pointed toward an administrative state. In
early 1886, Wilson developed the idea that the Constitution itself could
be seen as a scientific statement, as a set of "more or less successful generalizations of political experience" that exercised "much the same spell
upon the mind that other confident, roundly put generalizations exert."
But, "like other broad inductions," the Constitution commended itself as
"whole truths," although in fact it was "only partial truths." The bias of
the constitutional view was to assume that laws could enforce themselves,
while from a more comprehensive perspective it was clear that laws could
have no other reality than that which was given them "by the administration and obedience of men." Wilson began to see the Constitution in ad-

[21] "The Art of Governing," Nov. 15, 1885, *PWW,* v, 52.

[22] *Congressional Government, ibid.,* iv, 114–15. Robert D. Miewald, in "The Origins of Wilson's Thought: The German Tradition and the Organic State," in Rabin and Bowman (eds.),
Politics and Administration, pp. 17–30, argues that Wilson's essay was an exercise in state organicism and "a rephrasing of ideas then current in German administrative thought." The
result is some confusion because of Miewald's neglect of Wilson's distinction between the
state and government or administration. Generally speaking, Wilson considered the state in
organic terms and administration in mechanical terms: "If we are to put in new boilers and
to mend the fires which drive our governmental machinery, we must not leave the old wheels
and joints and valves and bands to creak. . . . We must put in new running parts." "The Study
of Administration," *PWW,* v, 375, and *passim.* It has also escaped notice that Wilson's state
was not the equivalent of *der Staat* in German theory but was substantiated in "common
habits" as a rough substitute for family and "civil society." It appears that the views that are
ascribed to Wilson would be better ascribed to John W. Burgess.

ministrative terms, an understanding that suggested that the organic base of the state would accommodate itself to a new reality of political power, the "new machine of government."[23] In contrast to the barren idea of inventing leadership by constitutional change, the development of administrative order would supply a visionary leadership with some of the stable prerequisites of power.

The crucial phrase is "administration and obedience," which signifies Wilson's awareness that "obedience" refers to different political processes, depending on the citizen's actual distance from the stage where decisions were being made. Obedience means one thing to the politician, who fights over the interpretation of constitutional restraints on power, and a different thing to the citizen who is far removed from the processes of power. Administration is constitutionalism writ small, the Constitution is administration writ large. A constitution is a set of "forms," "a violent presumption in favor of the reality of the substance" contained within it. Administration, on the other hand, is the practice of power: "The way in which men naturally exercise power must constitute the essence of every system" of constitutional form.[24] Just as constitutionalism provides the basic forms necessary for scientific inductions of political experience, administration supplies the forms necessary for inductions about political behavior. They supplement each other in a comprehensive picture of political regularities.

Like most Americans, Wilson had begun by assuming that administration and bureaucracy were the very opposites of constitutional self-government. One of the major themes of "Self-Government in France" had been that the habit of self-restraint had been stifled by the bureaucratic exercise of power. But Wilson gradually worked toward a level of abstraction in which the processes of "the exercise of power" could be dissociated from the taint of coercion and could be "reduced to science." As he pointed out in his notes, administration is, in a sense, ubiquitous, "as old as government itself." "Administration," he initially observed, "goes about *incognito* to most of the world." In his final draft, Wilson was able to sharpen his perception and aim with greater precision at the hiding place of administrative power: "A great deal of administration goes about *incognito* to most of the world, being confounded now with political 'management,' and again with constitutional principle."[25] The disentangle-

---

[23] "Responsible Government under the Constitution," Feb. 10, 1886, *PWW*, v, 107–108; "Notes on Administration," Nov. 15, 1885, *ibid.*, p. 49.

[24] "Responsible Government under the Constitution," *ibid.*, p. 108.

[25] "Notes on Administration," *ibid.*, p. 49; Notes to "The Study of Administration," Nov. 1, 1886, Woodrow Wilson Collection, Firestone Library; "The Study of Administration," *PWW*, v, 371.

ment of the bare process of administration is necessary if comparative study is to be realized and if the peculiar character of modern administrative needs is to be revealed. It is first necessary, Wilson thought, to free the mind of the "misconception that administration stands upon an essentially different basis in a democratic state from that on which it stands in a non-democratic state." In order to achieve a theory of a "perfected practice" of administration, it is necessary to see well-known phenomena in a new light.[26]

Two additional reasons apparently lay behind Wilson's turn to administration. One was his growing awareness of certain deficiencies in the traditional idea of leadership that appeared to require contradictory qualities in the leader. It is to ask too much to expect the modern leader "to *combine* wisdom in counsel and genius in action." The endless debates in the deliberative assembly require a patience that does not go well with the capacity for prompt and overwhelming action. Generals are seldom the greatest orators. The presidency of General Grant almost offered itself as an example of the disaster that ensues if ability in one field of leadership is presumed to carry over into another. Action in the modern world is dependent not primarily upon words but upon the organization and service of policies framed in the "nation's councils by far different men." Even the greatest modern generals were "but the instruments of statecraft" and had not themselves "hatched the wars in which they fought."[27] The revalorization of administrative functions implied a further depreciation of the common view of the political actor. In "The Study of Administration," Wilson challenged the reader: "Try to imagine personal government in the United States. It is like trying to imagine a national worship of Zeus. Our imaginations are too modern for the feat."[28]

The second issue that anticipated Wilson's turn to administration was a certain problematic feature of political habits. Although the very stability of popular habits is seen as a prerequisite for progressive change, the danger is that habits may become unchangeable. Wilson's early idea that oratory would electrify the popular constituency and spread like a wildfire was probably one of the casualties of the atmosphere at the Johns Hopkins, where the rapid advance of modern scholarship easily created a perception of popular backwardness. The suffocating weight of popular prejudice is another aspect of habits rooted in the population at large. "The Study of Administration" contained a strong statement about the

---

[26] "The Study of Administration," *PWW*, v, 377; "Notes on Administration," *ibid.*, p. 49.

[27] "Modern Democratic State," *ibid.*, pp. 89–90.

[28] "The Study of Administration," *ibid.*, p. 377.

ignorance of common people. While "progress" had earlier encountered
the selfishness and ignorance of the monarch, the problem is magnified
in the modern state. There is no "single ear" to approach. "The people"
are "selfish, ignorant, timid, stubborn, or foolish" by the thousands, Wilson argued.

> With opinions, possession is more than nine points of the law. It is
> next to impossible to dislodge them. . . . The grandson accepts his
> grandfather's hesitating experiment as an integral part of the fixed
> constitution of nature. . . . The bulk of mankind is rigidly unphilo-
> sophical, and nowadays the bulk of mankind votes. A truth must be-
> come not only plain but also commonplace before it will be seen by
> the people who go to their work very early in the morning; and not
> to act upon it must involve great and pinching inconveniences before
> these same people will make up their minds to act upon it.
>
> And where is this unphilosophical bulk of mankind more multi-
> farious in its composition than in the United States? . . . [O]ne must
> know the mind, not of Americans of the older stocks only, but also
> of Irishmen, of Germans, of Negroes . . . [and] influence minds cast
> in every mould of race, minds inheriting every bias of environ-
> ment.[29]

The establishment of administration would allow room for political experiment in "the daily details and in the choice of daily means of government." Abstract political education would be supplemented with drills in
the practice of government. Administration would "make public opinion
efficient without suffering it to be meddlesome."[30]

Wilson's turn to administration was a consequence of certain problems
inherent in his own thinking. His focus on administration was an out-
growth of his work on the concept of the modern state and its attendant
issues of constitutionalism, leadership, and political habit. Wilson had no
need for "an apolitical science of administration."[31] If additional evidence
for this conclusion is needed, the circumstances of the publication of Wilson's essay provide it. Wilson originally prepared the essay for an oral
presentation at the Cornell Historical and Political Science Association.
The editor of the *Political Science Quarterly*, Edwin R. A. Seligman heard
about the paper and asked permission to publish it. If Wilson had intended to launch a new science in America, one would expect that he
would eagerly seize upon the opportunity to have it published in a new

[29] *Ibid.*, pp. 368–70.

[30] *Ibid.*, pp. 374–75.

[31] Gerald E. Caiden, "In Search of an Apolitical Science of Administration," in Rabin and
Bowman (eds.), *Politics and Administration*, pp. 51–78.

but authoritative professional journal. This was not Wilson's response. In fact, he asked the editor to consider the content of the paper in view of his intentions behind its composition: "I did not prepare it with any thought of publication, but only as a semi-popular introduction to administrative studies." He had neither invented nor, for that matter, imported a science of administration. The paper, he said, "goes critically round the study [of administration], considering it from various outside points of view, rather than entering it and handling its proper topics."[32] His purpose had not been to enter the science but to consider it from the "outside," that is, from a general political point of view. He had intended to survey the prospects of the new science and to prepare the public for its possible establishment. The relevant question is therefore not whether Wilson succeeded in creating a new science but how he proposed to modify certain elements of American political culture that were traditionally seen to be opposed to the development of an administrative apparatus in America.

IT HAS generally been overlooked that Wilson's successful anticipation of critical attitudes toward administration is one of the most impressive achievements of his paper. Wilson's knowledge of American history and his respect for public opinion made it clear to him that most Americans were opposed to a science of administration and would happily "exchange a good deal of science for a little self-government."[33] Modern commentators, in contrast, have mostly taken for granted that the paper was to be read as an illustration of the assumption that Americans would be happy to exchange a good deal of self-government for a little bit of science. It is therefore worth pausing to observe the extreme cautiousness with which Wilson entered the new field. Much of "The Study of Administration," particularly its last section, is a discussion of the danger involved in the pursuit of administrative science and of the safety precautions required. The danger is spelled out with such warning signs as Wilson's references to the fear of getting any "diseases into our veins," the "apprehension of blood-poisoning," the "apprehension that we might perchance blindly borrow something incompatible with our principles," the danger of going "blindly astray," and the need to "filter" a foreign method over "a slow fire" to "distill away its foreign gasses." Wilson used such images of precaution as "the perfectly safe ground" of making use of comparative studies of administration. There was no need to "care a

---

[32] Nov. 11, 1886, *PWW*, v, 387–88.
[33] "The Art of Governing," Nov. 15, 1885, *ibid.*, p. 54.

peppercorn for the constitutional and political reasons" behind French and German administrative practices.[34]

How did Wilson propose to deal with these popular apprehensions, which earlier had impeded proposals for administrative government? Wilson's answer was to propose that administration be legitimated as a neutral means of obtaining government efficiency. This argument was sharpened in one of the central passages of the last section of the essay:

> If I see a murderous fellow sharpening a knife cleverly, I can borrow his way of sharpening the knife without borrowing his probable intention to commit murder with it; and so, if I see a monarchist died in the wool managing a public bureau well, I can learn his business methods without changing one of my republican spots. He may serve his king; I will continue to serve the people; but I should like to serve my sovereign as well as he serves his.[35]

Wilson had a complex idea of the kind of education that was necessary in order to allay public suspicion about administrative "methods." His parallel between watching preparations for criminal activity and the acceptance of administrative instrumentalities makes it clear that a dual process was to take place. The acceptance of administrative procedures was preceded by the suppression of another kind of knowledge. A politics of interpretation was taking place. The point of his parallel was that in order to remain attentive to administrative methods, the bystander—the student of administration and the public—must suppress knowledge about the ends of the action that is being observed. The observer must interpret the act as something neutral and should see the potential murderer as a knife grinder.

In retrospect, Wilson's argument is difficult to reconcile with the duties of good citizenship. The good citizen is obviously obliged either to talk the murderous person out of committing the act or to call the police. Wilson's parable is problematic, because the mere knowledge of criminal behavior makes the citizen-observer an accomplice in a conspiracy against justice. This aspect of the argument is covered up, because the attention is focused on the gain in public services that may possibly accrue to the private individual as a result of improved administrative methods. Public responsibility is replaced by an appeal to the benefits that may accrue to the citizen as a taxpayer or a consumer, such as cheaper and more efficient public services. Thus Wilson's argument is in effect a variation on the question of how to turn public vice into private benefit.

---

[34] "The Study of Administration," *ibid.*, pp. 376–80.
[35] *Ibid.*, p. 379.

As Wilson underscored by his choice of examples, administration is to be considered neutral only in the sense that it will be unconcerned with political justice. It is political in the sense that it will be preoccupied with the accumulation of power available for government purposes. Wilson constructed his example of incriminating observation of the development of instrumental skills in order to emphasize that the preference for the means of power over the ends is itself a fundamental choice of political identity, which could be defended only on administrative premises. The risk of citing instrumental power as a first priority is that the public will identify itself with the victim of administrative proficiency in the allegory rather than with the detached observer. It is therefore important that administration in America be promoted with reference to values that are very different from the values that sustain administration in Europe, where bureaucracy rests upon rituals and symbols referring to tradition, absolute authority, and popular submission.

Wilson argued that the debate about civil service, which culminated with the establishment of the Civil Service Commission in 1883, contained certain suggestions about values that appealed to many Americans. The creation of a civil service system, however, was "but a prelude to fuller administrative reform."

> We must go on to adjust executive functions more fitly and to prescribe better methods of executive organization and action. Civil-service reform is thus but a moral preparation for what is to follow. It is clearing the moral atmosphere of official life by establishing the sanctity of public office as a public trust, and, by making the service unpartisan, it is opening the way for making it businesslike. By sweetening its motives it is rendering it capable of improving its methods of work.[36]

To Wilson, "public trust" was the other side of "public responsibility," and these were perhaps the two political terms he took most seriously. He believed that in order to allay suspicion and to promote "conditions of trustfulness," administration should be associated with general American values, especially those concerning business practices, but should be kept at a distance from daily life by a more dignified purpose:

> The field of administration is a field of business. It is removed from the hurry and strife of politics. . . . It is a part of political life only as the methods of the counting-house are a part of the life of society. . . . But it is, at the same time, raised very far above the dull level of mere technical detail by the fact that through its greater principles it

[36] *Ibid.*, p. 370.

131

is directly connected with the lasting maxims of political wisdom, the permanent truths of political progress.[37]

To make administration acceptable to "our own politics," Wilson said, its practical value would be stressed, while its theoretical meaning would be repressed. "To suit American habit, all general theories must, as theories, keep modestly in the background, not in open argument only, but even in our own minds." The spirit of adaptation would have to be "the American how-to-do-it." In late-nineteenth-century America, nothing symbolized instrumental values more persuasively than business organization.[38] While references to business methods would underscore the utility of administration, references to science would indicate its separation from politics. Wilson first contrasted the scientific value of objectivity with existing administrative practices that he presented as an American law of the survival of the most corrupt, who flourished in "the poisonous atmosphere of city government, the crooked secrets of state administration, the confusion, sinecurism, and corruption ever and again discovered in the bureaus in Washington."[39] Second, administration was to be dissociated from common experience by the characteristic scientific quality of abstraction. Wilson presented a vivid picture of the typical way in which administrative practices would disconnect the popular view from the exercise of power:

> No lines of demarcation, setting apart administrative from non-administrative functions, can be run between this and that department without being run up hill and down dale, over dizzy heights of distinction and through dense jungles of statutory enactment, hither and thither around "ifs" and "buts," "whens" and "howevers," until they become altogether lost to the common eye not accustomed to this sort of surveying, and consequently not acquainted with the use of the theodolite of logical discernment.[40]

Wilson expected that appeals to scientific detachment and to business practices would follow different paths, but he was able to unify the two fields of activity in a remarkable definition of the study of administration, which bound the descriptive and the prescriptive ends of the new discipline closely together. It became virtually impossible for later commentators to unravel Wilson's knot and distinguish the "scientific" from the "political" elements.

[37] *Ibid.*, pp. 373, 370.
[38] *Ibid.*, p. 379.
[39] *Ibid.*, p. 363.
[40] *Ibid.*, p. 371.

In "The Study of Administration" Wilson wrote, "It is the object of administrative study to discover, first, what government can properly and successfully do, and, secondly, how it can do these proper things with the utmost possible efficiency and the least possible cost either of money or of energy."[41] He had adapted this formal statement from the precepts of political economy that he had been taught at the Johns Hopkins. Wilson also compressed it into a shorter formulation that explained how the new discipline was to present itself to the public. Its purpose, Wilson said, is to present the public as a customer of governmental service. The intention is simply to "open for the public a bureau of skilled, economical administration." Charges of "officialism" would best be fended off by endowing administration in America with the vestments of scientific objectivity combined with business efficiency.[42]

In addition, Wilson argued that there were two ways by which popular suspicions could be allayed. First, the class of administrators should be spread out geographically and assimilated institutionally. Ideally, administrative practices would trickle down to all levels of government:

In urging a perfected organization of public administration I have said not a word in favour of making all administration centre in Washington. I have spoken of giving new life to local organisms, of reorganizing decentralization. The end which I have proposed . . . is the discovery of the best means of constituting a civil service cultured and self-sufficient enough to act with sense and vigour and yet so connected with popular thought by means of elections and constant public counsel as to find arbitrariness out of the question.[43]

Second, Wilson applied the politics of light to public administration. The answer to popular distrust was the promotion of a spirit of popular vigilance. "Public attention must be easily directed, in each case of good or bad administration, to just the man deserving of praise or blame.

[41] *Ibid.*, p. 359. Wilson seems to have adapted this idea, not from German sources, but from the Belgian economist Émile Laveleye, who, according to Wilson, had "defined political economy as a branch of legislation, as 'the science which determines what are the laws which men ought to adopt in order that they may, with the smallest amount of effort or exertion, procure for themselves objects useful in the satisfaction of their wants, in order that they may distribute them in accordance with justice and consume them in conformity with reason.' " The phrase "a branch of legislation" is Wilson's addition. "History of Political Economy in the United States," May 25, 1885, *PWW*, IV, 654. See also his marginal note to Francis A. Walker, *Political Economy*, 2nd edn. (New York, 1887), Sept. 13, 1888, *ibid.*, VI, 8.

[42] "The Study of Administration," *PWW*, V, 366.

[43] "Editorial Note: Wilson's 'The Study of Administration,' " *ibid.*, pp. 358–59; this note quotes in full the two last paragraphs of the second section of the essay, which Wilson left out of the published version.

There is no danger in power, if only it be not irresponsible," Wilson argued. It followed that if the exercise of power was understood as a matter of public trust, the administrative system was not weakened but instead strengthened when an offender is found out. Wilson certainly did not want to see the adoption and enforcement of an ideology of official infallibility, which would run contrary to the American tradition. Popular suspicion was better allayed by occasional exposures of administrative breaches of faith, so that procedures could be revised and rules refurbished. The idea of authority, which was central to European notions of administration, could be translated as "clear-cut responsibility" in order to apply it to a more democratic culture.[44]

GIVEN THE SCOPE and purpose of "The Study of Administration," it is hardly surprising that Wilson tended to stress the passive, instrumental side of administrative functions. Although he took care to add that the administrator should not be considered "a mere passive instrument," it was tempting to picture administration in liberal terms as an act of supervision of the rules and plans that had been firmly established by the legislative assembly.[45] When Wilson worked on his second set of notes for the lectures at Johns Hopkins, he revised this view. Reviewing his earlier courses, he stated that he wanted to "advance 'from form to meaning'— from a description of the existing organs and machinery of Administration to a discussion of its standing problems, its general tests of efficiency, its essential principles."[46] As noted by the editors of *The Papers of Woodrow Wilson*, Wilson's readings in German jurisprudence, particularly Georg Jellinek's *Gesetz und Verordnung* and Karl von Gareis's *Allgemeines Staatsrecht*, inspired Wilson to state that administration should be regarded as a "subject in *Public Law*."[47] This turn from an understanding of administration drawn from the social sciences and political economy in particular to an understanding oriented toward legal doctrine explains, at least in part, why Wilson's article rather than his lectures became of primary interest to students of public administration as the field developed in the twentieth century. But what may have been lost in relevance for the field of public administration was gained in relevance for constitutional theory.

Wilson underscored that the definition of administration as public law

---

[44] "The Study of Administration," *PWW*, v, 373.

[45] *Ibid.*, p. 372.

[46] Notes for lectures on administration, Feb. 3 —March 10, 1890, *ibid.*, vi, 484–85. Wilson's emphasis deleted.

[47] "Editorial Note: Wilson's Lectures on Administration at the Johns Hopkins, 1890," *ibid.*, pp. 483–84; notes for lectures on administration, Feb. 3–March 10, 1890, *ibid.*, p. 485.

allowed him to pursue administration as a form of executive rather than legislative action. While he had earlier presumed that administrative activities were derived from legislation, he now emphasized that administration was "*itself a source of Law*" when viewed as ordinances that created "the *detail* of law." Ordinance as a form of public law should be understood as executive management rather than as a legislative function. Earlier he had tried to move administration and executive power into Congress in order to create a cabinet government that would dominate the legislative function. He was now convinced that it was possible to move administration away from the legislature in order to stake out the practical areas of executive autonomy. As Wilson summed up his view in a later revision of the lectures, his main point was to show that the exercise of administrative control depended on the ability "to get rid of our present pernicious system of *legislative* interference." His lever was the idea of prerogative power, that is, "the power of supplementing as well as of shaping the law to fit cases." For the first time Wilson began to quote extensively from John Locke.[48]

Wilson's readings in German theory led him to a reconsideration of Locke, but not the Locke who had fathered the social contract and had established the liberal ideas of individual rights. Wilson characterized the debate between Filmer and Locke as "nothing else than a contest touching the fundamental distinction between law and ordinance." Locke was fascinating to Wilson, because the discussion of the prerogative made clear that government authority was not only directed toward maintaining order among the citizens in civil society but was also established to secure the national welfare in the state of nature that existed among national powers. Locke had pointed out, Wilson noted, that "the law-making power is not always in being," that it is "usually too numerous and too slow for the dispatch requisite to execution," and that its access to relevant information was limited. Wilson argued that the significance of this discussion was to preserve the early modern power of the Prince as lawgiver and as the supreme guardian of public welfare in the prerogative.[49]

Wilson chose the budget as an example that showed the limitations of the traditional view of legislative authority. The budget, he wrote, is "a sort of *middle ground* bet[ween] law-making proper and administrative

---

[48] *Ibid.*, p 485, a later addition to the lectures as quoted in "Editorial Note: Wilson's Lectures on Administration at the Johns Hopkins, 1890," *ibid.*, 484; Wilson's emphasis. Wilson's discussion of the prerogative was based on Locke's doctrine of the executive power in *Two Treatises on Government*, chapter XIV, "Of Prerogative" (notes for lectures on administration, Feb. 3–March 10, 1890, *PWW*, VI, 508–509).

[49] *Ibid.*, pp. 508–509, 507. Wilson's emphasis deleted.

regulation" where the two fields would often "overlap," particularly "if taxation have also for its object the direction of economic life of the people." The "budget-supported State" had grown out of the self-supported state. The appropriation and allocation of means, which are the essence of modern budgets, are symbols of the interchange between decisions that relate both to interest and efficiency. Wilson concluded that "the representative body sh[ould] have the guidance of the administrative body." Lawmaking in this field is best performed "only when done under the guidance of men trained in the observance of political fact and force." *"The heads of administration are the most convenient leaders,"* Wilson emphasized.[50]

From the beginning of the 1890s, Wilson seemed to return to the study of law. His new definition of administration went hand in hand with his vigorous campaign to promote the plans for a law school at Princeton that would integrate the study of law with the social, political, and economic sciences within a broad liberal arts curriculum.[51] These efforts rested on an understanding of law that was very different from the legalistic doctrines he had encountered at the University of Virginia. It is a conception that is better described as a "field, not of law, but of the exercise (realization) of legalized function."[52] The legal battlefield was becoming more prominent in the 1890s, and Wilson realized that new administrative functions for government would have to be translated into an acceptable juridical form.

Wilson suggested the general scope of administrative activity in *The State*. He proposed to divide the functions of government into "constituent" and "ministrant" functions. Constituent functions would be those concerned with individual rights, primarily "the protection of life, liberty, and property, together with all other functions that are necessary to the civic organization of society." Ministrant functions, in contrast, would be those that would assist the development of "social organization." These functions, Wilson warned, should not be undertaken "by way of *governing*" society but "by way of advancing the general interests of society." They are optional and "necessary only according to standards of convenience or expediency." The ministrant functions would deal with broad areas, such as the regulation of labor and of trade and industry, internal improvements, communication, the manufacture and distribution of public forms of energy, education, and the conservation of human and natural resources.[53]

---

[50] *Ibid.*, pp. 517–19. Wilson's emphasis.

[51] "Editorial Note: Wilson's Plans for a School of Law at Princeton," *ibid.*, VII, 63–68.

[52] Notes for lectures on administration, *ibid.*, VI, 518–19. Wilson's emphasis deleted.

[53] *The State*, pp. 638–40.

Wilson intended the basic division as a mirror of the constitutional and administrative fields of politics. He constructed the constituent functions so that they would not be offensive "even in the eyes of strictest *laissez faire*." The ministrant functions, however, seemed open to charges of socialism. He argued them neither on constitutional nor on moral grounds but presented them as a matter of "the facts of government," subject to changes "in the method and extent" rather than to changes "*in kind*." The general idea is that the constituent functions maintain equal conditions, while the ministrant functions assist in social differentiation.[54]

Wilson's interest in the state and his projection of the needs of social organization brought him into contact with the ideas of state socialism. His most detailed discussion appears in "Socialism and Democracy," a short, unpublished essay he wrote in August 1887. The immediate occasion was his reading of Richard T. Ely's *The Labor Movement in the United States* and John Bates Clark's *The Philosophy of Wealth*.[55] Ely's work attempted to demonstrate that the labor movement was rooted in American Utopian and evangelical experiments no less than it was derived from foreign sources. Clark's book had a more ambitious theoretical scope. It sought to develop a comprehensive theory of social value and social distribution based on an organic conception of society. It was a serious attempt to bridge the gap between the economics of self-interest and the ideas of cooperation and harmony inherent in organic conceptions of society. Clark's work is usually seen as an early theory of marginal utility. Its basic contention is that exchange does not take place between individuals but between "an individual and society as a whole." "In every legitimate bargain," Clark wrote, "the social organism is a party. Under a regime of free competition, whoever sells the thing he has produced, sells it to society." From this idea, Clark stipulated that price is a measure of social value. "It is society, not the individual, that makes the estimate of utility which constitutes a social market valuation. That is part of our definition,—measure of service rendered to society as an organic whole."[56]

While Ely's work drew some critical remarks from Wilson's pen, Clark's book met Wilson's enthusiastic approval. He immediately wrote Clark to introduce himself and to acknowledge his "special obligations to its au-

[54] *Ibid.*, pp. 638, 640. Wilson's emphasis.

[55] New York, 1886, and Boston, 1885.

[56] Clark, *Philosophy of Wealth*, pp. 21, 83–85. Gunnar Myrdal, in *The Political Element in the Development of Economic Theory* (London, 1953), pp. 148–50, argues that Clark must be understood as a "harmony economist" who looked upon "existing conditions as the realization of social values, possibly with some reservation about free competition," rather than one who sought an examination of conditions "in the light of an ideal."

thor." "I feel," Wilson wrote, "that it has fertilized my own thought not only in the field of economics but also in the field of practical politics." "I shall, I am sure, return to your book again and again with undiminished pleasure and sympathy."[57]

In his essay, Wilson made clear that socialism is best understood as a matter of using the state to develop such "forms of organization" that would provide employment for each individual according to his talents and reward the individual according to his "diligence and merit."[58] Wilson stressed that "in fundamental theory" there is a correspondence between democratic and socialistic principles regarding the "omnipotence of legislation" as "the first postulate of all just political theory." Both systems rest "at bottom upon the absolute right of the community to determine its own destiny and that of its members. Men as communities are supreme over men as individuals." "Democracy is bound by no principle of its own nature to say itself nay as to the exercise of any power." The difference between democracy and socialism is not a question of what should be done but of how to do it. Democracy does not see any easy way to supply a substitute for the capital of the industry, and it lacks "adequate organization and suitable hardihood" to replace the system of credit. It has, therefore, recognized a distinction between social and political questions as a matter of convenience and expediency. Even faced with "dangerous combinations and individuals" in the modern age, the question is how to "act with practical advantage—a question of *policy*." "A question of policy primarily," Wilson concluded, "but also a question of organization, that is to say of *administration*."[59] Wilson's line of reasoning led to the conclusion that the system of private enterprise is better defended by reference to its organizational performance than by appeals to abstract rights or abstract purpose.

In a note hastily jotted down on an invitation to join the American Economic Association, Wilson gave some clues to the vital function of the

[57] WW to John Bates Clark, Aug. 26, 1887, *PWW*, v, 564–65. In his marginal notes to Ely's *The Labor Movement in America*, Wilson stated his objection: "And by what means is cooperation to supply a substitute for the capital of the industry?" (*ibid.*, p. 558).

[58] Aug. 22, 1887, *ibid.*, pp. 559–63. An early draft of this essay contains the conclusion: "May not the principle, to every man according to his honest toil and endeavour, be better realized by observing the natural limitations of state government [action?] than by having no fear of overstepping them? May we not achieve the objects of the socialist without sharing his opprobrium? How does Harvard College gain the confidence of the public, and its subscriptions? By a publication of its accounts. Is there no way to render all ways of money making clearly absorbed by the public? Is not *disinterest* the only obstacle to the objects of the socialists?" (Aug. 22, 1887, Woodrow Wilson Collection, Firestone Library).

[59] "Socialism and Democracy," *PWW*, v, 560–62.

administrative point of view, which was to be placed at the intersection of the economy and politics:

> One notable advantage of the Democratic state with a view to organic wholeness and all-round adjustment and development: all interests will have representation and a voice. The state will not have to depend for its progress upon the eye or upon the limited knowledge of a "Government": but will itself direct, from many sides (through great endeavour but finally with solid success) its own composition of conduct and development.[60]

The state, then, is not in opposition to private enterprise but is the theoretical expression of the conditions of social growth.

Wilson's grasp of the possibility of an agency in charge of organizing and accumulating knowledge of "the circumstances of society's case, the general conditions of social organization," raised the problem of regulation from a peculiar angle. The problem was to certify the development of self-interest according to social needs. In *The State*, Wilson described the purpose behind the administrative point of view:

> The hope of society lies in an infinite individual variety, in the freest possible play of individual forces. . . . It should be the end of government *to accomplish the objects of organized society*: there must be constant adjustments of governmental assistance to the needs of a changing social and industrial organization. . . . The regulation that I mean is not interference: it is the equalization of conditions, so far as possible, in all branches of endeavour; and the equalization of conditions is the very opposite of interference.[61]

Wilson envisioned an administrative order that would effect a liberation of individual energies: "The individual must be assured the best means, the best and fullest opportunities, for complete self-development." The end is the "variety and strength" of society: "Every means . . . by which society may be perfected through the instrumentality of government, every means by which individual rights can be fitly adjusted and harmonized with public duties, by which individual self-development may be made at once to serve and to supplement social development, ought certainly to be diligently sought, and, when found, sedulously fostered by every friend of society."[62]

One senses the compelling character of Wilson's vision of administration: an encompassing, continuing process in which the mass of individ-

[60] Pencil note, Aug. 1, 1888, Woodrow Wilson Collection, Firestone Library.
[61] *The State*, pp. 661, 660–611.
[62] *Ibid.*, pp. 661, 659.

uals, organized by society in economic relationships and stimulated as well as restrained by government, was held together by administrative knowledge and directed toward the end of the national state. The end was marked by the "diffusion of vitality and diversity of habit and capacity that make for structural and functional strength and for individual liberty."[63]

WILSON'S CONTRIBUTION to the origins of public administration in America came, not from an attempt to create a new science, but from an attempt to establish the foreign discipline in America. Administration needed some room of its own in America, because administrative skills and knowledge were commonly seen as an extension of absolute government, and thus as inherently hostile to democracy. The idea of "the modern democratic state" provided Wilson with some of the means whereby he could begin theoretical modifications of the conception of democracy that would allow ample scope for the study of and experiments with the new machinery of power. The most important issue was how to make Americans receptive to administration.

Wilson argued, in short, that administration in America should exchange its European regalia for attitudes and values that suited the American political environment. It should assimilate the spirit of science and the spirit of business when accounting for administrative necessity. The new class of administrators should be stimulated by American principles of motivation. Wilson conceived of administration in America as political power that appeared as the reflection of a predominant social need for growth. Whereas administration had traditionally been seen as a matter of rules and regulations imposed by the absolute state, Wilson argued that this picture could be reversed in America. Administration was to be located in America as a service demanded by various interests in society that would be faced with less opportunity and more social friction in the years to come. Wilson saw clearly that administration could not be imposed upon the republic from above. His achievement was to see that if administrative needs were perceived as spontaneously developed by social interests, the result would be to create political conditions that were highly favorable to leadership. The reason is that administrators, whether as public officers or as voters, by definition would be in need of political direction and national purpose. The assembly of administrative power would produce the prerequisites for leadership.

[63] Notes for a proposed book on the "Philosophy of Politics," Jan. 12, 1891, Woodrow Wilson Collection, Firestone Library.

VII

★ ★

THE POLITICS OF AMERICAN

HISTORICAL IDENTITY

In the 1890s and early 1900s, Wilson produced a series of books and essays that dealt with historical subjects. In addition to reviews and several articles that discussed the method and craft of historical writing, he published three major works: in 1893 a survey of recent history, *Division and Reunion, 1829–1889*; in 1897 a biography of George Washington; and in 1902 a five-volume work, *A History of the American People*.[1] Although he continued to teach and lecture on law and administration, and also wrote occasional notes for a philosophic treatise on politics, it seems clear that historical writing absorbed the better part of his energies during this decade. Engagements as a public lecturer also took an increasing amount of his time. In 1896 he suffered a stroke, which warned him about trying to do more than his health permitted. For some time he was forced to write with his left hand.

After his recovery, Wilson became involved in the politics of Princeton University, and in 1902 he was elected president of the university. His scholarly career seemed at its end. As he wrote in a private letter, "No doubt I shall have to give up writing for the next three or four years, and that is a heartbreaking thing for a fellow who has not yet written the particular thing for which he has been in training all his life." But he had had a "duty to accept." "It was a singularly plain, a blessedly plain, case."[2] His political career had begun. In May 1902 he was endorsed as the Democratic candidate for the presidency by an anonymous party member who had attended one of his lectures in Chicago.[3] Wilson was not entirely unprepared for such suggestion. Earlier he had written Frederick Jackson Turner, explaining why he would not agree to write a new

[1] *Division and Reunion, 1829–1889*, Epochs of American History series, ed. by Albert Bushnell Hart (New York, 1893); *George Washington* (New York, 1897); *A History of the American People* (5 vols., New York, 1902).

[2] WW to Edith Gittings Reid, July 12, 1902, *PWW*, xiv, 3.

[3] An Old–Fashioned Democrat to the editor of the *Indianapolis News*, *ibid.*, xii, 356–58.

book of history: "After all, I was born a politician, and must be at the task for which, by means of my historical writing, I have all these years been in training."[4]

WILSON'S TURN to historical subjects has been somewhat puzzling to his biographers. Since he continued to make notes for "The Philosophy of Politics," which he planned as a substantial contribution to the field of political science, the preoccupation with history has seemed a diversion. It has been suggested that Wilson made use of "his facile pen to write popular books" in order to meet his growing financial responsibilities and to pay for the house that he was building in Princeton. Wilson sold both *George Washington* and *A History of the American People* at a good profit to *Harper's* magazine, which serialized them before they were published as books. The commission that Wilson received on his *History of the American People* was the highest ever paid for such a work up to that time, and Wilson's personal correspondence does point to his concern for the income derived from these books.[5] Yet as a key to the works themselves, these considerations do not lead very far. In a commercial culture there is very little, indeed, that cannot ultimately be related to one's means of subsistence. In any case, as an early enterpriser in the market for national history, Wilson displayed an uncommon sensitivity to the subjects and style that filled a popular demand, and the implication of this is that Wilson used the writing of history as an opportunity to get in touch with common perceptions and values. His writings in the field of political science had been based on English and German literature, and his contribution depended in large measure upon his ability to view American politics from a distance. His books in American history Americanized his own nationalism, which was originally drawn primarily from European writings.

Generally speaking, historians do not hold Wilson's historical scholarship in high regard. Although the content of *Division and Reunion* has been praised for its modern outlook on the social causes of the Civil War, *George Washington* and *A History of the American People* have been seen as a step backward into the quagmire of heroic romanticism from which professional history was trying to disengage itself at the turn of the century. None of the books were based on primary research and they have been deemed guilty of "superficiality."[6] Indeed, Wilson's private corre-

[4] Jan. 21, 1902, *ibid.*, p. 240.

[5] Osborn, *Woodrow Wilson*, p. 280; Bragdon, *Woodrow Wilson*, p. 251; Harper and Brothers to WW, Jan. 27, 1900, *PWW*, xi, 380; Cooper, *The Warrior and the Priest*, pp. 52–54.

[6] George Louis Beer, review of *A History of the American People*, New York *Critic*, Feb. 1903, *PWW*, xiv, 338–46; Mulder, *Woodrow Wilson*, pp. 154–56.

spondence contains an admission that resembles Wilson's confession that he had not visited Congress in preparation for *Congressional Government*. Wilson replied to Richard Watson Gilder, who called his attention to some factual errors, "That was an amusing blunder in dates you caught me in; but it does not embarrass me. I am not a historian: I am only a writer of history, and these little faults must be overlooked in a fellow who merely tries to tell the story, and is not infallible on dates."[7] The most useful comments have been put forward by Eric F. Goldman, who argued in an influential article that Wilson, together with Frederick Jackson Turner and William A. Dunning, represented the historical views of a rising professional middle class that used the university to promote a national idea of history as seen from the states "in between." In contrast to established northern and southern historiography, these men exemplified what Goldman termed "middle states regionalism." Arno J. Mayer has pointed out that after 1902 Wilson, historiographically speaking, came to identify himself with the early progressive historians. More recently, John M. Mulder has shown that Wilson rejected the scientific view of history that was becoming generally accepted in these years and instead subscribed to history as a form of literary communication that used imagination to convey "the object lessons of history in compelling fashion."[8]

The problem of specifying the political intentions behind Wilson's historical works is compounded by the difficulty in accounting for Wilson's relationship to Edmund Burke. Wilson reread Burke in the early 1890s and seemed increasingly preoccupied with his writings, especially Burke's *Reflections on the Revolution in France*. It has not, however, been easy to point out what Wilson found most rewarding in Burke, apart from Burke's insistence upon the general priority of justice—meaning social order—over liberty. After his stroke in 1896, Wilson returned to the path of individualism, it has been suggested, although it is not clear why the stroke in itself would cause Wilson to move away from "his emphasis on social order and cohesion to an exaltation of individual liberty."[9] The seeming rapidity of the shift in his views may be the result of a failure to

[7] WW to Richard Watson Gilder, Jan. 28, 1901, *PWW*, xii, 84.

[8] Eric F. Goldman, "Middle States Regionalism and American Historiography: A Suggestion," in Eric F. Goldman (ed.), *Historiography and Urbanization: Essays in American History in Honor of W. Stull Holt* (Baltimore, 1941), pp. 211–20; also, see Louis Martin Sears, "Woodrow Wilson" in William T. Hutchinson (ed.), *The Marcus W. Jernegan Essays in American Historiography* (Chicago, 1937), pp. 101–21. Arno J. Mayer, "Historical Thought and American Foreign Policy in the Era of the First World War," in Francis L. Loewenheim (ed.), *The Historian and the Diplomat: The Role of History and Historians in American Foreign Policy* (New York, 1967), pp. 73–90; and Mulder, *Woodrow Wilson*, p. 139.

[9] Mulder, *Woodrow Wilson*, pp. 274, 146–47; Cooper, *The Warrior and the Priest*, p. 57.

distinguish between Wilson's religious views, which took the conscience of the individual as its primary value, and his political views, which depicted liberty as a consequence of social order. Perhaps the briefest indication of Wilson's distance from Burke's reverence for premodern "prejudices" is contained in Wilson's question: "How far are these crystals of experience to be crushed, how far respected as true jewels of conservatism worthy of a comely setting?"[10] Historical tradition in America, Wilson argued, was closely connected with the idea of the frontier, a theme he developed in conversations with Frederick Jackson Turner. A sensitivity to the significance of the West became a basic element in Wilson's view of American history, visible beneath his idea of the importance of economic interests for an explanation of the Constitution, Jacksonian democracy, and the outbreak of the Civil War.

Having abandoned the idea of "family history and the consequent inherited nature of popular government" as the essence of "political progress," Wilson was left with his ideas on the instrumental character of administration and the factual sovereignty of leadership.[11] He had a structure of power but no grounds on which to argue the legitimacy of government. In the outline of the projected "Philosophy of Politics," he noted that "the rule of lawyerly conceptions and *formalism*" had made it difficult to see and understand the "growth of national sentiment" in the United States.[12] Wilson's answer was intimated in a flourish of organic expressions, such as the "vitality and diversification of habit," the "diffusion of vitality," the "diffusion of power," and the "development of a diffused political vitality and diversification of the governing habit." These terms are repeated so often in the brief outline that Wilson seems to have encountered a barrier of language. In the margin, he finally added: "The essence of the matter is in the nation itself."[13]

The problem of connecting Wilson's political writings with his historical writings and the difficulty in acknowledging his contribution to the concept of the American West is that from the beginning Wilson had insisted upon the English origins of American political experience and upon the Continental European origins of administrative practices. It has therefore been easy to overlook that Wilson's ideas about political economy were largely based on his reading of American economists and that

[10] WW to Horace Elisha Scudder, May 12, 1886, *PWW*, v, 219. A fine discussion of Burke's reverberations in American liberalism appears in Louis Hartz, *Liberal Tradition in America*, pp. 145–58; and Arnold A. Rogow, "Edmund Burke and the American Liberal Tradition," *Antioch Review*, xvii (June 1957), 255–65.

[11] WW to Horace Elisha Scudder, May 12, 1886, *PWW*, v, 219.

[12] Outline of the Preface to "The Philosophy of Politics," Jan. 12, 1891, *ibid.*, vii, 98.

[13] Outline of "The Philosophy of Politics," Jan. 12, 1891, *ibid.*, pp. 99–100.

his main criticism of the historical school was its disregard of the American practice of political economy on the basis of common sense rather than abstract doctrine. Wilson repeated this criticism in his review of John W. Burgess's *Political Science and Comparative Constitutional Law*, in which he severely criticized a style of language that reduced political philosophy to "logical analysis" at the expense of its relevance to the interpretation of history. "There is no 'style' about such writing," Wilson noted sharply, "words are simply used as counters, without regard to the material out of which they are made, or to the significance which they bear in their hearts." "Politics can be successfully studied only as life."[14] To lack a vocabulary, as Wilson argued elsewhere, was to lack knowledge. "The facts do not of themselves constitute the truth." What is needed is "the just idea, the right revelation of what things mean. It is evoked only by such arrangements and orderings of fact as suggest meanings."[15]

In his historical writings Wilson seems to have been released from the spell of philosophical abstraction that slowed down his work on "The Philosophy of Politics." His criticism of Burgess's language is indicative of his own problems in regard to political theory. Wilson's historical work may be seen as the historical exercise of his political vision. His primary motive for engaging in historical writing was to state a political theory. "Our theory unorganic, our practice organic," Wilson noted about the essence of "the nation itself."[16] The new theory should therefore incorporate an antitheoretical bias that suited an admirer of Edmund Burke, but at the same time it should call forth the forces of national interest and make them "self-conscious." Industrialism should be made the crown of organic development and located where it is least expected: in the West. In a paragraph that deserves to be quoted at length, Wilson had told Turner about his idea:

> I want especially to form and express a right judgment as to the contribution of the West. And this on a somewhat peculiar line. Enough has been said, perhaps, of the spread of population and of the *material* development of the West (though doubtless even this could be said better, by being given a better perspective); but little or nothing has been said of the *self-consciousness*, so to say, of the West during this period and now,—of its own conception of its relations to the Union and of its own part in national development. My attention was called at one time to very interesting conventions held in the South not long before the war, conventions looking towards the industrial

[14] May 1891, *PWW*, vii, 201–202.
[15] "On the Writing of History," *ibid.*, ix, 295.
[16] Outline of the Preface to "The Philosophy of Politics," *ibid.*, vii, 98.

development of the South so that she might be put more upon an equality in wealth and resources with the other sections of the country. . . . Now, do you know of any similar conventions or any like expressions of policy in the West, any conventions looking towards the extension and perfection of railroad systems, of water connextions, or of manufactures, and accompanied by debates expressive of sectional ambitions in material development? . . . It occurs to me also that biographical material, of men active in the development of the West, might serve a similar purpose. But you catch my idea. It is that *self-expression* by the West in some authentic manner touching it[s] material and political ambitions.[17]

The intellectual connection between Frederick Jackson Turner and Woodrow Wilson appears to be an appropriate testimony to Herbert Baxter Adams's influence on American historical writing. What had been, in Adams's writings, an abortive attempt to graft German national historiography upon the American past was brought to a rounded and powerful conclusion by two of his ablest students. Wilson and Turner had first met in 1889, when they roomed together at Miss Ashton's boardinghouse in Baltimore.[18] They became intimate friends, and as soon as Wilson had decided to write the volume covering the years from 1829 to 1889 for the Longmans, Green series Epochs of American History, edited by Albert Bushnell Hart, Wilson wrote to Turner and asked for assistance. In his letter, Wilson referred to "our talks in Baltimore on the growth of the national idea, and of nationality, in our history, and our agreement that the rôle of the west in this development was very great, a leading, rôle, though much neglected by our historians."[19]

Wilson's idea of the West does not support the claim that some historians have made that the emergence of the frontier idea at the turn of the century implied a return to nostalgic notions of "the virgin land" and therefore signified a continuation of agrarian mythology in the midst of industrial society.[20] Wilson's idea of the West was clearly based on a recognition of the existence of an industrial order, including modern manufacturing, a system of transportation, and the replacement of local markets with a national market. His notion of "self-consciousness" drew upon an understanding of politics that saw a crucial connection between ma-

[17] WW to Frederick Jackson Turner, Aug. 23, 1889, *ibid.*, vi, 369–70.
[18] Frederick Jackson Turner to Caroline Mae Sherwood, Jan. 21, 1889, *ibid.*, p. 58.
[19] WW to Frederick Jackson Turner, Aug. 23, 1889, *ibid.*, pp. 368–69.
[20] Ross, "Liberal Tradition Revisited," pp. 116–21 in Higham and Conkin, eds., *New Directions in American Intellectual History*; Henry Nash Smith, *Virgin Land: The American West as Symbol and Myth* (Cambridge, Mass., 1950).

terial interests and political opinions, and that took its principle of reality from the national economy. Thus Wilson used the West to attempt to combine his concept of political place with political economy.

As pointed out by Richard Hofstadter and others, it is no coincidence that modern professional history in the United States is usually dated from the appearance of Turner's essay on the frontier.[21] The frontier theme was capable both of absorbing older ideas and forms of American history—such as notions connected with "the virgin land" and the idea of a spacious, popular republic—and of creating a new form appropriate to an industrial, rather than an agrarian, mode of production. The creation of the nation as a historical text depended upon a prior act of "vision" or interpretation, which may be understood as the discovery of a favored position from which to make the claim of being able to survey the whole of American development, or at least its essential parts. Turner's choice of the Cumberland Gap is perhaps the most famous point of vision from which American history came to appear as a coherent whole, visualized in "the procession of civilization, marching single file—the buffalo, following the trail to the salt springs, the Indian, the fur-trader and hunter, the cattle-raiser, the pioneer farmer."[22]

Wilson's choice of a location from which to achieve the distance necessary for a total view has received less attention. However, in his reminiscences about the creation of the frontier, Turner later called attention to Wilson's "splendid first chapter of his *Division and Reunion*," which contained Wilson's "own vision in its appreciation of the West."[23] Here, in a subchapter on American development entitled "A Material Ideal," Wilson wrote that he had attempted to disclose the secret of "the history of the country and the ambitions of its people."

> The obvious fact is that for the creation of the nation the conquest of her proper territory from Nature was first necessary; and this task, which is hardly yet completed, has been idealized in the popular mind. A bold race has derived inspiration from the size, the difficulty, the danger of the task.
>
> Expansion has meant nationalization; nationalization has meant strength and elevation of view.
>
> "Be strong-backed, brown-handed, upright as your pines.

[21] Hofstadter, *Progressive Historians*, pp. 47–48; Higham, *History*, pp. 171–76.

[22] "The Significance of the Frontier in American History," first published in the *Proceedings of the Forty-first Annual Meeting of the State Historical Society of Wisconsin* (Madison, 1894), pp. 79–112, and reprinted in *The Frontier in American History* (New York, 1920), pp. 1–38. The passage quoted is from p. 12 of the reprint.

[23] Wendell H. Stephenson (ed.), "The Influence of Woodrow Wilson on Frederick Jackson Turner," *Agricultural History*, XIX (Oct. 1945), 252.

By the scale of a hemisphere shape your designs," is the spirited command of enthusiasm for the great physical undertaking upon which political success was conditioned.[24]

In 1895, Wilson referred to the lines quoted above as "an inspiring programme" and as "the moral of our history."[25] Rather than writing a more conventional sort of history, Wilson sought to formulate principles, emotions, and practices that identified society as a whole both to itself and in relation to the outside world. "The spirited command of enthusiasm" is, it appears, directly addressed to the reader as citizen. "Elevation of view" refers to Wilson's interpretive concern. The act of interpretation is contained in Wilson's claim that the spirit of American life is to be found in its material order, its "physical undertaking," prior to its "political success"—meaning, presumably, its political institutions.

In *Congressional Government*, Wilson had already noted Alexander Hamilton's administrative genius and his role in creating federal conditions for national development. In *Division and Reunion*, he reformulated and developed this view:

> The federal government was not by intention a democratic government. In plan and structure it had been meant to check the sweep and power of popular majorities. The Senate, it was believed, would be a stronghold of conservatism, if not of aristocracy and wealth. . . . Only in the House of Representatives were the people to be accorded an immediate audience and a direct means of making their will effective in affairs. The government had, in fact, been originated and organized upon the initiative and primarily in the interest of the mercantile and wealthy classes. . . . It had been urged to adoption by a minority, under the concerted and aggressive leadership of able men representing a ruling class . . . possessed of unity and informed by a conscious solidarity of material interest.
>
> Hamilton, . . . the author of the graver and more lasting parts of its policy . . . had consciously and avowedly sought to commend it by its measures first of all and principally to the moneyed classes,—to the men of the cities, to whom it must look for financial support. . . . That such a policy was eminently wise there can of course be no question. But it was not eminently democratic. There can be a moneyed aristocracy, but there can be no moneyed democracy. There were ruling classes in that day, and it was imperatively necessary that their interest should be at once and thoroughly enlisted.[26]

[24] *Division and Reunion*, pp. 3–4.
[25] "The Course of American History," May 16, 1895, *PWW*, ix, 273.
[26] *Division and Reunion*, pp. 12–13.

Thus, behind the solemn event of the creation of the Constitution, Wilson saw an even more significant national compact of political economy. It was formed as a bargain struck between the monied interests and political reason as voiced by the Federalists in general and fashioned by Hamilton in particular. The purpose was to create a strong executive aligned with the vested interests and to shatter the popular forces that had temporarily asserted themselves in the revolutionary struggle. The legitimacy of the deal, confirmed by the creation of the first Bank of the United States, was provided with reference to the compelling needs of the postrevolutionary situation, as Wilson explained. The purpose of the bank was not only to furnish the country with a "sound and stable currency" but also to serve as "the fiscal agent of the government" and "to interest men with money in the new federal government."[27]

Despite the attention afforded *Division and Reunion* by contemporary American newspapers, it was the London *Daily Chronicle* which pointed out the theoretical implications of Wilson's historical argument. It wrote that Wilson had "first brought out very clearly that the United States at first were not only not democratic, but that the Constitution was very carefully framed in the interest of money and monopoly." In addition, Wilson had shown "with almost equal clearness the economic basis of the whole of American political controversy," beginning with the bank and tariff issues, and including the conflict over slavery.[28] J. Allen Smith clearly acknowledged Wilson's contribution to the economic interpretation of the Constitution in *The Spirit of American Government* in 1907 and quoted at length from the crucial passage cited above. In his work of 1913, *An Economic Interpretation of the Constitution*, Charles A. Beard briefly noted Wilson's account of the political formation of class interest behind the movement for a new constitution. But while the point of Beard's work was to show the narrowness of economic motives behind the Constitution, Wilson intended to show the priority for the nation of "the political and economic experiment we were making" over the constitutional experiment.[29]

---

[27] *Ibid.*, p. 70. In *A History of the American People*, iv, 44–45, Wilson repeated that the object of the first bank was to forge an alliance between the vested interests and the federal government. The bank was "by design a political institution. It had been Mr. Hamilton's object . . . to bring the money transactions of the country under a central control, to check the experimental banking operations of the States, and to draw the capitalists of the country and the greater organizers of industry to the active support of the federal government upon grounds of interest." See also Wilson's description of Hamilton's role in *George Washington*, pp. 255, 283–84, 287, 295.

[28] April 21, 1893, *PWW*, viii, 195–97.

[29] Smith, *The Spirit of American Government*, ed. by Cushing Strout (Cambridge, Mass.,

Wilson reiterated the argument that economic interests were absorbed and elevated in the prospect for national strength in his 1897 biography of George Washington. The West, Wilson argued, was opened by an act of political vision. The biography afforded Washington's youth and early travels so many pages that it has caused a later biographer of Wilson to complain that the work is "unbalanced."[30] But in fact the account of Washington's western possessions was vital to Wilson's whole argument, which claimed a revolutionary role for Washington in the West rather than in the East.[31] In his essay of 1897, "The Making of the Nation," Wilson repeated this argument in a more condensed form:

> Washington had been among the first to see the necessity of living, not by a local, but by a continental policy. Of course he had a direct pecuniary interest in the development of the Western lands,—had himself preëmpted many a broad acre lying upon the far Ohio, as well as upon the nearer western slopes of the mountains,—and it is open to any one who likes the sinister suggestion to say that his ardor for the occupancy of the Western country was that of the land spec-ulator, not that of the statesman. . . . It ought to be nothing new and nothing strange to those who have read the history of the English race the world over to learn that conquests have a thousand times sprung out of the initiative of men who have first followed private interest into new lands like speculators, and then planned their oc-cupation and government like statesmen. . . . The circumstance which it is worth while to note about [Washington] is, not that he went prospecting upon the Ohio when the French war was over, but that he saw more than fertile lands there,—saw the "seat of a rising empire," and, first among the men of his day, perceived by what means its settlers could be bound to the older communities in the East alike in interest and in polity. Here were the first "West" and the first "East," and Washington's thought mediating between them.[32]

1965), pp. 51–52; Beard, *An Economic Interpretation of the Constitution of the United States* (1913; reprint, New York, n. d.), p. 61; Wilson, *Division and Reunion*, p. 45.

[30] Bragdon, *Woodrow Wilson*, p. 244.

[31] *George Washington*, pp. 64–66, 142, 242, 245. See also "Mr. Goldwin Smith's 'Views' on our Political History," *PWW*, VIII, 354–55: "Washington had not had much of European culture. He had got his experience and his notions of what ought to be done for the country from actual contact with the wilderness, and actual life on the western frontier. He conceived the expansion of the country much more liberally than others of his generation, and looked confidently forward to many a great national enterprise. . . . The qualities that made him a great commander and a great president were qualities which would have made him an equally great frontiersman."

[32] April 15, 1897, *ibid.*, x, 225–26.

The passage is a representative example of how Wilson turned historical actors into carriers of forces of the national economy. Wilson intended his reconstruction of the birth of the national "design" to convey important meanings about the nature of the American nation. Washington's vision, as Wilson continued to explain, was directly translated into the politics of the Constitution. Most striking is Wilson's stress on material self-interest as a factor in the conception of the nation. It is a far cry from the national mythology steeped in religious connotations with which most nations cover the secrets of their origins. Wilson scornfully rejected the mysticism of his contemporaries who made much of "physical heredity" and spoke of "the persistence of race characteristics."[33] While it is not difficult to detect remnants of Moses' vision of the Promised Land in Wilson's description of the scene and its setting, Washington's vision is wholly secularized. This hard-nosed perception of Washington's motives supplemented rather than denied the sentimentalism that is often attributed to Wilson's historical works. Wilson's references to "direct pecuniary interest," "private interest," and the "speculator" hidden in General Washington contrast remarkably to conventional biographies of him. The choice of words makes clear, however, what Wilson saw as the key to national history.[34] The secret of nationality in America, he believed, was the transformation of economic interests, of private vices, as it were, into statesmanship and public virtues. The promise was continental expansion. The compact was between "interest and polity," a synonym for a national economy.

So far, Wilson seems to follow what is generally associated with the Turner thesis, yet Wilson's idea of the West had quite a different thrust. In Turner's essay, the nature of man was released by the frontier, whereas in Wilson's understanding civilization imposed itself upon nature. For Turner, the frontier created American individualism, or at least gave American culture its distinctive individualistic mark. For Wilson, the frontier inspired a new economic organization. While Turner stressed the sectional divergence of different stages of evolution, Wilson saw the West not in terms of sectional contrasts but as the resolution of contrasts in a continental political economy as a partnership in national perfection:

> Change had entry and freedom only in the great westward migration which followed the parallels of latitude further to the north, and

[33] "The Significance of American History," *ibid.*, xii, 183. Wilson had earlier repudiated notions of political heredity that had been associated with Bagehot, probably because of the confusing title of his book *Physics and Politics, or, Thoughts on the Application of the Principles of "Natural Selection" and "Inheritance" to Political Society* (1867; reprint, New York, 1948). See Wilson's note on Bagehot's *Physics and Politics* in PWW, vi, 335. See also, "Walter Bagehot— A Lecture," Feb. 24, 1898, *ibid.*, x, 437–38.

[34] "Making of the Nation," *ibid.*, 225–26.

in the great industrial expansion of the East. It was a process there which obliterated old political boundaries, fused diverse elements of population, created community in enterprise, quickened throughout wide regions the sense of co-operation, and made the nation itself seem to those who took part in it a single great partnership in material and political development.[35]

In writing about Wilson's influence on his conception of the frontier, Turner later recalled: "All my ideas and ambitions were broadened and enriched by Woodrow Wilson's conversations." The notion of the frontier, Turner explained, "was kindled by his imagination. His emphasis upon Bagehot's idea of growth by 'breaking the cake of custom' left a deep impression on me when I came to consider what part the West had played."[36] If Turner began with sectional geography, Wilson began with the dynamics of political power, and his intentions were normative rather than descriptive. Turner's aim was to account for the rise of sectionalism in American history. Wilson, in contrast, aimed to account for the rise of nationalism. If Turner asked what the frontier had done for the nation, Wilson asked what the nation had done for the frontier. Whereas Turner consistently stressed the dichotomy between the East and the West, Wilson toned down the clash of interests between the sections and attributed the conditions for western expansion to the origins of American nationality.

What Turner called the reading of American history from the west to the east became in Wilson's writing a forceful statement to the effect that the political constitution did not in itself possess the vitality and integrity that was needed to engage its citizens. Throughout the first chapter of *Division and Reunion*, Wilson elaborated this interpretation. It implied primarily that the two events—the Revolution and the Civil War—which had earlier commanded the understanding of American history, were drawn apart by the wedge of Jacksonian social democracy. Carefully weighing its symbolic content, Wilson took the idea of "a new nation," which vibrated with the meaning conferred on it by Lincoln's Gettysburg Address, and gave it a different form: "A new nation had been born and

[35] "State Rights (1850–1860)," Dec. 20, 1899, *ibid.*, xi, 312. See also a newspaper report of a public lecture, "Liberty and Government," *ibid.*, ix, 113. David M. Potter's influential essay "The Historian's Use of Nationalism and Vice Versa," *American Historical Review*, lxvii (July 1962), 924–50, investigates the shift from a descriptive to a classificatory or normative approach to the Civil War and brings it to bear on the equation of the North with nationalism and the South with sectionalism. Wilson's contribution, especially his replacement of moral and cultural values with political economy, is not mentioned.

[36] Quoted in Stephenson, "Influence of Wilson on Turner," p. 252. See also Billington, *Frederick Jackson Turner*, pp. 58–107.

nurtured into self-reliant strength in the West." It came to dominate the national stage beginning in 1829, the year that was "a turning point in the history of the United States." The "revolution in politics" was signaled by the presidency of Andrew Jackson. It was "the culmination of a process of material growth and institutional expansion," and it marked the "beginning, for good or for ill, of a distinctively American order of politics," which overshadowed "the apparent 'revolution' involved in separation from England," a revolution that in reality concealed "an almost unbroken continuity in our politics from the first until 1824." In contrast, the election of Andrew Jackson marked "a point of significant change in American politics,—a change in personnel and in spirit, in substance and in method," which led directly to "the period of the civil war, and, beyond that, to the United States of our own day."[37]

Wilson's book offended some contemporary critics for what they considered its insufficient appreciation of "the part played by the purely moral element in the irrepressible conflict."[38] In contrast, Wilson has offended some modern historians, who have spotted moral judgments behind Wilson's treatment of slavery and have charged him with "a moralized version of history."[39] In some ways, contemporary criticism displays the more correct understanding of Wilson's own intentions. He placed the political issue of slavery within the context of economic expansion.[40]

Wilson's account of the "causes" of the Civil War can be approached as a particular application of his larger theory of the national dynamics. He attempted to legitimize the republic in its national and continental form. In *Division and Reunion* he claimed that his understanding of the Civil War relied on "historian's facts," not on " 'lawyer's facts.' "[41] In a private letter, however, written to a critical reviewer after the publication of the book, Wilson made clear that not even "historian's facts" had been sufficient to make his basic point: "A Constitution must hold (contain) *the prevalent opinion*, and its content must change with the national purpose." "Otherwise," Wilson continued, "we must come to this (quite intolerable) practical conclusion, that lawyers and historians—at length antiquarians—are to determine what the course of national affairs shall be, bind-

---

[37] *Division and Reunion*, pp. 2–3, 11, 10, 9. Albert Bushnell Hart wrote to Wilson that he considered the first chapter the best thing Wilson had ever written. It had "electrified" Mrs. Hart. Wilson had hit upon "the true explanation of Jacksonianism—the rise of a national democracy which swept over its own local boundaries." Nov. 12, 1892, *PWW*, VIII, 43.

[38] Hermann Eduard von Holst, review of *Division and Reunion* in *Educational Review*, VI (June 1893), *PWW*, VIII, 223.

[39] Bragdon, *Woodrow Wilson*, pp. 237–38; Mulder, *Woodrow Wilson*, p. 142.

[40] *Division and Reunion*, pp. 125, 164–67.

[41] *Ibid.*, p. 212.

ing up new situations, new exigencies, in old conceptions produced by old conditions."[42] Thus the question for Wilson was not only how the Northern victory could be justified, but also the kind of power the war had brought to bear on political life.

Wilson's explication of the Southern secession and the Confederacy's eventual defeat was more complex, since he retained concern for the legitimacy of the outcome of the war even as he provided the basis for a socioeconomic explanation. At stake was the question of consent, that is, the right of the states to withdraw from the obligations of the Constitution. On the one hand, Wilson clearly stated as a constitutional right the concept that a "State could withdraw from the federal arrangement, as she might have declined to enter it."[43] On the other hand, Wilson was hesitant to leave sheer military superiority without a semblance of right. The result was an argument that combined some features of the idea of the modern state as a family with the idea of the nation as a compact based upon political economy.

The Constitution, Wilson argued, had been ratified by states of "corporate individuality." In the course of the nineteenth century, new territories had been "projected, stretched out, and energized" in the West. They had been added as states, as the "actual creations" of the federal government, and had received a mixed population "from all parts of the Union," "proceeding forth from the Union" as a homogeneous and national force. The South was no longer in a position to insist on local sovereignty, or physical integrity. The fault of the South was not treason but, rather, the sin of backwardness. "She had stood still while the rest of the country had undergone profound changes." She had refused to honor her "interest and purpose" in the national economy. To exaggerate Wilson's language a bit, the South was like a mother who claimed the right to leave her marriage, not to find a new lover, but to retrieve her lost innocence, the "old principles which had once been universal." At long last, the South was caught in the "national drift" and overwhelmed.[44] In a letter to the historian Hermann Eduard von Holst, who had reviewed his work, Wilson wrote that the South had "paid the inevitable penalty." She had been "lagging behind the national development, stopping the normal growth of the national constitution." The North should not be condemned at the "bar of history" for the war: *"I think the North was wholly right then,"* Wilson emphasized.[45]

---

[42] WW to Hermann Eduard von Holst, June 29, 1893, *PWW*, viii, 271–72.

[43] *Division and Reunion*, p. 211.

[44] *Ibid.*, pp. 211–12.

[45] June 29, 1893, *PWW*, viii, 271–72. See also the article "State Rights (1850–1860)," which Wilson wrote for the *Cambridge Modern History*, *ibid.*, xi, 303–48.

Wilson returned to his idea of national legitimacy inherent in "any power which our own growth had bred" when he concluded that national life was threatened by populist stirrings. His quarrel with populism was aroused by his opposition to sectionalism rather than by a fear of democratic upheaval.[46] In "The Making of the Nation," Wilson summed up his argument that the "cement" of interest and its political expression is the basis for the nation. "The temporary danger is that, not being of a common mind, because not living under common conditions, the several sections of the country, which a various economic development has for the time being set apart and contrasted, may struggle for supremacy in the control of the government and that we may learn by some sad experience that there is not even yet any common standard, either of opinion or of policy, underlying our national life." "We still wait for its economic and spiritual union," Wilson explained.[47]

WILSON understood political economy to be a knowledge of the conditions for economic growth that could be nationally motivated and directed from the political center. His elevation of this knowledge to become the saving form of political experience in America proceeded side by side with his criticism of liberal economics. Wilson often expressed this criticism with reference to Edmund Burke's condemnation of pure theory, which expounded the implications of the social contract or the idea that self-interest should be considered the basis of economic theory. He condemned both theories as "speculative politics."[48] Characteristically, Wilson combined his defense of the idea of the state with an attack both on the liberal understanding of society and on radical democracy. In July 1894, in the second lecture in a series of three at the School of Applied Ethics at Plymouth, Massachusetts, Wilson emphasized the

> Danger of confounding the 'State,' i.e., 'a people *organized*,' *with Society*, the field of individual initiative and endeavour, and of combination in small groups as contrasted with universal organization for common and general objects.
> We may be helped to a vivid perception of the difference by asking the following questions:
> Are the People, the whole body of citizens, *an Organ of the State?* Certainly not, for they cannot have *the same purpose at the same time.* Is the environment an organ of the body? Does the force wh[ich] re-

[46] *A History of the American People*, v, 260–67.
[47] *PWW*, x, 222, 220, 218.
[48] "Edmund Burke: The Man and His Times," Aug. 31, 1893, *ibid.*, VIII, 342.

sults from a correlation of the forces consist of the forces correlated?[49]

The title of the lecture was "The Organs of the State and Its Means of Advancement," a clear indication that Wilson intended to work out his idea of "political progress," which he had conceived as early as 1886 as a chapter in his projected work "The Philosophy of Politics."[50] He stated the theme of the lectures at the outset: "*An Age of Science* seems about to give place to *an Age of Right*: for which Science is responsible, inasmuch as it has produced modern social (cities) and industrial conditions." In 1898, working from the same set of notes, Wilson gave a new gloss on his distinction, one that is easier to follow. He described society as a number of persons who are "habituated to living together, conscious of common ties and interests, instinctively united, accustomed to co-operation." He saw "people Organized," in contrast, as an "acting" body, "under a more or less elaborate discipline, i.e., under authority,—an authority which serves to keep *individuals* from any breach of the common habit or understanding" and to secure "the maintenance of definite relationships and fixed rules of action, established principles and duties."[51] Thus the search for concepts that were more compatible with the need for national action led Wilson to distinguish between an "inorganic" and an "organic" social state, which seems to be a rough equivalent of the celebrated contrast between *Gemeinschaft* and *Gesellschaft* that was to dominate the political sociology of the twentieth century.

Another explicit attack on liberal economics followed in a lecture on "Liberty and Government" on December 19, 1894. This lecture is known from a verbatim report in the *Boston Herald*. Several sets of notes, some prepared before and some after this lecture, attest to its significance in Wilson's political philosophy.[52] Interestingly, the parts that in retrospect appear to be the most basic to Wilson's argument are not written out in the notes. The formulation has a spontaneous tone, which suggests that in the course of his lecture, Wilson discovered that he needed to spell out some of the interconnections he had taken for granted when he had prepared the notes.

[49] Lecture notes, July 2–10, 1894, *ibid.*, VIII, 600–601.

[50] WW to Horace Elisha Scudder, *ibid.*, V, 219; outline of the Preface to "The Philosophy of Politics," *ibid.*, VII, 98.

[51] Lecture notes, July 2–10, 1894, *ibid.*, VIII, 597; lecture notes, March 5, 1898, *ibid.*, X, 464–65.

[52] *Ibid.*, IX, 106–18. The best way to see the continuity and the continuous reformulation of Wilson's political ideas during the 1890s is to compare the sets of notes on the state and its study; July 2–10, 1894, *ibid.*, VIII, 596–608; Dec. 18, 1894, *ibid.*, IX, 102–106; and March 5, 1898–April 29, 1900, *ibid.*, X, 464–76.

Liberty is not synonymous with what we call scientific anarchy. By scientific anarchy we mean anarchy where there is no disorder. Ordinary anarchy means where everybody does what he pleases, following his passions.

Scientific anarchy is a state in which everybody is following his virtues. We are to have scientific anarchy in heaven, because we are told there is to be no rule there—that is, no constraint—because we shall all desire the good and follow it.

If every man desired good and were wise enough to follow his knowledge, there would be no need for government and restraint, and that would be scientific anarchy. . . .

As human nature exists at present, we are a great many of us following our passions, and following them very diligently. We say we are following scientific law, namely, the law of self interest. Nobody has ever studied this law. If he has, he has observed that self interest is a pasison [passion]—that a man's desire to promote his own interest is something that will inevitably lead, unless checked by very many virtues, to his trampling other men under his feet and crowding the men to the wall.

You have only to look around you to the men who are following that passion without regard to humanity. That is as dangerous for a man to follow as his lusts, because it is irregular.

I judge of my interest because of my understanding. My understanding may not be strong. . . . We don't want to follow that sort of understanding. Therefore as human nature is at present, we must adjust some sort of government to the needs of society, and see to it that we secure order.[53]

"Scientific anarchy" was a criticism that Wilson normally directed against "as *little* government as possible,—the notion of Jefferson," and against "such puerile doctrine" as that of the French Revolution, which held "that government is a matter of contract and deliberate arrangement" and "that the object of government is liberty, whereas the true object of government is justice."[54] But what began as a Burkean attack on radical democracy turned in Wilson's lecture into an attack on laissez-faire liberalism. The argument that Wilson presented is not the least interesting, because it virtually paraphrased Madison's famous argument in the *Federalist* papers for a balanced Constitution with sufficient checks on popular representation. Wilson, as had Madison, argued that government and restraints are necessary to keep humanity's vices within

[53] *Boston Herald*, Dec. 20, 1894, *ibid.*, ix, 108–109.
[54] *Ibid.*, x, 468; "Edmund Burke: The Man and His Times," *ibid.*, viii, 341.

bounds. Wilson turned Madison's argument for a balanced constitutional structure into an argument for a balance between the organized, authoritatively structured processes of society, on the one hand, and the improvised, voluntary, and private motives of interest and lust on the other. The purpose of government is to create restraints that secure the continuation and vitality of individual interests. Government, in other words, should keep "scientific anarchy" within such bounds as will insure the continuation of a growing national economy.

Wilson's views can hardly be adequately described as a conservative position in a decade that adopted English liberal economics as a creed and Herbert Spencer as its social prophet. The praise of "rugged individualism," the contempt for community, the glorification of property and capital, were the main elements in what Clinton Rossiter labeled "laissez-faire conservatism."[55] Neither of these elements has much descriptive value in regard to Wilson in the 1890s. Faced with economic views that hardly fit the expected pattern of political conservatism, historians have generally tended to see Wilson as a philosophical conservative. The argument is usually based on a letter from Wilson of May 13, 1893, in which he wrote: "If I should claim any man as my master, that man would be Burke."[56] Two comments seem necessary. First, claiming someone as a master is an indication of reverence. It is not necessarily a matter of becoming a follower in the sense of joining an ideological movement. Second, the context of Wilson's statement is not simple and obvious. Actually, it occurs in a letter in which Wilson explained why he did *not* want to edit Burke's papers. Thus, if Wilson joined the party of Burkean conservatives in words, he left it again quite soon in spirit. The statement was little more than a way to express interest in the project and at the same time to ask to be excused.[57]

[55] *Conservatism in America: The Thankless Persuasion*, 2nd rev. edn. (New York, 1962), pp. 151–54.

[56] WW to Caleb Thomas Winchester, May 13, 1893, *PWW*, VIII, 211.

[57] Wilson's relationship to Burke has long been a subject of discussion. Baker, in *Woodrow Wilson*, II, 102, suggested that if a man might be " 'interpreted by his admiration,' " Wilson should be considered a Burkean conservative. Diamond, in *The Economic Thought of Woodrow Wilson*, p. 40, also stressed that Burke was the source of Wilson's "historical conservatism." See also Link, *Wilson: The Road to the White House*, pp. 26, 32, and "Editorial Note: Wilson's First Lecture on Burke," *PWW*, VIII, 313–18. Mulder, in *Woodrow Wilson*, pp. 126–27, concluded that Wilson "abandoned his political mentor, Walter Bagehot, to become a follower" of Burke. Cooper, in *The Warrior and the Priest*, pp. 53–56, argues that what Bagehot had been for *Congressional Government*, Burke was to be for the projected "Philosophy of Politics." The problem in this interpretation is, not to account for Wilson's praise of organic institutions and his attack upon abstract political reason, but to account for his persistent interest in administrative science and the concept of leadership, which he defined simply and to the point as "initiative in choice and change" (lecture notes, April 28, 1900, *PWW*, x, 474). The

Seen from Wilson's point of view, Burke was useful because he provided a strong attack on rationalist political thought—"like Hobbes, Locke, Rousseau, *et id omne genus*"—and because of his defense of anti-rationalist ideas of order, such as "habit" and "political prejudice." But by the same measure, Burke had no idea of rational social evolution. Wilson saw Burke as "the apostle of the great English gospel of Expediency." Expediency pointed to a set of values that would offend established interests the least. It embodied a spirit of compromise and accommodation which identified what was "just" with what seemed "convenient" but which did not supply guidance where powerful groups were in conflict, and it contained little that would appease a majority that was capable of pressing a charge of injustice against the established order. Wilson's intentions may be described as an attempt to turn Burke's regard for the inherited order around and make it a promise for the future. Wilson's problem was not a Burkean problem of how to keep inherited inequalities in their proper place but one of how to devise a plan for their political evolution.[58]

In contrast to Burke's fears that a zealous elite would disturb the order among the common people, Wilson understood the idea of progress to be a resolution of the contradictions between stability and change, habit and rational choice, popular control and leadership initiative. Throughout the eighteenth and nineteenth centuries, the term *progress* was the catchword for the struggle against an inherited feudal order, the hierarchies of church and monarchy, and the suppression of popular majorities.[59] Wilson's hope, was to make progress a term for the modern dependence upon leadership. Discussing "the State's relationship to Progress," Wilson described the "material element" in progress as "an assured mastery over nature," and the "immaterial element" as the prevalence of order and stability in a governmental system "accommodated to existing needs and conditions." He believed that the key to progress, however, was the mobilization of the masses by the able few, because the "*relation of the Masses to Progress* is passive, depending upon the effect wrought by the discipline of life and the enlightenment of education and experience. There cannot be progress without the masses, but they are its material, not its effective cause. Progress works upon them, rather than by means of them."[60]

---

close relationship between Hegel and Burke is discussed in George H. Sabine, *A History of Political Theory*, 3rd ed. (London, 1951), pp. 519–20.

[58] WW to Horace Elisha Scudder, July 10, 1886, *PWW*, v, 303; "Edmund Burke: The Man and His Times," *ibid.*, viii, 342; memorandum, Sept. 10, 1899, *ibid.*, xi, 239.

[59] Sheldon S. Wolin, "From Progress to Modernization," *democracy*, iii (Fall 1983), 9–21; Arthur Alphonse Ekirch, *The Idea of Progress in America, 1815–1860* (New York, 1944).

[60] Lecture notes, *PWW*, viii, 599–600; lecture notes, *ibid.*, x, 465.

Perhaps the simplest way of putting the Wilsonian heritage in regard to the notion of progress is to note that he conceived of progress as an idea and as governmental practice that would restrain both the liberal belief in economic individualism and the belief in majoritarian democracy. Progress was no longer to be the rallying cry of the dissatisfied and the rebellious but the voice of moderation and reasonable expectations. The new leadership would be a leadership of "ordinary ideas, extraordinary abilities," as Wilson noted with reference to Walter Bagehot. It would rely on "a power of effective presentation, progressive modification, a power to conceive and execute the next step forward and to organize the force of the State for the movement." He defined leadership as "the practicable formulation of action, and the successful arousal and guidance of motive in social development."[61]

Wilson carried his frank exposition of modern elitism over into an attempt to reinterpret some of the key concepts of radical liberalism from the Age of Revolution: liberty, equality, and fraternity. While he rejected fraternity outright as a "word of motive, of sentiment, and not of organization," he read equality into the conventional understanding of the market economy: "equality at the starting-point, natural inequality at the goal." In this approach, liberty is to be understood not as individual choice but as "the best all-round adjustment of authority and individual choice,—the least friction bet[ween] the will of government and the will of the citizen." Neither liberty nor equality are the expression of popular or individual spontaneity but are "works of organization."[62] "There used to be a time when we took the Declaration of Independence literally," Wilson explained in 1899, "but we don't, we take it now in a Pickwickian sense. At any rate, if we believe that all men are born free and equal, we know that the freedom and equality stops at their birth."[63] Unlike traditional liberals, who tried to maintain a strict separation between market and government, Wilson's formulations stand out by their attempt to read the political meaning of American capitalism.

WILSON'S VERSION of American history combined modern historiographical realism with a style and a sense of romance that belonged to the Victorian era. His works contain important suggestions about his conception of elitism or "leadership," which centered on the interconnection between government and the economy and between leaders and popular work habits. Although these suggestions were covered by layers of lan-

---

[61] Memorandum, May 5, 1902, *ibid.*, XII, 365. Wilson's emphasis deleted.

[62] Lecture notes, *ibid.*, X, 468–72. Wilson's emphasis deleted. See also "Patriotism in Education," Oct. 13, 1899, *ibid.*, XI, 255–60.

[63] *Ibid.*, XI, 258.

guage that were intended to appeal to the popular imagination, they were nonetheless identified by such scholars as Frederick Jackson Turner, Charles A. Beard, and J. Allen Smith, who used some of Wilson's ideas in a language that contrasted sharply with Wilson's version of lyrical popular history. Wilson's didn't use his historical works to present a theory of elitism but to make his national audience fit for leadership. Unlike contemporary European ideas of elitism, which were addressed to an established elite, he dedicated his ideas to what he imagined to be the people themselves.[64]

In particular, Wilson went out of his way to sentimentalize a popular sense of national achievement. Time and again he praised the rugged virtues of the common American and referred to the moral values of common thought. In contrast to European theorists, and also in partial opposition to the gentile overtones of Theodore Roosevelt's ideas, Wilson did not sharpen the distinctions between the elite and the masses but emphasized instead their mutual dependence both in thought and in action. There was always enough of the shrewd real estate booster in George Washington and enough of the unpolished country lawyer in Lincoln to identify the popular values with political leadership. Wilson believed that he did not have to prove the necessity of leadership, only to present it in a language fit for the popular taste. Elitism in America was to be *of* the people, not just *for* the people as claimed by European theorists. Leadership was not pictured as an imposition but as the outcome of popular choice. In this way, Wilson's historical writings revealed their political purpose, which was to demonstrate in a historical context the existence of what Wilson at one point called "a mighty fund of unsurpassed civil capacity" ready to be developed for national purposes. He tried to exemplify his deep conviction that, as he put it in 1891, "We live in a nation that waits to be led."[65] The outbreak of the war with Spain in 1898 added a new dimension to this understanding.

[64] On European theories of elitism at the turn of the century, see H. Stuart Hughes, *Consciousness and Society: The Reorientation of European Social Thought, 1890–1930* (New York, 1958), pp. 249–77; and Peter Bachrach, *The Theory of Democratic Elitism: A Critique* (Boston, 1967), pp. 10–25.

[65] "Democracy," *PWW*, VII, 358–59. Wilson's emphasis deleted.

VIII

★ ★

WILSON'S IDEA OF

AMERICAN PATRIOTISM

It was not economic policy that came to preoccupy Wilson around the
turn of the century. Instead, his attention was increasingly drawn to the
concept of patriotism. Wilson's interest in the idea of patriotism may have
been stimulated by the stroke he suffered in May 1896. For the present
consideration, however, it is probably more relevant to note that Wilson
made his first trip to England and Scotland to recuperate. He traveled
alone from the beginning of June through August 1896. The long separation from his family, his homesickness for America, his search for
ancestors, and his visits to the shrines of both Adam Smith and Edmund
Burke may all be indicative of Wilson's need for a recovery of personal
and spiritual identity.[1] Wilson returned from England with an enhanced
sense of the importance of national duty which was first expressed in his
sesquicentennial address in October 1896, "Princeton in the Nation's
Service."[2] Whatever weight should be given to medical and personal factors, the course of political events was a primary factor in Wilson's turn
to patriotism. He worked out his ideas against the backdrop of a new
threat of sectional conflict, an upsurge of populism, and the outbreak of
the war with Spain in 1898, which established the United States as a
world power in competition with the European imperialist powers.

This phase of Wilson's political thought is of interest because patriotism became a persistent theme in his public addresses over the following
years and because it made it possible for him to formulate a concept of
popular leadership that supplemented his earlier emphasis on administrative competence. In addition, Wilson's analysis of the nature of American patriotism, especially its relationship to religion, sheds light on the
emergence of some of the values that seem, at least in retrospect, to have
become permanent features of American foreign policy in the twentieth

[1] WW to Ellen Axson Wilson, July 5, June 19, and July 26, 1896, *PWW*, ix, 533, 522, 547.
[2] Oct. 21, 1896, *ibid.*, x, 11–31.

162

century. The rise of imperialist sentiment in the nation stimulated and challenged Wilson to suggest a set of motives behind American expansionism that contrasted with traditional European imperialism, with its motives of territorial occupation, strategic domination, and economic gain. He suggested that overseas engagement could be incorporated into the American system of government as a means of strengthening the popular ideals of patriotic service and discipline. The importance of American world power was not a matter of unleashing economic self-interest but of restraining liberalism.

TOWARD the middle of the 1890s, Wilson renewed his emphasis on the primacy of politics over economic development. The rise of populism in the South and in the West seemed to warn that the ghost of sectional conflict was capable of returning to haunt the nation. Even though Wilson resented the very phrase "a new sectionalism" and paused to "rejoice to believe that there are no longer any permanent sectional lines in this country," he took the challenge from the Populists seriously enough to press his case for a national conception of the economy. In an important address to the Virginia State Bar Association on August 5, 1897, Wilson discussed the sectional divisions that issued from the "industrial revolution." The result of economic growth had been "an unprecedented diversification of interests," which produced "differences of region and of development" that were now "more sharply marked than they ever were before." Economic progress created its own regions of backwardness. "Here and there communities have a fixed life, and are still and quiet as of old, but these lie apart from the great forces that are making the nation, and the law is change." Accumulated economic change, however, was likely to stimulate political conflict. The real problem was that the major issues, such as "foreign policy, our duty to our neighbors, customs tariffs, coinage, currency, immigration, [and] the law of corporations and of trusts" could only be discussed in strictly economic terms:

> These are questions of economic policy chiefly; and how shall we settle questions of economic policy except upon grounds of interest? Who is to reconcile our interests and extract what is national and liberal out of what is sectional and selfish? These are not questions upon which it is easy to concentrate general opinion. It is infinitely difficult to effect a general enlightenment of the public mind in regard to their real merits and significance for the nation as a whole. Their settlement in any one way affects the several parts of the country unequally.[3]

[3] "Leaderless Government," *ibid.*, pp. 300–301.

As Wilson put it a few months later; "It requires more and more vision to conceive society as it grows more and more vast, more and more complex and various." The only hope, which Wilson expressed with an obvious note of disbelief, was that the temporary setback for economic nationalism could be overcome by political means. What Wilson had to offer was not a solution but a desperate hope, "an idea—a way out of chaos; the nationalization of the motive power of the government, to offset the economic sectionalization of the country."[4]

Within a few months this gloomy picture had totally changed. The public display of nationalistic sentiment before the war with Spain, the celebration of the quick victory, and later the general determination to continue the occupation of the Philippines despite the uprising of Emilio Aguinaldo convinced Wilson that foreign policy contained the key to a restoration of national unity. In a short personal memorandum entitled "What Ought We to Do?", apparently written shortly after the end of the fighting, possibly on August 1, 1898, Wilson noted that "a brief season of war has deeply changed our thought, and has altered, it may be permanently, the conditions of our national life." Wilson curtly dismissed jingoist arguments that proposed to see the war as the beginning of American imperialism. "It need make no difference to us," Wilson wrote, "whether we end it [the war] in a way to please the jingoes or not." In contrast to those who sought to emphasize the economic or strategic spoils of the war, Wilson argued that it should be appraised as the enactment of a drama that was politically significant because it demonstrated a common resolve. The war had not affected the different parts of the country unequally but had stimulated a sentiment of a shared fate. Its military actions had "strangely quickened our blood," as Wilson put it.[5]

The importance of the war was that it led to the articulation of a set of values that had little appeal in the normal course of liberal politics, with its emphasis on prudence, instrumental action, and self-interest. "It was for us," Wilson wrote, "a war begun without calculations, upon an impulse of humane indignation and pity,—because we saw at our very doors a government unmindful of justice or of mercy, contemptuous in its every practice of the principles we professed to live for." The war had generated "a manifest earnest passion for service." At the same time, however, Wilson was hesitant about the American entrance into an international environment in which civilization had become aggressive and in

---

[4] Notes for a lecture on patriotism, Dec. 10, 1897, *ibid.*, p. 349; "Leaderless Government," *ibid.*, p. 304. See also "The Making of a Nation," *ibid.*, p. 231, where Wilson argues that "authoritative national leadership" is a prerequisite for "a safe nationalization of interest and policy."

[5] *Ibid.*, pp. 574–76.

which England, Russia, Germany, and France were rivals in "the new spoliation" of Africa and Asia. The memorandum ends, significantly, with a restatement of the title, indicating Wilson's renewed attempt to formulate an idea of nationalism that was not asserted against domestic sectionalism but in opposition to foreign countries. "*What ought we to do?*" Wilson emphasized, "It is not simply a question of expediency: the question of expediency is itself infinitely hard to settle. It is a question also of moral obligation. What *ought* we to do?"[6]

The inconspicuous change of emphasis in Wilson's question marked the beginning of his work of redefining the liberal conception of the citizen in the modern state under the terms of foreign engagement. On the whole, Wilson showed little interest in either the theoretical or the practical aspects of imperialism. In view of his broad reading in European political literature, it is surprising that he made no reference to the stream of books that promoted and justified European imperialism in the late nineteenth century. His few comments on the future constitutional status of the Philippines and other practical aspects of long-term overseas involvement were largely overshadowed by his attention to the restoration of leadership as a legitimate part of American self-government. Although there were certainly elements in his thinking that pointed to the advocacy of an imperial foreign policy, he was surprisingly uninterested in colonies for their own sake. Since imperialism was usually argued with reference to interests of class, race, economic advantage, religion, or strategic advantage in relation to other great powers, Wilson's attitudes diverged from imperialism in the style of a Theodore Roosevelt, for example.[7] The dominant issue for Wilson was less a matter of action abroad

[6] *Ibid.*, pp. 574, 576.

[7] Robert Endicott Osgood, *Ideals and Self–Interest in America's Foreign Relations: The Great Transformation of the Twentieth Century* (Chicago, 1953), pp. 27–107. The liberal disgust with war and contempt for the notion of a "balance of power," which Richard Cobden saw as an aristocratic hoax to prepare the public for war, is well covered in Michael Howard, *War and the Liberal Conscience* (New Brunswick, N. J., 1978), pp. 31–51. The general American public reaction to the idea and practice of imperialism is covered in Walter LaFeber, *The New Empire: An Interpretation of American Expansion, 1860–1898* (Ithaca, N. Y., 1963), pp. 63–79, 150–96, where LaFeber describes reactions based on the frontier doctrine, the missionary calling, and economic ideas. Ernest R. May, in *American Imperialism: A Speculative Essay* (New York, 1968), pp. 44–72, describes the career of European imperialist literature in American establishment circles. Göran Rystad, in *Ambiguous Imperialism: American Foreign Policy and Domestic Politics at the Turn of the Century* (Lund, Sweden, 1975), pp. 25–69, presents a comprehensive overview of both the popular and the academic press. Among other places, Wilson's responsiveness to imperialist sentiment is testified to in his remark to the Lotos Club of New York on February 3, 1906, that "there are moments when I actually regret being an imperialist, because the anti–imperialists are put down as though they had no right to their opinions" (*PWW*, xvi, 297).

than of an impulse toward leadership that was disclosed as a consequence of popular patriotism in the wake of the war. Foreign policy seemed to reverse the traditional American distrust of leadership.

Wilson's response to the war of 1898 is therefore better described as an attempt to reflect on the vitality of national emotions than as an attempt to clarify the ambiguities in the actual goals and means of foreign policy. The formula he hit upon and repeated numerous times stated briefly that patriotism is "a principle, not a sentiment." He proposed to see patriotism, not as a matter of individual choice or as an extension of self-love, but as the embodiment of a structure of positive obligations deposited in the human character. It is "a sort of energy ... which expressed itself outside the narrow circle of selfish interests. It was not blind loyalty to the flag, for on the flag was written more than loyalty; there was written resolution. The springs of patriotism were in character—instructed, chastened, purified, unselfish character."[8]

There are obvious affinities between Wilson's heritage of Calvinist attitudes and his idea of patriotism. His perception of patriotism as an exercise in mental purification owed not a little to Puritan culture, with its stress on self-discipline and its ardent hope for a release from impure motives. In several public addresses, Wilson emphasized that "patriotism [is] the duty of religious men."[9] In view of the important role that religion was to play in Wilson's conception of patriotism, a general observation may be useful at the outset.

Quotations such as those listed above appear to make it easy to place Wilson within the general frame of Protestantism. Unlike Lutheran theology, which attempted to build a great wall of doctrine to separate the religious sphere from the political, the original Calvinist teachings stressed the interconnection between the religious and the political order. Since Wilson remained a devout Presbyterian all his life, historians have frequently been tempted to reduce his political ideas to their religious fundamentals. Recently there has been a tendency to argue that Wilson's political views are best understood as an expression of a deep wish to reestablish Christianity as the foundation of political life in America and elsewhere.[10]

---

[8] "Spurious versus Real Patriotism," Oct. 13, 1899, *ibid.*, xi, 244; notes for an address on patriotism, Jan 16, 1898, *ibid.*, x, 365: "What Patriotism Means," news report in the *New York Times*, Dec. 11, 1897, *ibid.*, p. 351.

[9] Notes for an address on patriotism, *ibid.*, p. 365.

[10] The political views of Luther and Calvin are compared in Wolin, *Politics and Vision*, pp. 141–94; Sabine, *History of Political Theory*, pp. 304–18; and Niebuhr, *Kingdom of God in America*, pp. 17–44. The political background is surveyed in Hans Baron, "Calvinist Republicanism and Its Historical Roots," *Church History*, viii (1939), 30–42. A recent example of the

Broadly speaking, this interpretation needs qualification because of its failure to appreciate that most of Wilson's references to religion were offered as comments on the cultural and political significance of religious sentiments, attitudes, and beliefs in America. While it is no doubt true that Wilson's views were deeply informed by Calvinist moral psychology, his writings and the record of his readings contain no evidence of a sustained interest in Calvinist theology. Wilson's intellectual concerns were simply oriented toward political rather than religious purposes. Two brief examples may suffice. His notes for a chapel talk in 1898 underline his keen perception that Christianity, by its reverence for the name of the Savior, had prepared men for political leadership. Wilson noted the popular need for "*a concrete image or example* instead of [an] abstract principle or conviction to serve men for action: cries, mottoes, emblems, *names*,—the most powerful, because the most definite, of all."[11] In his lectures he discussed the political benefits that might follow from religious arrangements. He emphasized that the Roman Catholic church had prepared the ground for the modern democratic state by creating "*a perennial fountain of individual capacity*" to offset "the exclusive class privileges of the feudal system," by which he meant "equality *at the start* for every man in orders, of whatever origin . . . though *at the top hierarchy, the preference of the fittest*, the most able." Most of Wilson's comments upon religion reveal his fundamental argument that religion provides one of the main pillars of order and progress in America.[12] This claim is as old as Tocqueville's observations on civil religion in America.

More specifically, Wilson's idea of patriotism as "the duty of religious men" was no part of orthodox Calvinist or Puritan thought. While Calvin had originally been intent on asking what kind of political order would serve to uphold and further the true religion, Wilson asked the exact opposite. In this period Wilson did not exhort Americans to join in a national or international crusade for world evangelization, and he did not demand that American patriotism be religiously inspired. He asked instead how people in a Christian culture were to serve their country.

WILSON's growing attention to the idea of patriotism changed the general tenor of his political thinking considerably. His public addresses became more attuned to the harmonies of common uplift and moral im-

---

religious interpretation of Wilson's foreign policy is Loren Baritz, *Backfire* (New York, 1985), pp. 132, 145–47, 150–53. See also Mulder, *Woodrow Wilson*, pp. 132, 145–47, 150–53, where Mulder explains Wilson's turn to religion as a reflection of his health problems.

[11] Notes for a chapel talk, March 13, 1898, *PWW*, x, 477.

[12] Lecture notes, *ibid.*, p. 470; see also "The Clergyman and the State," April 6, 1910, *ibid.*, xx, 329.

provement that were to distinguish progressive rhetoric after the turn of the century. Wilson's earlier focus on popular habit and obedience as the most obvious characteristics of mass behavior was toned down, while he gave popular allegiance and devotion to national political symbols a prominent place. Wilson continued to call attention to an element of fear as a stimulus to obedience—"fear of disapproval, if not of punishment,—apprehension arising out of our consciousness that we cannot determine the way in which others will regard our acts or deal with them." But in addition Wilson now stressed a more positive and active element behind obedience. He saw patriotism as "a means to individual character," as an act of identification with the national purpose which effected a transformation of the patriot himself.[13]

The importance of these changes may be assessed against the background of the general uneasiness in liberal theory in regard to the challenge from late-nineteenth-century nationalism. The general problem was that a philosophical system that cherished a view of humanity in constant pursuit of self-interest could not easily explain why citizens might occasionally be required to sacrifice their private interest in the name of national strength and honor. Another facet of the liberal problem was indicated by Adam Smith, who had underlined that the routines that followed from the division of labor tended to undermine "the martial virtue." The inevitable result of the advance of industry, he wrote, is an increasing corruption of the capacity for courage and "tender sentiment" in "the great body of the people," whose lives are confined "to a few very simple operations" in the chain of production. The growth of manufacture is likely to make workers look "with abhorrence" upon "the irregular, uncertain, and adventurous life of the soldier." These doctrines had gradually worn thin in the course of a century of revolutions and nationalistic wars. Still, at the turn of the century the fear of liberal effeminacy can be seen in the sharp reactions of Theodore Roosevelt and others who began to preach the virtues of the strenuous life.[14]

Wilson shared the discontents of liberalism. His notion of patriotism, however, was stated in explicit contrast to the nostalgic attempts to revive the martial spirit of the frontier. He did not deny that the settlement of the American continent had called for "*rough and unthoughtful strength*," but he denied that such virtues were suited to the modern condition that had come "with the filling in of the free lands of the West." This condition, with its necessity to "*stay where we are* and spend our lives in a single

[13] Lecture notes, *ibid.*, x, 465; notes for an address on patriotism, *ibid.*, p. 365.

[14] Adam Smith, *Wealth of Nations*, ii, 302–304, 306–309; T. J. Jackson Lears, *No Place of Grace: Antimodernism and the Transformation of American Culture, 1880–1920* (New York, 1981), pp. 97–117.

community," required a contrasting set of virtues, such as the cultivation of self-restraint, "a patient perseverance in details," and "a purged temper." Wilson's ideal war heroes were not the volunteer Rough Riders but "the christian gentlemen" who had gone through long training and who went to battle, not with a "love of slaughter," but with "a great pity, rather, for those whom they destroy."[15] In contrast to the then-current idea of patriotism as an expansive sentiment of military glory and conquest, Wilson's idea centered on values of balance, order, and restraint. This notion of patriotism—where violence is softened by Christian observances—was obviously more congenial to traditional liberal values.

Indeed, it might even be said that Wilson smuggled patriotism and its intimations of the public good into American liberalism. He raised the issue in terms that could offend no liberal. Taking the individual and the reputation of the individual as points of departure, Wilson carefully chose some of his crucial terms from political economy rather than theology. Wilson began by sketching patriotism as the manifestation of "a certain energy of character expressing itself outside of the narrow circle of self-interest." He took care to assert that the idea of private interest was not being undermined by his argument but was still to be considered necessary, desirable, and "in many forms praiseworthy." Yet "we are not so small as to live only for ourselves," he reminded his audience. Thus the liberal idea of the individual as a bundle of self-interests did not exhaust the variety of human energies. There is always, Wilson said, "a margin, a surplus, a free capital of character," which some individuals will seek to "expend" in undertakings "for the general welfare." The citizen is not "consumed" and "used up in serving himself"; there is occasionally a "generous remainder" that could be shared "with his neighbors and with his fellow-citizens and with his friends." Patriotism is not derived from a divine purpose but from man's location in a social context.[16]

The next step in Wilson's analysis was inspired by Calvinist doctrine. It explained how social sentiments could be turned into obligations and clear duties. Sentiments of love and devotion, he said, are transformed when they are subjected to the discipline that emanates from the object of devotion. As Wilson explained with reference to secular courtship, "You cannot compel a sentiment of sympathy unless you display the lovable qualities which inhere in the object which you would have loved."[17] The process of moral elevation occurs when the devoted subject transforms himself in the image of the beloved object. The same transforming

[15] Notes for a lecture on patriotism, Dec. 10, 1897, *PWW*, x, 350; "What Ought We to Do?" *ibid.*, p. 576.

[16] "Spurious versus Real Patriotism," *ibid.*, xi, 245.

[17] *Ibid.*, p. 249.

power is at work when the object of friendship or love is not a single person but a collective body capable of stimulating the moral aspirations of its individual members. Wilson did not believe in the natural goodness of the individual, but he believed that tested human institutions and ideals provide the means of self-improvement by setting a stage where man can transcend his natural limitations and develop his own character. The importance of patriotism is to display a basic human urge that is amenable to improvement by the examples of civil behavior and social duties inherent in the political order. Wilson did not dispute the low view of general human nature which prevailed in traditional liberal doctrine, but his whole idea of patriotism implied a sharp criticism of liberalism for neglecting the means of popular improvement. Doctrinaire liberals seemed to rejoice that men were so small as to live only for themselves.

Although Wilson would have found it highly improper to question the constitutional separation of church and state, he noticed that sentiments of friendship and love are dispersed through both the religious and political spheres. These sentiments, when recast into principles of duty by institutional arrangements, bind the members of the religious and the political communities into a state of cohesion that embodies an opportunity for the collective development of character. Wilson urged religious Americans to demand more from the realm of politics than "scientific anarchy":

> And so it seems to me that religion connects itself with patriotism, because religion is the energy of character which, instead of concentrating upon the man himself, concentrates upon a service which is greater than the man himself. And how a religious man can fail to have the fine impulse of patriotism I cannot perceive; for when you reflect upon it, the atmosphere we create is the atmosphere in which other men live, and national character is nothing but the atmosphere of motive and of action which we create for each other. . . . In proportion as we create the right corporate feeling in any body of men, we have lifted the individual man to the level of endeavor to which we desire to lift all men. And so it seems to me that religion unites itself with the patriotic purpose, because there is no motive which elevates like the religious motive.[18]

This is not to say that the political and the religious institutions share the same end. Wilson was never in doubt that the end of religion is the salvation of the individual by way of repentance and divine grace. The nation, in contrast, has "only this life in which to live." There is "no mercy

---

[18] "Religion and Patriotism," July 4, 1902, *ibid.*, XII, 475–76.

for a nation. A nation must save itself on this side of the grave," Wilson pointed out. But while religious and political orders can easily be distinguished, they intersect at crucial points by their appeal to complementary human motives. Both realms are dependent upon the "means of moralization."[19]

The result of these ideas is to set the nation up as a body of moral principles that nourish the individual. Constitutional government had been capable of enforcing restrictions and grooming the habits of civil behavior, but the nation aims much higher. Its purpose is to elicit the desire for moral achievement. It enables the citizen to reach for the highest form of personal freedom: the capacity for moral action in matters of common concern. "I believe it is every man's duty to be saved," Wilson told an audience at a student conference, "but there is a duty which crowns that, and that is the duty to lift other men along with him in that great process of elevation; and that is the patriotic duty just as much as it is the religious duty."[20] Thus the nation is far more than the sum of private interests, as liberal doctrine would have it. The nation is even more than the sum of the moral aspirations entertained among its members. The idea of the nation promises nothing less than a release from self-interest and an overcoming of the tension between self and society; the nation provides the basis for an argument that aims to combine perfect communal unity with absolute freedom for the individual. As Wilson put it: "National character [is] a means to individual character."[21]

Unlike the jingoists and the imperialists, who wanted to make Americans comrades in arms or partners in economic ventures, Wilson's consideration of patriotism was primarily concerned with the American moral community. This intent brought him to high levels of abstraction. As Wilson himself admitted, "the whole matter [of the nation] is abstract and of the mind, and it is clothed with the ideals of the mind."[22] A modern reader may often find it difficult to develop much feeling for a vocabulary and a style of expression that were stamped with the conventions of late Victorian rhetoric. Yet, if some of Wilson's central ideas, such as "moralization" and "spiritual elevation," are thought of as the equivalent of the modern quest for improved health, one may gain a sense of Wilson's reasoning, which turned upon the potential of modern society for the development of individuals by engaging them in matters of common symbolic meaning. Perhaps Wilson's position and its capacity for

---

[19] *Ibid.*, p. 476; notes for an address on patriotism, *ibid.*, x, 365.

[20] "Religion and Patriotism," *ibid.*, xii, 476.

[21] Notes for an address on patriotism, *ibid.*, x, 365.

[22] "Religion and Patriotism," *ibid.*, xii, 478.

generating controversy is best illustrated with reference to a concrete issue debated at the turn of the century.

The war with Spain gave rise to a public discussion of whether school-
children should salute the flag in a daily ritual. The issue contained most
of the elements of Wilson's idea of patriotism. The ritual involved a form
of political education directed toward the masses. Habit and moral aspi-
ration were blended in the ceremony, and Wilson was aware that the ritual of saluting the flag had borrowed rather freely from the practices of
religious worship. At the same time, it is clear that Wilson believed that
certain liberal principles were being offended. He argued, however, that
the ritual might be seen as a form of public education that preserved the
citizen's loyalty to the country without attenuating the regard for individual rights:

> When I see schoolrooms full of children, going through genuflec-
> tions to the flag of the United States, I am willing to bend the knee
> if I be permitted to understand what history has written upon the
> folds of that flag. If you will teach the children what the flag stands
> for, I am willing that they should go on both knees to it. But they
> will get up with [the right to] opinions of their own; they will not get
> up with the opinions which happen to be the opinions of those who
> are instructing them. They will get up with [the right to be] critical.
> They will get up determined to have opinions of their own. They
> will know that this is a flag of liberty of opinion, as well as of political
> liberty in questions of organization.[23]

This view of American patriotism is distinguished by Wilson's attention
to both the origins and the character of moral concordance. The key to
Wilson's argument is his emphatic demand that the elements of personal
authority be minimized. He understood that the solemn compact could
easily be compromised even by the teachers or others who were to direct
the ritual. The elements of compulsion behind the display of national
loyalty were exclusively to derive from the act itself, which allowed each
participant to lift his conscience into collective regard.

The sketch of the ritual of saluting the flag may be seen as an attempt
to reformulate the social contract of early liberalism under the impact of
nationalism. Unlike the liberal contract, in which individuals with prior
rights of property and opinions constituted the government, the patriotic
compact involved an act of submission that now signified the rights of
individual dissent, private opinion, and private interest. *E pluribus unum*

---

[23] "Spurious versus Real Patriotism," *ibid.*, xi, 247. I have supplied the words in brackets
to clarify Wilson's meaning.

became *Ex uno plures*. But, as Wilson's comments suggest, American patriotism would be masked as spontaneous diversity, as the practice of individual loyalty and private conscience. Wilson noted the contrast with German nationalism, where patriotism was turned into a confirmation of state power and where the symbols of national pride were paraded through the streets in order to insure a civic appreciation of national purpose.[24] American patriotism would not depend upon state uniformity but upon the cultivation of popular conformity.

Wilson first presented this exposition of the dynamics of American patriotism in outline form at a conference of the New England Association of Colleges and Preparatory Schools at Harvard University in October 1899, and he often returned to it in public addresses over the following five years. Wilson's explicit references to the worship of the flag were most likely to stimulate controversy. Newspaper reports of later addresses often interpreted his comments as a criticism of the ritual itself.[25] Almost five years after his first discussion of flag worship as a symbol of national civic education, Wilson received a letter from Robert S. Dana, who identified himself as a "Special Aide of the Grand Army of the Republic." Dana asked Wilson to repudiate a newspaper report that noted Wilson's " 'doubting the utility of the worship of the flag.' "[26] In his reply, Wilson repeated that if patriotism did not serve the purpose of fortifying a moral consensus as to "what the flag stood for," it was merely an exercise in "blind reference." As if rehearsing his original argument, Wilson objected strongly to Dana's self-assertive nationalism, which confused national obligations with personal predilections, and he asserted that the vigilant tone of the letter compromised the integrity of the national community. The underlying assumption of the letter "that the Grand Army of the Republic is at liberty to call their fellow-citizens to account for public utterances, *seems to me both offensive and ridiculous*," Wilson concluded, as if to insure that he had left no room for misunderstanding.[27]

The idea of patriotism that Wilson proposed depended upon an immediate and direct confrontation between "the nation" and the individual conscience. He was therefore deeply offended by Dana's suggestion that one's private conscience be carefully examined by some kind of agency before the individual was admitted into the national community. Unlike Dana, Wilson did not demand that private convictions conform to

---

[24] Speech on patriotism in Worcester, Mass., Jan. 30, 1902, *ibid.*, xii, 260; address on patriotism to the Washington Association of New Jersey, Feb. 23, 1903, *ibid.*, xiv, 367.

[25] Speech on patriotism in Worcester, Mass., *ibid.*, xii, 258, reported in the *Worcester Daily Telegram* under the heading "Flag Worship Is Cried Down."

[26] Robert Shoemaker Dana to WW, March 15, 1905, *ibid.*, xvi, 30.

[27] WW to Robert Shoemaker Dana, March 21, 1905, *ibid.*, 35.

preestablished patterns; he required only that individual opinion and interest be able to be defended with reference to national values. This did not lead Wilson to an exaltation of individualism in the political sphere. On the contrary, Wilson repeatedly issued strong warnings against the cultivation of individual personality, "the object of the individual being character," as he put it. "I believe that the curse of the age is the man who spends so much time thinking of himself," he said on one occasion. On another he pointed out that the man who tried to make his own character only succeeded in making "a precious prig" of himself. The nourishment of patriotic "virtue and highmindedness" had as its corollary that individual conviction be left alone "to take care of itself." How could Wilson combine his regard for individual rights with his outspoken criticism of individualism and personal persuasions, the great love-objects of the age? The answer seems to be that personal character lost its quality of inner necessity once it lost a monopoly on its sanctum in the human soul. When compared to the deep mysteries of collective concord, individual character came to look more like outward affectation. "Your character is no more to live for than is your dress," as Wilson remarked sharply.[28] When self-consciousness is relieved of its moral and political bearings, Wilson believed, it becomes incoherent and capricious. This condition makes the individual the natural object of national power, and the highest expression of national power in the 1890s centered on the issue and practices of imperialism.

WILSON'S COMMENTS on imperialism were characterized by a striking absence of concern for the international context of American expansionism. His support for official policy was largely limited to broad arguments that the Philippines and Puerto Rico should be kept under "tutelage" in order to prepare the indigenous population for self-government. The hesitation that marked his initial response to the news of the conquest was gradually abandoned, and by 1900 Wilson was talking about the acquisition of the Philippines both as an intimation of "an ordering of Providence" supported by "the willful fortune of war."[29] But his primary interest was directed toward the spiritual or moral import of imperialism, which was to become a school of self-discipline. He was more interested in the effects upon the tutor than upon the pupil of self-government. In an article in the *Atlantic Monthly*, Wilson wrote that Americans might need to govern the Philippines temporarily "with a strong

[28] Address on state education, Jan. 3, 1903, *ibid.*, xiv, 319; address on patriotism in Harrisburg, Pa., Feb. 23, 1903, *ibid.*, p. 368; speech on patriotism in Worcester, Mass., *ibid.*, xii, 260–61.

[29] "Democracy and Efficiency," Oct. 1, 1900, *ibid.*, p. 18.

hand that will brook no resistance, and according to principles of right gathered from our own experience, not from theirs, which has never yet touched the vital matter we are concerned with. . . . They are children and we are men in these deep matters of government and justice." Completely discarding the historical experience that lay behind Philippine culture and institutions, Wilson began to see the occupation of the Philippines as an American learning experience. "We must govern as those who learn," Wilson wrote. "We expect as much from schoolteachers as from the governors in the Philippines and in Porto Rico: we expect from them the *morale* that is to sustain our work there."[30] Wilson outlined three major consequences for America that followed from the venture overseas: changes in political opinions, changes in political institutions, and changes in political science.

The best illustration of the effects of the war upon political opinions, Wilson pointed out, was the abandonment of a whole range of old issues. The war had broken "the constant reargument, *de novo*, of the money question" and of "easy currency." The turn of international events dispelled American "false self-confidence" and belief in self-sufficiency almost overnight. Nearly half of the population, Wilson argued, had formed their opinions on the assumption that the United States was "a divided portion of mankind, masters and makers of our own laws of trade." The war had relieved public opinion of its "most childish errors" and submitted it to "the well-known laws of value and exchange." "There is no masking or concealing the new order of the world," Wilson wrote in October 1900. "A new era has come upon us like a sudden vision of things unprophesied, and for which no polity has been prepared."[31]

Wilson also registered the second impact of the war, the impact on American political institutions. "The center of gravity has shifted in the action of our Federal government," as he wrote in late 1901. "It has shifted back to where it was at the opening of the last century," to the era of the federalists, when the republic was fighting for its survival, and foreign policy therefore "dominated our politics." "Once more it is our place among the nations that we think of; once more our Presidents are our leaders. . . . And this centring of our thoughts, this looking for guidance in things, . . . this union of our hopes, will not leave us what we were. . . . Here is a new life to which to adjust our ideals."[32]

The final consequence of the war was its affect on American political thinking. As Wilson's disregard of Philippine culture made clear, the na-

---

[30] "The Ideals of America," Dec. 26, 1901, *ibid.*, pp. 223, 225; "Democracy and Efficiency," *ibid.*, p. 19.

[31] "Democracy and Efficiency," *ibid.*, pp. 13–14, 11.

[32] "The Ideals of America," Dec. 26, 1901, *ibid.*, pp. 226–27.

tional vision assumed the features of abstract method as soon as it was extended beyond the national borders. Although some of these changes may be said to have been registered in Wilson's writings on administration and on political progress, the experience of imperialism made them more visible in his thinking. The notions of historical experience and political habits were displaced in favor of a new emphasis upon "political and economic experiment." Wilson made the most direct argument in favor of a new political methodology in his essay on "The Significance of American History," written in 1901 for *Harper's Encyclopædia of United States History*.[33]

The importance of American history, Wilson argued, is to unveil "the deepest of all secrets, the genesis of nationality, the play of spirit in the processes of history." Historically, the continent had not been burdened with loyalty to a place, and it was free of the personal and class dependence that plagued Europe. The history of the United States was "modern history in broad and open analysis, stripped of a thousand elements which, upon the European state, confuse the eye and lead the judgment astray." "Complex things of government" were reduced "to their simples" in the New World. The natural environment had tended to draw government back to "its essential qualities, stripped of its elaborate growth of habit." Principles that elsewhere had been developed by "the long and intricate processes" of older cultures were put to "experimental test" in the United States, where "every element of life" was simplified and "every problem of government" had been "reduced to its fundamental formulæ." The result was that America exuded a new form of political knowledge, based on practice, not on abstract theories. Wilson hoped for the discovery of "a few of the first principles of the natural history of institutions." The new science of politics, with its emphasis on the "comparative study of institutions," would be directed against the radical democratic theories of revolution. It would "yield us a sane philosophy of politics which shall forever put out of school the thin and sentimental theories of the disciples of Rousseau," as Wilson phrased it. The new science was to focus on the principles of nation building:

> As a stage in the economic development of modern civilization, the history of America constitutes the natural, and invaluable, subject-matter and book of praxis of the political economist. Here is industrial development worked out with incomparable logical swiftness, simplicity, and precision,—a swiftness, simplicity, and precision impossible amidst the rigid social order of any ancient kingdom. It is a study, moreover, not merely of the make-up and setting forth of a

[33] Sept. 9, 1901, *ibid.*, pp. 179–84.

new people, but also of its marvellous expansion, of processes of growth, both spiritual and material, hurried forward from stage to stage as if under the experimental touch of some social philosopher, some political scientist making of a nation's history his laboratory and place of demonstration.[34]

America was, as later political scientists would phrase it, the first new nation.[35] The extension of the borders of the new science of political order in changing societies was more important to Wilson than any material benefits that might accrue from the temporary possession of dependencies. The acquisition of Puerto Rico and the Philippines suggested obvious places to experiment with the methods of self-government.[36]

Wilson most clearly spelled out his plea for a new political method in "Democracy and Efficiency," written in 1900. This essay demonstrated that it was not difficult for Wilson to apply some of the dynamic principles of domestic westward expansion to foreign affairs. "The frontier" became "the frontage." The "odd mixture of selfish and altruistic motives" that had carried continental expansion forward was to be reproduced overseas: "Our interests must march forward, altruists though we are; other nations must see to it that they stand off, and do not seek to stay us," Wilson claimed. To those who feared that the foreign venture would hamper the development of political institutions at home, Wilson answered that "such experiments in the universal validity of principle and method" might well make American democracy more efficient: "We may ourselves get responsible leadership instead of government by mass meeting; a trained and thoroughly organized administrative service instead of administration by men privately nominated and blindly elected; a new notion of terms of office and of standards of policy."[37]

MANY OF Wilson's early ideas about the meaning of foreign policy had a tentative character. They indicate a direction of thinking rather than a set of finished formulations. It should also be kept in mind that the present account of his views has drawn upon several, and somewhat disparate, sources, some of which were intended as contributions to patriotism itself rather than to the study of patriotism. Nevertheless, a distinctive feature is apparent in Wilson's general assumption that patriotism should

[34] *Ibid.*, pp. 180–84.

[35] See Seymour M. Lipset, *The First New Nation: The United States in Historical and Comparative Perspective* (Garden City, N. Y., 1967); and Samuel P. Huntington, *Political Order in Changing Societies* (New Haven, 1968) on modern theories of nation building.

[36] See, for instance, "The Theory of Organization," and "Our Congress and Its Powers," as reported in the Richmond *Times*, Nov. 2 and 4, 1898, *ibid.*, XI, 66, 71.

[37] Oct. 1, 1900, *ibid.*, XII, 11–13, 20.

be understood, not as the source of national power, but as its emotional supplement. In Wilson's view, patriotism did not motivate the war with Spain but followed in the wake of the war as a form of popular acceptance of the inevitable. As Wilson's discussion of the ritual of saluting the flag made clear, he understood citizenship to be a form of initiation that confirmed but did not create state power.

Although American patriotism had its roots in the national experience, Wilson's discussion made clear that its principles of loyalty were to reflect a context of modern power that went beyond national borders. He developed this idea in a brief article, "Education and Democracy," written in 1907 as a contribution to a collection of essays on citizenship and higher education. The book was never published, but the essay is sometimes cited by historians searching for clues to Wilson's opinions on imperialism.[38] Wilson's primary intention, however, was to advocate a two-tier system of education in which the majority of students received the proper technical training, while the minority received a broader liberal education that prepared them for leadership. In order to outline the qualities needed for leadership, Wilson produced his sketch of the conjunction of powers that pushed progress forward and seemed destined eventually to rule the world without serious opposition. There is a note of prophetic urgency in the essay, a note confirmed by Wilson's complete rejection of any sentimentality that might disturb the clear outline he presented. There is also a note of predetermination that may recall Wilson's early essay on "Christ's Army."

In Wilson's description the ruling powers are completely impersonal. They are largely unaffected even by systems of government. It is only through education that human beings come into contact with them. Each of these powers is described as a world unto itself, but as Wilson made clear, it is their advancing integration that makes their progress inexorable. The first is the power of "exact science applied." The second is the power of "extensive enterprise," oriented toward competition and profit. The third is the power revealed in "the irresistible energy and efficiency of harmony and cooperation," which is displayed in "coordinations of organizations" and in "vast combinations" encompassing public administration and private industrial structures in the attempt to overcome wasteful competition and harmful rivalry.

These are the powers of progress. They seem autonomous, but Wilson called attention to an evolutionary relationship among them. The science of nature had produced vast new opportunities for competitive enter-

---

[38] The most recent example is Lloyd Gardner, *Safe for Democracy: The Anglo-American Response to Revolution, 1913–1923* (New York, 1984), p. 41.

prise, which in turn had overstepped the boundaries of localism and produced the need for coordination between national government and industry on a national, and later an international, scale.

While modern power had advanced, human beings had stayed the same. They had the "same passions, loves, cupidities; the same innocences to be deceived, the same shrewdness to observe their interest" as when their horizon had been set by local business and politics. The impotence of human motives stands out in contrast to the potent logic of modern progress. The distinctive feature of Wilson's article is its strong insistence that progress cannot proceed before older structures are cleared away. The ruling forces are the expression of anarchy and selfishness. Knowledge is created for "tangible profit," enterprise for rivalry and "economic advantage." Large-scale violence, exploitation, and disregard of settled law follow in the wake of progress:

> If the individuals combine, government must seek to regulate not individuals but combinations; must lay itself alongside the complex structures of industry and multiply its function, in order to adjust law to the change. Since trade ignores national boundaries and the manufacturer insists on having the world as a market, the flag of his nation must follow him, and the doors of the nations which are closed against him must be battered down. Concessions obtained by financiers must be safeguarded by ministers of state, even if the sovereignty of unwilling nations be outraged in the process. Colonies must be obtained or planted, in order that no useful corner of the world may be overlooked or left unused. Peace itself becomes a matter of conference and international combination. Cooperation is the law of all action in the modern world.[39]

This description was hardly intended as a celebration of imperialism, but it reveals Wilson's understanding of violence as the necessary accompaniment of modern economic and political rationality. In order for the transformation from war to cooperation to take place, it is necessary to stimulate the growth of a fourth power, the power of leadership. Obviously, this is the type of leadership that Wilson hoped to create at Princeton. The question is not whether Wilson advocated imperialism but how he imagined that the new leadership could contain and integrate forces as powerful as modern science, capitalism, and organization.

Wilson's answer was that until now the forces of progress had depended upon the human ability to see and act within a very small range. Applied science was specialized, and it produced men who saw only "the

[39] "Education and Democracy," May 4, 1907, *PWW*, xvii, 134–36.

little interior pieces" of reality. The capitalist enterpriser who produced industrial miracles was driven by the limited motive of gain. Combinations of private and national organizations were effected in order to "weave an international network of gain and power." The key to modern leadership is to overcome this localism of skill, vision, and motive. True leadership, developed upon the grounds of pure science and liberal learning, would match the modern forces with "coordinations of thought" on the broad scale of academic disciplines and within a broad historical view. Modern education for the gifted minority should be conceived of as a new regimen of mind, "the government of right thinking, of clear, thoughtful planning of minds trained to see things in wholes and combinations, divorced from special interests." The key to Wilson's argument, as well as to his ambivalence about the issue of imperialism, is that he saw the large scale itself as the means by which to lift progress from its violent and anarchic stage. In this way the lifting of enterprise and politics to a worldwide scale transformed it qualitatively from "the limits of a single locality" to the stage where it was in effect forced to be "able to look far afield." The divorce from self-interest would be accomplished simply by entering the "general field of thought and observation."[40] Wilson's argument was a testimony to his enduring bias against localism and sectionalism in almost any conceivable form. Distance and separation implies conflict. Interdependence spells harmony. Occasionally, there is a note of internationalism and an appeal to business interests, but most of Wilson's opinions about imperialism center on his belief that power is ennobled as it is expanded and extended. He often formulated this as a reversal of the liberal understanding that interest is safest when most closely attached to the self. This understanding also represents, at least in part, an attempt to compensate for the loss of general political reason which was effected when "practical politics" was exalted as the substitute for general theories.

THUS for Wilson the challenge of the war and the issue of the occupation of the Philippines had less to do with founding new empires than dealing with power and the consciousness of power at home. Patriotism itself taught the people to measure up to a new standard of service that had unmistakable republican roots. "The Romans furnished us with types of public duty and self-sacrifice," as Wilson put it in a religious talk. Patriotism prepared the public for an evolution of administrative techniques that seemed foreign to the American experience. It destroyed provincialism and the belief in American exceptionalism. It was a sign of

[40] *Ibid.*

AMERICAN PATRIOTISM

political maturity that pointed in the direction of responsible leadership. As Wilson argued in 1900, "May it not be that the way to perfection lies along these new paths of struggle, of discipline, and of achievement? . . . What self-revelation will it afford; what lessons of unified will, of simplified method, of clarified purpose[?]" The promise of foreign involvement was therefore not only "that authority may be for leadership" but equally important "that the people may be the state."[41]

These formulations make clear that Wilson envisioned a sharp abridgment of the traditional understanding of democracy as a form of government. Democracy was instead to be understood as a set of principles that tolerated no established privilege to interfere with the right of each citizen to contribute to the national power to the best of his or her ability. "It is for this that we love democracy," Wilson declared with reference to Tocqueville, "for the emphasis it puts on character; for its tendency to exalt the purposes of the average man to some high level of endeavor; for its just principle of common consent . . . for its ideals of duty and its sense of brotherhood."[42] The issue of imperialism severed the notion of democracy from government practice. Democracy became, instead, a term for American social values. Individualism on the social level is not a contradiction but an affirmation of governance.

[41] Notes for a religious talk, Nov. 2, 1899, *ibid.*, xi, 273; "Democracy and Efficiency," *ibid.*, xii, 10, 20.
[42] *Ibid.*, pp. 6–8.

181

IX

MODERNIZING

THE LIBERAL TRADITION:

CONSTITUTIONAL GOVERNMENT

From the time he assumed the presidency of Princeton University until he was elected governor of New Jersey in 1910, Wilson was preoccupied with three broad areas of activity. The first claim on his attention was the reform of academic and social standards at Princeton and Princeton's promotion to the first rank among the nation's universities. The second was Wilson's own political ambitions and his growing commitment to opinions that would soon identify him as a leading opponent of William Jennings Bryan within the Democratic party. And the third was Wilson's continuation of his theoretical interests, primarily his last academic work, which consisted of a discussion of the political nature of the Constitution. Each of these three concerns was addressed to a special audience. The reforms at Princeton were directed to its faculty, students, trustees, alumni, and financial supporters. Wilson's political ambitions were directed primarily to leaders and supporters on the right wing of the Democratic party. Finally, the audience for Wilson's theoretical writings was made up of the reading public in general and of commentators and colleagues in the field of political science in particular.

Although activity in each of these fields had its own purpose, and its own rules and restraints, Wilson did not deal with his three fields in complete isolation of one another. Each area had a meaning for the nation as a whole, whether it be the proposals for educational reforms, the expression of political opinions, or the formulation of political ideas. In each area, Wilson was preoccupied with the opportunities and responsibilities of modern leadership, and in each case he would try to seek out a point of view that could be identified with the national scope and with his perception of the demands of the modern age for efficient action and common moral sentiment. He criticized forms of power that appeared to him to be closed off, self-sufficient, dated, or self-serving. In contrast, he offered his own values as those of vision and light, as means of moral improvement, or as measures of national direction and purpose. He used conservative as well as liberal and progressive labels for his own views. Perhaps his basic intentions are best described with an expression from recent English politics: "breaking the mold without rocking the boat." Wilson himself sometimes characterized his goals as serving liberal and progressive ends with conservative means.

Wilson's theoretical work during this period centered on an outline of the new constitutional system that appeared to be in the process of replacing traditional liberal constitutionalism. Most commentators have seen Wilson's attitudes toward the great corporations as the key to his partisan views. This approach, however, can easily obscure the general level of his thinking. Wilson knew that to indicate sympathy for or animosity toward the corporations was the most important move in the game of party politics in the whole era. At the theoretical level, Wilson's problem was how the corporations were to be used in the quest for national unity and strength. What kind of institutions were best suited to work out the adjustment between government and the corporations, between public needs and private rights? Should these institutions be closely connected with partisan politics or should they be placed on more neutral ground?

DURING his first years as president of Princeton University, Wilson succeeded in fulfilling his plans for three major areas of academic reorganization. First, he rearranged the undergraduate curriculum. Second, he instituted the celebrated "preceptorial system," which created fifty new positions for instructors, young scholars whose function was to mediate between the professorial lectures and the students' own interests in order to awaken their academic curiosity and train them academic thinking. Third, he established a presidential prerogative over the hiring and firing of members of the faculty, subject only to the formal approval of the board of trustees, whose capacity to judge academic performance was obviously limited. The new procedures ended the Presbyterian influence on the teaching of academic disciplines at Princeton, but in all three cases, Wilson's reforms were adopted with a minimum of opposition.[1] Coming after the years of his passive, almost subdued predecessor, Francis Landey Patton, Wilson's bold initiatives, abundant administrative vitality, and rhetorical enthusiasm, along with the high academic respect

[1] "Editorial Note: The New Princeton Course of Study," *PWW*, xv, 277–92; Link, *Wilson: The Road to the White House*, pp. 39–45; Mulder, *Woodrow Wilson*, pp. 162–65, 168–74, 176–78; Cooper, *The Warrior and the Priest*, pp. 89–95.

that surrounded his own work, inaugurated a time of expansion and improvement at Princeton. In the course of his brief presidency, Wilson changed the identity of the university, not least by virtue of a vast program of construction that was dependent upon his ability to maintain a cordial relationship with wealthy industrialists and businessmen willing to invest both time and money in matters of higher learning.

When Wilson moved from academic matters to a reform of the social life of the students, the atmosphere surrounding his leadership changed. His two major social reform proposals—the so-called "quad" plan and his attempt to secure the building of a graduate college on campus—were both defeated after long and bitter fights. He launched the quad plan in late 1906 as an attempt to replace a number of upper-class eating clubs that had grown up close to campus and cultivated social exclusiveness in well-endowed private houses. In their place, Wilson wanted to create "quadrangles" on campus where students of all classes could live and eat together, supervised by resident members of the faculty.[2] Despite its initial support, the board of trustees ultimately rejected this proposal.

Soon after, a conflict arose over the location of the new graduate college. Wilson wanted it to be placed conspicuously on campus to have a maximum effect on the academic and social life of the undergraduates. His opponents, led by Andrew F. West, the dean of the Graduate School, chose a site located a mile away from campus. While Wilson's priorities derived from his idea of graduate students as the natural leaders and role models for the undergraduates, the opposition was more concerned about the development of a separate graduate culture at some distance from the campus. When Wilson lost this fight, mainly due to Dean West's ability to secure funds for his own plans, Wilson's presidential authority was deeply shaken.[3] But these conflicts, not the least those that Wilson lost, gave him a national reputation both as a progressive educator and as a man undaunted in the face of conservative opposition. On the eve of his election as governor of New Jersey, Wilson resigned from the presidency of Princeton University.

The political content of these battles can easily be overrated, according to several historians. Wilson did not present his proposals as a progressive reform against the forces of organized wealth and educational privilege until fairly late, when it was clear that he would have to leave Princeton sooner or later. He did not engage in these conflicts because of progressive views, but the fights themselves influenced his political opin-

[2] Link, *Wilson: The Road to the White House*, pp. 45–57; Mulder, *Woodrow Wilson*, pp. 187–203; Cooper, *The Warrior and the Priest*, pp. 95–102.

[3] Link, *Wilson: The Road to the White House*, pp. 59–91; Mulder, *Woodrow Wilson*, pp. 203–28; Cooper, *The Warrior and the Priest*, pp. 102–105.

ions.[4] Laurence Veysey has argued, that compared to ideals nurtured in other universities at the time, Wilson's college ideal was "conformitarian" rather than liberal. "Although etiquette forbade him to say so directly," Veysey maintained, "Wilson apparently envisioned the production of a class of public servants in the spirit of Oxford." Certainly, many of Wilson's ideals of higher education were of British collegiate origin. But if Wilson wanted to emulate British social ideals, his experience at the Johns Hopkins had also given him a great admiration for the German ideals of scholarship, which combined intellectual discipline with a high national purpose.[5]

In a witty and elegant address at Harvard University, Wilson contrasted the liberal policy at Harvard with the spirit of discipline at Princeton. Harvard was telling its students to choose freely among the offered courses, mirroring the dominant contemporary culture in America, or as Wilson saw it: "Seek what you want; get what you please." Princeton, in contrast, was doing for America "what she should wish to do," which was "to combine men in a common discipline" consisting of such values as continuity, idealism, and "common social endeavor."[6] Before his appointment as president of the university, Wilson had noted privately that "higher education should be made an ally of the state." The best example was the University of Berlin which had been founded by William von Humboldt and Baron von Stein and which Wilson saw as a model of a beneficial interaction between government and higher learning. "A body of able and disinterested critics" had been placed "at the very doors of the gov[ernmen]t. They can see the small, the technical, things which the nation could never see," Wilson wrote. Universities might produce candidates fit to be "the eyes of the nation in finding out the personal and particular features of administration" and thus develop administrative methods "derivable no-other-whence." But even the best bureaucracy could not rule a liberal country. "There must be a personality in affairs large enough for the whole country to see and understand."[7] Wilson's view of the university embraced the encouragement of both special professional skills and scientific methods, but it also included a persistent and eloquent affection for a broad liberal education, the importance of

[4] Link, *Wilson: The Road to the White House*, pp. 51, 82–86, 123; Mulder, *Woodrow Wilson*, pp. 221–22.

[5] Laurence R. Veysey, "The Academic Mind of Woodrow Wilson," *Mississippi Valley Historical Review*, XLIX (March 1963), 630–31; see also, *idem, Emergence of the American University*, pp. 241–46; and Cooper, *The Warrior and the Priest*, pp. 89–90 on the origins of Wilson's ideal university.

[6] Address at Harvard University, June 26, 1907, *PWW*, XVII, 226–28.

[7] Random notes for "The Philosophy of Politics," Jan. 26, 1895, *ibid.*, IX, 131.

which was its ability to serve as a bridge between modern science and the general culture. His ideal was, not the creation of class rule in the imperial style, but the education of a political elite, defined not by social origins, but by governmental needs in a culture that celebrated social mobility and equal opportunity. For Wilson, at least, there was a significant difference between asking what the universities could do for the privileged classes and what they could do for the government of the nation.

The spirit of community that Wilson hoped to stimulate at Princeton was to be animated by a sense of national service. The discovery of a national perspective had been the overwhelming experience of his own college days, and among the scores of addresses Wilson gave every year on educational aims and methods, only a few did not emphasize the achievement of national purpose and outlook.[8] The removal from parents and local surroundings, the compensation of new friendships formed with fellow students from other parts of the country, and the guidance by teachers and by institutional discipline entailed nothing less than the remaking of the student's imagination "in the nation's service" and "for the nation's service."[9] The ideals and values of college life could be for the nation what industrialism was for the economy and what modern communication was for government: the overcoming of particularism and the beginning of a truly national life. As Wilson argued in his first public address after his appointment as president of Princeton, the university was to be seen as both the institutional expression and the custodian of "this touch of an idealist that makes the man, this conception of conduct as a whole, this love of integrity for its own sake, this idea of what he owes to the man in the other business, and to his rival or comrade in the same business, this feeling of the subtle linking of all men together, and behind it all the country itself, the country's welfare, the progress of America."[10]

It is quite clear that Wilson did not envision a system of mass education. He argued instead that the university should be seen as an exemplar of a form of community that was able to preserve its distinctive features despite its location in the midst of modern society. He saw the university as a profusion of national good will, carried primarily by its graduates into all areas of social and political life, quieting the nation's social conflicts and mellowing its harsh competitive features by cherishing a com-

---

[8] See, for instance, his address at the Brooklyn Institute of the Arts and Sciences, Dec. 12, 1902, *ibid.*, xiv, 283–85; and "The University and the Nation," Dec. 15, 1905, *ibid.*, xvi, 267–71. Mulder, in *Woodrow Wilson*, pp. 158–228, analyzes incisively Wilson's organic view of the university as a community.

[9] Oct. 21, 1896, *PWW*, x, 11–31; Oct. 25, 1902, *ibid.*, xiv, 170–85.

[10] "The Relation of University Education to Commerce," Nov. 29, 1902, *ibid.*, xiv, 244–45.

mon morality that could link individuals together in public concerns and national obligation. And, indeed, his own advance to the White House was bound to overshadow even his most eloquent rhetoric in persuading the public that the modern liberal university had something important to offer in solving what Wilson in 1907 called "the greatest question for the country now," namely, "the question of government."[11]

In retrospect, Wilson's most lasting and significant contribution to the institutional growth of modern American universities came less through his academic or educational reforms than through his conception of the place of the university in the country as a whole. The ideas and the temper expressed above were in obvious contrast to the contemporary English and German ideologies of higher learning, with their pride in the preservation of high culture and the high authority of erudition, contained in institutions that were apt to keep the vulgar masses at a respectful distance.[12] Wilson's view may also be contrasted to the modern ideology, which sees the university largely as the producer, not of a political class with national obligations conferred by a liberal education, but of a class of professional technicians, administrators, and scientists. Wilson was probably the most eloquent spokesman for the view that prevailed until the middle of the twentieth century—that the modern American university should be seen, not as an imposition by the governing class or by government itself, but as a natural and almost instinctive expression of forceful ideals and values inherent in society.

WILSON'S ENTRANCE into partisan politics took place in several stages from 1904 to 1907 as his political ambitions matured. His political initiation was largely arranged by conservative forces in the Democratic party. As Arthur S. Link has identified them, "Wall Street bankers, utility magnates, conservative editors representing these interests, even Cleveland's secretary of the treasury, hated by the agrarian radicals for his success in maintaining the gold standard—all these were among Wilson's early supporters."[13] To what degree did this alliance effect a change in Wilson's convictions? It seems clear that Wilson was intent on working his way toward leadership of the Democratic party from within the group that opposed the agrarian radicalism associated with William Jennings Bryan. To what extent did Wilson find it expedient or even necessary to compromise his academic views on government action to suit the opinions of his mentors? A tentative answer to this question must involve at least

[11] Address at Harvard University, *ibid.*, XVII, 227.

[12] Arno J. Mayer, *The Persistence of the Old Regime: Europe to the Great War* (New York, 1981), pp. 253–73.

[13] Link, *Wilson: The Road to the White House*, p. 102.

three elements. First, it must consider Wilson's convictions before he began to address himself to factions within the Democratic party. Second, it must consider Wilson's own terms for entrance into the political arena. Third, it must consider Wilson's relationship to big business, both at the psychological and at the conceptual level.

The most striking feature of Wilson's progressivism before 1904 is that it developed from sources that may be described as American republicanism. Wilson's progressive views concerning the primacy of government over the economy as a whole were clearly embodied in a temper that was thoroughly conservative in its respect for law, the social structure, and patriotism. In contrast to later progressives, Wilson's ideas did not originate in an outcry against social or economic injustice. The word *poverty* appears but a few times in his academic writings. From his first use of it, Wilson keyed the term *progress* to the theory and practice of national government, its authority, efficiency, and responsibilities, including the maintenance of a harmonious relationship between federal authority and state rights. Considerations of social inequality are largely absent from Wilson's early work.

One of the remarkable results of the publication of *The Papers of Woodrow Wilson* has been to reveal the consistency and unbroken continuity of Wilson's political temper throughout his academic career. His capacity for comprehending and absorbing new ideas, new methods, and even new areas of scholarship was strikingly matched by his ability to adapt them to his original political loyalties and dispositions. Obviously, his formulation of problems and questions changed with the passing of time as old issues were replaced by new ones. But Wilson probably never felt that he changed his basic views and attitudes, only that he restated his ideas as required by new circumstances. The premise that Wilson made a sharp turn toward conservatism after 1900 tends to underestimate how deeply Wilson's convictions were rooted in conservative values long before his entrance into partisan politics.

Wilson's conservatism, however, was very different from the brand of conservatism that prevailed in American business circles around the turn of the century. Wilson's deep and abiding belief in order was obviously at odds with the contemporary conservative celebration of laissez faire, and his equally abiding faith in the supremacy of government institutions did not go well with a contemporary conservatism that hoped to roll government back to a minimal police function and longed to emancipate the corporations from all social and political constraints. Wilson's idea of the individual as the expression of a collective conscience—shaped by the struggles of economic life but infused by cultural values transmitted through family, religion, and education—had no easy way to make peace with an understanding of individualism that was based on the individual's natural right to prevail over those less fit for survival. Wilson's rejection of the idea of natural rights was not based on compassion for the poor but on his understanding of new political conditions that were forcing America "to fall back upon her conservatism [and] pull herself together, adopt a new regimen of life, husband her resources, concentrate her strength, steady her methods, sober her views, restrict her vagaries, trust her best, not her average members." This was for Wilson the time for progressive change in response to new circumstances.[14] His rejection of individualism based on natural rights followed from these premises. In 1903 Wilson told a visiting student that he did not believe in "the inherent Rights of Man . . . when written in capitals." Referring to a recent discussion with a colleague, Wilson said that he might admit "that a man had the right to as much of this world's goods as might be necessary for subsistence and as might be acquired without damage to the same right of his fellow man, but that man had the natural right of storing up these acquired goods, he could not accept." Wilson stressed "that there were no rights of property except as developed by the law," and he regretted that his colleague had been "incapable of discussing the question calmly."[15] Thus, for Wilson, conservatism was not a matter of unleashing the economic forces contained in business and organized in the great corporations. It was a matter of harnessing these forces to national progress.

WILSON'S CONNECTIONS with conservative businessmen of the Democratic party were established in the course of two short after-dinner addresses in which Wilson presented himself and was accepted by informal but very influential groups of party leaders. The first event took place at the Waldorf-Astoria Hotel in New York on November 30, 1904, where Wilson addressed the Society of Virginians and announced himself as a strong critic of Bryan's leadership. The second address was before the prestigious Lotos Club in New York on February 3, 1906. After Wilson spoke, the editor of *Harper's Weekly*, George Brinton McClellan Harvey, proceeded to announce the symbolic nomination of Wilson as a potential presidential candidate. Soon afterward, *Harper's Weekly* printed a picture of Wilson on its front page, and Harvey began to feel out and stimulate the political contacts that eventually led to Wilson's nomination as a gubernatorial candidate in New Jersey. The address to the Lotos Club was followed by a long series of speeches that exposed Wilson to party leaders

[14] "Bryce's American Commonwealth," *Political Science Quarterly*, IV (March 1889), 153–69, *PWW*, VI, 61–76. Statements quoted here are from *PWW*, VI, 72.

[15] Edward Graham Elliott's memorandum of a conversation with WW, Jan. 5, 1903, *PWW*, XIV, 325.

and supporters in many states, beginning with his address on Thomas Jefferson at a dinner at the Democratic Club in New York on April 16, 1906.[16]

The addresses to the Virginians and to the Lotos Club are of special interest because they contain clear evidence of Wilson's awareness that he was crossing a line between political scholarship and partisan politics. Both addresses contain stronger attacks upon popular politics than was customary for Wilson. But juxtaposed with a bow to the prejudices of the party potentates, one finds the self-assured presentation of a claim to the leadership of the party. Wilson did not come to take orders but to teach a new vision of politics. It may therefore be important to note, first, how Wilson was able to disarm his audience with professions of good will, and, second, in what terms he presented his candidacy.[17] Thus, Wilson by no means attempted to enter the political arena with the sword of righteousness in hand, but affirmed instead that he was returning to where he belonged. Still, his play on "the outside" (appearance) and "the inside" (intentions) is striking:

> I feel that I am where I belong among you here. There was once a rather unsophisticated old woman who went to one of those side shows where they have marvellous pictures on the outside of things that are not to be seen on the inside. And in the show she saw a man who read a newspaper, or pretended to read a newspaper, through a two-inch plank. "Come right along out of here, Silas," the old lady said to her husband. "This is no place for me with these thin clothes on!" (Prolonged laughter) Now I have no such feelings here among you to-night. I feel that I am of you: that I belong here.[18]

In one sense, Wilson's presentation can be said to measure up well to the eloquent prefatory statements with which supplicants for the role of adviser to a European monarch would approach the prince. What could be more convincing of honest and transparent intentions than a confession of nakedness? It is therefore easy to overlook that Wilson placed his confession in a setting of make-believe, where things were not what they were supposed to be. Behind Wilson's elegant show of political naiveté and inexperience, he actually presented a striking ambition and self-con-

[16] *Ibid.*, xv, 545–49; xvi, 292–301, 362–69.

[17] The two addresses are closely related to each other. Colonel Harvey even linked them together in his remarks after Wilson spoke on February 3, 1906. On both occasions Wilson introduced himself with the same story, which he frequently used to establish cordial relations with a new audience.

[18] Address on the South, *ibid.*, xv, 546–48.

fidence on behalf of his political ideas. The profession of unpretentious-
ness covered his bid for leadership.

Wilson set out the terms of leadership in another innocent story that
he related to the Lotos Club as he proceeded to intimate to the party men
that perhaps they needed his assistance even more than he needed theirs.
He told a story of "the Methodist divine down in Tennessee who spent a
quarter of an hour praying for power. One of his deacons said to him,
taking him aside, 'Parson, you are praying for the wrong thing; what
are you praying for power for? You don't need any power; you ought to
pray for ideas.' " The parable was designed to show the party bosses the
limits of their power and to prepare the stage for Wilson's own vision of
the nation. But before he sketched out his own saving ideas, Wilson made
his conservative credentials clear. To the ex-Virginians, he proposed that
the agrarian radicals be read "out of the party as an alien faction," as "a
noisy minority." To the Lotos Club he presented the same offer, pointing
to the need for "civic manhood firm against the crowd." The Democratic
party, in return, was to become the "party of conservative reform," acting
in performance of "a great national service." Wilson promised "reform
without loss of stability" and "careful use of the powers of the Federal
Government in the interest of the whole people of whatever class or occupation."[19] On the face of it, these vague promises of reform could
mean whatever one took them to mean. To get a full picture of the situation, it may be useful to suggest a rough outline of the general thinking
of the traditional, non-Populist wing of the Democratic party.

As Samuel Beer has pointed out, the modern division in America between conservatism and progressive liberalism awaited the resolution of
the earlier and more fundamental division that dominated American politics until "well into the present century." The idea of a fundamental social conflict that is inherent in industrial society and that is projected into
the opposition between government and big business was not established
conclusively in party politics until the New Deal, which imposed the modern meaning of conservatism and progressive liberalism upon the American political mind.[20] It is abundantly clear from Wilson's use of the terms
"conservative" and "progressive" that the words did not yet have a definite resonance in political language. Wilson was therefore relatively free
to change their meaning from address to address. Before the early 1930s,
Beer argued, the "issue of overwhelming importance was the national

[19] Address to the Lotos Club, *ibid.*, xvi, 293, 297–98; address on the South, *ibid.*, xv, 547–
48.

[20] Samuel H. Beer, "Liberalism and the National Idea," in Robert A. Goldwin (ed.), *Left,
Right and Center: Essays on Liberalism and Conservatism in the United States* (Chicago, 1965), pp.
142–69.

question." The main cleavage of political forces was made up this way: on one side there was "a national party, tending towards elitism," such as may readily be associated with the Federalist, the Whig, and the Republican parties; on the other side there was an "antinational" or "provincial" party, tending to be democratic or populist in spirit, such as the Jeffersonian Republican and the Democratic parties, both of which were associated with localism, individualism, and minimal government. As late as 1909, Herbert Croly concluded in *The Promise of American Life* that the Democratic party could not "become the party of national responsibility without being faithless to its own creed." It was irreparably the party of state rights, of laissez faire, and of local elitism, and it advocated a "system of unrestricted individual aggrandizement and collective irresponsibility." It was the party of "drift."[21]

If this assessment of the state of the Democratic party is accepted in broad terms, Wilson's attempt to redirect the vision of the party toward national power becomes essential to an understanding of his political project as a whole. It becomes clear with what care Wilson measured his words when he told the Virginians that the university possessed a form of knowledge with certain claims to political neutrality. Announcing his willingness to participate in partisan politics, Wilson reminded his audience that he came from an institution that specialized in disinterested knowledge. He emphasized that "while it did not become him, as a person in an academic position such as he held, to discuss politics from a partisan point of view, he felt that he might well say something on general lines about matters affecting the country as a whole." Before the Lotos Club, Wilson elaborated his idea that "the business of the university" is to remind the public constantly of the need to resort both "to pure science" and to "a philosophy of life and conduct" in order to embrace the true "size of America."[22] Having argued his credentials for mastering the power of ideas, Wilson proceeded to give his audience in the Lotos Club a brief but distinct glimpse of a new conception and a new practice of national leadership in an age of mass politics:

Gentlemen, we are lifted from achievement to achievement by imagination. No man ever demonstrated an achievement; he conceived the achievement. There was a vision dreamed in some moment of lofty feeling, and . . . therefore, he is guided by feeling or by imagination; and that is the way of the men who lift their figures above

[21] *Ibid.*, pp. 151, 156–59; Herbert Croly, *The Promise of American Life* (1909; reprint, New York, 1963), pp. 27–51.

[22] Address on the South, *PWW*, xv, 546; address to the Lotos Club, *ibid.*, xvi, 295–96.

the general crowd and are picked out as the leading men, the distinguished men, the achieving men of our generation.[23]

Undoubtedly, the assembled party men had no clue at all as to what lay behind Wilson's stories and his lofty claim to national leadership. Of those at the dinner, as Arthur S. Link has put it, apparently only Wilson took Harvey's proposal of a Wilson candidacy seriously.[24] The point here is to see the meaning of Wilson's addresses in the light of his thirty years of thinking about politics. From his earliest writings Wilson had been preoccupied with the mystical moment when a true leader steps into the political arena. In "Leaders of Men," Wilson had concentrated much attention upon the power of imagination that came into being when a leader whose time had come began to absorb and formulate what was on the public mind. Clearly, Wilson did not enter the stage of party politics with the ideas of the New Freedom on his lips. Wilson presented himself as a man from outside politics who for several decades had reflected upon the role of the popular political leader as "a man of ordinary opinions and extraordinary abilities."[25] But behind the bland remarks about conservative reform that he offered to the assembled party leaders, he pledged to himself to modernize the Democratic party in return for its support. This pledge contained the outline of a new direction that promised to engage the party with an imagination fit for the national scale.

To ENTER American politics during the years after the turn of the century was to take a public stand regarding business power. Such a stand involved both an assessment of the personal power of wealthy businessmen and an idea of the general power of corporations. Wilson's personal relations with party managers and wealthy conservative businessmen cannot be described in terms of bargaining for mutual advantage, because Wilson seems to have been immune to the psychology of haggling. He was quite aware that he needed support from these sources in order to succeed in politics. Business support was necessary at the early stages of his political career for approximately the same reasons that contributions from wealthy industrialists were a precondition for turning Princeton University into an institution of national preeminence, and Wilson's success in getting business to pay for what was needed at Princeton depended in large measure on the effect of his numerous appeals to benefactors. Wilson wrote many "begging" letters without too many secret

[23] Address to the Lotos Club, *ibid.*, xvi, 297.

[24] Link, *Wilson: The Road to the White House*, p. 99. Before Wilson went to bed, he wrote Harvey to thank him. "It was most delightful to have such thought uttered about me . . . and I thank you with all my heart," Wilson wrote. *PWW*, xvi, 301.

[25] *Ibid.*, vi, 664–68; address to the Lotos Club, *ibid.*, xvi, 296.

qualms, and with a clear view of his goals, which he considered superior both to the money that he received and to whatever apprehensions he harbored privately.[26] To read these letters as a matter of negotiation for mutual advantage is to miss a striking element of Wilson's temper. He probably did not feel that he was begging for money any more than a minister would feel that he was begging when asking people to save their souls. To think that business could propose its own terms for supporting his educational or political leadership was the equivalent of a sinner pretending to bargain with the minister over the terms of salvation. One of Wilson's most vivid childhood memories, which continued to make "a very profound impression" upon him, was of a time when, unobserved, he had watched his father "in a company of gentlemen." One of them had said an oath, "and then, his eye resting upon my father," said "with evident sincerity: 'Dr. Wilson, I beg your pardon; I did not notice that you were present.' 'Oh,' said my father, 'you mistake, sir; it is not to me you owe the apology.' " "I doubt," Wilson said in 1906, "if any other remark ever entered quite so straight to the quick in me . . . that the offense was not to him but to his Master."[27]

In addition to Wilson's experience in dealing with businessmen in connection with the remaking of Princeton, it deserves attention that he seems to have had rather definite opinions about the limitations of business influence on political life. Business had to buy its way into political institutions, and to Wilson this need revealed the narrow confines of business power. Despite the occasional public uproar about the corruption of American political institutions by business, Wilson viewed the situation with detachment.[28] In his view, business was forced to buy votes because of its inability to produce a coherent political opinion that could persuade people. For obvious reasons, Wilson did not express his full view of the matter very often. He formulated his sharpest outline of the political limits of the business mind during 1907, when his relationship with conservative business interests was fairly close:

> In those hot centres of trade and industry, where a man's business grips him like an unrelaxing hand of iron from morning to night

[26] See, for instance, WW to James Hay Reed, Jan. 13, 1904, *ibid.*, xv, 124–26. See Mulder, *Woodrow Wilson*, pp. 163–65, for a full account of Wilson as a fund raiser.

[27] "The Minister and the Community," March 30, 1906, *PWW*, xvi, 350.

[28] "The Banker and the Nation," an address to the American Bankers' Association in Denver, Sept. 30, 1908, is the first clear evidence that Wilson was moving to the left on the issue of corporate capital. Instead of attacking only illegitimate business methods, Wilson now began to contrast "organized capital" with "the general masses of the people and the movements of business throughout the country." *Ibid.*, xviii, 426; Link, *Wilson: The Road to the White House*, pp. 120–22.

and lies heavily upon him even while he sleeps, few men can be said to have any opinions at all. They may bury their heads for a few minutes in the morning paper at breakfast or as they hurry to their offices, may dwell with dull attention upon the afternoon paper as they go wearily home again or drowse after dinner; but what they get out of the papers they cannot call their opinions. They are not opinions, but merely a miscellany of mental reactions, never assorted, never digested, never made up into anything than can for the moment compare in reality and vitality with the energetic conceptions they put to use in their business.[29]

Wilson's severe estimate of the political deficiencies of the business mind is easily overlooked because of its corollary—an undisguised admiration for business competence when it operated within its own field. Thus he was ready to defend business from government interference, not because he had any principled argument against government regulation, but because he believed that regulation should conform to standards of business convenience and efficiency. He opposed "direct regulation of corporate business through governmental commissions," both to distinguish his platform from that of Theodore Roosevelt and because he feared that regulation at the management level represented an overextension of government, which ran the risk of sapping "the energy of private enterprise."[30]

The final element in Wilson's attitude on the corporate question was probably the most important, because it represented the continuation of his earliest perception of the national economy. It was Wilson's conviction that business and industry had rendered the nation an invaluable service despite their interference in politics. Few modern historians would disagree with Wilson's contention that business and industry were primary factors in tying the country together after the shattering experience of the Civil War. When Wilson considered the issue of business reform, expediency therefore had to be formulated on a national scale. As he put it in one of his most conservative addresses, "One of the distinguishing characteristics of our time is that our processes of business have ceased to be local and have become national, and one of the most important results of this is that the old contrasts between the different sections of the country are disappearing." This "nationalization of conditions" was the basis for the "union of sections," which had finally overcome "every

---

[29] *Constitutional Government*, PWW, XVIII, 148. The description of the businessman is embedded in a comparison between the Senate and the House of Representatives.

[30] "Credo," Aug. 6, 1907, *ibid.*, XVII, 336.

intimation that the interests of different parts of the country are hostile and rival interests."[31]

In view of the national value of corporate business and industry as the material expression of social growth, both Theodore Roosevelt and Wilson seemed prepared to deny the wisdom of the old lament that "corporations have no bodies to be kicked and no souls to be damned." While Roosevelt's political temperament dictated that he choose the more vigorous and militant approach to the issue of corporate power, Wilson chose the moralizing route. Both men seemed to agree that in the long run the federal government and corporate business would have to grow together. Wilson did not oppose the regulation of business, except when regulation was tied to Roosevelt's idea of acting primarily through independent government commissions. Wilson advocated a technique for regulation that relied mainly on the courts; it was to be "legal regulation and not direct management."[32] He opposed commissions because they seemed, like congressional government, to shield rather than to expose entrenched power. Wilson argued that the corporate question was a matter of the incorporation of modern economic forces into the moral and political order of the nation. Roosevelt's proposal, he said, would fortify corporate power with political authority. The question was how "to restrain and control" the corporations. "It would be infinitely worse" if the corporations were "combined with government itself, and a partnership formed which could not be broken up without attacking our very governors themselves."[33] The question of control would be better solved by allowing new corporations to enter the market than by government regulation of those already in a position of dominance.

A central feature of Wilson's approach to the issue of corporate power was to insist upon a sharp distinction between means and ends. As he put it before the Cleveland Chamber of Commerce,

> For my part, I don't believe that fining corporations is of the least use for the ends we seek. . . . If a chauffeur goes too fast, I have heard some of my fellow-citizens propose that we lock up the machine. I had a great deal rather lock up the chauffeur. I suppose that if a railway accident occurs you will lock up the locomotive presently—you will lock up our tools, because we do not have sense enough or humanity enough to use them properly. Corporations, these imaginary persons, are our tools; they are not ourselves. And

[31] "False and True Conservatism," Nov. 12, 1907, *ibid.*, 493–94.
[32] *Ibid.*, v, 361; "The Ideals of Public Life," Nov. 16, 1907, *ibid.*, xvii, 502–503; address to a Democratic Dollar Dinner, March 29, 1910, *ibid.*, xx, 301.
[33] Address to a Democratic Dollar Dinner, March 29, 1910, *ibid.*, p. 301.

the responsibility is not to rest upon them to the incommoding of the whole business development of the country, but is to rest upon the individuals who are misusing them.[34]

Despite the obvious conservative intentions behind Wilson's argument, his logic was rather flexible. What Wilson was implying was, not that the corporations could not be regulated, but that such regulation must be defended with reference to the "whole business development of the country." It is tempting to see, at least in retrospect, that Wilson's choice of metaphors gave away his conservative rhetoric as soon as the public demand was interpreted to mean, not that the locomotive be imprisoned, but that better brakes be installed.

Wilson's emphasis on legal prosecution seems to have provided certain rhetorical advantages. It left him free to pursue a line of agitation with certain populist undercurrents, as when he demanded that business point out its culprits for speedy trial. Thus, at a Fourth of July celebration in Norfolk, Virginia, in 1907 Wilson was almost able to outbid Governor Charles Evans Hughes of New York. Wilson raised the question of corporate greed and concretely insisted upon "the arrest and imprisonment of corporation heads instead of the fining and dissolution of corporations themselves."[35] Wilson's repeated proposals to "moralize" the corporations were usually not intended as appeals to a corporate sense of Christian charity. On the contrary, he wanted to reorganize corporate structures for legal purposes so that the guilty could be prosecuted.

Wilson's emphasis on law and on action by the courts appealed to the business interests, because of the courts' demonstrated willingness to adjust to business wishes while barring legislative action on both the state and federal levels. For conservatives, the courts came to look like a dike holding back the rising tide of the masses. Wilson played on these reactions all the more freely, since he himself held a very flexible view of the law, as expressed in his last academic work, *Constitutional Government*. The best example of this flexibility is contained in the so-called Credo, a private memorandum Wilson wrote to the wealthy owner of the New York *Sun*, William M. Laffan, and to Thomas Fortune Ryan, a prominent New York banker, both of whom feared that the panic of 1907 would tempt Roosevelt to bring business "to bondage." They were, as a friend wrote to Wilson, "beating the bushes for some Moses to lead them into a land of promise."[36] Wilson repeated the views he had set forth in his recent

---

[34] "Ideals of Public Life," *ibid.*, XVII, 503.

[35] News report of a celebration at the Jamestown Exposition, *ibid.*, pp. 247–48.

[36] John Allan Wyeth to WW, March 9 and 26, 1907, *ibid.*, pp. 65, 93. The early political clash between Wilson and Roosevelt is laid out in Cooper, *The Warrior and the Priest*, pp. 130–

lectures at Columbia, stating his belief in a "constitutional system" understood in the light of "the nation that we are." The "freedom of contract" was an essential element in this system. The first sentence set the tone of the memorandum: "My training has been that of the law, and it has been under the influence of that discipline that I have formed my conception of our constitutional system."[37] Obviously, Wilson found no reason to upset the two gentlemen by telling them that he had left the discipline of law in order to write a book on political leadership and that his new work on the Constitution was a vindication of presidential leadership.

Constitutional Government was Wilson's last book, and in some respects it was his most mature work, despite the unusual circumstances of its production. Since it was based on a series of lectures at Columbia University financed by the George Blumenthal Fund, it is tempting to read the work as a set of largely independent essays. Also, the very title invites the conclusion that *Constitutional Government* was basically an attempt to revise *Congressional Government*, a suggestion that Nicholas Murray Butler, the president of Columbia University, made in April 1906, when inviting Wilson to inaugurate the Blumenthal Lectures.[38] Wilson accepted the invitation, which obliged him to publish the lectures afterward, on the condition that a stenographer be present while he was speaking. He simply did not have the time to write the lectures out in full and therefore needed a complete record of what he had said for the final revision of the manuscript. The preparation of the lectures was further delayed by a stroke that Wilson suffered a few days after he received the invitation. For the rest of his life he had only peripheral vision in his left eye.[39] Although his appearance at Columbia was postponed a few months, it is hard to believe that Wilson gained much time. The fall of 1906 was occupied both by Wilson's preparation of the quad plan and by the development of his hopes for a political career.

Recent biographies of Wilson have given varying assessments of *Constitutional Government*. Henry W. Bragdon found the result to be conservative because of Wilson's opposition to progressive proposals for new voting rights, such as the initiative and the referendum. He also noted Wilson's warnings against economic paternalism, his "defense of the states against federal encroachments," and a tone of celebration sur-

36. See also Alan Seltzer, "Woodrow Wilson as 'Corporate–Liberal': Toward a Reconsideration of Left Revisionist Historiography," *Western Political Quarterly*, xxx (June 1977), 192.

37 "Credo," *PWW*, xvii, 335, 337.

38 Nicholas Murray Butler to WW, April 25, 1906, *ibid.*, xvi, 374.

39 WW to Nicholas Murray Butler, April 26 and May 14, 1906; Ellen Axson Wilson to Eloise Hoyt, June 12, 1906, *ibid.*, pp. 375, 395, 423–24.

rounding Wilson's remarks on "rural and small town America."[40] Both John M. Mulder and John Milton Cooper, Jr., have noted the persistence of contradictory tendencies in Wilson's political thinking between an emphasis on the individual and an emphasis on the state. His work, they observe, esepcially his public addresses, turned from an earlier "statist emphasis" toward a celebration of the individual.[41] These conclusions, however, may be taken to imply that Wilson worked to harmonize conflicting groups within the Democratic party rather than as an indication that he had changed his conceptual framework, which permitted him to dismiss as spurious the contradictions between agrarian and industrial production, and between the individual and the state.

Most political scientists have read *Constitutional Government* as a continuation of *Congressional Government*. In 1958, A. J. Wann reviewed the book as an attempt to relocate the potential of political leadership from the earlier legislative setting to an executive setting. "One may conclude," Wann wrote, "that the more Wilson's theory of the Presidency seemed to change, the more it continued to be the same."[42] Only two years later, in 1960, Richard E. Neustadt laid the basis for most of the present attention to the book as a foreboding of the strategic rather than the constitutional power inherent in the presidential office. Neustadt urged that the last words in Wilson's chapter on the presidency, "action making for enlightenment," be "engraved over the White House door." Wilson's declaration that the president retained the liberty to "be as big a man as he can be," was at the center of the modern expansive view of the office.[43] Without any intention of reducing the recent debate about the book in contemporary political science, one may conclude that it reflects both the opportunities and the disenchantments in regard to the modern idea and practice of executive aggrandizement.

The current focus upon the presidency can easily obscure the comprehensive scope of Wilson's work. He conceived the book, not as a theory of executive government, but as a "theory of politics." In his brief preface he also promised a "fresh analysis" from "a fresh point of view," directed toward "policy and practice."[44] The scope of his subsequent chapters contrasted significantly with *Congressional Government*. In his first book Wilson was absorbed with the attempt to create a constitutional framework that would enhance the quality of deliberative contests among members

[40] Bragdon, *Woodrow Wilson*, pp. 346–48.

[41] Mulder, *Woodrow Wilson*, pp. 242–44; Cooper, *The Warrior and the Priest*, pp. 125, 135.

[42] "The Development of Woodrow Wilson's Theory of the Presidency: Continuity and Change," in Latham (ed.), *Philosophy and Policies of Woodrow Wilson*, pp. 61–66.

[43] *Presidential Power: The Politics of Leadership* (New York, 1960), pp. 5, 106.

[44] *Constitutional Government*, PWW, xviii, 69.

of the legislative branch of the government. Out of the ordeal of debate, oratorical leadership was to emerge, guiding national opinion. In *Constitutional Government* Wilson both broadened his scope and changed his focus. Formally, he added chapters on the courts and on political parties. But in reality he changed the context in which leadership was to take place. The citizen of *Congressional Government* was largely understood as a member of an attentive public, gazing from the galleries or discussing the newspaper accounts of the recent battles in the political arena. Wilson conceived of the citizen as basically a listener, ready to receive great words, ready to be educated by his representatives, and finally, ready to make up his mind and choose among the gifted contestants. The picture Wilson painted of the American citizen was very different in *Constitutional Government*. He now pictured the context, not as a public mesmerized by oratorical excellence, but as a dynamic society densely populated with busy citizens who had little time to spend on following oratorical contests. The public was preoccupied with the tasks of settling the continent, of producing and consuming, of taking care of their families, and of hoping for good things to come.

This simple new premise suggested a different relationship between the citizen and the government. Wilson now presumed that the individual was brought into contact with government primarily in the course of the pursuit of economic objectives. This implied that the new citizen was less interested in listening and more ready to ask for, or even to pressure the government for, help in the realization of material interests. Although the citizen had several institutions at his disposal for the political expression of his interests, (his party or the state legislatures, for example), it was the courts that mattered most to the citizen's daily life. The courts were the primary governmental institution that settled disputes between varying and conflicting interests. The courts also settled disputes between government and the individual, sorting out and determining individual rights in relation to the general interest. Hence, an understanding of the true nature of constitutionalism lay in seeing the judiciary, rather than the legislature or the executive branch of government, as the primary source for civic preparation and education. The courts are, as Wilson put it repeatedly, "the people's forum."[45]

Wilson presented this argument as part of his overall view of constitutionalism. "There is a sense in which it may be said that the whole efficacy and reality of constitutional government" resided in the courts. "So far as the individual is concerned," Wilson wrote, "a constitutional government is as good as its courts; no better, no worse." The American system

[45] *Ibid.*, pp. 162, 178.

of law was not distinguished by its end—the accomplishment of justice—but by its reliance on a better method. The courts did not protect the individual but provided him with the means of self-protection. The American system of law in a sense forced the individual to be free and to fight for his rights.

> Nothing in connection with the development of constitutional government is more remarkable, nothing commends itself more to the understanding of . . . the real bases of human dignity and capacity, than the way it has exalted the individual, and not only exalted him, but at the same time thrown him upon his own resources, as if it honored him . . . to see and seek his own rights. The theory of English and American law is that no man must look to have the government take care of him but that every man must take care of himself, the government providing the means and making them as excellent as may be, . . . but never itself taking the initiative, never of its own motion intervening. . . . Such an attitude presupposes both intelligence and independence of spirit. . . . The individual must seek his court and must know his remedy, and under such compulsion he will undertake to do both.[46]

Just as it was the pursuit of happiness, rather than its actual achievement, which had nurtured the virtues of self-reliance in the early republic of open space, so the pursuit of liberty through legal action renewed the sturdiness of character in modern society, with its dense population and crowded conditions. Modern society had room for neither the citizen soldier of classical republicanism nor the yeoman of agrarian republicanism. In their place, Wilson put a new and very modern citizen, fending for himself or herself in an interest-ridden, competitive, litigious society with its ever-changing meaning for the terms *individual rights* and *property*. The courts provided the "balance and means of energy,—this means of energy for the individual citizen," Wilson wrote. The courts blunted the sharp edges of individualism, harmonized opposing interests, and coordinated them in the interest of the material development of the nation. As Wilson pointed out, "the weightiest import of the matter is seen only when it is remembered that the courts are the instruments of the nation's growth."[47]

It may be clear at this point why Wilson chose to write about "the constitutional system" and about "constitutional government" rather than about the Constitution. He decapitalized the idea of the Constitution be-

[46] *Ibid.*, pp. 80–81.
[47] *Ibid.*, pp. 166, 178–79.

cause he wanted to bypass the legal discussion and look at constitutionalism as a means of changing the citizen. He wanted to show how a long
period of constitutionalism had shaped the soul of the citizen and had
come to form human character in America, to become, finally, the soul
of the nation itself. On this reading, the spirit of the Constitution was to
be understood, not as a set of legal guarantees for the individual, but as
"the whole expansion and transformation of our national life that has
followed its adoption."[48]

Wilson's choice of the courts as the unifying administrative agency of
American constitutionalism was both descriptively and theoretically important. Progressive historiography would later remember the courts of
the decades around the turn of the century as the bulwarks of reaction-
ary conservatism. But as Morton Keller has pointed out, the courts
played a conspicuous role in America's industrialization, because they
solved a host of administrative functions that neither legislatures, nor
parties, nor the underdeveloped public administration had the skills and
authority to deal with. "The result," Keller concluded, "was a void in governance that was often filled by the pervasive and authoritative structure
of the courts."[49] It is therefore not difficult to see the element of realism
that made Wilson's idea persuasive. But his theoretical depiction of the
role of the courts was hardly less important. Wilson's rejection of the tradition of natural law could not have been more emphatic. The political
purpose of the courts was to read liberal rights into his idea of state interest.

One side of Wilson's view captured and promoted the understanding
of American courts as the political essence of the free-enterprise system.
The courts were both the manifestation and the symbol of individual interests in constant movement, colliding and rubbing against each other
as a supreme expression of American social and economic vitality. While
the courts on the European continent had invariably expressed the coercive power of the state, the American courts signified a political confirmation of individual interests. The confirmation, however, did not depend upon natural rights but upon equal access to the courts, where
government officials and private citizens met and contested each others'
claims on the same terms. Justice, accordingly, was not a substantive issue
but a question of how to secure the right of due process. At bottom, Wilson argued, this was becoming a social issue: "I fear . . . that a rich litigant
can almost always tire a poor one out and readily cheat him of his rights
by simply leading him through an endless maze of appeals and technical

---

[48] *Ibid.*, pp. 163, 172.
[49] *Affairs of State*, pp. 343, 369–70; Skowronek, *Building a New American State*, pp. 39–46.

delays." From the point of view of Wilson's legal realism, the real issue was how to make the courts accessible and "serviceable to the poor man as well as to the rich." The republican virtue of self-dependence, as practiced in legal contests, was needed by rich and poor alike: "The individual of whatever grade or character must be afforded opportunity to take care of himself, whether against the power of his neighbor or against the power of the government."[50] Individual rights were not a rejection of natural rights but a means of building up republican character.

The other side of the American system of courts did not certify individual interests but instead controlled them. The function of the courts was to absorb, administer, authorize, and direct individual interests and energies toward the national interest. The courts "adapted" individual interests to the common interest. How were the courts themselves adjusted to this function? There was, Wilson argued, "the statesmanship of adaptation characteristic of all great systems of law since the days of the Roman prætor; and there can be no doubt that we have been singular among the nations in looking to our courts for that double function of statesmanship, for the means of growth as well as for the restraint of ordered method." The great statesman of constitutional adaptation, he wrote, was John Marshall, America's Roman prætor, of "the school and temper of George Washington," who had conquered the Newtonian mechanical conception of the Constitution and replaced it with a Darwinian conception and in so doing had made "the constitution a suitable instrument of the nation's life." Marshall's achievement was to create "the principles of interpretation which have governed our national development." Marshall saw the Constitution, not as "mere negations of power," but as "grants of power, and he reasoned from out the large political experience of the race as to what those grants meant, what they were intended to accomplish." There could be no denial of the political role of America's courts: "We have married legislation with adjudication and look for statesmanship in our courts."[51]

It is possible to view Wilson's discussion of constitutional government as an attempt to add flexibility to settled practices in order to allow more room for the modern presidency. It appears, however, that his idea of

[50] *Congressional Government*, PWW, XVIII, 170.

[51] *Ibid.*, pp. 179–80, 173. Having gone so far toward a principled statement of the political role of the judiciary, Wilson took several steps back on concrete issues, such as the question of federal regulation of the "conditions of labor in field and factory." Wilson observed that the conditions of production were then "recognized as the undisputed field of state law" (p. 181). Later Wilson pictured the states as the federal laboratories of experimentation in this as in other areas of the economy (pp. 190, 196–97). See Wolfe, "Woodrow Wilson: Interpreting the Constitution," for a fine analysis of the legal issue of constitutional adaptation.

constitutionalism implied a more decisive break with past liberal understandings. In the traditional liberal view, constitutional doctrines served
as the individual's bulwark against government power and its abuse. Wilson, in contrast, viewed constitutionalism as a political authorization of
the growth and development of national power. The "grants of power,"
their meaning and direction, expressed a fundamental political truth that
was no less self-evident than the truth of human equality had appeared
to the generation of the American Revolution. Wilson persuasively identified the character of the renewed or transformed Constitution as a system of powers destined for growth and accomplishment in the two great
images of power he found operating beneath or behind the American
consciousness. The first was the influences of the great westward movement. The second was the "silent and unobserved" influence of the economic and social changes that were uniting Americans by "working a
great synthesis upon us," carrying "the nationalizing process steadily and
irresistibly forward to the same great consummation."[52] The question was
therefore: Which of the representative government institutions was capable of bringing to self-consciousness the immense forces of national
energy that constitutionalism had nurtured and restrained through the
courts?

As MIGHT be expected, Wilson repeated much of his earlier criticism of
congressional practices and deplored the fact that Congress had acquired
power over legislative activity that rightly belonged to the executive. The
result had been that the House of Representatives had become little more
than a stock exchange for special interests. "Its ideal is the transaction of
business," as Wilson put it. It was a business of selling favors, exchanging
"concession for concession." In this process, the House had compromised
its true function of public "counsel and criticism." The result was that
even the limited measure of discussion and "common counsel" that was
generated in the House was "hidden away in committee rooms." The
House had abandoned its greatest political asset—its opportunity to be
"in the most direct communication with the nation itself." "In its effort to
make itself an instrument of business, to perform its function of legislation without assistance" from the executive, the House had "in effect si-
lenced itself." Predictably, the public reacted to this paradox with suspicion about the trusted representative of the people. Whether business in
the House was honest or dishonest mattered less than the inability to see
what was going on. "The people, finding things done they do not just
know why or how in their legislative assemblies, indulge suspicions which
deeply disturb them and make them unjust critics of the whole repre-

[52] *Congressional Government*, xviii, 100–101.

sentative system. . . . Anything hidden is suspected, no matter how honest it may be."[53]

What the House of Representatives was for specific and local interests, the Senate was for regional interests. The Senate was the organized expression of provincialism, understood as "the general absence of national information, and, by the same token, of national opinion." While the Senate admirably reflected the country "in its many sections," it was unable to represent the people as a whole. Wilson exonerated the Senate of most of the charges of corruption voiced by the progressives, but he was concerned about the wholesale change in the public image of the Senate which these charges implied. "There was a time when we were lavish in spending our praises" upon the Senate, Wilson said. "In our own day we have been equally lavish of hostile criticism. We have suspected it of every malign purpose, fixed every unhandsome motive upon it, and at times almost cast it out of our confidence altogether."[54]

Popular attitudes toward state governments were no less problematic. "There are many evidences that we are losing confidence in our state legislatures," Wilson wrote. Since state legislatures had been at the center of popular politics until the Civil War, the loss of confidence indicated an important change in the balance of the system as a whole. "To lose faith in them is to lose faith in our very system of government," Wilson warned. Taking care not to offend the conservative belief in state rights, Wilson outlined the paradox that state governments got most of the blame for what was in fact federal encroachment upon state prerogatives: "We are impatient of state legislatures because they seem to us less representative of the thoughtful opinion of the country than Congress is. We know that our legislatures do not think alike, but we are not sure that our people do not think alike."[55] The cruel dilemma was that state legislatures could hardly be expected to create homogeneous legislation on their own, and by the same token, federal authorities could achieve homogeneity only at the expense of state rights. The dilemma itself betrayed a significant change in public attitudes. People no longer judged the federal government by local standards, but they increasingly judged local government according to a standard that was essentially national in spirit. The revolution in commerce and communication had forever transformed the public perception of the general interest. Despite its fragmentation, Congress was still more in touch with the national spirit of the population than were the state legislatures.

A similar shift of public attitudes revealed itself in regard to party pol-

[53] *Ibid.*, pp. 133, 136, 137–38, 141, 139.
[54] *Ibid.*, pp. 152, 142–43.
[55] *Ibid.*, pp. 192–93, 195.

iticians. Local bosses were probably no better and no worse than members of Congress. But increasingly local politicians seemed petty in their concerns. Even their capacity for corruption seemed substandard, having neither the size nor the ambition that citizens would expect from the leaders of a national republic and an emerging world power. The parties had served important national functions, offsetting the divisions and separations of constitutional power and restraining "the very compulsion of selfishness" that was generated during the period of westward expansion. But as economic conditions were tending toward a state of coordination and homogeneity, the status of party government was becoming unclear.[56] The civic affection associated with the parties was essentially oriented toward the past, not the future, of American politics.

The reorientation of public sentiment toward the parties displayed itself in the standing of the local bosses. These political figures had served an important function during the nineteenth century. "A system of so-called popular elections like ours could not be operated successfully without them," Wilson claimed. But these same bosses were now reduced to "managers whom the people obey and affect to despise." The failure of party government was registered in the growth of dissatisfaction with the innumerable nominations and elections for petty as well as for important political offices. It was the party system itself that made people "look about for new means by which to obtain a real choice in affairs." The system of "farming the functions of government out to outside parties" had reduced even the president to the position of a "national boss," "doling out his local gifts of place to local party managers in return for support." The "enormous patronage," which was the material basis for party government, was increasingly viewed with distress by the public. "We have made the task of the voter hopeless and therefore impossible," Wilson concluded.[57]

As most commentators have noted, *Constitutional Government* contained a clear outline of the two structural features that supplied new rules for the constitutional game of checks and balances and gave the presidency a strong hand in American politics. The first was Wilson's em-

[56] *Ibid.*, p. 214.

[57] *Ibid.*, pp. 194, 211–12. The analysis of "party government" was new for Wilson, despite his longstanding interest in parliamentary government. While preparing the last lecture in Bermuda during the winter of 1907, he admitted to his wife that it was most difficult to write on the parties, which, he said, "I have never elaborated in my thought before." The lecture required "a good deal of reading and digesting." WW to Ellen Axson Wilson, Jan. 30, 1907, *ibid.*, xvii, 26. His lecture relied heavily on Henry Jones Ford, *The Rise and Growth of American Politics: A Sketch of Constitutional Development* (New York, 1898).

phasis upon the new technical preconditions, primarily the revolution of communications. The second was Wilson's insistence upon the revolution in foreign affairs that had made the republic a permanent member of the great powers of the world. There could be no leaving the world arena once the republic had involved itself in the Far East, and Wilson's achievement was to see that this involvement would forever alter the shape of the presidential office, leaving it with the best credentials to serve as the representative of the nation as a whole.[58] When these two features were combined, the effect was to make the presidency the focus of national unity, not just during election campaigns, but on a continuous basis as the directing center of policy and as a primary object of public attention. The briefest checklist of new opportunities for expanding the office and improving the efficiency of national government included proposals for coordinating executive and legislative functions in the interest of government performance and proposals for expanding the president's opportunity to set the legislative agenda and influence deliberation in the congressional committees, including the possibility of bringing public pressure to bear on the various stages of the legislative process.[59]

Wilson's theoretical contribution to the concept of the presidency, as distinguished from his ideas about the various strategic possibilities offered by the Constitution, consisted of his discussion of the interrelationship between the two basic functions of the president. On the one hand, the president was the chief executive, and in Wilson's view, the natural head of efficient and responsible government. On the other hand, the presidency was destined to become the primary symbol of American national power as Americans moved consciously toward becoming "a single community." Wilson was aware of an inherent disharmony between the two functions. As head of government, the president was the natural target of civic suspicions and distrust, but as the head of the nation, the president seemed the natural point of reception for the trust that gravitated toward the only political office that embodied the legitimacy expressed in the general suffrage. Wilson clearly favored the legitimating function over the executive, administrative function. He predicted that "with the growth and widening activities of the nation itself," presidents would eventually tend to view their office "in its truest purpose and with greatest effect," less as a matter of providing administration than as a matter of providing legitimacy, as "directors of affairs and leaders of the nation," as "men of counsel and of the sort of action that makes for en-

[58] *Constitutional Government*, *PWW*, xviii, 99–100, 108, 120–21. See also Lee Benson's seminal ideas on the communications revolution in *Turner and Beard: American Historical Writing Reconsidered* (Glencoe, Ill., 1960), pp. 42–46.

[59] *Constitutional Government*, *PWW*, xviii, 115–21, 141.

lightenment." The people's "instinct is for unified action," Wilson argued, "and it craves a single leader."[60]

Thus the president represented unified popular opinion and will over and above the fragmented governmental system created by the Constitution. At the same time, the president represented governmental competence and administrative necessity against unrealistic popular wishes. This double position explained, at least in part, why Wilson did not have any pronounced fear of demagogues capturing the presidency. Demagoguery might bring a man the office, but governmental administration would soon transform him into a humble servant of administrative necessity. Public opinion was a much more plastic and pliable material than what was offered by administrative leadership, and Wilson was more attracted to its potential, because it afforded the president an opportunity to shape his own constituency. The natural object for legitimation was "the imagination of the country." As Wilson put it, the president who was trusted could not only lead "the whole people" but could even "form it to his own views."[61]

While *Congressional Government* had focused on the need to provide a training ground for political talent and had depicted the citizen as simply an admiring spectator of the contests of the debating elite, *Constitutional Government* largely dispensed with the issue of how to provide political skills for the leader. "If the matter be looked at a little more closely," Wilson now argued, "it will be seen that the office of President, as we have used and developed it, really does not demand actual experience in affairs so much as particular qualities of mind and character." "What the country will demand of the candidate will be, not that he be an astute politician, skilled and practiced in affairs, but that he be a man such as it can trust, in character, in intention, in knowledge of its needs, . . . [and] in capacity to prevail by reason of his own weight and integrity." It was useless, then, to try to make a theory of leadership qualities, because these characteristics did not lend themselves to generalization. It was enough to show that there was open space at the very top of a tightly regulated constitutional structure. "The President is at liberty, both in law and conscience, to be as big a man as he can. His capacity will set the limit."[62]

Although Wilson now had less to say about the training for statesmanship, he had more to say about the conditions that allowed for a grateful reception of what is now often referred to as "charisma." Because the

[60] *Ibid.*, pp. 102, 123, 114.
[61] *Ibid.*, p. 114.
[62] *Ibid.*, pp. 112–13, 116.

genius of statesmanship came full-bodied into politics from the outside and therefore did not lend itself to political inquiry, the more important question concerned the conditions that prepared the citizens for an immediate recognition of the statesman's special abilities. In summarizing his work, one may distinguish between three major points in Wilson's consideration of the current governmental conditions that encouraged the citizens to look for political fulfillment to a strong and vigorous exercise of presidential power.

The first was the obvious default of the major political institutions, parties included. As Wilson had noted, every government institution, formal or informal, was surrounded with a suspicion of corruption, with distrust (with a credibility gap in modern parlance). While some of these suspicions were rooted in constitutionalism itself—in its warning of the necessity of being on constant guard against politics itself—it was also clear that the possibilities for political participation were greatly reduced in a modern republic.

Second, Wilson showed that the citizen's confrontation with power in its national form, such as had happened most dramatically during the war of 1898, induced people to identify with national power rather than to reject the symbols of national greatness. This was probably the first American war since the Revolution which immediately seemed to reduce rather than to exacerbate tensions between the sections. The growth of national power in both its political and economic forms would sooner or later translate itself into a popular demand for a human figure on which to focus political attention. The steady and inexorable growth of complex systems of administration and production, not least in the private sector, stimulated the need to identify with a political figure who seemed to inherit the remaining elements of democratic power. The presidency was to become the personal symbol of popular authority by offering assurance that people were not subject to impersonal and abstract forms of power wholly beyond their vision. The presidency offered reassurance by representing a force that "no other single force" could withstand and that "no combination of forces" would be expected to overpower.[63]

Third, and perhaps most important, Wilson sketched a new picture of the political psychology of the modern citizen as a searcher for community in a society that constantly assailed him with its demands for change and competition. Wilson's idea of the new citizen, always under pressure to adjust to changing social and economic demands, contrasted sharply with not only the liberal image of the self-confident economic man of enterprise and the agrarian image of the self-dependent farmer, but also

---

[63] *Ibid.*, p. 114.

with the picture of the senselessly conformist industrial mass-man that Tocqueville had painted and that Nietzschean political theory had made the prevalent image on the European continent.[64] Wilson asked political scientists to look for another political type: "Look at all men everywhere first of all as at human beings struggling for existence, for a little comfort and ease of heart, for happiness amidst the things that bind and limit them." The new citizen was a man of good will. His interests were shaped by society and were both stabilized and dignified by cultural accumulations of religious practices, educational discipline, and familial concerns. A long republican tradition had taught him to feel "put upon his honor" to fulfill his role as "a man with his thought upon the general welfare, his interests consciously linked with the interests of his fellow-citizens, his sense of duty broadened to the scope of public affairs." The presidency offered the most promising outlet for these emotions.[65]

Wilson's idea of national leadership pictured the presidency as the natural trust or depository for civic urges and republican instincts that had nowhere else to go in the modern constitutional system. This conception of leadership sought to reconcile a modernized version of republican virtue with the structural conditions of an industrial economy. Wilson wanted to teach the citizen to demand more of his government than spoils and the promotion of self-interest. The provision of understanding, even comfort, was a prominent element in Wilson's identification of the statesman as "a great human being, with an eye for all the great field upon which men like himself struggle, with an unflagging pathetic hope, towards better things. . . . He is a guide, a comrade, a mentor, a servant, a friend of mankind."[66] Wilson's description of the needs fulfilled by modern leadership contained an early but suggestive picture of the helplessness and dependence that became the dominant characteristics of the voter in the twentieth century.

WILSON'S DISCUSSION of the question of leadership in *Constitutional Government* was important, but the real significance of the book lay in its sensitivity to the political importance of large-scale industrialization and its use of constitutionalism to describe the authorization of economic change. Civil society—the system of production, transportation, and communication—was expressed politically in the nation state by virtue of the unique American legal system. The political function of the administration of law—as opposed to the legal function of guarding the body of abstract, general rights—had been to encourage the development of

[64] *Democracy in America*, II, part IV; Mayer, *Persistence of the Old Regime*, pp. 275–329.

[65] "The Law and the Facts," presidential address to the American Political Science Association, Dec. 27, 1910, *PWW*, XXII, 271; *Constitutional Government, ibid.*, XVIII, 84.

[66] "The Law and the Facts," *ibid.*, XXII, 271.

unequal practical needs, abilities, opportunities, and interests and to empower these in conformity with the national interest. Having read the economy into the constitutional system, it became obvious to Wilson that the notion of citizenship needed to be reconsidered. His awareness of the inability of certain groups to gain access to the courts was only one indication to him that individual rights were largely inoperative unless they were sanctioned administratively. The transformation of the citizen into a voter who looked to leadership for reassurance of his political existence was another indication of the shifting basis of citizenship.

In retrospect, one is tempted to conclude that Wilson deliberately softened some of the sharper theoretical features of his work. It seems clear that his idea of the administrative function of the courts was constructed in categories that could contain the question of the corporations, but for the most part Wilson quietly bypassed the host of legal issues that surrounded the corporations. Wilson's last academic work, his presidential address to the American Political Science Association in December 1910, displayed fewer inhibitions.[67] As he told the political scientists, the state had put its power behind the expansion of business forces but had done so unsystematically and on a piecemeal basis: "Any one who clamored for legislative aid and brought the proper persuasive influences to bear could get assistance and encouragement. . . . A free field and all the favour the law could show was our rule of life, our standard of policy. Interests of this, that, or the other sort grew so big that they necessarily touched and interlaced." The courts had mediated between interests but had lacked general guidelines.[68] With the rise of the great corporation, the breakdown of the traditional distinction between state and society, or between government and business, had become total. Corporations, seeking profit as their form of power, operated on a scale and performed acts of social disruption and reorganization that had previously been a government monopoly. Business forces had become the most powerful forces in modern politics, "the hardest to correlate, tame, and harness."[69] At a governors' conference a month earlier, Wilson had been even more explicit:

> Business has spread itself with a new organization and volume. As it
> has spread it has been interwoven, in actual organization as well as
> in the rapid interchange of goods. The organization of business has
> become more centralized, vastly more centralized than the political
> organization of the country itself. Corporations have . . . excelled
> States in their budgets and loomed bigger than whole common
> wealths in their influence over the lives and fortunes of entire com-

[67] *Ibid.*, pp. 263–72.
[68] *Ibid.*, p. 266.
[69] *Ibid.*, pp. 268–69.

munities of men. . . . Amidst a confused variety of States and statutes stands now the colossus of business, uniform, concentrated, poised upon a single plan, governed, not by votes, but by commands.[70]

How was the student of politics to approach these basic facts of modern life? What were the terms of their interpretation as the highest political law? As an answer, Wilson sketched two forms of political reason. The first he described as the study of "these great phenomena . . . in their pure and separate force." Political science and economic science were basically devoted to this task and were oriented toward the formulation of policy on the basis of a systematic "segregation" of facts. Wilson made it clear, however, that there was a second form of political reason directed, not toward policy, but toward politics and political action. This form of reason was synthetic in nature and deeply suspicious of "formulas," such as the use of constitutions and traditions as the standards of interpretation. In place of the separation of forces, the new political reason was aimed at "the correlation of forces." Its basic interpretive guidelines were the values of "adjustment, synthesis, coordination, harmony, and union of parts."[71] In a striking paragraph, Wilson outlined the idea of a system of forces that was to contain politics in the modern state. It was a system predicated upon the breakdown of constitutional reasoning under the impact of modern forms of power:

> We must look away from the piecemeal law books, the miscellaneous and disconnected statutes and legal maxims, the court decisions, to the life of men, in which there is always, of necessity, an essential unity, which, whether it will or no, whether it is conscious of it or not, *must* be of a piece, *must* have a pattern which can be traced. Here are the fragments: the laws, the separate forces, the eager competing interests, the disordered *disjecta membra* of a system which is no system, which does not even suggest system, but which must somehow be built together into a whole which shall be something more than a mere sum of the parts.[72]

Wilson argued that behind a vocabulary that betrayed its debt to German terminology, a new configuration of "facts" seemed to be taking shape in modern political reasoning. The new nation was to be conceived, not in liberty, but on the basis of modern power, with a high regard for its varied parts and their unequal growth. At present, Wilson suggested, political science offered a picture or a whole range of interests

[70] Address to the Conference of Governors in Frankfort, Kentucky, Nov. 29, 1910, *ibid.*, p. 106.
[71] *Ibid.*, pp. 269, 271, 267.
[72] *Ibid.*, p. 267.

and powers in search of a system, a conception of itself. "Interests" each had their own "separate and complicated development" and needed to be made the subject of separate "regulation and adjustment." The new system was intended to institutionalize flexibility between government and the "sections" of the economy. Even corporations were to be seen as "instrumentalities, not objects in themselves." As Wilson put it,

> Suppose we define business as the economic service of society for private profit, and suppose we define politics as the accommodation of all social forces, the forces of business of course included, to the common interest. We may thus perceive our task in all its magnitude and extraordinary significance. Business must be looked upon, not as the exploitation of society, not as its use for private ends, but as its sober service; and private profit must be regarded as legitimate only when it is in fact a reward for what is veritably serviceable,— serviceable to interests which are not single but common, as far as they go; and politics must be the discovery of this common interest, in order that the service may be tested and exacted.[73]

The function of government is to maintain and adjust the "law" to contain "the actual circumstances of social experience." "Law," Wilson said, "is an effort to fix in definite practice what has been found to be convenient, expedient, adapted to the circumstances of the actual world. Law in a moving, vital society grows old, obsolete, impossible, item by item." It would have to be continuously reformulated to serve the nation. Wilson's emphasis upon the values of "adjustment" and "correlation" indicates that the object of the new system was its own maintenance and growth. Unlike a regular constitution, the new system could not and need not be adopted in any formal sense, if for no other reason than because it lacked an end or a purpose that would justify its being. Instead of a purpose, Wilson argued, it required continuous interpretation. In one interesting passage Wilson seems to suggest that the new system would depend, at least in part, on the modern inclination to be "very obedient to our men of science." It appeared, however, that the general provision of legitimacy was to be the task of a partnership between the "statesmanship of thought" and "the statesmanship of action."[74] This partnership, based on a common language consisting of elements gathered from various fields—such as literature, "human relationships," and the social sciences—was charged with the responsibility for shaping the outline of the new system in the public mind.

[73] *Ibid.*, pp. 265, 271, 268.
[74] *Ibid.*, pp. 263, 269.

X

★ ★

CONCLUSION:

RECONSTRUCTING THE NATION

The basic pattern of Wilson's political thought was formed over the period from the end of Reconstruction to the war with Spain, a period of distinct political features. Many contemporaries saw the political reconstruction of the country after the Civil War as requiring a new form of the legitimation of government. As Ralph Henry Gabriel pointed out in 1940, "When Beauregard's batteries ceased firing, the breached and crumbling walls of Sumter perfectly symbolized American political democracy when Americans appealed from reason to force. Responsibility for the disaster rested with the American people."[1] The notion of "the people" as a corporate political body was undermined so violently that the only comparable discrediting of democracy that comes to mind is the widespread belief in Europe after World War II that the phenomenon of Nazism was somehow a creature of democratic mass politics.

The political disaster of the Civil War was inherent not only in the appeal from reason to force, but also in the modern means of violence. The war is often seen as the first modern industrial war. It was modern not only in regard to weapons and bloodshed but also in regard to the systematic use of political ideas that served to mobilize the masses for the trenches and for the factories. The result was that the war gradually assumed the appearance of a violent clash between two distinct political cultures that had been bridged by an intricate institutional structure consisting of the Constitution as supplemented by the compromises that had been built upon it. When the bridge collapsed, the South came to be seen as the inheritor of institutions derived from state and local politics, encapsulated in traditionalistic social and racial structures. The North became the exponent of free labor, equal citizenship, liberalism, and industrialism.

[1] *The Course of American Democratic Thought: An Intellectual History since 1815* (New York, 1940), p. 111. See also the fine discussion in Dunning, *History of Political Theories*, pp. 249–92, 332–39.

Accordingly, the progress of the war highlighted the fact that the constitutional props had collapsed in the North as power had become centralized and the Constitution itself had been overruled in the process of winning. The social structures that supported northern liberalism and capitalism were asserted on the battlefield, but the Constitution itself was severely weakened in the process.[2] The picture was different in the South. The Constitution appeared to be restored in the South, at least in a formal sense, but here the underlying social structure appeared to have fallen apart. But unlike wars in the twentieth century, the result was not the exhaustion of ideology. On the contrary, it appeared to contemporary theorists that when traditional constitutional and social structures were attenuated, the result was not popular cynicism but the rise of popular enthusiasm. Political passions and theory were unleashed.

In 1876, William Graham Sumner drew a picture of the theoretical backdrop to the birth of a new academic political science, of which for many years he was the foremost practitioner.[3] It was not a republic in which the elite needed a science with which to govern, as Hamilton had argued in the 1780s.[4] Sumner's picture was a far cry from the bland idea of a "crisis of legitimacy." In his view, the war had given birth to a republic in which ideas had gripped the masses, in which the passions of theoretical reason reigned supreme. The normal politics of interest had been overruled. What Sumner called "the proper domain of politics"—the politics of selfishness, of material gain and loss for groups and individuals—had been replaced by a new politics of "unselfishness and moral and religious motives," deeply influenced by "heroic elements,—sacrifice for moral good, and devotion to right in spite of expediency."

> Every schoolboy could dogmatize about natural and inalienable rights, about the conditions under which men are created, about the rights of the majority, and about liberty. The same doctrines are so held to-day by the mass of the people, and they are held so implicitly, that corollaries are deduced from them with a more fearless logic than is employed upon political questions anywhere else in the world. Even scholars and philosophers who reflect upon them and

[2] John W. Burgess, "The American Commonwealth: Changes in Its Relation to the Nation," *Political Science Quarterly*, I (March 1886), 9–35; William A. Dunning, "The Constitution of the United States in Reconstruction," *ibid.*, II (Dec. 1887), 558–602; Woodrow Wilson, "The Reconstruction of the Southern States," *Atlantic Monthly*, LXXXVII (Jan. 1901), 1–15, *PWW*, XI, 459–79.

[3] "Politics in America, 1776–1876," *North American Review*, CXXII (Jan. 1876), 47–87.

[4] *The Federalist*, No. 9, p. 51.

doubt them are slow to express their dissent, so jealous and quick is the popular judgment of an attempt upon them.[5]

Only gradually did this situation change, and in most modern fashion Sumner welcomed the return of popular "indifference and apathy." People would soon demand no more from politics than "good government, honorable and efficient administration, business-like performance, and exactitude." Sumner expected the new political identity to take its cue from the economy.[6] The growth of the industrial economy soon tempted many Americans to see their country with the eyes of millions of immigrants, who, it was widely assumed, had chosen the United States as the best road to material prosperity. The republic of political passions became the land of private opportunity. The publication of *The Papers of Woodrow Wilson* has revealed that Wilson's writings contain a distinct expression of the changes in academic political thought ensuing from the war and the victory of nationalism.

IT HAS BEEN EASY to overlook Wilson's role as an academic political thinker, not only because his published writings seemed unsystematic and because most of his private notes were unavailable until recently, but also because he soon developed a characteristic view of the role of the political theorist. He tended to consciously suppress the active and creative contribution of political theory in favor of the perception of political reality. While the sense of theoretical achievement still figured prominently in Wilson's early plea for parliamentary leadership in *Congressional Government*, his turn toward the idea of the modern state implied a humbling of the theorist. Only gradually did Wilson develop the view that leadership could arrogate to itself the creative role that the theorist had lost.

In Wilson's mature view, the political thinker was no longer to aim to transform political reality but instead simply to register its existing tendencies. His function was not to furnish new ways of grasping reality but to promote factualism in politics and to associate himself with the forces of progress and promote the general acceptance of expedient or inevitable changes. The new theorist was an imaginative administrator of existing facts and commonly accepted ideas, not the herald of dramatic discoveries. He was to bring "light, *not heat*," "warmth," but not "warping heat," to the national organism. His role as an interpreter was not to enter a pitched battle between power and justice but to show the interconnections between authority and community. The ground rules for the

---

[5] Sumner, "Politics in America, 1776–1876," pp. 79, 78.
[6] *Ibid.*, pp. 80–81.

new kind of theory were stated most clearly in Wilson's confidential journal of 1889. His goal was to set forth a professional self-portrait, but also a portrait of a new professional ethos that rejected an "ideal conception" in favor of a method that sought to formulate "the laws of social development" on the basis of "facts" understood as political "*relationships*."[7] "I *receive* the opinions of my day, I do not *conceive* them," Wilson wrote.

> But I receive them into a vivid mind, with a quick imaginative realization, and a power to see as a whole the long genesis of the opinions received. I have little impatience with existing conditions; I comprehend too perfectly how they came to exist, how *natural* they are. I have great confidence in progress; I feel the movement that is in affairs and am conscious of a persistent push behind the present order. . . . It is a task, not of origination, but of interpretation. Interpret the age: i.e. interpret myself. Account for the creed I hold in politics. . . . No one can give a true account of anything of which he is intolerant. I find myself exceedingly tolerant of all institutions, past and present, by reason of a keen appreciation of their reason for being—*most* tolerant, so to say, of the institutions of my own day which seem to me, in a historical sense, intensely and essentially reasonable, though of course in no sense *final*.[8]

The most important feature of these ruminations was Wilson's insistence that the new method or approach to the study of social relationships be distinguished by an interior, tolerant point of view. The theoretical mind should not impose its standards on society from the outside but should enlist itself in the modification of the social environment. This step, in which mind becomes conscious of its ability to anticipate social events, was the crucial step that brought Social Darwinism into an evolutionary phase, where the ability to anticipate implied the ability to modify and turn to social advantage, as Edward S. Corwin pointed out in 1950.[9]

WILSON'S IDEAS of political economy, administration, and leadership were deeply dependent upon his idea of American nationality. In the twentieth century, nationalism is often regarded as a popular insistence upon some kind of inherent superiority in regard to other nations. This meaning does not capture the origins of Wilson's understanding. Nation-

---

[7] Notes for a chapel talk, *PWW*, XII, 287; confidential journal, Dec. 29, 1889, *ibid.*, VI, 464.

[8] Confidential journal, Dec. 28, 1889, *ibid.*, 462–63.

[9] Edward S. Corwin, "The Impact of the Idea of Evolution on the American Political and Constitutional Tradition," in *Corwin on the Constitution*, ed. by Richard Loss (Ithaca, N. Y., 1981), pp. 187–89; Richard Hofstadter, *Social Darwinism in American Thought*, rev. ed. (Boston, 1955), p. 136.

alism is best regarded, at least for the present purposes, as a general term that articulates the perceived interconnections between population and place. The meaning of the term is dependent upon the historical circumstances, the origins, and the values that are expressed when these interconnections are named.[10] One kind of nationality has grown under conditions of popular struggle against foreign occupation; a different kind may develop in the process of conquest; a third kind may develop as a result of civil war. Wilson, of course, did not invent American nationalism. His use of the term was necessarily colored by earlier formulations, such as Alexander Hamilton's and Henry Clay's ideas about national economic independence, John C. Calhoun's ideal of a national sentiment nourished by the rights of the states, Daniel Webster's constitutional nationalism, and Abraham Lincoln's union of free individuals. At this point, the outward features of Wilson's concept of nationality stand out with sufficient clarity. They may briefly be summed up as his modification of the constitutional basis and the substitution of the majoritarian idea of "the people" as the principle of legitimacy with an idea of the nation, which consisted of inherited loyalties and habits, on the one hand, and of directing sovereignty on the other. The interior origins of Wilson's idea of nationality may require further discussion.

Such inquiry should not begin with the mood of complacency and trust in historical progress that one finds in Wilson's confidential journal of 1889. A better point of departure would be the political tensions that had originally turned his attention to political writing in 1876. His earliest attitudes are not well described as those of a conservative southern Democrat. They are better described as those of a British Loyalist who had gone into hiding in 1776 and, half unwillingly, had returned to American society a century later and found himself in a foreign land. In Wilson's experience, the acceptance of the "facts" of history,—the defeat of the South and the imposition of general suffrage—were conditions that made the formulation of American nationality a matter of emotional necessity and intellectual will rather than sentimental and intellectual convention.

In 1880, more than a year after he had published his first essay, "Cabinet Government in the United States," Wilson noted in the margin of a speech by John Bright about the causes of the Civil War that "I have

[10] A short genealogy of the idea of nationalism is found in Hans Kohn, "Nationalism," *Dictionary of the History of Ideas: Studies of Selected Pivotal Ideas*, ed. by Philip P. Weiner (New York, 1973), III, 324–39. General discussions of the term abound. I have found the following most useful: Alexander Passerin d'Entreves, *The Notion of the State* (London, 1967), pp. 170–81; and John H. Schaar, "The Case for Patriotism," in Schaar, *Legitimacy in the Modern State* (New Brunswick, N. J., 1981), pp. 285–312.

reached maturity at a time when the passions it stirred have cooled. . . . In this calmer period I can clearly see that the suffering of the Confederacy was an inestimable [?] blessing, that the doctrine of states rights was a danger settled, and that the abolition of slavery was, even for us, a lasting benefit."[11] "To *me*," Wilson underscored, attempting to overcome the political impressions from his earliest years, "the Civil War and its terrible scenes are but the memory of a short day." This last phrase is one of the single most expressive phrases concerning Wilson's idea of nationality. It covers his reactions to a prolonged state of fear and insecurity about the survival of settled ways of life. It was also a precise expression of a reconstructed nationality that abounded in attempts to unify the themes of light, progress, and power in a symbolism of biological metaphors and resurrectional allusions.

One may wonder why Wilson did not refer to "the memory of a short *night*." The shorter the day, if a Freudian note be permitted, the longer is the night. The reason behind Wilson's breach of the cliché was that there could be no denial that Abel had been slain in the field and that it was senseless, even sinful, to cover this fact by darkness and night. There could be no progress, no national rise and reconciliation until the war was made part of the day. Historians who see Wilson as a nostalgic man who longed for the return of a political state of innocence or an economic state of Jeffersonian yeomanry have missed the point that it was the overcoming of the past, not its repetition, which made *progress* such a prominent term in his historical writing. *"Political sin,"* he believed, is simply "the transgression of the law of political progress." What could not be repressed would have to be sublimated and made as bloodless as the pages of history and as redeeming as the blessings of social and economic advance. The war and the occupation of the South could not be left as the night, in which the powerful asserted their might, but were to be clothed in right and seen as a process of cleansing of the nation of its obsolete structures and sentiment, of burning civil life to the ground to make room for national growth. For Wilson it was therefore not a matter of preserving the ruins of the broken constitutional covenant but of setting off on a new beginning in which material development served as the preamble for a reconstructed economic body. As Wilson knew, Cain's offspring was Tubal, "an instructor of every artificer in brass and iron." "The dem[ocracy] of the U.S. has succeeded because of the press and the steam engine, the telegraph and the speeded post. These agencies, partly created out of its originating strength, have gone before it and prepared the way for it," Wilson wrote in a note for the preface to his unwritten

[11] Marginal notes, July 19, 1880, *PWW*, I, 664–65.

"Philosophy of Politics."[12] The spirit was another matter. The partnership between the brothers of the Union was destroyed. The blood cried from the ground.

There is no answer to this problem in the long and somewhat self-satisfied account of the war and occupation with which Wilson later tried to commend the white southern reaction to readers from other sections of the country.[13] The answer, at least from a theoretical point of view, was Wilson's turn from parliamentary constitutionalism to state organicism. The symbolism of organicism allowed a process of "healing and oblivion" to be consummated. The blood must be swallowed; the war became intestinal. Brotherhood was not enough. Hence, a movement from brotherly competition back to Adam, back to the familial organicism whose symbolism best reaffirmed the "new tissue of nationality," the "links stronger than links of steel round the invisible body of common thought and purpose which is the substance of nations." Organicism was primarily a symbolic representation that expressed a biological understanding of society.[14] Modern readers mostly find it either silly or meaningless, because it seems to veil what we want revealed. But it was attractive for Wilson for exactly the same reasons that it is rejected by the modern reader. It was a language of adumbration, with deep meanings taken from Christian symbolism and mysticism.

This idea of state organicism lended itself to rhetorical exploitation. It often allowed Wilson to tell the owners of corporations to go full speed ahead while at the same time telling the exploited that they need not lose hope. But organicism did even more for political science. It taught the first generation of political scientists that innovation and social cohesion could coexist, that progress could be administered, and that the social environment was amenable to manipulation and reform. Organicism taught what kind of society was best fit for survival. It was not a society that was distinguished by conflict among its members, as the Social Darwinists had said. It was, on the contrary, a society characterized by the suppression and diversification of struggle.[15]

WILSON'S IDENTIFICATION of his own theoretical personality and his insistence that theory accommodate itself to perceived historical necessity

[12] Memorandum for "The Philosophy of Politics," Jan. 26, 1895, *ibid.*, ix, 129; Gen. 4:11–22; notes for "The Philosophy of Politics," Dec. 1–20, 1885, Woodrow Wilson Collection, Firestone Library.

[13] *A History of the American People*, v, 1–114.

[14] "The Reconstruction of the Southern States," *PWW*, xi, 478.

[15] Corwin, "Idea of Evolution," in *Corwin on the Constitution*, p. 185; Eric F. Goldman, *Rendezvous with Destiny: A History of Modern American Reform*, rev. ed. (New York, 1956), pp. 66–101.

go a long way toward explaining why Wilson never wrote his projected major work, "The Philosophy of Politics." His plans were first put on paper in the course of writing "The Democratic State" soon after he left the Johns Hopkins. From outlines, scattered notes, and Wilson's private letters it is clear that he conceived the project to be an elaboration and continuation of the ideas behind this essay. Early in 1891, in 1895, and again in 1901 and 1902, Wilson resumed work on his "Immortalia," as he only half jestingly called his work. The central categories, such as "political morality," "political expediency," and "political prejudice," that Wilson arranged for discussion were clearly inspired by Burke.[16]

The project had great importance for Wilson, because it seemed to offer him the opportunity to refute the tradition of Jeffersonian philosophical radicalism in America. He was well aware that both agrarian populists and American socialists regarded themselves as the natural inheritors of the Jeffersonian legacy, just as the French revolutionaries had been the children of Rousseau, according to Burke. In a popular survey of American statesmen he wrote in 1893, Wilson almost read Jefferson out of American history as "a great man, not a great American." Although Wilson noted "a native shrewdness, tact, and sagacity" in Jefferson's practical leadership, he saved his Burkean invectives for Jefferson's political theory: "It is his speculative philosophy that is exotic, and that runs like a false and artificial note through all his thought. It was un-American in being abstract, sentimental, rationalistic, rather than practical. . . . The very aërated quality of Jefferson's principles gives them an air of insincerity."[17]

Even in 1906, when Wilson was called upon to demonstrate his own loyalties in politics by delivering the address at the annual Jefferson Day dinner of the National Democratic Club, there was a note of ambivalence both in his manuscript and in his speech. In terms of theory, it is hardly surprising that he sought to please conservative Democrats by turning down what he now called Jefferson's "gentle lambent flame of theory" and turning up "the eager flame of action." True Democrats, he said, must see to it that "it is the spirit, not the tenets of the man by which he rules us from his urn," Wilson declared. Wilson now took the criticism of radical philosophy beyond Burke. He accused Jefferson's practice of theory of betraying his genteel aspirations. Jefferson had declined to make

---

[16] WW to Horace Elisha Scudder, May 12, 1886, *PWW*, v, 218–20; WW to Ellen Axson Wilson, Jan. 26, 1895, *ibid.*, ix, 128; WW to Richard Watson Gilder, Jan. 6, 1901, *ibid.*, xii, 67–68; WW to Frederick Jackson Turner, Jan. 21, 1902, *ibid.*, 240. Cooper, *The Warrior and the Priest*, pp. 52–54.

[17] "A Calendar of Great Americans," *PWW*, viii, 373–74; Cooper, *The Warrior and the Priest*, pp. 122–23.

public appearances, "he preferred the closet. . . . We think of him, not as a man who mixed with the people, but rather as a man withdrawn, aristocratic, exclusive, . . . [with] a sort of secret, Machiavellian, Italian hand in politics." Wilson intimated that Jefferson's democratic legacy contained both a spirit of popular action and a form of theory that was vaguely conspiratorial, indeed, a "ghost." Thus, Wilson went two significant steps further than simply repeating the Burkean animus against abstract political reason.[18]

First, instead of viewing radical liberalism as a consequence of giving the masses access to voting, Wilson attached it to aristocratic and conspiratorial inclinations. He turned Burke's celebration of popular inertness upon its head by establishing an American connection between political action and the popular habits of economic and moral individuality. These practices had furnished the material growth of the American state from the bottom up, and Wilson was now prepared to find them as authentically expressed in Jefferson's teaching as he had earlier seen them in Hamilton's "conservative genius." Second, regarding the constitutional continuity that was at the very heart of Burke's political universe, Wilson emphasized that Jefferson had been the first to break the constitutional mold that had limited the natural growth of state power. Jefferson had clearly and correctly understood that the Constitution did not warrant the Louisiana Purchase, but as Wilson put it, "he preferred to make waste paper of the Constitution rather than make a waste of America."

Taken together, the two steps constitute the beginning of what Wilson obscurely referred to as the construction of "a real, sound, water-tight theory of Democracy." Surprisingly, Wilson was able to use the example of Jefferson to present a version of Burke that suited a "popular" America rather than an aristocratic England. He achieved this, it should be noted, while keeping a demonstrable distance from liberal versions of individual rights or even conservative versions of Jeffersonian economic individualism, insofar as these versions all depended upon a prescriptive doctrine that found the source and limits of political authority in individuals' purposes. Not individualism but "individualization of men" was the key to American power and liberty. The state was to be understood as the seat of manifest national freedom, not abstract individual liberties. As Wilson put it to his audience, "I cannot make Democratic theory out of each of you, but I could make a Democratic theory out of all of you."[19]

As Wilson realized, Burke had addressed a nation in which political

---

[18] Address on Thomas Jefferson, *PWW*, xvi, 359, 360, 363.

[19] "A Calendar of Great Americans," *ibid.*, viii, 370; address on Thomas Jefferson, *ibid.*, xvi, 364, 366. See also, Steven Lukes, "Types of Individualism," in *Dictionary of the History of Ideas*, ii, 601.

tradition was enshrined in customs and institutions that bespoke of a long, continuous history. Wilson, in contrast, was to address his "Philosophy of Politics" to a political culture in which, as he put it, "the past seems dead." In view of the narrow limits of social and political traditionalism in America, Wilson seems to have intended to make "The Philosophy of Politics" an appeal to the family as the source of time-honored morality, selfless devotion, individual responsibility, and sturdy work habits. The soul of his project was the idea that family history could be projected into the development of the state as "a moral person" and in its conclusion portrayed as the moral profile of leadership in the modern nation.[20] As one might put it today, the study was intended as an anthropology of political ethics, which uncovered the familial relations behind the constitution of modern rulership. Wilson wanted to show that the outward behavior of government both derived from and stimulated the internal principles of human conscience. He wanted to historicize the "self" in "self-government" as an alternative theory of the democratic nation, which worked its way through history by way of what Wilson called *induction*, not through the ideas of the social contract, which he termed *deduction*. Yet Wilson had no psychological or sociological language with which to express himself on such topics as political "responsibility," "trust," and "character." He had conceived a project for which there was hardly any vocabulary available. When such a vocabulary did begin to form after the turn of the century, it was too late. If a vocabulary had been available, the informing intentions might have been closer to Continental social science, such as Durkheimean sociology, than to Burkean conservatism.[21] The problem with this artificial comparison is that Wilson was largely uninterested in the scientific method per se and betrayed little awareness of the methodological problems involved when the inductive method is applied to social and political phenomena. Instead, he consciously and consistently oriented his scholarly writings away from a spec-

[20] Notes for "The Philosophy of Politics," Jan. 26, 1895, *ibid.*, IX, 131; WW to Horace Elisha Scudder, May 12, 1886, *ibid.*, V, 219.

[21] WW to Horace Elisha Scudder, July 10, 1886, *ibid.*, V, 303–304. The comparison with Durkheim is intended to suggest that Wilson, perhaps because of his need to criticize French political thought, especially Montesquieu and Rousseau, had absorbed more of its spirit than he cared to admit. These writers were also important for Durkheim, who was, incidentally, very interested in family history. See Wolin, *Politics and Vision*, pp. 368–74; and Steven Lukes, *Émile Durkheim, His Life and Work: A Historical and Critical Study* (New York, 1972), pp. 125–27, 179–90, 279–89. Graham Wallas's book *Human Nature in Politics* (1908; reprint, London, 1948) was the first modern dicussion of political psychology within Anglo-American political science, although some of Wallas's tenets had been anticipated in Bagehot's *Physics and Politics*; see Fay Berger Karpf, *American Social Psychology: Its Origins, Development and European Background* (1932; reprint, New York, 1972), pp. 158–64.

ulative understanding and toward an intuitive grasp of "practical politics."

Wilson kept the idea of a philosophical work in mind for a number of
years, but he was largely content to let the subject "*simmer* without coming
to a hard boil."[22] In view of his meticulous attention to the strengths and
weaknesses of his own intellect, this decision may have been a wise one.
One example of his difficulties may suffice. The methodological point of
departure was to be his criticism of contemplative theories of government: "As we can know persons only from what they say and do, and the
manner of their acting and speaking, so we can know governments from
what *they* say and do and the manner of their speech and action. But in
governments and persons alike we can look beneath the surface, if we
have discernment enough, and so discover more of *character* than any
amount of *a priori* speculation can reveal."[23] The problem was that Wilson's notion of character, as something that emerged from "beneath the
surface" cannot be distinguished from the "dissected qualities" that he
accused the theorists of the social contract of putting in the place of "real
persons." But unlike these authors, Wilson was unaware that he was dealing with theoretical fictions, no matter how strongly he exhorted the
spirit of practical and historical reason to breathe life into his imaginative
constructions. Furthermore, his work was founded on a distracting paradox. It was planned as a warning against political utopianism, but it was
conceived on the basis of a true scientific utopianism that intended nothing less than to unify the appearance and the meaning of political phenomena: "The ideal thing to do would be to penetrate to [the] *essential
character* [of the spiritual oneness of government] by way of a thorough
knowledge of all its outward manifestations of character."[24] This choice
of words not only discloses the problematic character of the project, it
also gives a hint of why Wilson could never come to a close encounter
with his own inspired vision in order to try to resolve the problems of
method.

As indicated by his use of sexual metaphors, the project was a forbidden love. When he tried to lay out his plans in a letter to the author and
editor Horace Elisha Scudder, Wilson realized that his governing ideas
could barely be written out. The subject could only be broached orally.
Instead of writing, Wilson longed for an intimate conversation to "*talk* it
over." "*Then* I might go at least a little way *inside* the subject I so love to
explore, but whose outside only I have been able to touch here." In ad-

[22] WW to Ellen Axson Wilson, Jan. 26, 1895, *PWW*, ix, 129.
[23] WW to Horace Elisha Scudder, July 10, 1886, *ibid.*, v, 304. Wilson's emphasis.
[24] *Ibid*. Wilson's emphasis.

dition, the project betrays its ambiguous character from the point of view of behavioral psychology. It was conceived in the spirit of a Wanderjahr by a man deeply devoted to strenuous, systematic, even excruciating, habits of daily work.[25]

If a religious double bind is preferred as an explanation, Wilson's simultaneous yielding to the attraction and the repulsion of his project may be seen as the equivalent of the Puritan approach to the notion of predestination, a subject that Calvin had introduced with horrible threats. Calvin's intent was to deter the believers from an exploration that tempted the inquirer to strip naked such "things that the Lord has willed to be hid in himself." "No restraints can hold [curiosity] back from wandering in forbidden bypaths and thrusting upward to the heights. If allowed, it will leave no secret to God that it will not search out and unravel." Such inhibitions on the quest for knowledge may be foreign to the modern reader. But they may still throw light on the allurements and the firm repression of any projected work that revealed a dangerous ambition to thrust upward to obtain control over progress, even as Wilson prefaced his notes with warnings against "hope without moderation."[26] Thus the fate of "The Philosophy of Politics" was not the accidental outcome of temporary distractions or bad luck. The project was immortal for Wilson, because it was never consummated and, hence, never abandoned. Condemned as well as lifted up to a state of perpetual virginity, Wilson's project may not be approached as the victim of progressive self-restraint in the practice of political theory but as its spiritual embodiment.

The upshot was that Wilson's academic political thought was unable to impose itself on American political science, simply because his major work did not materialize. No major academic political scientist in the twentieth century has claimed to be directly inspired by Wilson. Even in the field of executive leadership, where Wilson's present influence may be most pronounced, Wilson's ideas are largely discussed as an American version of theories that came to the nation's attention by way of Max Weber's political sociology. Seen from the viewpoint of American political science, Wilson's contribution was a theory *mancando*. It was primarily directed not toward fellow political scientists but toward the public. Wilson's later career seemed to confirm the suspicion that his ideas contained too much politics and not enough science. Undoubtedly Wilson himself realized his complicated standing in the profession. He gave

[25] *Ibid.*; WW to Richard Watson Gilder, Jan. 6, 1901, *ibid.*, xii, 68. Wilson's emphasis.

[26] *Calvin: Institutes of Christian Religion*, ed. by John T. McNeill, trans. by Ford Lewis Battles (2 vols., Philadelphia, 1960), ii, 922–23; random notes for "The Philosophy of Politics," Jan. 26, 1895, *PWW*, ix, 128.

voice to it when he declared, standing at the pinnacle of professional recognition as he gave the presidential address to the American Political Science Association in 1910, "I do not like the term political science. . . . I prefer the term Politics."[27] His remark contained a note of open defiance. He had just been elected governor of New Jersey.

What was the legacy that Wilson bequeathed to American political science in the twentieth century? This legacy was eventually to be worked out in a highly abstract and rationalistic language that made it easy to repress its antecedent. In place of Wilson's state came the notion of "the system," as Sheldon S. Wolin has suggested. In place of Wilson's notion of a political and economic drive toward diversification, specialization, and a differentiation of function, political scientists soon developed the concept of American pluralism.[28] They inherited Wilson's reformulation of the Burkean rejection of abstract political reasoning but worked it out as the distinction between normative and descriptive theory. Wilson's critique of constitutional reasoning as unable to fulfill the needs of power that befit an industrial polity with expanding international interests has grown to become a major theme in modern political science. But unlike Wilson, who wanted to celebrate the spirit, while banishing the ghost, of Jefferson's political ideas, modern political scientists—proceeding from Arthur F. Bentley's work on the *Process of Government*—often seem more inclined to exorcize the Wilsonian spirit while remembering his ghost of the state, his "metaphysical spook," in Bentley's epithet.[29]

The adoption of organic metaphors allowed Wilson to presume a historical unity between government and economic growth, a process that assumed the existence of a national state, registered, not in the Constitution, but in the advance of national power. Wilson expressed his idea of national organicism in his portrait of the personality of the state that had overcome its childhood, when it had been under the guidance of a self-contained political elite that had brought the United States safely from independence to constitutionalism. The next phase of national youth was the popular political experience that had begun with Jackson's presidency and that had run its course by the beginning of the Civil War. The current phase was a period of "maturity" and "self-consciousness." This advanced stage—the modern democratic state—was reflected in Wilson's insistence upon wholeness, upon the life and growth of nationality, the integration of diverse functions, the stability of habits, the necessity of organs, the prevalence of diffused sentiment, and the sover-

[27] "The Law and the Facts," *PWW*, xxii, 271.

[28] Sheldon S. Wolin, "The Idea of the State in America," *Humanities in Society*, iii (Spring 1980), 164.

[29] *Ibid.*, p. 162.

eignty of leadership, which were intended as the spiritual expression of the material growth of national power. What had fallen apart in political reality because the constitutional center could not hold was to be reconstructed as social and economic advance under political direction.

The significance of Wilson's political views may be assessed against the political values that he rejected. In his intellectual inclination and accomplishment, Wilson belonged to a group of writers engaged in both a "revolt against formalism" and the founding of a new set of political and social sciences. Historians have afforded this group of writers the unusual privilege of allowing them to name their adversaries.[30] If for no other reason, Wilson deserves a place in American intellectual history because his papers make clear that the intellectual criticism of formalism in significant part was aimed at the majoritarian, localist, and populist understanding of power in America. While this understanding was mainly based upon John Locke, the Declaration of Independence, and the Preamble to the Constitution, the practice of majoritarian politics was for the most part associated with Jacksonian democracy. Its central belief was that government is rooted in popular involvement, consciousness, desires, and will. The strength of this tradition and Wilson's growing appreciation of habitual popular dispositions dictated that the attack on majoritarianism be carried out in the name of democracy itself. It is "absolutely prerequisite to any competent study . . . that the democracy which is now becoming dominant is a *new* democracy . . . informed with a life and surrounded by controlling conditions altogether modern," Wilson wrote in "The Modern Democratic State." "Properly organized democracy is the best govt. of the few."[31]

The majority was to be contained rather than attacked directly. It was given certain characteristics that raised it to a form of historical inevitability, but Wilson stripped it of any claim to political reason. "The efficient majority" became a mass, unified by being bound to irrational sentiment and by the self-assurance of power. It "had seen its legions and felt its might in the field," Wilson wrote in 1900. During the Civil War, the majority was animated by the "dangerous intoxication of an absolute triumph." It was then that "the ultimate foundation of the structure was laid bare: physical force, sustained by the stern loves and rooted predilections of masses of men, the strong ingrained prejudices which are the fibre of every system of government."[32] As Wilson saw it, the veil of sen-

---

[30] *Social Thought in America: The Revolt against Formalism* (Boston, 1957), p. 12; Thomas L. Haskell, *The Emergence of Professional Social Science: The American Social Science Association and the Nineteenth-Century Crisis of Authority* (Urbana, Ill., 1977), pp. 9–14.

[31] *PWW*, v, 80, 85.

[32] "Reconstruction of the Southern States," *ibid.*, xi, 474–75.

timent would hardly cover the brutality of majoritarian numbers organized for modern warfare. The majority had burst out of the confines of constitutionalism. To the extent that constitutionalism had attempted to divide the majority, it had failed. The task for modern leadership was therefore, not to break up the majority, but to govern the mass by harnessing its energies to the national state while modifying its "loves" and "prejudices."

Political economy and administration were the primary means of forging the material power of the national state. Both sciences taught how the majorities were incorporated within the system of government. Political economy was a study of the use of private interest for the purpose of public strength. Human motives could be developed "by deliberately *breeding an interest*," as Wilson put it.[33] Administration referred to the practical skills involved in bringing the principles of political economy to bear upon society. Administration was not the enemy of liberal political economy, as many conservatives argued, but its natural complement, especially "in the field of *competitive interests*, like those of trade and manufacture," Wilson pointed out in 1898. Political economy and administration systematized expediency and transformed it from a Burkean "gospel" into progressive reform policy. The importance of Wilson's notion of the state was to permit him to argue that administration was both a reflection of new social needs and an affirmation of the governability of society. Administration referred to the promotion of "the conscious, deliberate, studious, almost ceaseless *adjustment of law to social conditions*, and, by intended consequence, of the alteration of those conditions."[34]

Wilson's contribution is of an order that justifies a comparison with the political science that lay behind the creation of the Constitution. In Madison's view, one of the chief benefits of the Constitution was the discouragement of political leadership, which was feared to be one of the dangers of majoritarian democracy. The chief safeguard against majoritarianism was the system of checks and balances, which would divert political momentum from one institution by setting it against the authority of competing institutions. The second measure was a policy of geographical expansion, which would make it difficult for majorities to come to know their strength and endanger the minority's right not least, the right of property. The Constitution was designed "to prevent, not to achieve."[35]

Wilson's reversal of the Madisonian depreciation of leadership and his

---

[33] Notes for a lecture on patriotism, Dec. 10, 1897, *ibid.*, x, 350.

[34] Notes for lectures in a course on constitutional government, Dec. 11, 1898, *ibid.*, xi, 20.

[35] Wolin, *Politics and Vision*, p. 390; *idem*, "Idea of the State in America," 157–61.

rejection of Madisonian categories were already achieved by 1900. The double key to Madison's constitutionalism was its creation of institutional complexity and support for open space for territorial expansion. The key to Wilson's view was his idea of institutional simplicity, meaning an expanded role for the governmental direction of public opinion, combined with the restraints inherent in the social and economic complexity of the modern world. He replaced Madison's idea of the spacious republic with the idea of a republic of growth, where opportunity would be seen as a function of competitive ability rather than as an American birthright. His special contribution was to adopt the notion of progress, which in nineteenth-century liberal thought referred to the economic advance of society, and make it a term for a political regime. Rejecting the traditional American assumption of abundant space, Wilson redirected Madisonian constitutionalism toward a condition that required political direction. The notion of progress itself invoked an order of controlled advance and restrained energy.

The changing nature of political space was essential for Wilson's transformation of Madisonian reasoning. Madison had used the availability of space to marshal a profusion of private interests against a popular government that might be captured by the majority and employed to suppress the minority. Initially, unlike his friend Frederick Jackson Turner, Wilson had hailed the end of the frontier in the hope that the exhaustion of space would imply new opportunities for a compact government and for political leadership. When he received news about the American conquest of the Spanish colonies, Wilson was hesitant to welcome a return to expansionism. Soon after, however, he discovered that government was strengthened rather than weakened by its foreign engagement. Thus, in 1900 Wilson was able to draw a connection between the Civil War and the war with Spain: "It is evident that empire is an affair of strong government, and not of the nice and somewhat artificial poise or of the delicate compromises of structure and authority characteristic of a mere federal partnership. . . . The impulse of expansion . . . comes with a consciousness of matured strength, but it is also a direct result of that national spirit which the war between the states cried so wide awake."[36]

As the land was taken up and later became scarce, expansion became a matter, not of undermining political authority, but of strengthening the need for leadership in a government based upon popular suffrage. The Civil War was to be redeemed abroad. Perhaps there was even an element of atonement involved. Writing on Reconstruction thirty years after its end, Wilson confessed: "It is a wonder that historians who take

[36] "The Reconstruction of the Southern States," *PWW*, xi, 479.

their business seriously can sleep at night."[37] A national spirit that springs from internalized fratricide is a wandering and restless spirit. The taking of blood worked its way to an inevitable republican outcome in the Philippines.

Wilson's modification of Madison's ideas proceeded from a deepening of emotional intensity that flowed from the Civil War. Added to a changing conception of space there was a new conception of the control of private interests. While Madison had advocated the multiplication of interests by means of extending the national territory, Wilson conceived of administration as the governmental expression of a diversification of interests within settled boundaries.

> The object sought is, not the effectuation of a system of mechanical, or artificial, checks and balances, but only the facilitation and promotion of organic differentiation, with its accompanying diffusion of vitality and accession of vigour. The modern constitutional State seeks to support this differentiation with the positive sanctions of law. No part is to be overworked, but every part is to be disciplined and rendered skilful by specialization.[38]

While Madison's idea had been to diffuse the majority, Wilson's transfer of interest politics to the state organism resulted in the production of "a minority to be protected" and "a majority to be satisfied" by administrative means. Even the rights of private property were to be considered a matter "of policy, not of power," as Wilson put it. These issues were to be decided upon by agreement between administrative expertise and the actual experience of the parties involved, combining "the knowledge of experts and the more subtle inferences of special observation and experience." Such legislative subjects could not be presented to the voter, because their complicated nature dictated that "strong and general convictions" were left "out of the question."[39]

What distinguished Wilson's conception of administrative politics from that of other exponents of expert government was that he recognized the limited appeal of administration in a democratic culture. Administrative politics was therefore to be secured and legitimized by national leadership. In effect, Wilson broke Madison's idea of factionalism into two parts. Madison had argued that factions consisted of interests that were animated by passion, animosity, and bias of judgment. The very definition of a faction was a group of people who were unable to form a polit-

---

[37] *Ibid.*, p. 460.

[38] Notes on administration, *ibid.*, VII, 142. Wilson's emphasis deleted.

[39] Constitutional government notes, *ibid.*, XI, 20; *The State*, VI, 297. Wilson's emphasis deleted.

ical opinion of the "aggregate interests of the community."[40] The notion
of nationality supplied Wilson with the idea that diversification itself
would create a need for political authority as an embodiment of common
ideas. The actual conditions of struggle made the modern citizenry especially sensitive to attempts to bind together in spirit what was diversified in daily practice. "A democracy," as Wilson put it, "by reason of the
very multitude of its voters and their infinite variety in capacity, environment, information, and circumstance, is peculiarly dependent upon its
leaders." Wilson's answer was to construct a concept of ideological leadership as a corollary to his division between the mass and the elite. The
politics of leadership "where there is no absolute and arbitrary ruler to
do the choosing for a whole people—means massed opinion, and the
forming of the mass is the whole art and mastery of politics."[41]

Wilson's idea of leadership both incorporated and preserved the remains of majoritarian attitudes and some of the vestiges of traditional
political theory. It appears that some historians have tended to locate
Wilson's conception of ideology within the realm of administrative politics, where, as Wilson insisted, "strong and general convictions" were out
of place. Wilson conceived of leadership neither in terms of a grand vision nor as a system of values from which a list of policy priorities can be
extracted. Instead, leadership is a method of perceiving and formulating
common premises; it is an act of "reading the common inclination." The
"ear of the leader must ring with the voices of the people. He cannot be
of the school of the prophets; he must be of the number of those who
studiously serve the slow-paced daily demand." "The nineteenth [cen-
tury] has established the principle that public opinion *must* be truckled to
(if you *will* use a disagreeable word) in the conduct of government," as
Wilson put it.[42] Leadership was restrained as well as promoted by the
fund of common ideas produced in the course of popular identification
with a national purpose. The strategic function of leadership, in Wilson's
conception, was to mediate between an increasingly complex and fragmented social condition and the need to form a set of common ideas as
the basis of nationality.

Perhaps the best summary of Wilson's idea of democracy is contained
in "The Real Problem of Democracy," an essay he published in 1901.
Wilson developed his basic argument with reference to a comparison between the English and French political traditions, which embodied two
radically different principles and practices of democracy. The French

[40] *The Federalist*, No. 10, pp. 57–59.

[41] "The Real Idea of Democracy," Aug. 31, 1901, *PWW*, xii, 179; "Leaderless Government," *ibid.*, x, 290.

[42] "Leaders of Men," *ibid.*, vi, 661, 660, 658.

231

tradition, associated in America with ideas of revolution and Jeffersonian theory, tended to focus on the idea of "the sovereignty of the people" and dreamed of a "state in which no man shall have mastery over another without his willing acquiescence and consent." Equality was seen as "a political birthright which is without bound or limitation." The other tradition, English liberalism, was based on "the consent of the governed" (understood as the practical matter of how to "choose between leaders") which should provide "the chief guiding force of a free people." Three features characterized the English tradition. First, it sought out its leaders from the broadest possible base in society. Second, it left the choice between competing political elites to the people in general. Third, it intended the result of its elections to be an authoritative statement of advice to the rulers. In an early formulation of a theory of the popular mandate, conferred by the governed on the governors by the election of representatives, Wilson claimed that the legitimacy of democratic government lay in the open popular declaration of "the needs and temper and interests of the nation," whereby the constituency assured beforehand its "cordial assent to every measure of government." The idea of popular consent, the "concord and counsel" between "those who governed and those who are governed," was no longer "guessed at or risked upon some blind calculation." It was "systematically ascertained."[43] Popular sovereignty was to be understood as a problem, not of popular political participation, but of effective leadership. Wilson's distinction between the French and the English practice of democracy disappeared for several decades, probably as a result of two wars that aligned both traditions against the German devotion to the state. It was rediscovered by George H. Sabine in 1952.[44]

Although Wilson hoped to restore the rhetorical grandeur of political leadership, it is clear that his view of the modern leader allowed a scope for action that was both narrow and distinctly modern. The severe restrictions that hem in the modern leader, Wilson believed, are not only a function of his dependence on popular election. Perhaps more important, the leader is surrounded by economic, political, and administrative sciences that keep political initiative within the narrow limits of expediency, understood as the priorities of established interests. While Wilson considered the leader to be the spiritual minister of national unity, he is but the highest functionary of national power. This idea is mirrored in Wilson's insistence again and again that the range of leadership be considered a matter of "ordinary ideas, extraordinary abilities," restricted to

[43] "The Real Problem of Democracy," *ibid.*, XII, 175–79.
[44] "The Two Democratic Traditions," *Philosophical Review*, LXI (1952), 451–74.

a notion of progress as "a power to conceive and execute the next step forward and to organize the force of the State for the movement."[45] This, incidentally, may be the simplest and best definition of progressivism that historians of the period will come across.

Wilson's academic writings constitute an important link in American political thought. He substantially revised Madisonian constitutionalism and paved the way for a theory of group politics predicated upon administrative arrangements. His political scholarship came at a point when the notion of the state was being revived in a form that could readily be absorbed into the presuppositions of the modern social sciences. Wilson was a crucial figure in the transition from a substantive idea of American democracy to the idea of democracy as a method for the free election of the leaders. Democracy should not be understood as the right to participate but as the right to vote. He turned American liberalism towards conservative notions of order and functional inequality, but at the same time he liberalized American conservatism by reorienting the idea of the state and the practice of government toward the advancement of national power. He purified the idea of power as he distanced it from the citizenry. Wilson left the conservatives an idea of power that was elevated above human frailty and political suspicion by its association with nationality and its intimations of ultimate destiny. Liberalism inherited an idea of power that was lowered beneath political suspicion and presented as a technical means, as an applied science, or as a principle of administrative efficiency. The most important Wilsonian legacy is therefore the creation of reasoning, metaphors, and concepts that support the practice of the systematic accumulation of power by dispelling the opposition to state power that remained as a vestige of liberal and majoritarian strands in American political culture.

A considerable part of Wilson's contribution to American political ideas is contained in a passage from 1901 in which Wilson claimed that a new collective identity would emerge, "not in the uncertain light of theory, but in the broad, sunlike, disillusioning light of experience." He defined political knowledge as "clear experimental knowledge of what are in fact the just rights of individuals, of what is the equal and profitable balance to be maintained between the right of the individual to serve himself and the duty of government to serve society."[46] This formulation implied that the sources of political knowledge extend well beyond individual experience. In the place of Madison's constitutive values: "To secure the public good, and private rights," Wilson substituted: To "secure

---

[45] Memorandum on leadership, *PWW*, xii, 365.
[46] "The Ideals of America," Dec. 26, 1901, *ibid*., pp. 223–24.

233

private rights and yet concerted public action, a strong government and yet liberty also."[47] In Wilson's formulation, government becomes the active center of political activity, both as the guardian of private rights and as the organizer of national progress.

WILSON'S ACADEMIC contribution to American political thought may be described as the replacement of the political notion of the people with the idea of nationality, the formulation of an idea of administration that was to reshape the perception of politics, and finally, his attempt to reformulate American democracy as a problem of the selection of leaders and the functioning of leadership. These transformations of American political thought may be characterized as the emergence of the idea of an American national state as a distinctive phase within the liberal tradition, that made up the general political background of American progressivism. In short, Wilson supplied progressivism with a modernized version of constitutional government. Constitutionalism was to be seen less as the protection of individual rights against government encroachment than as a set of procedures and behavioral norms that made society governable. Wilson formulated some of the important elements in an understanding of progress that tied the themes of power and purity together at the level of the national state. From this followed many of the goals and techniques of progressive reform policy as well as an acknowledgment of the restricted possibilities for popular participation in political deliberation and action.

[47] *The Federalist*, No. 10, p. 61; "Democracy and Efficiency," *PWW*, xii, 9.

XI

★ ★ ★ ★ ★ ★ ★ ★ ★ ★ ★ ★ ★ ★ ★ ★ ★ ★ ★ ★

ESSAY ON HISTORIOGRAPHY

AND METHOD

Historical investigations of Wilson's academic writings can be arranged according to a few general interpretations. The first was inspired by Charles A. Beard, although Beard acknowledged, but never commented in detail on, Wilson's scholarship. Apparently Beard had trouble placing Wilson unambiguously within the framework of the great political division in American history between the Hamiltonian and the Jeffersonian parties, a division that had been outlined earlier by Wilson as the English and French traditions of democracy. The typical Beardian solution to this problem was to insist upon the chastening effect of Wilson's departure from academia and his meeting with political reality. Wilson had to go through some kind of political conversion to progressivism before or soon after he entered politics. Wilson was "made progressive by experience," which was to say that his progressivism was not founded on ideology. Beard described professor Wilson as a Jeffersonian of the preindustrial South, inspired by Manchester liberalism and largely ignorant of the facts of American industrialism: "Trained in the classics and mathematics at Princeton, [Wilson] escaped the more dissolving influence of natural science and the socializing provocations of political economy. . . . Judged by his career and his writings, Wilson was everywhere regarded as a conservative Democrat of the old school. . . . Speaking concretely, his philosophy was a concept that pleased southern planters without alarming merchants who imported goods and capital".[1]

Charles A. Beard served as an advisor to William Diamond, who began his study of Wilson in the early 1940s. Beard pointed out to Diamond that although the main outlines of Wilson's economic world view were known, his ideas had not been studied systematically and in detail.[2] Although Diamond modified Beard's interpretation in some respects, he

[1] Charles A. Beard and Mary R. Beard, *The Rise of American Civilization*, rev. and enl. ed. (New York, 1930), pp. 605–606.

[2] Diamond, *Economic Thought of Woodrow Wilson*, pp. 7–8.

retained the framework. A central point of Diamond's was that Wilson's meeting with modern scholarship, especially his reading of political economy and German writings on the state, did not have a lasting effect on his thinking. Diamond's study, in turn, influenced the image of Wilson that Richard Hofstadter, Louis Hartz, and Eric F. Goldman created. Arthur S. Link's work on Wilson's road to the White House also used Diamond's interpretation. Later, Henry W. Bragdon added many details to this composition.[3]

A different line of interpretation was followed by historians and political scientists who saw psychohistory in one form or another as the key to Wilson's behavior during the distressing conflicts at Princeton and later over the ratification of the Treaty of Versailles. This body of literature is already quite extensive and is probably destined to grow with the advance of medical knowledge. The first works in this genre stressed Wilson's compulsive dependence on his father's views. The result was to emphasize an authoritarian cast of mind and Wilson's alleged intolerance of dissent. This understanding now has few protagonists. Martin J. Sklar was the first historian to suggest that Wilson's works were much more preoccupied with organic unities than with laissez-faire liberalism. This view was provided with strong psychological underpinnings, originally by John M. Mulder, who analyzed the parents' biographies exhaustively and came to the conclusion that Wilson's attachment to his mother was no less significant for his emotional development than his relationship with his father.[4] Wilson actually took his mother's name, Woodrow, at her special request, because it allowed him to use the names of both parents in his signature. A psychological reading of Wilson's political ideas on the basis of the present study seems to support the new view, with its added attention to Wilson's dependence on his mother. The Civil War was the war of the fathers for Wilson's generation. In contrast, typically maternal values, such as love, reconciliation, and concern for health and healing were associated with a nation with unified leadership. The shift from stern (paternal) justice to maternal care and security may also be implicit in

---

[3] Hofstadter, *American Political Tradition*, p. 375; Hartz, *Liberal Tradition in America*, pp. 295–96. Goldman supervised parts of Diamond's study; see also Goldman, *Rendezvous with Destiny*, pp. 165–66; Link, *Wilson: The Road to the White House*, pp. 24, 26; Bragdon, *Woodrow Wilson*.

[4] Freud and Bullitt, *Thomas Woodrow Wilson*; George and George, *Woodrow Wilson and Colonel House*; Martin J. Sklar, "Woodrow Wilson and the Political Economy of Modern United States Liberalism," in James Weinstein and David W. Eakins (eds.), *For A New America: Essays in History and Politics from* Studies on the Left, *1959–1967* (New York, 1970), pp. 46–100; Weinstein, *et al.*, "Woodrow Wilson's Political Personality"; Mulder, *Woodrow Wilson*, pp. 30–31, 37, 46; Weinstein, *Woodrow Wilson*, 10–13, 21–23, 44–45, 190. Cooper, *The Warrior and the Priest*, p. 18; Ross, "Woodrow Wilson and the Case for Psychohistory," pp. 667–68.

Wilson's carrying the Hegelian *Staat* over into his own notion of society, oriented toward the general welfare. Finally, Wilson's constitutional writings may be described as an attempt to read the doctrines of the Founding Fathers into the tissue of political experience of the mother country, England. Such a reading would probably choose Melanie Klein's elaboration of the relationship between the ego and the mother as a complement to Freud's theory of the interconnection between the superego and the father.[5]

The publication of *The Papers of Woodrow Wilson* has revealed new source material relating to Wilson's early years. It has become abundantly clear that Wilson early admired the Federalists, and Alexander Hamilton in particular, and only made his peace with Jefferson belatedly and reluctantly. John M. Mulder's biography of Wilson's intellectual development upon which the present study has relied extensively, was the first study to make full use of these papers.[6]

Mulder's book was conceived basically as a religious biography, but it also made the claim that Wilson's political writings could be understood in large measure as reflections of his religious beliefs, in particular as expressions of the so-called covenant theology that Wilson had absorbed in his home and in the Presbyterian church. This interpretation depends on the establishment of two links between Wilson's political ideas and his religious upbringing. Mulder presents the first connection as the claim that the notion of the covenant played a large psychological role in Wilson's thought. He presents as evidence the famous letter Wilson wrote to his fiancée about a "solemn covenant" with his classmate. As I have argued earlier (p. 45), the importance of this letter can easily be overestimated, because Wilson in fact was explaining, not why he felt committed to "the covenant," but why he had broken it. The term is used without any religious connotation and refers to a simple agreement between friends.

Mulder's second assumption is that deep in his mind Wilson connected modern constitutions (those for debating societies as well as the United States Constitution) with Abraham's covenant as it was expressed in the theology of the Puritan revolution. In this reading, both laid down a social order in fundamental law, fixed in time and presented as a mutual commitment between the Lord and man. The argument cannot come to grips with the liberal idea of a constitution as a contract.[7] Furthermore,

---

[5] WW to Robert Bridges, Nov. 7, 1879, *PWW*, I, 583; Melanie Klein, *Love, Guilt and Reparation, and Other Works, 1921–1945* (New York, 1975).

[6] *Woodrow Wilson*, p. 280.

[7] *Ibid.*, pp. 56, 124–26, 269–77; H. Richard Niebuhr, "The Idea of Covenant and American Democracy," *Church History*, XXIII (June 1954), 126–35, where Niebuhr actually warns

the argument fails to note that, constitutionally speaking, Wilson was much closer to the Pauline conception than the orthodox Jewish position. If Wilson had ever discussed the idea, he would certainly have subscribed to Paul's rejection of the written covenant: "For the letter killeth, but the spirit gives life" (II Corinthians III:1–6). But in fact no such discussion is to be found. The term *covenant* appears in Wilson's writings very few times before 1910. It appears that Mulder has backdated the term, which came to play a more prominent role during the contest over the League of Nations. In any case, an overemphasis on the religious traces in Wilson's idea of constitutionalism is likely to result in a wholesale dismissal of his contribution to modern American political science.

Another problem for a religious interpretation of Wilson's work is to represent his understanding of religion as an important feature of American life. In Wilson's view, religion was the primary language of moral significance in America, and it was the language that had taught America about the nature of power and the necessity of leadership. That Wilson considered himself a devout Presbyterian is probably less important for a consideration of his political writings than that he deemed Americans to be a highly religious people. The failure to make this distinction clear results in a picture of Wilson as a premodern religious man, much as Hofstadter pictured him as a politician of premodern morality. Such an approach is apt to lead away from his political writings not into them. An interpretation of this sort may be suitable if one is interested in uncovering Wilson's religious development. The argument here is only that much of the substance of Wilson's political thought cannot be examined by such a method.

THE DISCIPLINE of political science has not yet produced a full study of Wilson's intellectual development, despite increasing attention to his ideas in recent years. In a poll taken in the early 1960s, Albert Somit and Joseph Tanenhaus reported that teachers of political science named Wilson as number seven—almost on a par with Arthur Bentley—among the so-called immortals of professional political scientists before 1945. This high standing apparently surprised the pollsters, who explained the result with reference to Wilson's article on public administration.[8] In the last decade, however, a reconsideration of Wilson's political science slowly got under way, taking its cue from the revival of constitutional and presidential studies that appeared from the middle of the 1970s. In particu-

---

against equating *covenant* and *constitution*. The latter was born with John Locke's idea of a *contract*.

[8] Albert Somit and Joseph Tanenhaus, *American Political Science: A Profile of a Discipline* (New York, 1964), p. 66.

lar, Wilson's writings have been linked to the modern "post-imperial presidency," or the personal or rhetorical presidency. The most comprehensive arguments have been put forward by Jeffrey Tulis and by James W. Ceaser and his coauthors.[9]

The central theme of the idea of the rhetorical presidency is that Wilson's writings and his actions as president should be seen as a sharp break in American constitutional development. Whereas previous presidents had perceived their constitutional role as public officers, carrying out an administrative task that was supposed to conform to conventional constitutional principles, Wilson formulated a doctrine according to which the presidency became the place where unspoken popular desires were articulated. Rhetoric came to replace deliberative skills as the first condition for presidential greatness. According to Jeffrey Tulis, the Founders had rested the authority of the president upon the independent constitutional position of his office. For Wilson, in contrast, "power and authority are conferred directly from the people. *The Federalist* and the Constitution proscribe popular leadership. Woodrow Wilson prescribes it." Thus Wilson formulated the doctrine and later shaped the practices that issued in the present dilemma, in which presidents are tempted to promise more than they can deliver, because the leadership of popular opinion often inhibits control of the legislative and administrative processes. The result is a "constitutional hybrid" that feeds cynicism and paralyzes political action.[10]

This interpretation restores Wilson to a prominent place among American constitutional theorists, and the present study is dependent on its insistence that Wilson's own work proposed a conceptual revaluation of presidential politics. It is also an interpretation that is marked by the disenchantment with the presidency that followed from the experiences of the "imperial presidency." It attests to the strong influence of Max Weber upon contemporary American political science. The division between the constitutional presidency and the popular presidency seems to have been

---

[9] Jeffrey Tulis, "The Two Constitutional Presidencies," in Michael Nelson (ed.), *The Presidency and the Political System* (Washington, D. C., 1984), pp. 59–86; James W. Ceaser *et al.*, "The Rise of the Rhetorical Presidency," *Presidential Studies Quarterly*, xi (Spring 1981), 157–71; and James W. Ceaser, *Presidential Selection: Theory and Development* (Princeton, N. J., 1979), pp. 170–212. See also Harry Clor, "Woodrow Wilson," in Morton J. Frisch and Richard G. Stevens (eds.), *American Political Thought* (New York, 1971), pp. 191–218; Paul Eidelberg, *A Discourse on Statesmanship* (Urbana, Ill., 1974), pp. 279–362; Robert Eden, *Political Leadership and Nihilism: A Study of Weber and Nietzsche* (Tampa, 1983), pp. 1–35; and Theodore J. Lowi, *The Personal President: Power Invested, Promise Unfulfilled* (Ithaca, N. Y., 1985), pp. 22–43.

[10] Tulis, "The Two Constitutional Presidencies," in Nelson (ed.), *The Presidency and the Political System*, pp. 81–83.

largely derived from Weber's division between legitimacy based on rational and legal grounds and legitimacy based on charismatic grounds, that is, "resting on devotion to the . . . exemplary character of an individual person." The concept of the rhetorical presidency is itself in close correspondence with Weber's "plebiscitary democracy."[11] The paradox is that a theory of plebiscitary leadership informed by Max Weber leads contemporary commentators to criticize Wilson for a doctrine that based the presidency "on words, not power."[12]

Thus it has been easy to overlook that Wilson was as concerned to dispel what he considered the illusion of popular sovereignty as he was to overcome constitutional fragmentation. The problem for constitutional theory seems to be to recognize the full scope of Wilson's attempt to read society and the civic character of the modern voter into the new system of governance, or, as Wilson put it, "the modern democratic state." Between Wilson's first and his last book there occurred more than twenty years of reading and lecturing on such concepts as "the state" and "the nation" that are only partially captured by a reconsideration of his writings in terms of constitutional theory, with its tendency to view government as a system of institutions external to the self and society. My own interpretation has attempted to stress Wilson's politicization of society, which occurred in tandem with his tendency to depoliticize the president by stressing the genius of popular leadership that the modern voter was prepared for and waiting for. Finally, it appears from the present study that Wilson himself saw his ideas as a renewal of the Federalist political mentality, not as a fundamental break with Madison's and Hamilton's ideas.

THE PROBLEM of reading Wilson's political writings is in large measure a problem of context. It is tempting, indeed, to interpret Wilson's works in the light of his later rise to political office. Wilson himself was quite aware of this danger of reading history backward, that is, of having one's "eye on the future always rather than directly on the present." In a review of a biography of Abraham Lincoln, he complained about "the foolish habit of most biographers, of beckoning their great men impatiently on to their greatness, wondering the while and fretting at their laggardliness and blindness to the destiny in store."[13]

What is the appropriate context for a consideration of the economic and political writings that Woodrow Wilson produced in the course of his

[11] Max Weber, *Economy and Society*, ed. by Guenther Roth and Claus Wittich (2 vols., Berkeley, 1978), I, 215, 266–71.

[12] Ceaser *et al.*, "Rise of the Rhetorical Presidency," p. 168.

[13] "Anti–Slavery History and Biography," Aug. 1893, *PWW*, VIII, 296.

academic career? The answer depends, of course, on the general purpose of the investigation. The most common procedure has been to consider these writings with a view to Wilson's public actions as president of the United States. Themes and quotations from the early works seem obvious points of reference with which to explicate Wilson's decisions on issues relating to national and international policy. Some of Wilson's writings were even made a political issue in the campaign of 1912.[14] There may be nothing wrong with this procedure as long as it is understood that it necessarily imposes certain limitations on the understanding of arguments that were produced with other purposes in mind. The historian's art is in great measure to discover factual resources and remove them from one established social and intellectual context in order to construct the imagination of another context. In this process, the coherence and integrity of alternative possibilities are necessarily weakened.

There are, however, certain structural reasons that favor an attempt to consider Wilson's academic writings separately from his opinions as a candidate for political office and as president. The contest for political office, as well as the occupation of the office, tend to produce a certain kind of political opinion. Although the formulation of general political principles may occasionally seem to play a role, such attempts are understood, not as a search for truth, but as a means of persuasion. The American electoral system has frequently been noted for its tendency to bring candidates into a political situation where only a limited number of issues are up for debate and where disagreement is kept within certain boundaries. The campaign process serves to focus public attention on a range of initiatives that are within the conventional reach of governmental influence and that can be demonstrated to be able to be attained within a definite period of time. When issues of a more philosophical nature are drawn into the contest, they are mostly presented as matters of style or personal principle, both of which are intended to create a favorable impression of the candidate's character. While the purpose of a campaign is to get the candidate elected, the purpose of the election is to resolve political disagreements and conflicts by rules that are respected by most or all of the electorate, as well as by the competing candidates. The election process is intended to make conflict manageable by serving as a symbol of consensus. Similarly, the function of decision making is to reach

[14] Diamond, *Economic Thought of Woodrow Wilson*, p. 192; Sklar, "Woodrow Wilson and Political Economy," in Weinstein and Eakins (eds.), *For A New America*, pp. 46–54; Seltzer, "Woodrow Wilson as 'Corporate-Liberal,'" pp. 187–88, 190–91; Osborn, *Woodrow Wilson*, viii, 120. One issue that developed during the campaign with reference to Wilson's characterization of recent groups of immigrants is related in Link, *Wilson: The Road to the White House*, pp. 24, 26.

agreement on specific issues, to harmonize conflicting opinions, to build a basis for lasting compromise, and, possibly, to exclude and isolate unmanageable dissent.[15] All of these functions shape political opinions and set them off from political theory.

The point of these remarks is that the accepted structure of American politics—the system of parties, elections, and government—puts certain limits on what is considered both to be worthy of sustained attention and to lie within the boundaries of conventional political propriety. To consider theoretical formulations on the basis of opinions that are generated as part of the political process itself is, therefore, to incur the risk of overemphasizing certain issues or of excluding others. Thus the importance of the tariff question at the beginning of the first Wilson administration has been projected onto the early writings and has caused a disproportionate view of Wilson as an ardent advocate of Manchester liberalism from the professorial chair.[16] An example of the process of exclusion is Wilson's notion of the state, which played virtually no role during Wilson's years as a politician. Indeed, the term itself was banished from respectable political discussion because it became tainted with German officialdom and militarism after the outbreak of World War I. The result has been that Wilson's idea of the state as reflected in his academic writings has hardly been considered a subject worthy of inquiry.[17]

Behind the reluctance to treat Wilson's theoretical views extensively, one may detect the general assumption that the essence of political knowledge within the framework of American politics is expressed under competitive conditions, typically in the contests for office or in the processes of bargaining and decision making. According to its nature, such knowledge is best appraised on the basis of its consequences. Thus progressive historiography usually centers attention on reform proposals and the efficacy of reform. But political theory, by convention, exemplifies a category of knowledge that is traditionally defined with reference to concepts of truth that are derived from religious, philosophical, historical, or scientific thought. The outcome is typically appraised, not in

[15] The structural prerequisites of the two-party, representative political system are discussed, for example, in Frank Sorauf, *Political Parties in the American System* (Boston, 1964), and in Michael A. Sego, *Ship of State: Foundations and Fragmentation of American Democracy* (Brunswick, Ohio, 1982), pp. 89–193.

[16] Diamond, *Economic Thought of Woodrow Wilson*, pp. 25–26, 51–54, 66–67, 97–98; Sklar, "Woodrow Wilson and Political Economy," in Weinstein and Eakins (eds.), *For A New America*, pp. 48–49, 81–85.

[17] Diamond has only one brief reference in *The Economic Thought of Woodrow Wilson*, on p. 57; the state is not discussed by Sklar in "Woodrow Wilson and Political Economy," in Weinstein and Eakins (eds.), *For A New America*, or by Seltzer in "Woodrow Wilson as 'Corporate-Liberal.'"

terms of consequences, but in terms of presuppositions, premises, and procedure. Claims to truth are not regarded as directly affected by the practical application of such knowledge to detailed problems. Instead, the importance of a theory often rests with the success of its attempt to deal with and shed light on a broad range of political phenomena rather than to solve isolated problems.[18] The proposition that Wilson's academic writings reflect an interest in political theory that should be distinguished from his speeches and actions as a politician is the major methodological assumption behind the present study.

What is the alternative context for a discussion of Wilson's early political and economic writings, if it is accepted that these writings cannot be adequately investigated in the context of his political career? The most satisfying answer is one that can be argued with reference to the writings themselves. At first glance, there appear to be different answers corresponding to the different academic fields in which Wilson chose to work. But on further reflection, there may also be a more general answer, one that depends on the degree to which it can be shown that there was an internal consistency behind Wilson's varied academic pursuits. As presented in this study, the underlying motive behind Wilson's early writings may be described as a keen intellectual interest in a sort of power that may be called political power, because Wilson understood it to be the energy that expressed coherence, order, and purpose throughout American society.

The guiding principle in Wilson's different academic and literary undertakings was his intellectual preoccupation with different human manifestations of power that tied Americans to each other and that generated further power in the process of unification. Thus Wilson's early choice of the profession of law was not primarily motivated by a wish to become a lawyer but by his belief that the study and practice of law provided the obvious way to move closer to the political order expressed by American legal institutions. Wilson's study of political economy indicates his appreciation of the importance of economic relationships for an understanding of the modern processes of the generation of material wealth and their consequences for political power. His studies of the state and of modern administration reflected his interest in the institutionalization and rationalization of power. He did not conceive of his historical writings as contributing to the discipline of history but as serving the broader purpose of establishing a framework for the growth of national sentiment. These considerations may also explain why Wilson's academic writings should be considered a contribution to American political thought rather than

---

[18] Wolin, "Political Theory," 325.

to American political science. I have used the different studies of American political science that seek to place Wilson's contribution within the particular fields of constitutional theory or public administration throughout chapters 3 through 9, and they have been very helpful on numerous points. But they cannot supply the general framework for an investigation of Wilson's varied academic writings without a distortion of the scope and intentions behind his work.

Wilson's academic studies represent a continuous attempt to set forth an inclusive understanding of political power. His intention was to formulate a vision or theory of power that would make it possible to explain power, to legitimize its existence, its divisions, and its distribution, as well as to account for its historical evolution and consider its future development. The main objection to this claim about Wilson's project is that he did not succeed in formulating a comprehensive theory of power in the way that the major political theorists of Western culture may be said to have constructed a theoretical whole. Apart from scattered notes and a brief exploratory draft, Wilson did not begin, let alone finish, what he considered to be his major study of the philosophy of politics. His academic career was cut short first by his decision to accept the presidency of Princeton University and later by his decision to run for governor of New Jersey. But if there is no final theoretical product, there is at least a set of theoretical beginnings—characteristic preoccupations, metaphors, and perceptive ideas—that together make conclusions about Wilson's theoretical intent plausible and worthwhile.

The chronological limit of the present study may appear somewhat arbitrary. The purpose is not to suggest that Wilson stopped thinking about politics when he became governor of New Jersey but that the terms of his theory changed. Wilson's political views had to be reformulated according to some of the conventions of the American system of politics, which he had been free to ignore as long as his political ambitions were expressed in the idiom of a man of letters. For Wilson, the choice between the study and the practice of politics presented itself, not as an alternative, but as a matter of postponement. His failure to recover his health after he left the presidency made it impossible to resume scholarly work.

The attempt to set Wilson's academic writings apart for special inquiry and the assumption that these writings constitute a whole, rather than a series of explorations in different disciplines that have no intrinsic connection with each other, may be argued to be simply a choice of method. One's choice of method, however, is likely to have substantive implications. In the present case, these implications apply, not only to Wilson's early career, but also to the later part of his life, which is not covered here. It seems clear that Wilson's writings would have provided him with a distinctive place in the history of American political thought if he had not held a political office that was bound to overshadow his academic work. But such an argument would miss the point. The methodological focus upon Wilson's theoretical interests does not imply a suppression of the fact that Wilson eventually became the president of the United States. It only requires that attention be paid to the coherence of his theoretical concerns and to his role as a teacher of political institutions. Indeed, one of the benefits of a focus on Wilson's study of politics is the different viewpoint it offers from which to assess his presidential activities. Although most commentators would probably agree that the presidency is necessarily involved in the political education of the public, it seems clear that this responsibility has been considerably reduced in modern treatments of presidential politics. It is most often treated as a function of policy making, and it is disguised as "public relations" which is approached as the art of image making and as the use of the media to present policy options and decisions.

Yet most students of politics would agree that American politics and the predictability of the public response to decision-making depend importantly upon a continuous political language, which teaches the public how to react and what to expect in the realm of politics. In recent years there has been a growing attention to Wilson's role in shaping the political language that prepared Americans for industrial conditions and for permanent foreign engagement. It may be that a consideration of Wilson's own study of politics provides a vantage point from which to obtain a glimpse of the lasting features of his education of the public, that is, his impact upon political language and culture. Thus, in the final analysis, the importance of an investigation of Wilson's political and economic thought lies in the light it sheds on his historical role as one of the American public's primary instructors in a comprehensive language of powers and instrumentalities that became synonymous with the American state of the twentieth century.

BIBLIOGRAPHY

★ ★

Manuscripts in the Firestone Library, Princeton University

Archives of the American Whig Society
Princetoniana Collection
Woodrow Wilson Collection

Works by Woodrow Wilson

Division and Reunion, 1829–1889. Epochs of American History series, edited by Albert Bushell Hart. New York: Longmans, Green, 1893.

George Washington. New York: Harper and Bros., 1897.

A History of the American People. 5 vols. New York: Harper and Bros., 1902.

The Papers of Woodrow Wilson. Edited by Arthur S. Link *et al.*, 55 vols. to date. Princeton, N. J.: Princeton University Press, 1966–.

The State: Elements of Historical and Practical Politics, A Sketch of Institutional History and Administration. Boston: D. C. Heath, 1889.

Contemporary Books

Adams, Herbert Baxter. *Methods of Historical Study.* Johns Hopkins University Studies in Historical and Political Science, 2nd series, i–ii. Baltimore: Johns Hopkins University, 1884.

Addresses Delivered at the Funeral of L. H. Atwater. New York: Randolph, 1883.

Atwater, Lyman Hotchkiss. *Ethics and Political Economy from Notes Taken in the Lecture Room.* Trenton, N. J.: Princeton College, 1878.

Bagehot, Walter. *The Collected Works of Walter Bagehot.* Edited by Norman St. John–Stevas. 9 vols. to date. Cambridge, Mass.: Harvard University Press, 1968–.

———. *The English Constitution.* Garden City, N. Y.: Doubleday, n. d.

———. *Physics and Politics.* 1867. Reprint. New York: Alfred A. Knopf, 1948.

Bluntschli, Johann K. *The Theory of the State.* Authorized English translation. Oxford: Clarendon, 1885.

Bryce, James. *The American Commonwealth.* 3 vols. London: Macmillan, 1888.

Burke, Edmund. *Reflections on the Revolution in France.* 1790. Reprint. New York: Dolphin Books, 1961.

Calvin, John. *Calvin: Institutues of the Christian Religion.* Edited by John T. McNeill and Ford Lewis Battles. 2 vols. Philadelphia: Westminster Press, 1960.

Carlyle, Thomas. *On Heroes, Hero-Worship and the Heroic in History.* London: Chapman and Hall, 1872.

Catalogue of the College of New Jersey for the Academic Year 1878–79. Princeton, N. J.: Princeton Press, 1878.

Clark, John B. *The Philosophy of Wealth: Economic Principles Newly Formulated.* Boston: Ginn and Co., 1885.

Croly, Herbert. *The Promise of American Life.* New York: Macmillan, 1909. Reprint. New York: Arcon Books, 1963.

Ely, Richard T. *French and German Socialism in Modern Times.* New York: Harper and Bros., 1883.

———. *Ground under Our Feet: An Autobiography.* New York: Macmillan, 1938.

———. *An Introduction to Political Economy.* New York: Chautauqua Press, 1889.

———. *The Labor Movement in America.* New York: Thomas Y. Crowell, 1886.

———. *The Past and Present of Political Economy.* Johns Hopkins University Studies in Historical and Political Science. 2nd Series, iii. Baltimore: Johns Hopkins University, 1884.

———. *Recent American Socialism.* Johns Hopkins University Studies in Historical and Political Science. 3rd Series, iv. Baltimore: Johns Hopkins University, 1885.

Fawcett, Henry. *Free Trade and Protection: An Inquiry into the Causes Which Have Retarded the General Adoption of Free Trade since Its Introduction into England.* London: Macmillan, 1878.

The Federalist. Edited by Jacob E. Cooke. Middletown, Conn.: Wesleyan University Press, 1961.

Ford, Henry Jones. *The Rise and Growth of American Politics: A Sketch of Constitutional Development.* New York: Macmillan, 1898.

Gilman, Daniel Coit. *The Launching of a University and Other Papers: A Sheaf of Remembrances.* New York: Dodd, Mead, and Co., 1906.

Goldsmith, Oliver. *The Works of Oliver Goldsmith.* Edited by J.W.M. Gibbs. 5 vols. London: George Bell and Sons, 1884.

Hamerton, Philip G. *Round My House: Notes of Rural Life in France in Peace and War.* Boston: Roberts Bros., 1877.

Lowell, Abbott Lawrence. *Essays on Government.* 1892. Reprint. New York: Johnson Reprint Corporation, 1968.

Macaulay, Thomas Babington. *The Miscellaneous Writings of Lord Macaulay.* 2 vols. London: Longmans, Green, 1860.

Maine, Henry Sumner. *Ancient Law: Its Connections with the Early History of Society, and Its Relation to Modern Ideas.* 4th ed. London: John Murray, 1870.

————. *Popular Government.* New York: H. Holt, 1886.

Merriam, Charles Edward. *History of the Theory of Sovereignty since Rousseau.* New York: Columbia University, 1900.

Morley, John. *Edmund Burke: A Historical Study.* 1879. Reprint. New York: Knopf, 1924.

Morris, George Sylvester. *Hegel's Philosophy of the State and of History: An Exposition.* Chicago: S. C. Griggs, 1886.

Mulford, Elisha. *The Nation.* New York: Hurd and Houghton, 1875.

Smith, Adam. *An Inquiry into the Nature and Causes of the Wealth of Nations.* Edited by Edwin Cannan. 2 vols. Chicago: University of Chicago Press, 1976.

Stickney, Albert. *A True Republic.* New York: Harper and Bros., 1879.

Sumner, William Graham. *Alexander Hamilton.* New York: Dodd, Mead, 1890.

————. *Andrew Jackson as a Public Man.* Boston: Houghton, Mifflin, 1883.

————. *A History of American Currency.* New York: H. Holt, 1875.

Thorpe, Francis Newton. *The Constitutional History of the United States, 1765–1895.* 3 vols. 1901. Reprint. New York: Da Capo Press, 1970.

Tocqueville, Alexis de. *Democracy in America.* Translated by George Lawrence. Garden City, N. Y.: Doubleday, Anchor, 1969.

Turner, Frederick Jackson. *The Frontier in American History.* New York: Henry Holt, 1920.

Walker, Francis Amasa. *Political Economy.* New York: H. Holt, 1889.

Wayland, Francis. *The Elements of Political Economy.* Edited by Aaron L. Chapin. New York: Sheldon, 1879.

Woolsey, Theodore D. *Political Science; or, The State Theoretically and Practically Considered.* 2 vols. New York: C. Scribner's Sons, 1878.

Contemporary Articles

Atwater, Lyman Hotchkiss. "The Currency Question." *Presbyterian Quarterly and Princeton Review,* New Series, iv (October 1875), 721–42.

————. "The Great Railroad Strike." *Presbyterian Quarterly and Princeton Review,* New Series, vi (October 1877), 719–44.

Atwater, Lyman Hotchkiss. "Our Industrial and Financial Situation." *Presbyterian Quarterly and Princeton Review*, New Series, IV (July 1875), 518–28.

Bagehot, Walter. "Adam Smith as a Person." *Fortnightly Review*, New Series, XX (1876), 18–42.

Burgess, John W. "The American Commonwealth: Changes in Its Relation to the Nation." *Political Science Quarterly*, I (March 1886), 9–35.

Dunning, William A. "The Constitution of the United States in Reconstruction." *Political Science Quarterly*, II (December 1887), 558–602.

Ely, Richard T. "Political Economy in America." *North American Review*, CXLIV (February 1887), 113–19.

——. "Report of the Organization of the American Economic Association." *American Economic Association Publications*, I (1886), 5–46.

Jameson, John Alexander. "National Sovereignty." *Political Science Quarterly*, V (June 1890), 193–213.

Laughlin, J. Laurence. "The Study of Political Economy in the United States." *Journal of Political Economy*, I (December 1892), 1–14.

Leslie, Thomas Edward Cliff. "Political Economy in the United States." *Fortnightly Review*, New Series, XXVIII (1880), 488–509.

North American Review, CXXVI (1878), 171–74.

The Princetonian, April–May, 1879.

Sumner, William Graham. "Politics in America, 1776–1876." *North American Review*, CXXII (January 1876), 47–87.

SECONDARY BOOKS AND DISSERTATIONS

Alsop, Em Bowles, ed. *The Greatness of Woodrow Wilson, 1856–1956*. Port Washington, N. Y.: Kennikat Press, 1956.

Avineri, Shlomo. *Hegel's Theory of the Modern State*. Cambridge: Cambridge University Press, 1972.

Bachrach, Peter. *The Theory of Democratic Elitism: A Critique*. Boston: Little, Brown, 1967.

Baker, Ray Stannard. *Woodrow Wilson: Life and Letters*. 8 vols. Garden City, N. Y.: Doubleday, Page and Co., 1927–39.

Baritz, Loren. *Backfire*. New York: William Morrow, 1985.

Barker, Ernest. *Political Thought in England, 1848–1914*. London: Oxford University Press, 1915.

Beam, Jacob N. *The American Whig Society*. Princeton, N. J.: 1933.

Beard, Charles A. *An Economic Interpretation of the Constitution of the United States*. 1913. Reprint. New York: Free Press, n. d.

——. *Public Policy and the General Welfare*. New York: Farrow and Rinehart, 1941.

Beard, Charles A., and Mary R. Beard. *The Rise of American Civilization.* Rev. and enl. edn. New York: Macmillan, 1930.

Benson, Lee. *Turner and Beard: American Historical Writing Reconsidered.* Glencoe, Ill.: Free Press, 1960.

Bentley, Arthur F. *The Process of Government: A Study of Social Pressures.* Chicago: University of Chicago Press, 1908.

Billington, Ray Allen. *Frederick Jackson Turner: Historian, Scholar, Teacher.* New York: Oxford University Press, 1973.

Black, R. D. Collison, *et al.*, eds. *The Marginal Revolution in Economics: Interpretation and Evaluation.* Durham, N. C.: Duke University Press, 1973.

Bledstein, Burton. *The Culture of Professionalism: The Middle Class and the Development of Higher Education in America.* New York: Norton, 1976.

Blum, John Morton. *Woodrow Wilson and the Politics of Morality.* Boston: Little, Brown, 1956.

Boller, Paul F., Jr. *American Thought in Transition: The Impact of Evolutionary Naturalism, 1865–1900.* Chicago: Rand McNally College Publishing, 1969.

Boorstin, Daniel J., ed. *An American Primer.* New York: Mentor Books, 1967.

Bragdon, Henry Wilkinson. *Woodrow Wilson: The Academic Years.* Cambridge, Mass.: Belknap Press of Harvard University Press, 1967.

Brown, Bernard Edward. *American Conservatives: The Political Thought of Francis Lieber and John W. Burgess.* New York: Columbia University Press, 1951.

Bryson, Gladys. *Man and Society: The Scottish Inquiry of the Eighteenth Century.* Princeton, N. J.: Princeton University Press, 1945.

Buechner, John C. *Public Administration.* Belmont, Mass.: Dickenson Publishing Co., 1968.

Buenker, John D. *Urban Liberalism and Progressive Reform.* New York: Charles Scribner's Sons, 1973.

Ceaser, James W. *Presidential Selection: Theory and Development.* Princeton, N. J.: Princeton University Press, 1979.

Chandler, Alfred D. *The Visible Hand: The Managerial Revolution in American Business.* Cambridge, Mass.: Belknap Press of Harvard University Press, 1977.

Coben, Stanley, and Lorman Ratner, eds. *The Development of an American Culture.* Englewood Cliffs, N. J.: Prentice-Hall, 1970.

Coker, Francis W. *Organismic Theories of the State: Nineteenth Century Interpretations of the State as Organism or as Person.* Studies in History, Economics and Public Law, xxxviii, No. 2. New York: Columbia University, 1910.

Collini, Stefan, Donald Winch, and John Burrow. *That Noble Science of Politics: A Study in Nineteenth-Century Intellectual History*. London: Cambridge University Press, 1983.

Conkin, Paul K. *Prophets of Prosperity: America's First Political Economists*. Bloomington: Indiana University Press, 1980.

Cooper, John Milton, Jr. *The Warrior and the Priest: Woodrow Wilson and Theodore Roosevelt*. Cambridge, Mass.: Belknap Press of Harvard University Press, 1983.

Corwin, Edward S. *Corwin on the Constitution*. Edited by Richard Loss. Ithaca, N. Y.: Cornell University Press, 1981.

Crick, Bernard. *The American Science of Politics: Its Origins and Conditions*. Berkeley: University of California Press, 1959.

Crunden, Robert M. *Ministers of Reform: The Progressives' Achievement in American Civilization, 1889–1920*. New York: Basic Books, 1982.

Dahl, Robert A. *A Preface to Democratic Theory*. Chicago: University of Chiacgo Press, 1982.

Daniels, Josephus. *The Life of Woodrow Wilson*. Philadelphia: John C. Winston, 1924.

D'Entreves, Alexander Passerin. *The Notion of the State*. London: Oxford University Press, 1967.

De Witt, Benjamin Park. *The Progessive Movement: A Non-Partisan, Comprehensive Discussion of Current Tendencies in American Politics*. 1915. Reprint. Seattle: University of Washington Press, 1968.

Diamond, William. *The Economic Thought of Woodrow Wilson*. Johns Hopkins University Studies in Historical and Political Science, Series LXI, No. 4. Baltimore: Johns Hopkins Press, 1943.

Dictionary of American Biography. 24 vols. New York: Charles Scribner's Sons, 1928–79.

Dorfman, Joseph. *The Economic Mind in American Civilization*. 3 vols. New York: Viking Press, 1946–59.

Dunning, William A. *Essays on the Civil War and Reconstruction*. 1897. Reprint. New York: Peter Smith, 1931.

———. *A History of Political Theories: From Rousseau to Spencer*. New York: Macmillan, 1920.

Easton, David. *The Political System: An Inquiry into the State of Political Science*. New York: Alfred A. Knopf, 1963.

Eden, Robert. *Political Leadership and Nihilism: A Study of Weber and Nietzsche*. Tampa: University of South Florida Press, 1983.

Eidelberg, Paul. *A Discourse on Statesmanship*. Urbana: University of Illinois Press, 1974.

Ekirch, Arthur Alphonse. *The Idea of Progress in America, 1815–1860*. New York: Columbia University Press, 1944.

Emerson, Rupert. *State and Sovereignty in Modern Germany.* New Haven: Yale University Press, 1928.

Faulkner, Harold U. *The Quest for Social Justice, 1898–1914: A History of American Life.* 1931. Reprint. Chiacgo: Quadrangle, 1956.

Fine, Sidney. *Laissez Faire and the General-Welfare State: A Study of Conflict in American Thought, 1865–1901.* Ann Arbor: University of Michigan Press, 1964.

Fischer, David Hackett. *Historian's Fallacies: Toward a Logic of Historical Thought.* London: Routledge and Kegan Paul, 1971.

Forgie, George B. *Patricide in the House Divided: A Psychological Interpretation of Lincoln and His Age.* New York: Norton, 1979.

Frederickson, George M. *The Inner Civil War: Northern Intellectuals and the Crisis of the Union.* New York: Harper and Row, 1965.

Freud, Sigmund, and William C. Bullitt. *Thomas Woodrow Wilson: A Psychological Study.* London: Weidenfeld and Nicholson, 1966.

Friedman, Lawrence M. *A History of American Law.* New York: Simon and Schuster, 1973.

Frisch, Morton J., and Richard G. Stevens, eds. *American Political Thought.* New York: Charles Scribner's Sons, 1971.

Furner, Mary O. *Advocacy and Objectivity: A Crisis in the Professionalization of American Social Science, 1865–1905.* Lexington: University Press of Kentucky, 1965.

Gabriel, Ralph Henry. *The Course of American Democratic Thought: An Intellectual History since 1815.* New York: Ronald Press, 1940.

Gardner, Lloyd. *Safe for Democracy: The Anglo-American Response to Revolution, 1913–1923.* New York: Oxford University Press, 1984.

Gay, Peter. *Style in History.* New York: McGraw-Hill, 1974.

George, Alexander L., and Juliette L. George. *Woodrow Wilson and Colonel House: A Personality Study.* New York: John Day, 1956.

Gerth, Hans, and C. Wright Mills. *Character and Social Structure: The Psychology of Social Institutions.* New York: Harcourt, Brace and World, 1953.

Godwin, Harold. *A History of the Class of '79.* Trenton, N. J.: Princeton College, n. d.

Goldman, Eric F. *Rendezvous with Destiny: A History of Modern American Reform.* Rev. edn. New York: Random House, Vintage, 1956.

————, ed. *Historiography and Urbanization: Essays in American History in Honor of W. Stull Holt.* Baltimore: Johns Hopkins University Press, 1941.

Goldwin, Robert A., ed. *Left, Right and Center: Essays on Liberalism and Conservatism in the United States.* Chicago: Rand McNally, 1965.

Gruber, Carol S. *Mars and Minerva: World War I and the Uses of Higher*

Learning in America. Baton Rouge: Louisiana State University Press, 1975.

Haddow, Anna. *Political Science in American Colleges, 1636–1900*. 1939. Reprint. New York: Octagon Books, 1969.

Hamburger, Joseph. *Macauley and the Whig Tradition*. Chicago: University of Chicago Press, 1976.

Hartz, Louis. *The Liberal Tradition in America: An Interpretation of American Political Thought since the Revolution*. New York: Harcourt Brace Jovanovich, 1965.

Haskell, Thomas L. *The Emergence of Professional Social Science: The American Social Science Association and the Nineteenth-Century Crisis of Authority*. Urbana: University of Illinois Press, 1977.

Hawkins, Hugh. *Pioneer: A History of the Johns Hopkins University, 1874–1889*. Ithaca, N. Y.: Cornell University Press, 1960.

Hays, Samuel P. *The Response to Industrialism, 1885–1914*. The Chicago History of American Civilization. Chicago: University of Chicago Press, 1957.

Heimert, Alan. *Religion and the American Mind: From the Great Awakening to the Revolution*. Cambridge, Mass.: Harvard University Press, 1966.

Herbst, Jürgen. *The German Historical School in American Scholarship: A Study in the Transfer of Culture*. Ithaca, N. Y.: Cornell University Press, 1965.

Hexter, J. H. *On Historians: Reappraisals of Some of the Makers of Modern History*. Cambridge, Mass.: Harvard University Press, 1978.

Hicks, John D. *The Populist Revolt: A History of the Farmers' Alliance and the People's Party*. Minneapolis: University of Minnesota Press, 1931.

Higham, John, with Leonard Krieger and Felix Gilbert. *History*. Englewood Cliffs, N. J.: Prentice-Hall, 1965.

Higham, John, and Paul K. Conkin (eds.). *New Directions in American Intellectual History*. Baltimore: Johns Hopkins University Press, 1979.

Hoeveler, J. David, Jr. *James McCosh and the Scottish Intellectual Tradition: From Glasgow to Princeton*. Princeton, N. J.: Princeton University Press, 1981.

Hofstadter, Richard. *The Age of Reform: From Bryan to F.D.R.* New York: Alfred A. Knopf, 1955.

———. *The American Political Tradition and the Men Who Made It*. 1948. Reprint. New York: Vintage, n. d.

———. *The Progressive Historians: Turner, Beard, Parrington*. New York: Random House, 1968.

———. *Social Darwinism in American Thought*. Rev. edn. Boston: Beacon Press, 1955.

Howard, Michael. *War and the Liberal Conscience*. New Brunswick, N. J.: Rutgers University Press, 1978.

Hruska, Thomas Joseph, Jr. "Woodrow Wilson: The Organic State and His Political Theory." Ph.D. Diss., Claremont Graduate School, 1978.

Hughes, H. Stuart. *Consciousness and Society: The Reorientation of European Social Thought, 1890–1930*. New York: Vintage, 1958.

Huntington, Samuel P. *Political Order in Changing Societies*. New Haven: Yale University Press, 1968.

Hutchinson, William T., ed. *The Marcus W. Jernegan Essays in American Historiography*. Chicago: University of Chicago Press, 1937.

Israel, Jerry, ed. *Building the Organizational Society: Essays in American Historiography*. New York: Free Press, 1972.

Karpf, Fay Berger. *American Social Psychology: Its Origins, Development and European Background*. 1932. Reprint. New York: Russell and Russell, 1972.

Keller, Morton. *Affairs of State: Public Life in Late Nineteenth Century America*. Cambridge, Mass.: Belknap Press of Harvard University Press, 1977.

Kennedy, David M., ed. *Progressivism: The Critical Issues*. Boston: Little, Brown, 1971.

Klein, Melanie. *Love, Guilt and Reparation, and Other Works, 1921–1945*. New York: Delta, 1975.

Kolko, Gabriel. *The Triumph of Conservatism: A Reinterpretation of American History, 1900–1916*. Chicago: Quadrangle, 1967.

Kramnich, Isaac. *The Rage of Edmund Burke: Portrait of an Ambivalent Conservative*. New York: Basic Books, 1977.

Kutler, Stanley I., and Stanley N. Katz, eds. *The Promise of American History: Progress and Prospects*. Baltimore: Johns Hopkins University Press, 1982.

LaFeber, Walter. *The New Empire: An Interpretation of American Expansion, 1860–1898*. Ithaca, N. Y.: Cornell University Press, 1963.

Lasch, Christopher. *The New Radicalism in America, 1889–1963: The Intellectual as a Social Type*. New York: Vintage, 1967.

Latham, Earl, ed. *The Philosophy and Policies of Woodrow Wilson*. Chicago: University of Chicago Press, 1958.

Lears, T. J. Jackson. *No Place of Grace: Antimodernism and the Transformation of American Culture, 1880–1920*. New York: Pantheon Books, 1981.

Lewis, Edward R. *A History of American Political Thought from the Civil War to the World War*. 1937. Reprint. New York: Octagon Books, 1969.

Link, Arthur S. *The Higher Realism of Woodrow Wilson, and Other Essays.* Nashville, Tenn.: Vanderbilt University Press, 1971.

————. *Wilson: The Road to the White House.* Princeton, N. J.: Princeton University Press, 1947.

————. *Woodrow Wilson and the Progressive Era, 1910–1917.* New American Nation Series. 1954. Reprint. New York: Harper Torchbooks, 1963.

Link, Arthur S., and Richard L. McCormick. *Progressivism.* American History Series. Arlington Heights, Ill.: Harlan Davidson, 1983.

Lippincott, Benjamin Evans. *Victorian Critics of Democracy.* New York: Octagon Books, 1964.

Lipset, Seymour M. *The First New Nation: The United States in Historical and Comparative Perspective.* Garden City, N. Y.: Doubleday, Anchor, 1967.

Loewenberg, Bert James. *American History in American Thought: Christopher Columbus to Henry Adams.* New York: Simon and Schuster, 1972.

Loewenheim, Francis L., ed. *The Historian and the Diplomat: The Role of History and Historians in American Foreign Policy.* New York: Harper and Row, 1967.

Lowi, Theodore J. *The Personal President: Power Invested, Promise Unfulfilled.* Ithaca, N. Y.: Cornell University Press, 1985.

Lukes, Steven. *Émile Durkheim, His Life and Work: A Historical and Critical Study.* New York: Harper and Row, 1972.

Lustig, R. Jeffrey. *Corporate Liberalism: The Origins of Modern American Political Theory, 1891–1920.* Berkeley: University of California Press, 1982.

McClosky, Robert Green. *American Conservatism in the Age of Enterprise, 1865–1910.* New York: Harvard University Press, 1951.

McConnell, Grant. *Private Power and American Democracy.* New York: Alfred A. Knopf, 1966.

Mann, Arthur, ed. *The Progressive Era: Major Issues of Interpretation.* 2nd edn. Hinsdale, Ill.: Dryden Press, 1975.

Marsden, George M. *Fundamentalism and American Culture: The Shaping of Twentieth-Century Evangelicalism, 1870–1925.* New York: Oxford University Press, 1980.

May, Ernest R. *American Imperialism: A Speculative Essay.* New York: Atheneum, 1968.

Mayer, Arno J. *The Persistence of the Old Regime: Europe to the Great War.* New York: Pantheon, 1981.

Merriam, Charles Edward. *American Political Ideas: Studies in the Development of American Political Thought, 1865–1917.* New York: Macmillan, 1923.

Merton, Robert K. *Social Theory and Social Structure*. Enl. edn. New York: Free Press, 1968.

Meyer, D. H. *The Instructed Conscience: The Shaping of the American National Ethic*. Philadelphia: University of Pennsylvania Press, 1972.

Miller, Perry. *Errand into the Wilderness*. Cambridge, Mass.: Belknap Press of Harvard University Press, 1956.

———. ed. *American Thought: Civil War to World War I*. New York: Holt, Rinehart and Winston, 1954.

Mommsen, Wolfgang J. *The Age of Bureaucracy: Perspectives on the Political Sociology of Max Weber*. New York: Harper and Row, Harper Torchbooks, 1974.

Mosher, Frederick C. *Democracy and the Public Service*. New York: Oxford University Press, 1968.

Mowry, George E. *The California Progressives*. Berkeley: University of California Press, 1951.

———. *The Era of Theodore Roosevelt and the Birth of Modern America, 1900–1912*. New American Nation Series. 1958. Reprint. New York: Harper and Row, Harper Torchbooks, 1962.

Mulder, John M. *Woodrow Wilson: The Years of Preparation*. Princeton, N. J.: Princeton University Press, 1978.

Myrdal, Gunnar. *The Political Element in the Development of Economic Theory*. London: Routledge and Kegan Paul, 1953.

Nelson, Michael, ed. *The Presidency and the Political System*. Washington, D. C.: CQ Press, 1984.

Neustadt, Richard E. *Presidential Power: The Politics of Leadership*. New York: John Wiley, 1960.

Newton, Bernard. *The Economics of Francis Amasa Walker: American Economics in Transition*. New York: Augustus M. Kelley, 1968.

Niebuhr, H. Richard. *The Kingdom of God in America*. 1939. Reprint. New York: Harper and Row, Harper Torchbooks, 1959.

Noble, David W. *The Paradox of Progressive Thought*. Minneapolis: University of Minnesota Press, 1958.

Oleson, Alexandra, and John Voss, eds. *The Organization of Knowledge in America, 1860–1920*. Baltimore: Johns Hopkins University Press, 1979.

Orum, Anthony M. *Introduction to Political Sociology: The Social Anatomy of the Body Politic*. Englewood Cliffs, N. J.: Prentice-Hall, 1978.

Osborn, George C. *Woodrow Wilson: The Early Years*. Baton Rouge: Louisiana State University Press, 1968.

Osgood, Robert Endicott. *Ideals and Self-Interest in America's Foreign Relations: The Great Transformation of the Twentieth Century*. Chicago: University of Chicago Press, 1953.

257

Ostrom, Vincent. *The Intellectual Crisis in American Public Administration*. Birmingham: University of Alabama Press, 1973.

Pocock, J.G.A. *The Machiavellian Moment: Florentine Political Thought and the Atlantic Republican Tradition*. Princeton, N. J.: Princeton University Press, 1975.

Polanyi, Karl. *The Great Transformation: The Political and Economic Origins of Our Time*. Boston: Beacon Press, 1957.

Quandt, Jean B. *From the Small Town to the Great Community: The Social Thought of Progressive Intellectuals*. New Brunswick, N. J.: Rutgers University Press, 1970.

Rabin, Jack, and James S. Bowman, eds. *Politics and Administration: Woodrow Wilson and American Public Administration*. New York: Marcel Dekker, 1984.

Rader, Benjamin. *The Academic Mind and Reform: The Influence of Richard T. Ely in American Life*. Lexington: University of Kentucky Press, 1966.

Rossiter, Clinton. *Conservatism in America: The Thankless Persuasion*. 2nd rev. edn. New York: Vintage, 1962.

Ruggiero, Guido de. *The History of European Liberalism*. Translated by R. G. Collingwood. 1927. Reprint. Boston: Beacon Press, 1959.

Rystad, Göran. *Ambiguous Imperialism: American Foreign Policy and Domestic Politics at the Turn of the Century*. Lund, Sweden: Scandinavian University Books, 1975.

Sabine, George H. *A History of Political Theory*. 3rd edn. London: George C. Harrap, 1951.

Schaar, John H. *Legitimacy in the Modern State*. New Brunswick, N. J.: Transaction Books, 1981.

Schiesl, Martin J. *The Politics of Efficiency: Municipal Administration and Reform, 1880–1920*. Berkeley: University of California Press, 1977.

Sego, Michael A. *Ship of State: Foundations and Fragmentation of American Democracy*. Brunswick, Ohio: King's Court Communications, 1982.

Skowronek, Stephen. *Building a New American State: The Expansion of National Administrative Capacities, 1877–1920*. Cambridge, Mass.: Cambridge University Press, 1982.

Smith, Bruce James. *Politics and Remembrance: Republican Themes in Machiavelli, Burke, and Tocqueville*. Princeton, N. J.: Princeton University Press, 1985.

Smith, Henry Nash. *Virgin Land: The American West as Symbol and Myth*. Cambridge, Mass.: Harvard University Press, 1950.

Smith, J. Allen. *The Growth and Decadence of Constitutional Government*. New York: Holt, 1930.

258

————. *The Spirit of American Government.* Edited by Cushing Strout. Cambridge, Mass.: Belknap Press of Harvard University Press, 1965.

Smith, James Ward, and A. Leeland Jamison, eds. *The Shaping of American Religion: Religious Perspectives in American Culture.* 4 vols. Princeton, N. J.: Princeton University Press, 1961.

Somit, Albert, and Joseph Tanenhaus. *American Political Science: A Profile of a Discipline.* New York: Atherton Press, 1964.

————. *The Development of American Political Science: From Burgess to Behaviorism.* Boston: Allyn and Bacon, 1967.

Sorauf, Frank. *Political Parties in the American System.* Boston: Little, Brown, 1964.

Sprout, John G. *"The Best Men": Liberal Reformers in the Gilded Age.* New York: Oxford University Press, 1968.

Stillman, Richard J., II. *Public Administration: Concepts and Cases.* Boston: Houghton Mifflin, 1976.

Stourzh, Gerald. *Alexander Hamilton and the Idea of Republican Government.* Stanford, Calif.: Stanford University Press, 1970.

Strout, Cushing. *The New Heavens and the New Earth: Political Religion in America.* New York: Harper and Row, 1974.

Tomsich, John. *A Genteel Endeavor: American Culture and Politics in the Gilded Age.* Stanford, Calif.: Stanford University Press, 1971.

Tuveson, Ernest. *The Redeemer Nation: The Idea of America's Millennial Role.* Chicago: University of Chicago Press, 1968.

Veysey, Laurence R. *The Emergence of the American University.* Chicago: University of Chicago Press, 1965.

Waldo, Dwight. *The Administrative State: A Study of the Political Theory of American Public Administration.* New York: Ronald Press, 1948.

Wallas, Graham. *Human Nature in Politics.* 1908. Reprint. London: Constable, 1948.

Walzer, Michael. *The Revolution of the Saints: A Study in the Origins of Radical Politics.* Cambridge, Mass.: Harvard University Press, 1965.

Weber, Max. *Economy and Society.* Edited by Guenther Roth and Claus Wittich. 2 vols. Berkeley: University of California Press, 1978.

————. *From Max Weber: Essays in Sociology.* Translated and edited by H. H. Gerth and C. Wright Mills. London: Routledge and Kegan Paul, 1948.

Weinstein, Edwin A. *Woodrow Wilson: A Medical and Psychological Biography.* Princeton, N. J.: Princeton University Press, 1981.

Weinstein, James. *The Corporate Ideal in the Liberal State, 1900–1918.* Boston: Beacon Press, 1968.

Weinstein, James, and David W. Eakins, eds. *For A New America: Essays in*

History and Politics from Studies on the Left, 1959–1967. New York: Vintage, 1970.

White, Leonard D. *Introduction to the Study of Public Administration*. New York: Macmillan, 1929.

White, Morton. *Social Thought in America: The Revolt against Formalism*. Boston: Beacon Press, 1957.

Wicksell, Kurt. *Lectures on Political Economy*. 2 vols. London: Routledge and Sons, 1957.

Wiebe, Robert H. *The Search for Order, 1877–1920*. New York: Hill and Wang, 1967.

Wolfinger, Raymond D., *et al. Dynamics of American Politics*. 2nd edn. Englewood Cliffs, N. J.: Prentice-Hall, 1980.

Wolin, Sheldon S. *Politics and Vision: Continuity and Innovation in Western Political Thought*. Boston: Little, Brown, 1960.

Woodward, C. Vann. *Origins of the New South, 1877–1913*. Baton Rouge: Louisiana State University Press, 1951.

Ziff, Larzer. *The American 1890's: Life and Times of a Lost Generation*. New York: Viking Press, 1966.

Secondary Articles

Appleby, Joyce. "What is Still American in the Political Philosophy of Thomas Jefferson?" *William and Mary Quarterly*, xxxix (April 1982), 287–309.

Baron, Hans. "Calvinist Republicanism and Its Historical Roots." *Church History*, viii (1939), 30–42.

Beer, Samuel. "Tradition and Nationality: A Classic Revisited." *American Political Science Review*, lxviii (September 1974), 1293–95.

Bryson, Gladys. "The Emergence of the Social Sciences from Moral Philosophy." *International Journal of Science*, xlii (October 1931), 304–23.

Caldwell, Lynton K. "Public Administration and the Universities: A Half-Century of Development." *Public Administration Review*, xxv (March 1965), 52–60.

Cashdollar, Charles D. "August Comte and the American Reformed Theologians." *Journal of the History of Ideas*, xxxix (January–March 1978), 61–80.

Ceaser, James W., *et al.* "The Rise of the Rhetorical Presidency." *Presidential Studies Quarterly*, xi (Spring 1981), 158–71.

Cox, Theodore S. "John Barbee Minor." *Dictionary of American Biography*, vol. xiii, pp. 26–27. New York: Charles Scribner's Sons, 1928–79.

Cuff, Robert D. "Wilson and Weber: Bourgeois Critics in an Organized

Age." *Public Administration Review*, xxxviii (May–June 1978), 240–44.

Cunningham, Raymond J. "The German Historical World of Herbert Baxter Adams, 1874–1876." *Journal of American History*, lxviii (September 1981), 261–75.

Dorfman, Joseph. "The Role of the German Historical School in American Economic Thought." *American Economic Review*, xlv (May 1955), 17–28.

Filene, Peter G. "An Obituary for 'The Progressive Movement.'" *American Quarterly*, xxii (Spring 1970), 20–34.

Fine, Sidney, ed. "The Ely-Labadie Letters." *Michigan History*, xxxiv (March 1952), 13–25.

Galambos, Louis. "The Emerging Organizational Synthesis in Modern American History." *Business History Review*, xliv (1970), 270–90.

George, Juliette L., and Alexander L. George. "*Woodrow Wilson and Colonel House*: A Reply to Weinstein, Anderson, and Link." *Political Science Quarterly*, xcvi (Winter 1981–82), 641–65.

Golembiewski, Robert T. "'Maintenance' and 'Task' as Central Challenges in Public Administration." *Public Administration Review*, xxxiv (March–April 1974), 168–76.

Higham, John. "Herbert Baxter Adams and the Study of Local History." *American Historical Review*, lxxxix (December 1984), 1225–39.

Horowitz, Daniel. "Genteel Observers: New England Economic Writers." *New England Quarterly*, xlviii (March 1975), 65–83.

Kirwan, Kent. "The Crisis of Identity in the Study of Public Administration: Woodrow Wilson." *Polity*, ix (Spring 1977), 321–43.

———. "Historicism and Statesmanship in the Reform Argument of Woodrow Wilson." *Interpretation*, ix (September 1981), 339–51.

Kohn, Hans. "Nationalism." In *Dictionary of the History of Ideas: Studies of Selected Pivotal Ideas*, edited by Philip P. Weiner, vol. iii, pp. 324–39. New York, 1973.

Link, Arthur S. "What Happened to the Progressive Movement in the 1920s?" *American Historical Review*, lxiv (July 1959), 833–51.

Lukes, Steven. "Types of Individualism." In *Dictionary of the History of Ideas: Studies of Selected Pivotal Ideas*, edited by Philip P. Weiner, vol. ii, pp. 594–604. New York: Charles Scribner's Sons, 1973.

McCormick, Richard L. "The Discovery that Business Corrupts Politics: A Reappraisal of the Origins of Progressivism." *American Historical Review*, lxxxvi (April 1981), 247–74.

Niebuhr, H. Richard. "The Idea of Covenant and American Democracy." *Church History*, xxiii (June 1954), 126–35.

Potter, David M. "The Historian's Use of Nationalism and Vice Versa." *American Historical Review*, LXVII (July 1962), 924–50.

Quandt, Jean B. "Religion and Social Thought: The Secularization of Postmillennialism." *American Quarterly*, XXV (October 1973), 390–409.

Riggs, Fred W. "Relearning Old Lessons: The Political Context of Development Administration." *Public Administration Review*, XXV (March 1965), 70–79.

Rodgers, Daniel T. "In Search of Progressivism," *Reviews in American History*, X (December 1982), 113–32.

Rogow, Arnold A. "Edmund Burke and the American Liberal Tradition." *Antioch Review* XVII (June 1957), 255–65.

Ross, Dorothy. "Historical Consciousness in Nineteenth-Century America." *American Historical Review*, LXXXIX (Oct. 1984), 909–28.

———. "Socialism and American Liberalism: Academic Social Thought in the 1880s." *Perspectives in American History*, XI (1977–78), 5–79.

———. "Woodrow Wilson and the Case for Psychohistory." *Journal of American History*, LXIX (December 1982), 659–68.

Sabine, George H. "The Two Democratic Traditions." *Philosophic Review*, LXI (1952), 451–74.

Seltzer, Alan. "Woodrow Wilson as 'Corporate-Liberal': Toward a Reconsideration of Left Revisionist Historiography." *Western Political Quarterly*, XXX (June 1977), 183–212.

Spring, David. "Walter Bagehot and Deference." *American Historical Review*, LXXXI (June 1976), 524–31.

Stephenson, Wendell H., "The Influence of Woodrow Wilson on Frederick Jackson Turner." *Agricultural History*, XIX (Oct. 1945), 249–53.

Stevens, Robert. "Two Cheers for 1870: The American Law School." *Perspectives in American History*, V (1971), 405–550.

Stillman, Richard J., II. "Woodrow Wilson and the Study of Administration: A New Look at an Old Essay." *American Political Science Review*, LXVII (June 1973), 582–88.

Thelen, David P. "Social Tensions and the Origins of Progressivism." *Journal of American History*, LVI (September 1969), 323–41.

Tucker, Robert C. "The Georges' Wilson Reexamined: An Essay on Psychobiography." *American Political Science Review*, LXXI (June 1977), 606–18.

Veysey, Laurence R. "The Academic Mind of Woodrow Wilson." *Mississippi Valley Historical Review*, XLIX (March 1963), 613–34.

Weinstein, Edwin A., *et al.* "Woodrow Wilson's Political Personality: A Reappraisal." *Political Science Quarterly*, XCIII (Winter 1978–79), 585–98.

Wolfe, Christopher. "Woodrow Wilson: Interpreting the Constitution." *Review of Politics*, XLI (January 1979), 121–42.

Wolin, Sheldon S. "From Progress to Modernization." *democracy*, III (Fall 1983), 9–21.

———. "The Idea of the State in America." *Humanities in Society*, III (Spring 1980), 151–68.

———. "Political Theory: Trends and Goals." *International Encyclopedia of the Social Sciences*, vol. XII, pp. 318–31. New York: Macmillan, 1968.

Xenos, Nicholas. "Classical Political Economy: The Apolitical Discourse of Civil Society." *Humanities in Society*, III (Summer 1980), 229–42.

"*Modern Democratic State, The*," 93–94, 221, 226; and the American Revolution, 106–7; composition of, 95; conception of, 96–110. See also *State, The*

Morris, George Sylvester, 69, 75–76, 94

"Mr. Gladstone," 52, 58–59

Mulder, John M., 143, 199, 236; Wilson as "covenanter," 45n, 237–38

Mulford, Elisha, 94

Neustadt, Richard E., 199

New Freedom, x, 193

New Nationalism, x

"New School" of political economy. *See* German historical school of political economy; political economy

"Notes for Lectures on Administration," 118, 134–36

"Of the Study of Politics," 86–88

"Old School" of British economists, 72. *See also* political economy

"Organs of the State and Its Means of Advancement, The," 155–56

Ostrom, Vincent, 121

Paine, Thomas, 105

panic of 1873, 4

panic of 1907, 197

Papers of Woodrow Wilson, The, 188, 237

patriotism: and religious service, 166–67, 169–71; transformation of the individual, 168–71, 172–74; and worship of the flag, 172–74. *See also* American imperialism

Patton, Francis Landey, 183

Perry, Arthur Latham, 83, 84

Philippines, 164–65, 174–75, 177, 230

"Philosophy of Politics, The," 142, 144, 156, 158n, 223; failure of, 224–26; methodological problems in, 224; problem of language in, 144–45

Philosophy of Wealth, The (Clark), 137

Physics and Politics (Bagehot), 94–95

Pitt, William, 28

political economy: and administration, 133; American and British economists, 80–81; anti-theoretical bias in America, 79–81; behind the Constitution, 148–49; and the Civil War, 108, 154; defined by Adam Smith, 83; and economic policy, 84; and fear of sectionalism, 163–64; German historical school of, 71–74, 94; and imperialism, 169, 176–77; at Johns Hopkins University, 69–70, 72–75; orthodox idea of, 24–25; at Princeton, 17; question of method, 71–73, 78–81; and space, 73n; and the state, 72, 75. *See also* "History of Political Economy in the United States"

political leadership, x, xiii, 26–31, 59–67, 232–33; in cabinet government, 30–35; and foreign policy, 67, 166; in the presidency, 208–10

political oratory, 27–28, 232–33; and Calvinist tradition, 27; in Congress, 32–33; in *Congressional Government*, 52–53, 63–64; and debating clubs, 18; as literary style, 55–56; in the modern state, 98–99; and power, 28; "the rhetorical presidency," 239–40

political science. *See* Wilson, Woodrow, *political ideas*: political science

Political Science and Comparative Constitutional Law (Burgess), 145

Political Science Quarterly, 128

"Political Sovereignty," 64–67

populism, 155; Wilson's reaction to, 163–64, 191

power, notion of: in Christian culture, 5, 8; as key to Wilson's political thought, 234–44; Wilson's conception of, 35–36. *See also* Wilson, Woodrow, *political ideas*: political power

Preamble to the Constitution, 227

presidency: in *Congressional Government*, 50, 53; in *Constitutional Government*, 206–10

"Princeton in the Nation's Service," 162

Princeton University, 20–21; academic reform, 182–87; dependent upon business support, 184; fight over location of the graduate college, 184; preceptorial system, 183; rejection of the plan for "quadrangles," 183, 198; Wilson's models for academic reform, 185–87

Princetonian, The: editorials in, 18n, 20–21, 29, 35n; Wilson as editor, 18

progress: in Bagehot's writings, 94–95; in Francis Amasa Walker's view, 85. *See also* Wilson, Woodrow, *political ideas*: progress

progressivism, 90, 168, 191, 202; Wilson's

Publication of Supplementary Volumes to *The Papers of Woodrow Wilson* is assisted from time to time by the Woodrow Wilson Foundation in order to encourage scholarly work about Woodrow Wilson and his time. All volumes have passed the review procedures of the publishers and the Editor and the Editorial Advisory Committee of *The Papers of Woodrow Wilson*. Inquiries about the series should be addressed to The Editor, Papers of Woodrow Wilson, Firestone Library, Princeton University, Princeton, N.J. 08544

Raymond B. Fosdick, *Letters on the League of Nations. From the Files of Raymond B. Fosdick* (Princeton University Press, 1966)

Wilton B. Fowler, *British-American Relations, 1917–1918: The Role of Sir William Wiseman* (Princeton University Press, 1969)

John M. Mulder, *Woodrow Wilson: The Years of Preparation* (Princeton University Press, 1978)

George Egerton, *Great Britain and the Creation of the League of Nations* (University of North Carolina Press, 1978)

Stephen L. Vaughn, *Holding Fast the Inner Lines: Democracy, Nationalism, and the Committee on Public Information* (University of North Carolina Press, 1980)

Robert C. Hilderbrand, *Power and the People: Executive Management of Public Opinion in Foreign Affairs*, 1897–1921 (University of North Carolina Press, 1980)

Inga Floto, *Colonel House in Paris: A Study of American Policy at the Paris Peace Conference 1919* (Princeton University Press, reissue 1981)

Edwin A. Weinstein, *Woodrow Wilson: A Medical and Psychological Biography* (Princeton University Press, 1981)

Arthur S. Link, ed., *Woodrow Wilson and a Revolutionary World*, 1913–1921 (University of North Carolina Press, 1982)

Klaus Schwabe, *Woodrow Wilson, Revolutionary Germany, and Peacemaking, 1918–1919* (University of North Carolina Press, 1985)

Frances Wright Saunders, *First Lady Between Two Worlds: Ellen Axson Wilson* (University of North Carolina Press, 1985)